Middle East Reviews
Second Edition

MIDDLE EAST REVIEWS

second edition

edited by
Mohammed M. Aman, PhD
Mary Jo Aman, MLIS

Westphalia Press
An Imprint of the Policy Studies Organization
Washington, DC
2018

Library of Congress Cataloging-in-Publication Data

Names: Aman, Mohammed M., editor. | Aman, Mary Jo, editor.
Title: Middle East reviews / edited by Mohammed M. Aman, Mary Jo Aman.
Other titles: Post Arab Spring.
Description: Second edition. | Washington, DC : Westphalia Press, an imprint
     of the Policy Studies Organization, 2018.
Identifiers: LCCN 2018023876 | ISBN 9781633916975 (pbk.)
Subjects: LCSH: Middle East--Book reviews. | Africa, North--Book reviews. |
     Arab Spring, 2010---Book reviews.
Classification: LCC DS44 .P67 2018 | DDC 956--dc23 LC record available at
     https://lccn.loc.gov/2018023876

ISBN-10: 1-63391-697-9
ISBN-13: 978-1-63391-697-5
Printed in the United States of America

Westphalia Press
An imprint of Policy Studies Organization
1527 New Hampshire Ave., NW
Washington, DC. 20036
info@ipsonet.org

Future reviews of books on the Middle East
will appear in the peer-reviewed journal,
Digest of Middle East Studies (DOMES),
published by Wiley-Blackwell

CONTENTS

Contents

MUSLIMS IN AMERICA

MUSLIMS IN EUROPE

NORTH AFRICA

Algeria

Egypt

Tunisia

OMAN

OTTOMAN EMPIRE

POLITICS AND GOVERNMENT

Contents

Contents

Introduction

The volume brings together reviews of books published about the Middle East and North African (MENA) countries in the fields of social sciences and humanities, in particular. It follows objectives similar to those of our previously published monograph of book reviews regarding this region. The first volume titled *The Middle East: New Order or Disorder?* was published by the Washington-based Policy Studies Organization (PSO)/Westphalia Press. As with the previous edition, the reviews published in the present volume include complete bibliographic information for each title and a detailed and analytical signed review for each listed book. An ISBN is included, but not the price, as there are various discounted and changing prices that appear on web sites such as amazon.com and others. The entries are arranged under broad subject and geographical headings.

In the first book, *The Middle East: New Order or Disorder?* the published reviews described what was, to a great extent at the time, a positive outlook for the region's attempts for reform, and open society, freedom for the majority of Arab citizens who had suffered lingering hereditary, authoritarian, and military regimes. There was a brief sense of optimism which, unfortunately, was marred by disorder and conspiracies that dashed the peoples' hopes for orderly change of power and restoration of semblance of much needed political and economic reforms. Instead of reforms, the Middle East witnessed chaos; instead of freedom and liberty, more authoritarianism and a tighter grip on power by military regimes, or armed insurgents that engage in war on their own citizens, and overwhelming destruction of their countries' economies and infrastructures, like those being waged in Libya, Syria, and Yemen.

The reviews are written by American and international scholars who are experts in their respective subject and geographic areas of the MENA region. The reviews cover established subjects such as history, social sciences, literature, as well as relatively new subjects that have emerged in the currently published literature on the Middle East and North Africa, among them: Islamophobia, Islamic terrorism, the war in Yemen, the Syrian civil war, Saudi social and political reforms.

It is our hope that this new book will be a valuable and significant contribution to the field of MENA Studies and of benefit to scholars worldwide including diplomats, policy-makers, and business leaders.

We are thankful to the Policy Studies Organization and its affiliate Westphalia Press, as well as the publishers whose books are reviewed in this volume for their continued cooperation in sharing with us their newly released books to be considered for review in *DOMES*. We are equally grateful to our panel of international reviewers for their cooperation, timely, and valuable reviews.

Professor Mohammed M. Aman, PhD   Mary Jo Aman, MLIS

ARAB SPRING

The Arab Spring and the Geopolitics of the Middle East: Security Threats and Revolutionary Change

Amr Yossef & Joseph R. Cerami. Basingstoke, UK: Palgrave Macmillan. 96 pp. ISBN: 978-1137504074.

Numerous theories have been suggested to explain the emergence of the Arab Spring. These include: widespread corruption, dictators who had been in power for decades, rising prices, a rapidly increasing population, whose "youth bulge" had few prospects for meaningful employment, and the new social media that enabled protesters to rapidly mobilize. In this slim volume, Amr Yossef and Joseph Cerami add another cause—the failure of state institutions to function properly, a phenomenon that was also to plague the post-2011 regimes in Tunisia, Egypt, Syria, and Libya, the countries that are analyzed in this book.

Leaning heavily on the work of Lisa Anderson and Joel Migdal, the authors argue that the failure of the state bureaucracies in these countries was a major factor in precipitating the Arab Spring, and once the old regimes had collapsed, the failure of the new governments to provide the necessary law and order contributed to public disapproval in countries like Tunisia and Egypt and to outright civil war in Libya and Syria. Given the authors' thesis, it is not surprising that they consider that the establishment of honest, competent, and well-functioning bureaucracies is the key to prevent a state from failing. This is the case, argue the authors, even if a regime with an efficient state bureaucracy is not a democracy. In this context, they approvingly cite the example of Singapore (p.70). The authors conclude their argument by asserting:

> [What] The societies of these countries most need is state-building in the form of a capable bureaucracy that not only monopolizes the legitimate use of force within the country's territory, but also enforces law, delivers services, and administers the country in a way that is efficient, just, and beneficial to its citizens (pp.70-71).

The final section of the book criticizes the approaches of the European Union and the United States to state building in the Middle East and calls for the US to have wise and far-sighted statesmen, to make policy in the region. The authors cite Robert Gates, who replaced Donald Rumsfeld as Secretary of Defense in the George W. Bush Administration, as an ideal example of such a leader (pp.80-82), while they condemn Rumsfeld as " a toxic leader and bad boss" (p. 83).

In general, I am sympathetic to the thesis of the authors about the need for a strong, competent, transparent, and honest bureaucracy as a vital component in state-building. However, I do not share the authors' position that democracy is not an important component of state-building. Lee Kwan Yew's Singapore is very dissimilar to the states of the Arab World, and a large part of its national cohesion was formed when Singapore broke off from Malaysia in 1965.

Nonetheless, for those interested in the challenges of state-building and the causes of the failures of the post-Arab Spring states, this is a book that can be recommended. ***ROF***

The Arab Spring: The Hope and Reality of the Uprisings; Beyond the Arab Spring in North Africa

Mark L. Haas & David W. Lesch, Eds. *The Arab Spring: The Hope and Reality of the Uprisings.* Boulder, CO: Westview Press, 2017 (2nd ed.). 338 pp. ISBN: 978-0813349749.

Daniel Křížek & Jan Záhořík, Eds. *Beyond the Arab Spring in North Africa.* Lanham, MD: Westview Press and Lexington Books, 2017. 241 pp. ISBN: 978-1498547239.

After Mohamed Bouazizi set himself on fire in Sidi Bouzid in Tunisia on December 17, 2010 in frustration at his poor condition and government restrictions, a series of violent street demonstrations ensued that ultimately led to the resignation of Tunisia's president and to political change in the country. This event was succeeded in Egypt, Yemen,

Libya, and other Arab countries by similar turbulent activities, prompting democratic change and promises of better life conditions—and the term "Arab Spring" was coined to denote them. Many articles and books were subsequently published to study and explain this unprecedented phenomenon, and the two books reviewed here are good examples.

The first book has 13 chapters in two parts: Part I (with 7 chapters, including a new one on Iraq, not found in the earlier edition) focuses on the Arab uprisings and concentrates on the tyranny, the anarchy, and the "democracy" prevailing in the Arab world; and Part II (with 6 chapters) discusses how non-Arab countries reacted to the Arab Spring and it has a completely revised conclusion ending the book.

The second book has 10 chapters that treat different aspects of the Arab uprisings, some dealing with specific topics like women's rights, or rights of LGBT individuals, or the role of the new social media fomenting the uprisings and reporting on them. But, they generally go *beyond* the uprisings to explore prospects and possible problems.

Both books have excellent contributions on the social, economic, and political conditions of the Arab countries leading to the Arab Spring. Western colonialism had been ousted for some time before, but had been replaced by mostly autocratic and authoritarian regimes. The aspirations of the Arab people for freedom and democratic rule were not achieved but were frustrated and thwarted; economic conditions, despite the oil boom and the surge of internal and international trade, were far from rewarding to the average Arab citizens. Pressure was building up for an explosion and the self-immolation of Mohamed Bouazizi, horrible as it was, was the spark that detonated the expectancy of the people, first in Tunisia, then in several other Arab countries.

Both books, in variable depths, deal with how the Arab rulers tried to repress the people's anger, to meet their demand, or to forestall disaster: sometimes by actual improvements and often by promises of such. In the end, when all was said and done, the Arab world was a new place, although there is debate still whether the Arab Spring has achieved all its goals.

It is interesting to note how non-Arab countries reacted to the Arab Spring. The Haas and Lesch book, in particular, discusses in Part II the response of Iran, Turkey, Israel, Russia, and the U.S.A. in separate chapters for each country; and, without being too pretentious, one can say the response of each was determined by its own interests — as indeed the authors of the chapters explained in detail.

These two books are a good read and are recommended to all students and scholars interested in the Arab world, its modern history, and politics;

the general reader is also a beneficiary if he or she wants to know more than is available in daily newspapers. *IJB*

Arguing Islam after the Revival of Arab Politics

Nathan J. Brown. Oxford, UK: Oxford: Oxford University Press, 2016, 296 pp. ISBN: 978-0190619459.

This book is original and timely. I think it has almost everything a modern book on Middle East politics following the Arab Spring should have — a reliance on both fieldwork and narrative techniques; an openness to new theories of public space, sociology, anthropology, and political science that promise better outcomes, illustrations with real data sets that show the cultural and political perspectives and specificities of this region of the world. The book raises useful questions with step-by-step answers that help the reader work out how to understand the challenges facing Arab politics and society in countries such as Egypt, Jordan, Syria, Kuwait, and Saudi Arabic in the post-Arab Spring era. It is a sophisticated book that truly provides an elegant and useful analysis of the interaction of religion and politics in the region.

This is a book for readers and researchers who are already familiar with theories of politics and public sphere, but who may not know the complexities of Arab and Muslim societies. The title of the book and the introduction seem to indicate that this book is suitable for those who are interested in Islam and the Islamic movement in the Middle East and North Africa and who want to know how political discourse, activism, and religion impact on policy-making and democratizing the region.

What is interesting about this book is that it focuses on several types of public sphere and analyzes how they interact. It investigates political conversations in small groups in public and private circles, debates in public squares and mosques, discussions that take place in social and regular media, and debates in institutions like parliaments, especially the political discussions and clashes that take place between opposing parliamentary groups before agreeing or voting on legislation.

However, I have two major concerns about this book. First, it gives the impression that religion and politics can go together, and that people should overcome their fear of religion. However, we know for a fact that one of the reasons for the violence and civil wars in the region is the overwhelming power of Islam and its utilization in politics as "the main language of public debate," as the author states. Religion has its own discourse and perspective, and it is actually problematic for public life and for human rights. The Middle East would do better if it could separate religion and politics.

Second, although the book discusses amply the role of religion in advancing political debate and democracy, it does not refer to jihadist groups systematically perhaps because they are violent or are situated outside recognized official institutions. But, I think one cannot discuss religion in politics without including jihadism and jihadists who use religion for political ends and who have their conversations displayed mainly in social media. They also aim at transforming society and at changing policy and the nature of politics. Moreover, they do have an impact on political debate and policy in many Muslim countries.

While the book focuses on religion, it develops a comprehensive approach to understanding the revival of Arab politics which has a significant impact on policy, and how Arab peoples assess their political systems and governance structures. The book also argues that there is much variability in religious debate and the revival of politics in Arab countries.

The book describes the various facets of the ideology crisis in the Arab world and the revival of the public's interest in politics despite the failure of the Arab Spring and the restrictions of public freedoms imposed by authoritarian regimes. It explores the numerous strategies used by politicians, religious groups, activists, and media to surmount these difficulties and to increase their chances of influencing policy-makers. It reveals the remarkable influence of political and religious conflicts and conflicts of interests, and the role they play in youth's integration, participation, and achievement. The book also nicely reveals how the government uses the political argument to silence public voices and shut out the opposition in this region. The book also thoroughly analyzes what happens when politics becomes a public issue, and people discuss it and argue about it in public.

The book is divided into three major parts. Part I begins by defining and explaining concepts such as "politics," "publicity," and "argument," and then turns to discuss publicity, religion, and the revival of politics (Chapter 1). The reader is slowly and clearly led through how Arab societies are struggling to achieve democratic rights by showing concern for political matters and by using religious discourse, wavering between tradition and modernity (Chapter 2).

Part II discusses a number of arguments used in the public and private spheres to describe and deal with political and social problems, in relation to the state's cultural and political perspectives and governance (Chapter 3). It investigates the various features of spaces where politics is discussed in the Middle East, and how these spaces interact with each other, and how Islam and the Islamic law (shari'a) are used and argued in the public debate (Chapters 4 and 5).

In Part III, the author describes Arab constitutions and the multitude of voices of the public sphere, tracing the socio-cultural ramifications of public politics for policy outcomes. He analyzes how politics and religion are discussed in the contentious public sphere leading a remarkable argument about religion (Chapter 6). In Chapter 7, the author focuses on the family law, showing a strong separation between the law as it is practiced and the law as it is understood and debated. He argues that such arguments which are divorced from reality are rarely taken into account in policy-making.

The book also researches the more practical issue of textbooks in schools and universities. It shows that the political and religious arguments operate in these textbooks, and provoke heated discussions and disagreements, thus "sharpening divisions" and widening the gap between different social and religious groups in society. However, these divisions do not have a significant impact on policy (Chapter 8).

The book ends by a reflection on the political revival of the Arab world in post-Arab Spring, illustrating that this political dynamism, which gave rise to powerful public debates, has been reduced by challenging political realities and structures (Chapter 9).

In sum, while the book brings out the deep-seated tensions and contradictions in the socio-cultural fabric of Arab societies, it underlines how Islam functions, impacts and integrates the political arena of the Arab world today. As such, the book is a significant contribution to understanding the Middle East politics and society, and the role of Islamic traditions and the ramifications for policy outcomes and governance across the region.

Reference

Ennaji, Moha, Ed. (2014). *Multiculturalism and Democracy in North Africa: Aftermath of the Arab Spring*. New York, NY: Routledge. **ME**

Armies and Insurgencies in the Arab Spring

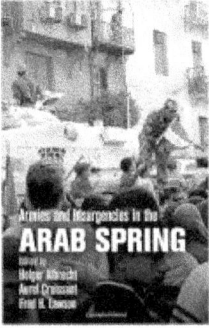

Holger Albrecht, Aurel Croissant, & Fred H. Lawson, Eds. Philadelphia, PA: University of Pennsylvania Press, 2016. 320 pp. ISBN: 978-0812248548.

The tumultuous events known as the Arab Spring began with the Tunisian Revolt of late 2010 and then swept the Middle East and North Africa (MENA) region becoming tsunami-like waves of influence that even reached the present. These demonstrations, protests, riots, terrorist attacks, coups, and civil wars of the period continue to intrigue a diverse global audience ranging from followers of the daily news to policy-makers. This extraordinary socio-political event not only remade the political landscape of the Middle East, but also marked these ancient lands with a message for the modern era that pundits continue to interpret.

Amid the enthusiasm generated by the subject, and the many political, social, cultural, gender, and interdisciplinary studies attempting to explain the phenomenon, a critical variable of the Arab Spring received only scant attention: the armies and security forces that waded into the streams of youthful and contorted faces crying out for reform and regime change. *Armies and Insurgencies in the Arab Spring,* edited by Holger Albrecht, et al. boldly marches through this obscure and complex terrain of military mindsets, cultures, cases, and resources that determined the hopes and dreams of millions.

No doubt *Armies and Insurgencies of the Arab Spring* emerged from the authors' recognition that the scholarly community had neglected the role of Arab militaries in the Arab Spring. Although the tone of the introduction and subsequent articles by the dozen authors of the study is not accusatory, these pundits nonetheless recognized the deficiencies of previous research on the subject due, in large part, to disinterest, distraction, and deficit (in academic background). The introduction notes, "Middle East Studies and political science were ill-equipped to analyze the Arab militaries' role in these events .... With few exceptions ... researchers had lost interest in the military" (p. 2).

But, *Armies and Insurgencies of the Arab Spring* is far more than a corrective approach to the study of the "final guarantor of regime security"—the military forces that were so critical to the outcomes of the Arab Spring. In addition to offering insight into the role the militaries played in determining courses and outcomes in the unrest of the period, the book provides a deep analysis of the political role of the security forces in the Middle East as well as the "corporate behavior" of the military in the wider context of popular unrest in the region. Questions regarding why militaries intervene in popular uprisings, and why they chose to either support or to defect from their respective authoritarian regimes, structure the book and lead the reader to critical variables such as resources, reputation (of the military), elites, history, and organizational cohesiveness—among other factors.

The reader will be pleasantly surprised that *Armies and Insurgencies of the Arab Spring* offers no central thesis. The personalities, contexts, histories, class structures, experiences, and organizational behaviors of the diverse military and security entities in the Mideast are far too diverse for the application of a general theory explaining these complex civilian–military relationships. Any attempt to create such a paradigm would produce more than a gross generalization, but also a misunderstanding that could potentially distort the decision-making of key leaders in government, partnered militaries (military to military engagements), civil society, and humanitarian organizations who find that civilian–military and related encounters are a common aspect of operating in the region.

Despite the lack of a central thesis, and the diversity of authors in this edited study, it remains focused on practical questions regarding the role of the security sector in the Arab Spring — an approach that tightly weaves each chapter together in a mutual search. Among the real-world questions explored in detail by each author is "How and why do military apparatuses actively intervene in politics, especially under conditions of mobilized opposition against authoritarian leadership?" (p. 3). More specifically, and tactically, the introduction queries again: "Which units or individuals within a military apparatus remain loyal to embattled incumbents, and which ones do not?" (p. 3). The authors answer these critical questions and similar ones by using case studies, historical analysis, and a broad regional and global context to find comparisons, theories, and key variables illuminating these civilian–military relationships. The book's comparison of militaries in the MENA to Asian and Latin American counterparts is an example of the quality methodology that underpins the study.

Armies and Insurgencies of the Arab Spring is also a very balanced work addressing large countries like Egypt as well as smaller ones like Tunisia and Bahrain. The result of this balanced approach is an analysis that skillfully navigates the diverse terrain of the region while furnishing understandings of the major issues shaping the Arab Spring. For instance, in Chapter 9, Cherine Chams El Dine calls attention to the dynamics of a divided civilian sector frustrated in its attempt to manipulate the Egyptian military toward one's respective political agenda. She notes the failure has left the military as the most powerful political arbiter replete with the financial, economic, and organizational autonomy requisite for its preeminence in Egypt's political affairs (pp. 199-200).

In addition to a much-needed refocusing on military issues in the Arab Spring, Holger Albrecht's edited book also provides clarification of the diverse elements of the military–security sector. Several chapters rightly call attention to the differences between the military and other security entities, with special attention to the role of the Mukhabarat (intelligence service) and relevant internal security agencies. These organizations have provided authoritarian regimes in the MENA with the cover, access, precision, deniability, and potency required to check popular uprisings. In contrast to national militaries, these security forces were often more active and more critical to outcomes in the Arab Spring, but they have not received the requisite attention (p. 69).

Armies and Insurgencies of the Arab Spring provides additional contributions to the subject of civilian–military relationships in the MENA by challenging key assumptions held by Western scholars. While all the chapters provide valuable insight into the subject, Risa Brook's chapter on Tunisia deserves special attention in this regard. In addition to addressing the "corporate ethos" (organizational culture) of the Tunisian military and its unique history and developments, the chapter addresses more fundamental questions. First, the author posits individual agency (and not just general political, social, and economic variables) critical for understanding the behavior of militaries in the MENA. She asserts: "In short, individuals do and can matter, not only in how they act upon their own preferences, but also in how they lead what is a very hierarchical organization like the military" (p. 220). Moreover, the author questions the prevailing notion that a transition to civilian rule is a quick fix to problems often associated with authoritarian regimes resisting the Arab Spring. She asserts again: "In part, future progress in securing the subordination of the military to democratic institutions will require civilians to resist any temptation to politicize officers" (p.220).

Armies and Insurgencies in the Arab Spring, edited by Holger Albrecht, et al. is a significant contribution to the study of the Arab Spring, and in a broader sense, an understanding of civilian–military relationships determining the quality of life in the MENA region. Academics, politicians, non-governmental organizations, and military–security professionals who study or operate in these areas will find the book particularly useful for understanding the nuanced dynamics of the nexus of military and civilian life. If peace indeed comes to the Middle East, the outcomes will be determined by a better understanding of the role of military leaders, cultures, organization, economics, and politics, the very issues addressed in this valuable study. **MSC**

Human Rights, Revolution and Reform in the Muslim World

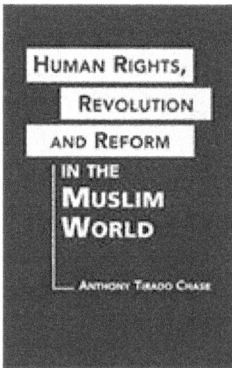

Anthony Tirado Chase. Boulder, CO: Lynne Rienner, 2013. 225 pp. $25.00. ISBN: 978-188268013.

In this book, Anthony Tirado Chase argues that human rights have been a strong and dynamic force in the Muslim world, working to frame contentious debates and shaping events. Chase contests the "false binary" of human rights as a Western imposition used to advance powerful global interests versus the assertion that those rights are universal. Instead, Chase uses the human rights regime to analyze the ongoing cultural, economic and political contestations in the Muslim world. In this conception, human rights are studied as sites of struggle rather than a set of fixed moral dictates. Human rights are important to the extent that Muslims have used those rights to comprehend and come to terms with their changing world, not because those rights are universal or because they have been upheld.

In Chapter 2, Chase provides a historical overview of the Muslim world's engagement with human rights. The important question, he notes, is not whether Muslims care about human rights, but why and in what ways they care. He briefly surveys the history of intellectual currents in the Muslim world, contesting the assertion, often voiced by authoritarian leaders in Muslim countries, that human rights are Western imports. Moreover, he shows that Muslim countries (along with others) played important roles in the establishment of international standards on human rights, including that of gender equality, and how human rights attained increased legitimacy in the Muslim world after the Arab defeat at the hands of Israel in 1967. Thus, human rights have largely supplanted the calls for self-determination made earlier in the immediate post-colonial period.

In Chapter 3, the cross-border transmission effects vis-à-vis human rights is explored. Chase shows how even Islamists — or otherwise anti-Western political forces — have come to articulate a narrative of human rights and democracy. Although some of these have been opportunistic, articulations of human rights have increasingly drawn from local sources, making extensive use of Islamist categories. In Chapter 4, Chase examines the factors that have supported the emergence of human rights. He argues that the philosophical impulse for human rights combined with globalization and the objective of stability after World War Two have worked to promote human rights. He shows how, in many instances, countries have worked to improve human rights — despite the absence of obvious sanctions or domestic pressure — when extra-national legal institutions, such as the European Court of Human Rights, established legal norms. In Chapter 5, Chase presents what he calls an 'antifoundational' theory of human rights, criticizing the cultural relativist critique of human rights as well as support for human rights that emanates from assumptions of natural law. Instead, Chase presents a view of human rights as the expansion of human agency, as defined, redefined and contested by diverse groups and individuals living and working in their respective societies.

Chase takes a deeper look into these contestations, concerning freedom of expression (political rights) and sexual identity (social rights), in Chapters 6 and 7. Political rights are normatively accepted in most of the Muslim world; the question is how are they defined and put into effect? Chase is highly critical of curbs on freedom of expression that are made in the name of religion because the denial of the essential rights jeopardizes the attainment of all other rights. Chase does not discuss how subtler self-censorship or institutional censorship — as opposed to blatant political repression — might (or might not) have broadly similar debilitating effects. Although he concedes that rights of sexual identity are less normatively accepted in much of the Muslim world, he argues that perceptions of rights over sexuality have recently experienced rapid change internationally, including in Muslim countries. Chase is unsympathetic to narratives that paint gay identity in Muslim countries as an imported trend — they both deny gay persons agency and thwart free expression that is vital to the realization of other rights, reinforcing existing power relations. Chapter 8 summarizes the main points made in the book and makes some extrapolations concerning human rights in the post-Arab Spring era. Chase advises against relying on the West, especially the United States, for leadership in the arena of human rights, stressing instead the importance of developing domestic groups that advocate for such rights in Muslim countries. He shuns the notion that human rights are an end in themselves, viewing them instead as a means to promote human agency and in turn break down rigid identities to advance pluralism in rigid and nationalistic polities.

A few themes run through this book. Chase appropriately views the Muslim world as basically unexceptional, responding to broadly similar structural forces and possessing internal dynamics that are general and analyzable. Human rights are seen not as fixed or natural, but dynamic and highly dependent on what people and social forces in Muslim countries make of them. An implication of this approach is that it has little to say about the ethical or moral dimension to rights, which in fairness, Chase does not intend to do. Another consequence is that Chase conceives of human rights in basically instrumental terms only: the extent to which they lead to an expansion in pluralism or other rights. This contrasts with, for example, the capabilities approach that posits both intrinsic and instrumental import to rights. The latter approach assumes there is an intrinsic human benefit to, for example, not being imprisoned when engaging in free expression, even if it does not result in increased pluralism or the promotion of other rights. ***BY***

Morbid Symptoms: Relapse in the Arab Uprising

Gilbert Achcar. London, UK: Saqi, 2016. 240 pp. ISBN: 978-0863561832; (Ebk). ISBN: 978-0863561788.

It is almost six years since the world media first fixed its attention on frustrated Arabs mobilizing from Tunis to San'a as they occupied city squares, staged mass demonstrations, and chanted "the people want the fall of the regime." Observers continue to seek to understand how protest movements that promised so much have degenerated into repression, extremism, war, and mass displacement. Following an earlier book and numerous other writings, Gilbert Achcar, of the School of Oriental and African Studies at the University of London, has made a significant contribution to this discussion. *Morbid Symptoms: Relapse in the Arab Uprising*, is both a detailed account of recent events in two of the Arab world's pivotal crises — Egypt and Syria — and an insightful analysis of the decisions and dynamics that transformed the promise of the 2011 uprisings into today's tragic malaise. The former is produced by a close documentary study which emphasizes interviews with significant actors; the latter through a simple but powerful conceptual model of the revolutionary and counter-revolutionary forces at work. *Morbid Symptoms…* provides a clear-eyed assessment of the lessons that can be learned from the decisions and actions of the aspiring Arab revolutionaries, while also providing a reminder — if any is needed — of the role of external actors in the region's ongoing crises.

Three poles

Central to Achcar's analysis is the concept of tripolarity in the post-uprising Arab world: "not a binary confrontation between revolution and counter-revolution — as in most revolutionary upheavals in history — but a triangular conflict between one revolutionary pole and two rival counter-revolutionary camps" (p. 10). The first of the counter-revolutionary forces is the political and military bureaucratic class. It is comprised of not only the political elite and its patronage networks, but the layers of society that depend upon the state for employment or other benefits and have an interest in regime survival. Critically, it encompasses the military — in whole or in part — which has a similar interest in the status quo. The second counter-revolutionary pole is represented by Islamic fundamentalism of various kinds, characterized by an "oppressive agenda" equal to that of the authoritarian state, at odds with the aspirations of the revolutionaries, and supported by regional actors including the Kingdom of Saudi Arabia, the State of Qatar, and the Islamic Republic of Iran (p. 8). The revolutionaries — the Egyptians, Iraqis, Libyans, Syrians, Tunisians, and Yemenis who participated in the Arab Spring uprisings — represent the revolutionary pole, a broad movement with "radical progressive and emancipatory potential" (p. 9). The relations between these three poles create an intractable crisis in which, as Antonio Gramsci wrote, "the old is dying and the new cannot be born; in this interregnum a great variety of morbid symptoms appear." Those who grasped this dynamic early, Achcar contends, should have been under no illusions that a resolution could be achieved without violence.

Equipped with this framework, Achcar guides the reader through a close examination of the events that have taken place in Syria and Egypt since he finished writing his prior book, *The People Want* (U. of California Press, 2013). In chapters dedicated to each country, he draws on, and quotes at length, contemporary media reporting and analysis, particularly where it is based on interviews with significant actors including activists and politicians.

13

The narrative produced in these two main chapters provides a valuable secondary source for students. Its main shortcoming is its lack of primary sources. This is understandable given the nature of Achcar's meta-level analysis and the political and security risks associated with fieldwork in the region at present; however, personal interviews would have added depth to the narrative. That said, Achcar's sources are broad and deep, multilingual, precisely referenced, and critically assessed. The book's endnotes provide additional insight and avenues for further enquiry. The slim volume concludes with brief observations on Libya, Tunisia, and Yemen, identifying similar tripolar dynamics with local variations.

Lessons to be Learned

The decisions and events that led the Arab world to its current situation contain lessons for the region's emancipatory social and labor movements. The Syria chapter describes how "[t]he new progressive forces that emerged in Syria with the beginning of the uprising in 2011 have been suffocated by the dynamics of a civil war for which they were totally unprepared" (p. 47) and examines the strategic approach of two key players: the Syrian government and the Obama Administration. Achcar compellingly portrays the Syrian government's relationship with the Islamic State group as pragmatically collusive, ambivalent, or combative, depending on the government's assessment of its priorities at a point in time. "The Syrian regime," he writes, "will fight ISIS only if, and to the extent to which, it believes that it enhances its position in the fight against its main enemy: the mainstream opposition backed by Turkey and the Gulf monarchies" (p. 42). On the one hand, we see a naïve opposition movement that lacks the capacity and capability to respond to repressive and chaotic violence; on the other, a government willing to "instrumentalize" violent extremists against forces that it fears may one day threaten its own survival.

Achcar's analysis joins a growing body of analysis critical of the Obama Administration's response to the Syrian uprising. At its core, US policy has sought the maintenance of the Syrian state — to avoid the collapse and chaos unleashed elsewhere — and to prevent the revolutionary emergence of political forces or structures that would challenge the "US dominated regional order" (p. 64). In practical terms, this meant no support for progressive forces at the start of the revolution, refusal to arm the opposition when it faced repression, and constraints on the provision of arms by US allies. As a result, the opposition is unable to counter the emergence of extremist groups or seriously threaten the government. Achcar concludes, "whereas the three previous presidents devastated Iraq by way of direct US military aggression, Obama contributed to the devastation of Syria by letting its dictatorial regime achieve it" (pp. 26-27).

The role of the US is also evident in Egypt; however, Achcar's primary foci are the missteps of the Egyptian revolutionaries and the maneuvers of the military and Islamist counter-revolutionary poles. The military and the Muslim Brotherhood are central actors, but Achcar also takes care to introduce the non-specialist reader to the important decisions and actions of the activist group Tamarrod (pp. 85-87), including its open collaboration with the *fulul* (remnants of the old order) (p. 91), and politicians such as Hamdeen Sabahy, who shifted from an independent position to accommodation with the military (pp. 97-100). The tripolar framework illuminates the outcome of the Egyptian uprising: the revolutionary pole achieves initial success only to find itself opposed by two larger and stronger counter-revolutionary poles which then proceed to contest power. The revolutionary leadership naïvely forms a tactical alliance with the military against the Muslim Brotherhood, only to find itself in an unbalanced partnership where it is essentially disempowered (pp. 104-106). This narrative unfolds against a backdrop of economic crisis, mass worker unrest (pp. 80-81), and, as the military seizes power, increasing detention, disappearances, and death. Under this new order, Achcar concludes, Egypt's near future holds militarized rentierism (pp 139-140).

The only optimistic observation is that the events of the past six years are "merely the first cycle in a long-term revolutionary process" (p. 106). Although, reflecting on the Rabi'a massacre — the anniversary of which was observed while writing this review, and which Achcar fears may be "a harbinger of the repression to come" (p. 146) — future cycles in this process may create more horror than hope.

Measured Optimism and a Strategic Challenge

"In the same way as in 2011 I was warning against the euphoria and the illusions that [the Arab uprisings] created," Gilbert Achcar recently remarked (Perth Indymedia, 2016), "I am nowadays in the position of warning against the reverse — this kind of full pessimism that exists regarding the Arab countries." Yet *Morbid Symptoms...*, as its title suggests, is decidedly light on optimism. Having explored Syria and Egypt in detail, and after touching upon Libya, Tunisia, and Yemen, Achcar concludes, "...the alternatives on offer [in the Arab world] remain, more than ever, radical progressive social and political change or a deepening clash of barbarisms" (p. 150).

Achcar's closes by addressing the strategic challenge facing "the Arab left." While he does not go into detail about "what is to be done," Achcar certainly sets out in stark terms what should not be done. Alliances — tactical or strategic — with counter-revolutionary forces, particularly where there is a power and size asymmetry, cannot provide a path forward for social movements seeking genuine revolutionary, emancipatory change. By incorporating genuinely progressive forces into one of the two counter-revolutionary poles, alliances in both Egypt and Syria have effectively closed off the opportunity to create a powerful third pole with the organizational strength to decisively remove the elite that it opposes. Successful revolutionary action will require greater "organization and strategic thinking" (p. 150). This can only be achieved by the emergence of "resolutely independent progressive leaderships" capable of replacing the current order with "one in which state resources and the national wealth are truly mobilized in the interests of the people" (p. 172). Achcar does not elaborate on how this might be achieved. Many will hope that another chapter is written soon.

References

Perth Indymedia. (2016). Morbid symptoms: Gilbert Achcar on the counter revolution in the Arab World. Retrieved September 13, 2016 from http://perthindymedia.net/morbid-symptoms-gilbert-achcar-on-the-counter-revolution-in-the-arab-world/. **DD**

The Muslim Brotherhood: The Arab Spring and Its Future Face

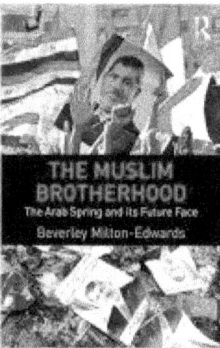

Beverley Milton-Edwards. New York, NY: Routledge, 2016. 234 pp. ISBN: 978-0415660013.

The Muslim Brotherhood (*alIkhwan alMuslimun*) is the largest, in terms of its membership, and most geographically widespread Islamist movement in the modern world. With national branches, which operate largely independently though they are technically connected to each other through their shared history and evolution from the thought of founder

Hasan al-Banna (19061949), in many Arab Muslim majority countries including Egypt, Jordan, the Palestinian Territories, Yemen, Iraq, Tunisia, and Syria, the Muslim Brotherhood has both enjoyed an unprecedented revival and major hurdles since the beginning of the 'Arab Spring' in December 2010 and January 2011.

Beverley Milton-Edwards, a professor of politics, international studies, and philosophy at Queen's University Belfast, is uniquely placed to write a primer on the history and evolution of the Muslim Brotherhood as an idea as well as the histories and contemporary trajectories of its various national branches/organizations. Previously, she has written studies on modern Islamic "fundamentalism," modern Middle East politics, the modern history of Jordan, and *Hamas*. Using the primary and secondary sources as well as interviews conducted with various players in different Muslim Brotherhood branches, such as *Hamas* official Mahmoud al-Zahar, she has written a useful, comprehensive introduction to the movement and its different branches. By including chapters on the movement's most important branches, Milton-Edwards provides readers with a handy single volume covering many aspects of this influential and multifaceted social movement and set of political organizations.

She argues that the Muslim Brotherhood today faces a watershed moment in its history, much like it did in 1967 following the humiliating defeat of pan-Arabism, led by Egypt's Gamal Abd al-Nasir, at the hands of Israel in the Six Day War, which opened the door to the rise of Islamism as an alternative transnational ideological competitor in the Arab World. Similarly, the 'Arab Spring' provided many of the movement's regional branches the first real opportunity at open participation in the political processes of their home countries. The resulting upheavals in the region from 2011 to the present have also presented the branches with a set of hurdles, such as in Egypt following the military coup that toppled the elected government of Muhammad Mursi, the Egyptian Brotherhood's candidate, as well as the parliament, which included powerful Brotherhood and Salafi contingents. In Egypt in particular, the country's Brotherhood faces the choice of whether to shift toward political violence in the wake of the Sisi regime's brutal crackdown on all forms of dissent, Islamist and otherwise, and the outlawing of the Brotherhood and mass arrests, torture, and political trials of the organization's leaders and members.

Before delving into the individual histories of the Muslim Brotherhood's national branches, Milton-Edwards provides a succinct introduction to the movement's founding history and ideology. Focusing on the life and career of Hasan al-Banna, the Egyptian school teacher, intellectual, and Muslim activist, the book's first chapter situates the rise of the movement in the historical, political, and social milieu of change in 1940s Egypt. She also highlights the challenge the movement faced with the rise to prominence, radicalization, and execution of the popular revolutionary Muslim Brotherhood ideologue and writer Sayyid Qutb as well as the return to the 'middle' path of pragmatism endorsed by the movement's general guide, Hasan al-Hudaybi. Qutb's most revolutionary writings, particularly his book *Ma'alim fi alTariq* (Milestones along the Path) and the revisions of some of his massive *tafsir, Fi Zilal alQur'an* (In the Shadow of the *Qur'an*), continue to be popular with revolutionary Islamists and particularly jihadi organizations such as Al-Qa'ida and its regional affiliates and the Islamic State.

In Egypt, the Egyptian Brotherhood organization's senior leadership was late in endorsing and joining the mass popular protests in Tahrir Square in Cairo and other parts of the country against the country's aging ruling autocrat, Hosni Mubarak, and his corrupt regime. However, it soon joined the bandwagon and, thanks to its well-established grassroots networks and history of activism and participation in civil society organizations such as labor and teachers' unions, as well as university student organizations, was better placed than most of its competitors to take advantage of the political openings, such as actual democratic elections, that followed Mubarak and the *ancien régimes.*

In Syria, the Syrian Brotherhood had been severely repressed by the ruling Ba'athist regime led by the al-Asad family since the 1970s and it had split into several competing factions including a more politically moderate "Damascus Wing," a more confrontationist Aleppo wing led by Marwan Hadid, and an extremely militant offshoot, the Fighting Vanguard (*al-Tali'a alMuqatila*). The surge in mass antigovernment protests in Syria in the spring of 2011 and the subsequent beginning of a brutal civil war presented the Syrian Brotherhood with potential opportunities as well as major challenges, particularly as it seemed to lose ground inside the country as the civil war has dragged on and become increasingly brutal, leading to the rise of more puritanical Islamist rebel groups with their own networks and ideologies.

In Tunisia, the Ennahda Party has perhaps been the most successful Brotherhood organization in post-'Arab Spring' politics, engaging in multi party competition in the wake of the flight of the country's former dictator, Zayn al-Abidin Ben Ali. The party's leader and founder, Rached Ghannouchi, is often described as a conservative democratic and he has steered Ennahda on a pragmatic course through postautocratic politics in the country. In Yemen, the Yemeni Brotherhood, which is one of the groups that make up the Islah Party, which is more of an uneasy coalition of the country's Ikhwan, tribal figures, and Salafi political actors.

Hamas, the Palestinian Islamic political and militant movement, continues to have a rocky experience with governance in the Gaza Strip and an uneasy on-again-and-off-again relationship with the Palestinian National Authority in the West Bank, which is dominated by its rival, the Fatah Party, formerly led by Yasir Arafat and now led by a coterie of his aides, including PNA president Mahmoud Abbas. Hamas also continues to be torn between its desire to participate in politics through its political wing and the interests of its military wing, the Martyr Izz alDin al-Qassam Brigades. Due to her previous in-depth research on the organization, the book's chapter on Hamas and the Palestinian Brotherhood is particularly insightful.

The Jordanian Brotherhood historically has maintained good relations with the ruling Hashemite monarchy, often serving as the 'loyal opposition.' Unlike its sister organizations in Egypt and Syria, the Jordanian organization has not suffered under the same forms of government repression as the former. Beginning in 2014, however, Jordan's King 'Abdullah II, who lacks the tribal connections and charisma of his late father, King Husayn bin Talal bin 'Abdullah, began to crack down on the Jordanian Brotherhood's political party, the Islamic Action Front due to pressure from his country's Arab Gulf state allies, who had recently declared the Muslim Brotherhood to be a banned "terrorist organization." The Jordanian monarch, surrounded by regional instability and fearful for the future of his regime, chose to pursue a confrontational policy toward the organization and the future trajectory of the Jordanian Brotherhood remains unclear.

The book also includes a chapter on the transnational aspects of the Muslim Brotherhood as a multi-country social movement. It includes a section on its extensive Internet presence and cyber activism, which Milton-Edwards dubs the "Cyberhood." This presence includes extensive web sites in Arabic and English as well as official Twitter accounts for the organization and individual leading members in the movement's various national branches. The Internet, however, has also presented the Muslim Brotherhood with a new set of challenges including how to effectively maintain a sense of unity and continuity in its messaging as well as how to counter anti-Brotherhood cyber activists who have launched hacking attacks on its web sites and social media accounts.

Overall, the book is a very useful and comprehensive introduction to one of the Middle East and North Africa's most influential and widespread sociopolitical movements. It includes extensive details concerning the Muslim Brotherhood's history and the histories of its national branches as well as insights into their future trajectories. Milton Edwards' volume is particularly well suited to classroom use, including by undergraduates. The individual chapters can also fairly easily be used independently of one another in university courses on Middle East politics, political Islam, and Middle East and North African history. **CA**

Routledge Handbook of the Arab Spring: Rethinking Democratization

Larbi Sadiki, **Ed.** London, UK: Routledge, 2015. 718 pp. ISBN: 978-0415523912.

The revolutionary tide that swept many Arab countries in 2011 has generated much controversy among scholars working on various subjects. The infamous argument of the so-called Arab exceptionalism appeared to have shaken the masses pouring into the streets demanding their freedom and dignity. *The Routledge Handbook of the Arab Spring* presents a valuable reference to the various narratives of the uprisings and their national, regional, and international dynamics.

In his introduction, the editor of the volume refutes any assumed correlation between the Arab Spring and democracy. For him, democracy in this context is about "the dynamic of unruliness, defiance against and resistance to authoritarian rule" (p. 1), rather than a particular type of government. In this view, this popular defiance of authoritarianism creatively manifested itself in three dimensions: time, space, and language. Clockwise demonstrations, occupying public spaces and speaking out what the people want are only examples of challenging the authoritarian grip.

The volume is divided into eight parts. The first part — "Introducing the Arab Spring: Reflections on Contexts and Contests of Democratizations" — spans four chapters that contextualize the Arab Spring within the literature on democratization. It begins with an interesting contribution by Lawrence Whitehead where he compares the Arab Spring with other "springs" across history to draw lessons and guidance. His comparison demonstrates a high lack of the inclusionary tendencies as well as the international stabilizing forces in the MENA experience — two factors that are important in reinforcing political liberalization. Drawing on his personal experience in Lebanon,

Michael Husdon rethinks Arab political legitimacy, calling for broadening our focus from state and regime to society, economy, culture, and exogenous influences and pressures. For his part, Raymond Hinnebush criticizes the democratization and post-democratization theories for not emphasizing an important aspect of the uprisings: the "underlying political economy motors of politics" (p. 49). Mustapha al-Sayyid emphasizes the similarities and differences among the Arab Spring countries to examine the immunity of other countries from the rising demands of democratization and good governance. The importance of many of the contributions in this part lies in their comparative study of the Arab Spring, which puts into question the exceptionalism argument.

Parts two and three highlight the structure vs. agency argument. While some chapters, especially in the second part, are focused on the political, historical, and socio-economic basis of the revolutions, others pay greater attention to the actors themselves, their historical developments, and how they responded to the different tactics of the incumbent regimes.

Part Two: "The 'Travel' of Revolution: From Tunis to San'a," discusses in ten chapters the roots and direct causes of the Arab uprisings and how the spark that started in Tunisia spread to other parts in the Arab World. The Tunisian and Syrian revolutions receive the most attention here. Amor Boubakri, for example, presents the main milestones in the long history of the struggle for political reforms in Tunisia before Bou'azizi. Sami Zemni lays emphasis to the class aspect to our understanding of the Tunisian revolution. He demonstrates how capitalist transformations in Tunisia since the 1980s have influenced the relationship between the state and different classes. Anas Buera sheds lights on the nature of the Libyan political regime under Gadaffi, whereas Anas El Gomati examines the main junctures in the history of Libya's Islamists, from 1843 until the 17th of February Revolution in 2011. In her chapter on the uprising in Bahrain, Kristina Ulrichsen examines the regional and international factors that led to the crackdown on the burgeoning reform social movement. In her view, this crackdown had a huge cost, not only economically, but also on the social cohesion of Bahrain.

Writing from an activist perspective, Obaida Fares presents his narrative of the Syrian revolution, arguing that "[i]n all its forms, foreign intervention has undermined the will of the Syrian people and contributed to the prolonging of the conflict" (p. 158). Approaching the Syrian revolution through the lenses of media coverage, Layla Saleh appears to confirm this conclusion. For her part, Elham Manae explains the failure of the youth revolt of Yemen with reference to the features and acts of the "cunning state" that is "run by ethnic core elites, who exploit the seams of international structures and capitalize on the fear on the international community over its perceived failure to perpetuate its grip on power" (p. 160).

Part Three: "Egypt in the Arab Spring: Islam, the State and the Military," is exclusively devoted to the January 2011 Egyptian revolution regarding its causes, dynamics, and the different actors involved therein. Among the significant contributions in this part is Irene Weiper-Fenner's chapter on "Making the crisis visible" where she exposes the power struggle within the ruling elite before the January Revolution through a discursive analysis of the Egyptian parliament. Her chapter demonstrates the usefulness of the institutional approach in understanding the complexity of authoritarianism in general. Khalil al-Anani challenges the "inclusion-moderation" hypothesis, which assumes that integration of anti-establishment parties and social movement would lead to their moderation. Studying the case of the Muslim Brotherhood in Egypt, al-Anani shifts the focus from the "outcomes" of the inclusion process to the dynamics of the process itself. He examines how the internal and external variables have influenced the Islamist movement's discourse, ideology, and tactics.

In his chapter, Khaled Abou el-Fadl examines "the cliental relationship between the military and the secular elite in a state that controls and defines religion" (p. 254). He argues that there are three main causes of the failure of the Egyptian Revolution: the military, the secular intelligentsia, and the Saudi Arabian role. Abou el-Fadl challenges the dominant narrative that puts all the blame on Egypt's Islamists for the failure of the Egyptian Revolution by exposing the secular intelligentsia's betrayal of both the revolution and the democratic principles. In his conclusion, without elaborating on how that would happen in current circumstances in Egypt, Abou el-Fadl presents quite a pessimistic view of Egypt's political future, arguing that "at the end Egypt will witness an Iranian-style theocracy" (p. 269).

The relatively short Part Four: "Women's Voices in the Arab Spring," is dedicated to the role of women in the Arab Spring, a subject that remains, nonetheless, underrepresented. The two chapters in this part focus on the Syrian and Tunisian women. Based on her various interviews with Syrian female activists mostly living outside Syria, Tamara al-Om discusses the varying roles that Syrian women played and continue to play in the revolution and their struggle to achieve equality and adequate representation in the society. Andrea Khalil discusses female activism in post-revolutionary Tunisia and demonstrates how it is embedded within the confrontation between "Islamist" and "secularist" discourses.

Part Five: "Arab Spring: Breakdown of the Old Social Compact," examines various agents of change, such as trade unions and social movements that seek to bring down the economic and social authoritarian structures. This part begins with Lachen Achy's chapter that shows how the fall of the political leadership in both Egypt and Tunisia did not necessarily lead to breaking down the foundations of their authoritarian regimes. Therefore, a new state-citizen relationship failed to materialize. In his view, what he calls the Arab Authoritarian Bargain Model (ABM) "relies on a strong network of alliances entrenched in the business sector and within a wide range of state institutions including the security sector, the bureaucracy, the media and the judiciary" (p. 304). In his chapter, Gianluca Solera studies the similarities among social movements around the Mediterranean to examine if these similarities "represent a space, an opportunity for common political action" (p. 331).

Part Six: "Uprisings: The Technology of Protest," highlights the different tools that political actors used to enact change. Armando Salvatore begins this part by discussing the notion of the public sphere and its relationship to the revolution and democratization. He emphasizes the importance of interdisciplinary and comparative approaches in discussing such developments. He warns that although a viable public sphere is a necessary condition for democratization, it is not in itself sufficient to bring about democratic change. Salvatore, however, focuses on the democratizing effect of social media but overlooks how authoritarian regime can use the same means to overcome the democratization challenge by tracking down activists and using counter propaganda tactics.

In the remaining six chapters in this part, contributors elaborate on a variety of empowerment tools used in resisting authoritarianism, including music, graffiti, poetry, as well as satellite media, particularly Al-Jazeera. Ezzeddine Abdelmoula's chapter discusses the democratizing role of Al Jazeera and the relationship between the Arab revolutions and the coverage of the channel, highlighting its role in revolutionizing the Arab media sphere long before the revolutions.

Part Seven: "The Arab Spring: The Wider Middle East," tackles the reflective influences of Arab Spring on the wider regional circle and the way other regimes reacted to the challenges to change. Michael Willis, for example, discusses how Morocco was able to avoid a popular uprising. The Moroccan exceptionalism, according to him, indicates the political acumen of the monarchy. However, he argues that the monarchy's response had only delayed rather than overcome the main problems of the country. While Youcef Bouandel argues that the series of reforms initiated by the Algerian government since February 2011 are just strengthening "façade democracy" (p. 452), Hamid Alkifaey claims that the Iraqi democracy is on the right track. In

Oman, James Worrall contends that while reforms taken by the Sultan may seem to be lacking a real substance, deeper analysis reveals possible long-term impacts.

The protest tide has also its repercussions on non-Arab Middle Eastern countries. Turkey's regime vs. opposition discourse, as Derya Gocer Akder and Marc Herzog argue, has been influenced by the new political conflicts in the region with negative results for Turkey's own transition. While contributors to this part are mostly interested in the different consequences of the "Arab Spring," Shabnam Holliday problematizes "the idea of an *Arab* Spring by examining the case of Iran" (p. 534). He argues that the same dynamics attributed to the Arab Spring already exist in Iran.

Part Eight: "The Arab Spring in a Global Context," discusses the impact of Arab Spring beyond the regional frontiers. For example, Tobias Schumacher outlines the EU's response to the Arab uprisings and argues that it reflects the same "structural weaknesses and contradictions of past policy approaches" (p. 560). On the contrary, Timo Behr finds that when it comes to Arab uprisings, Nordic countries have shown signs of change from "internationalism" to "interventionism." Karina Fayzullina explains the Russian reaction to the uprising, not on ideological bases, but based on its pursuit of power and prestige by influencing world events. Pragmatism has also characterized the Indian stance toward the revolutions, as Anwar Alam argues. For her part, Dalal Daoud demonstrates the rhetoric-action contradictions of North America's countries. She argues that the Canadian and American administrations attempted to control the uprisings via 'managed transitions;' transitions that would appease their concerns about the rise of Islamists and protect the future of Israel.

Useful as many contributions in this *Handbook...* may be, it could have been structured in a more meaningful way. It would have been useful for the comparative study of the cases to divide the volume along five main areas: the (traditional and new) actors, the structural causes of the uprising, the dynamics and tools of change, the (regional and international) context, and the repercussions of the protest movement. Many of the weaknesses found in some parts of the *Handbook...* are due to its rather random outline. For example, Part Three, which focuses on the Egyptian revolution, informs readers enough about Egypt's traditional political elites (the military, secularists, and Islamists), but very little about its youth social movement that stirred and largely shaped the protests. Moreover, it is not clear why the Syrian and Tunisian women were chosen as representative of the Arab women's role in the revolutions, but not Yemeni women, for example, even though one of them, Tawakul Karman, has won the Noble Prize for Peace for her influential role in the protests.

Dealing with the tools of change, a chapter on political satire and sarcasm — two phenomena that have flourished with the "Arab Spring" and became influential in challenging the cultural foundations of authoritarianism — would have been a great addition to part six. A more coherent organization would also demonstrate the reciprocal influence between the uprisings and the tools of change themselves. For example, the Arab Spring has influenced Al-Jazeera as much as it influenced the protests. This is reflected in the changing popularity of the channel during and after the revolutions in many countries of the Arab Spring.

When it comes to the regional level, readers may wonder why, except for Khaled Abou al-Fadl's contribution, the role that Saudi Arabia has played in these revolutions is not adequately discussed. The same question applies to the UAE given its clear support to the counter-revolutionary forces in the region. There is some unnecessary overlapping among some chapters in part eight. For example, while one chapter discusses the European Union's democracy promotion efforts in general, another focuses on the EU's democracy promotion in Tunisia, repeating some of the details mentioned in the former chapter. Finally, it is not clear why India is represented in this part, but not China, for example.

The main strength of this volume lies in its breadth, variety of views and approaches, and compacted information. But as is always the case with edited volumes, the contributions vary in their depths. While some contributions are thought-provoking and set the stage for further research on the Arab Spring, others are more descriptive and do not offer any new insights. Overall, the *Handbook...* is useful and will serve its purposes as an introductory reference for understanding the events that shocked the Middle East to its core in recent years. It will definitely contribute to the on-going discourse on the so-called Arab Spring and its potential trajectories. **MFAS**

Salafism after the Arab Awakening: Contending with People's Power

Francesco Cavatorta & Fabio Merone, Eds. New York, NY: Oxford University Press, 2016. 354 pp. ISBN: 978-0190274993.

What have been the theological and political impact of the Arab Spring on Salafism? This edited book addressed that question with a kaleidoscopic look at the Middle East and North Africa (MENA). In his concluding chapter, Roel Meijer argued that quietism has been vindicated and there has been a change in the nature of jihadism. In briefly locating *salafi-yya da'wiyya* (evangelizing Salafism) or *salafiyya 'ilmiyya* (scholastic Salafism) — quietist Salafism — in the context of the Arab Spring, particularly the thorny issue of *hizbiyya* (party politics) in fearing *fitna* (chaos), Laurent Bonnefoy argued that rejection of political participation is not necessarily apolitical. Noting that politicization is a two-way street, Bonnefoy stressed that quietist Salafists have their legitimacy and visibility intact. Organized into fourteen chapters, including an introduction and conclusion, the case studies included Egypt, Jordan, Kuwait, Lebanon, Morocco, Saudi Arabia, Syria, Tunisia, and Yemen. The introductory chapter laid out four research questions: What explained the robust and surprise emergence of Salafism? What were the conditions for the trajectory of one variant over another? How did the different national contexts explain common transnational trends? What will be the role of Salafism for regional political stability?

In revisiting the 2006 seminal work by Quintan Wiktorowicz that propounded purist, politico, and jihadi subcategories, Joas Wagemakers made a five-fold criticism: The similarity of *'aqida* (creed) was not related to *manhaj* (method), the method was restrictively related to only political authority, excessive reliance on Saudi experience, "quietist" was a better substitute for "purist," and incorrect assumption about a shared creed with differing method. He explained differences among Salafis in terms of political and societal variables of method. Arguing that they were not homogeneous subgroups, Wagemakers provided sub-subcategories within quietists (aloofists, loyalists, and propagandists), politicos (electoral politics versus political activism), and jihadis (defensive, revolutionary, and global). He introduced nuanced classifications that were an interesting contribution to the literature.

Addressing political Salafism in Saudi Arabia, Stephane Lacroix pointed to *al-sururiyyun* (Sururis) and *al-ikhwan al-muslimun al-sa'udiyyun* (Saudi Muslim Brotherhood) that were part of the somewhat secretive *jama'at* within the Sahwa movement. Given that the principle of *hisba* (social morality) can be broken into *maydaniyya* (on the ground), *bi-l-kitaba* (through writing), and *bi-l-ziyara* (through visits), there is an uneasy relationship among the groups comprising the *jama'at*. In comparing *Ittihad al-Rashad* (Rashad Union) with quietist Salafis and the al-Islah party, within a framework of political opportunity in Yemen, Judit Kuschnitzki used the broader term "activist" instead of politico. Revealing intra-Islamist competition, al-Rashad walked a fine line in identifying the conditions under which *hisbiyya* was justified. Aside from explaining the rift between al-Nahda and the Answar al-Shari'a movement in Tunisia (AST), Stefano Terelli observed that the leadership was quietist at home while supporting jihad abroad. In an interesting separate contribution on Tunisia, Iris Kolman looked at Salafi women. Even though reluctant to identify themselves as Salafis, she found the same three counterparts of quietist, political, and jihadi subgroups among female Salafis.

With moderate Muslim Brotherhood and other "extreme" Islamist groups dominating the political landscape, Khalil al-Anani identified four characteristics in Egypt since the January 2011 uprising: Proliferation of Islamist parties, politicization of Salafis, internal change within Islamist movements, and intra-Islamist competition. Salafi expansion was facilitated by acrimonious relationship between the political regime and the Muslim Brotherhood, return of educated middle-class from GCC, pre-existing charitable networks, and low educational level among the younger generation. Participation in competitive pluralist elections marked a dramatic shift in Salafi doctrine. For al-Anani, the "pragmatism" of al-Nour party — along with its patron *al-Da'wa al-Salafiyya* (Salafi Call) — was a calculated move to see decimation of the Muslim Brotherhood, filling the political vacuum, and anticipation of sizable seats in parliamentary elections.

The fluidity of Salafi movement led Mohammed Masbah to propose a four-fold typology for Morocco: Ideological versus pragmatism and politicized versus apolitical. Unfortunately, this framework was not cogently applied to a discussion of traditionalists, pragmatists, civil-society activists, and jihadis. However, he noted three moderating attitudes of the Salafis: Acceptance of monarchy, pivoting away from equality and individual rights, and softening toward Sufism. Zoltan Pall examined the issue of obedience to the ruler that created two factions within the Salafis in Kuwait: Purists who advocated unconditional obedience and activists who acquiesced to conditional obedience. Concentric with the concept of *hakim-iyya* (God's sovereignty), Salafi theology had identified three components of *tawhid* (unity of God): *Tawhid al-rububiyya* (unity of Lordship), *tawhid al-uluhiyya* (oneness of God), and *tawhid al-asma' wa al-sifat* (unity of the attributes). 'Abd al-khaliq introduced the fourth component of *tawhid al-hu-kum* (oneness of governance), which was opposed by al-Sabt as a tacit call for revolt against the ruler. The theological dispute between al-Khaliq and al-Sabt led to the expulsion of the former and his followers from *Jama'iyyat Ihya' al-Turath al-Islami* (Revival of Islamic Heritage Society, RIHS), an umbrella organization for political engagement by the Salafis. Others moved on in establishing *al-Haraka al-Salafiyya* (Salafi Movement, SM), a political organization, but further dispute led to splintering with the creation of *Hizb al-Umma* (Umma Party). The purists continued to be more pervasive in Kuwait society, however, remarked Pall.

Salafiyya 'ilmiyya and *salafiyya Jihadiyya (jihadi Salafism)* were the two main Salafi groups in Lebanon, remarked Adham Saouli. Pointing to three centers of power within the Sunni community — secular leadership, *Dar al-Fatwa* (House of Religious Edicts), and *al-Jama'a al-Islamiyya* (The Islamic Group) — he observed that the third group gained traction because of the perceived failure of the Sunni leadership to protect *ahl al-Sunna* (Sunni community) amidst deep sectarian divisions in the country. Aside from a tiny social base, competitive external funding from Kuwait, Qatar, Saudi Arabia, and the United Arab Emirates undermined political articulation and activism.

Foreign fighters and political competition among Kuwait, Qatar, Saudi Arabia, and Turkey shaped fragmentation and realignment in Syria, observed Thomas Pierret. He illustrated this point with insightful case studies: Jihadi *Jabhat al-Nusra li-ahl al-Sham* (Support Front for the People of the Levant), activist *Ahrar al-Sham* (Freedom of the Levant) and *al-Jabhat al-Is-lamiyyat al-Suriyya* (The Syrian Islamic Front, SIF), and quietist *Jabhat al-As-ala wa al-Tanmiyya* (Front for Authenticity and Development, FAD). Activist Salafis in Kuwait — relocated subsequently to United Kingdom, Jordan, and Qatar — also contributed money to *Jabha Tahrir Suriyya al-Islamiyya* (Syria Islamic Liberation Front, SLIF), which included non-Salafi commanders and maintained contacts with *Hay'at al-Sham al-Islamiyya* (Sham Islamic Committee) humanitarian organization leadership in Saudi Arabia and Bahrain. SIF and SILF later merged into *al-Jabhat al-Islamiyya* (The Islamic Front, IF), but the National Coalition and the Free Syrian Army (FSA) firewall against the Islamic State in Iraq and Syria (ISIS) suffered from Saudi-Qatari rivalry. The chapter provided a window into the sad dynamics of regional politics.

Different "reformist" and "activist" subcategories were introduced by Joas Wagemakers for Jordan and Judit Kuschnitzki for Yemen, respectively. Given the Jordanian regime's bureaucratic control over religious groups, *Jam'iyyat al-Kitab wa al-Sunna* (Association of the Books and Traditions of the Prophet) did not formalize into a political party but coupled political and social agendas into charitable works with monetary donations from Kuwait, Qatar, and Saudi Arabia. Correctly arguing that a puritanical streak is common to all, Kuschnitzki distinguished groups affiliated with only mosques or teaching institutions as "quietists." However, it was a stretch to label a group devoid of institutional politics but involved in only charitable work as "activist" (p. 101). In juxtaposing quietist Salafis and al-Islah party, she faced a particular challenge in pigeon-holing *al-Rashad* (well guided) in Yemen. That was because the al-Rashad leadership avoided the use of not only *'bid'a'* (innovation) and *'shirk'* (polytheism), but also "Salafi" to refer to the party and its programs. Kuschnitzki addressed the puzzle of the "new Islamic voice" with attention to the concept of *hizbiyya* (factionalism) and "duality of structure" by Anthony Giddens.

In invoking the distinction between procedural democracy and liberal democracy, Stefano Torelli accused *Jabhat al-Islah* (Reform Front) party in Tunisia of taking advantage of democratic means toward authoritarian ends in shunning coalition with secular groups (pp. 159-60). However, that overlooked being part of a coalition government with other religious parties. By the same token, should it be surprising that *al-Jam'iyya al-Wasatiyya li-l-Taw'iyya wa al-Islah* (Moderate Association for Awareness and Reform), categorized as a quietist Salafist by the contributor, would like to create a religious police? With al-Nahda forming a government, however, Torelli was at a loss in trying to classify the Ansar al-Shari'a movement in Tunisia (AST). That was because AST combined quietist Salafism and assertive charitable activism with support for jihad in Iraq and Syria — a similar challenge was also noted by Wagemakers in Chapter 2 in an analysis of the concept of *al-wa-la' wa al-bara'* (loyalty to fellow Muslims and disavowal of everyone else).

The book is a significant contribution to the literature on MENA and political Islam, particularly Salafism. The conceptual analysis and diverse case studies are insightful and interesting. Scholars of political parties and religious violence will find it a worthwhile reading. Graduate students in religion, comparative politics, and security as well as policy-makers will also benefit from the work. ***RGM***

Women's Movements in Post-"Arab Spring" North Africa

Fatima Sadiqi, Ed. New York, NY: Palgrave Macmillan, 2016. 325 pp. ISBN: 978-1137520470.

"Women's Movements in Post-'Arab Spring' North Africa", a collection of essays edited by Fatima Sadiqi, tears across the cultural, economic, legal, and political history of the region during the post-colonial era, presenting an exploration of how relatively static political images of male-female relations define the limitations of a revolution's ambition. The most vivid essays in the collection demonstrate how the patriarchy finds a way to co-opt, not only tradition, but modernity in North African societies. Women remain trapped in complimentary status: if not to males, then to male conceptions of modernity. As Rachida Kerkech summarizes in her contribution on cultural challenges facing Moroccan women: "women's development might be accepted, but only as long as it does not impinge on men's absolute power" (p. 277). Rachid Tlemçani, examining Algeria, writes that "modernization has been stronger than modernity in Muslim countries, and as a result, women have been marginalized in modern state-building" (p. 238).

In highlighting feminist involvement and interpretations of revolution in this volume, Miriam Cooke discusses "the Algerian lesson" from that country's revolution, in which women called on to join the fight were shunted back to traditional roles when hostilities ceased. Dina Wahba observes in her piece on gender in the Egyptian revolution that providing only limited, abstract political concessions regarding women's rights rather than altering longstanding socio-economic patterns is a method for the patriarchy to re-establish itself, strengthening its foundation even as its elaborate structures splinter in the storm of revolution. The principle of establishing a "new normal" (Margot Badran's phrasing in her essay on the Egyptian experience) regarding male-female relationships is the most difficult phase of social transformation; if it cannot occur in the ideologically-latent Algerian War, what hope for the patchwork of revolutions twisting across North Africa in recent years?

This volume also addresses the willingness of regimes that otherwise espouse modernist principles to rely on sexual violence or the threat of it to secure themselves during the rebellion. Cooke describes Muammar Qadhaafi's alleged use of mass rape as a tool to salvage his rule, and Wahba the crumbling Mubarak regime's attempts to degrade female activists as impious or debauched. Wahba further discusses the crucial role of women in helping to combat regime propaganda aimed at portraying Egyptian protestors as simply masses of angry young men, easily dismissed by international media as dangerous or radical. The very presence of unintimidated women in the crowd on television screens is a powerful disruptor of this narrative.

The often-facile attempts of modernist regimes to deal with women's rights on a meaningful level, in part, explain the tendency of Libyan and Tunisian society to revert to Islamist or traditional practices once "secular" leaders are removed. Such regimes have also shown a willingness to take retrograde stands on women's issues as it suits their needs. Tlemçani observes how, in 1980, the Benjadid regime in Algeria passed legislation prohibiting women from traveling without permission from a male guardian. It was incumbent on women to protest this law, which they did in a successful effort to have it canceled, in part, due to the negative attention the regime garnered internationally.

Some essays explore the history of women's activism in the region, whether in resistance to the colonial patriarchy or the masculinist, secular dictatorships and juntas to follow. Sondra Hale writes about how Sudanese women continue to see the struggle for their rights in terms of other than ideological, substituting the new term "activist" for terms such as "Islamist" or "communist" which may immerse women's causes in broader pantheons of political objectives.

Moha Ennaji's sweeping regional scope allows her chapter to serve as a bridge between the earlier contextual chapters and later focus on individual countries. It taps into the most stirring thematic concept of the collection, that the future of freedom in the region is absolutely tied to the future of women's emancipation (addressing this fundamental point more clearly than does even the volume's introduction). This principle, so clearly understood and articulated in anti-colonial struggles, is often forgotten in the absence of a state-level threat. Ennaji writes of how male leaders of the Islah Islamic organization advocated for women's emancipation during the colonial era across the Maghreb. The connection of women's rights to broader political freedom and development was understood by modernists, both Islamist and secular. But the lack of consideration of women's rights as an *inherent* good rather than simply a benchmark for supposedly weightier political and economic policies is a crucial question Ennaji underscores.

The essays which analyze post-2011 developments in context with earlier history are welcome additions. Moushira Khattab reviews Egypt's constitutional history and new challenges to women's freedom, like the 2012 repeal of FGM laws by the Islamist-controlled parliament. Ellen McLarney discusses the tactical importance of women's rights to Egypt's autocratic rulers, both in symbolism and in black-and-white constitutional guarantees. Her review of legal protections and considerations in Egypt's various constitutions is perhaps the best integration of history with recent events in this collection. The compromises Sadat and others made regarding the role of Shari'a as it relates to women are reviewed in this insightful essay, as is the ostentatious advocacy of women's issues by Jihan Sadat and Suzanne Mubarak. Many women's advocates believed the control of the few legal women's organizations by these autocrats' wives tarnished the women's movement among broad sectors of the public. Soumia Boutkhil includes Leila Trabelsi among these figures of "state feminism," and explains how their lack of commitment to freedom made them part of the problem, not the solution (p. 256).

Even when male leaders advocate for women's rights in the region, a disconnect remains between regime promotion and public demands. Khadija Arfaoui observes that Bourguiba's 1956 Code of Personal Status, providing significant individual freedoms for Tunisian women unknown elsewhere in the Arab World, was not the result of a demand by those women; it was a personal "gift" from the president in accordance with his preferences. Perhaps, the most exaggerated example is put forward by Amanda Rogers, who writes that while Qadhaafi heralded his own role in improving the lot of Libyan women with respect to the previous monarchy, his official Green Book philosophy still held them as subordinate to men in accordance with natural order. His regime had a role for the objectification of women and possibly even sexual violence when it found itself threatened. Nabila Hamza demonstrates how the mission of Tunisia's Islamist Al-Nahda party to justify women's roles in society in "complementary" terms to men's roles creates a tension with its need to be seen as a champion of democracy in the birthplace of the Arab Uprisings (p. 217). Like Islamist parties before it (e.g., Sudan's National Islamic Front in the 1980s), Al-Nahda has learned the symbolic and constitutional value of having strong female representation in legislative assemblies; the vast majority of female parliamentarians elected in 2014 were Al-Nahda members.

"Balance" is a term modernists may choose to reconcile a vision of a modern future with one in which women remain bound to "special" roles that they and only they can fill. Tlemçani quotes Prime Minister Recep Erdogan in 2008 describing the status of women in Turkey: "Our religion [Islam] has defined a position for women: motherhood. Some people can understand this, while others can't" (p. 247). Boutkhil's chapter ventures an idea on how patriarchy and conservatism feed on global conflicts and tensions to create the conditions of what the chapter refers to as women's transitional, "liminal" citizenship. In the Moroccan context, she writes that "tradition and modernity" is a narrative to promote the country as a balance between two concepts seen as at odds elsewhere. In Morocco, the contrast with the rest of the region's turmoil is meant to lead to a natural confidence in the establishment.

Highlighting another theme of this volume, Névine El Nossery cites Leila Ahmed's caution against the tendency of treating women as "oppressed" as a rule in Middle East rather than viewing them as articulate agents of their own will, free to put forward narratives that may contradict those of their supposed benefactors in the West (p. 148). Abdellatif Zaki argues that mass involvement of women in protests and revolution allows them to become even more aware of "the limitations of the scope of the discourse on issues related to their status and rights" (p. 308).

In conclusion, though the theme of the "Arab Spring" is certainly constant in this book, it seems to me the focus on this period unintentionally downplays the scope of what is covered. The book's primary theme is the role of women in expanding and progressing concepts of what constitutes "modernity". The events of December 2010 onward are important but only one of the latest transitions in this ongoing struggle, as the rich history reviewed in much of this work attests. **JDL**

ARTS AND ARCHITECTURE

The Bronze Age Towers at Bat, Sultanate of Oman: Research by the Bat Archaeological Project 2007-12

Christopher P. Thornton, Charlotte M. Cable, & Gregory L. Possehl, Eds. Philadelphia, PA: University of Pennsylvania Museum of Archaeology and Anthropology, 2016. 330 pp. ISBN: 978-1934536063.

As the title states, this book is a report of the archaeological work conducted by an international team led by the University of Pennsylvania during six seasons (2007-2012) at Bat in north-central Oman. Bat, the first pre-historic site in Arabia to become a UNESCO World Heritage Site, is the best-preserved Bronze Age (3rd millennium BCE) settlement in Magan, the name given to southeastern Arabia in ancient Mesopotamian texts. The work covers the three major Bronze Age periods in Magan: Hafit (3100-2800 BCE), Umm an-Nar (2800-2000 BCE), and Wadi Suq (2000-1600 BCE). This period is characterized as witnessing "the emergence of a new socioeconomic system in which independent states became reliant, if not entirely dependent, upon other states for the maintenance of their elaborate social, cultural, and religious behavior... that eventually collapsed around 2000 BCE due to environmental, demographic, and sociopolitical factors..." (p. 1). The team's specific goal was to determine the how, when, and why of the construction of Bat's distinctive towers while adding to the understanding of the social, political, and economic conditions underlying Magan's relations with Mesopotamia, Dilmun (Eastern Arabia), and Meluhha/Harappa (the Indus Valley).

The report begins with a geo-archaeological study of the site, focusing on water management and agricultural practices. The next six chapters focus on Bat's towers with detailed reports on Kasr al-Khafaji (Tower 1146), Matariya (Tower 1147), Kasr al-Sleme (Tower 1148), Tower 1156, preliminary discussion of two structures in the neighboring town of Ad-Dariz, and an overview of the five remaining towers (Kasr al-Rojoom, Husn al-Wardi, al-Qa'a, al-Khutum, and Wahrah Qala) in Bat. In presenting their findings, the authors also draw on previous, largely unpublished, archaeological work, most notably that conducted by Karen Frifelt during the 1970s and 1980s. The authors then examine the ceramics, chipped stone pieces, metal and metallurgical artifacts, and ground stone artifacts. Five appendices present information on archaeo-botanical studies, ancient water systems, Bronze Age mud bricks, radiocarbon dates, further information relative to two Wadi Suq Period tombs at Tower 1156, and a list of the field staff.

While determining the how and when of tower construction is relatively easy, the why remains elusive. All have in common an early period of mud-brick construction, usually associated with a well, during the Hafit Period, followed by the construction of a stone tower during the Umm an-Nar Period, and then a period of decline when the towers became the source of building materials for smaller Wadi Suq period grave structures. However, due, in large part, to their modification and re-use throughout the thousand years under consideration, their function, be it ritual, water management, or defense, is very difficult to establish. As the authors admit, they were unsuccessful in determining the exact function of the towers and "may never know precisely what the Bronze Age towers of Bat were used for" (p. 260).

What the archaeological evidence does serve to establish is Magan's interdependence with Mesopotamia and the Indus Valley and the overall decline of the region during the Bronze Age. Pottery artifacts provide evidence for both cultural and stimulus diffusion with imported wares from Mesopotamia, Iran, and the Indus Valley, followed by locally produced imitations, and then entirely local styles. Metal and metallurgical artifacts also serve to confirm Oman's importance as a source of copper for the southwest Asian region. What makes this evidence especially important is that, unlike other Bronze Age sites on the coasts of Oman and the United Arab Emirates, Bat is well inland and so demonstrates that commercial contacts existed well beyond the maritime realm. Finally, the geo-archaeological and ancient water system studies indicate steady aridification throughout the Bronze Age and a shift in water management practices from controlling excess surface water to increased dependence on irrigation.

Despite the failure to establish the function of the Bat towers, the publication of these results greatly expands our understanding of Bronze Age Oman and its world. Work continues at the site, and the preliminary data from the archaeo-botanical survey and mud brick studies provide fascinating glimpses into agricultural production and domestic life. *The Bronze Age Towers at Bat, Sultanate of Oman,* is a most welcomed addition to the literature on not just Oman, but also to the broader Bronze Age period of globalization. *CHA*

Contemporary Urban Landscapes of the Middle East

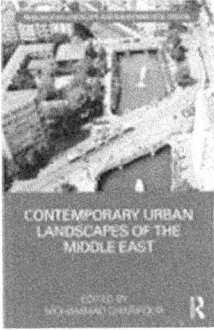

Mohammad Gharipour, Ed. New York, NY: Routledge. 307 pp. ISBN: 978-1138849594.

This is a timely and rigorous scholarly work that focuses on contemporary urban landscapes of the Middle East through case study analyses in selected settings. The book is composed of 12 chapters addressing diverse projects of landscapes in different cities including Cairo, Doha, Dubai, Eskişehir, Islamabad, Muscat, Tehran, and Tel Aviv. Illustrations, figures, and photos of parks and landscapes are provided in all chapters except for Chapter 1. In addition to a general bibliography at the end of the book, each chapter provides notes including references.

In Chapter 1, "Urban Landscape: Public Space and Environment in Cities of the Contemporary Middle East," Mohammad Gharipour provides an introduction to the edited book that tackles the development of urban landscape in the Middle East after the 1950s by investigating architecture, landscape, and urban design simultaneously. Gharipour highlights core concepts and elements of planned urban landscapes including identity, infrastructure, ecology, public space, and private development. For instance, he argues that each urban landscape encompasses objective and subjective elements. While the objective aspect includes physical features such as streets or plants, the subjective element refers to human perception. In Chapter 2, entitled "Between Garden and Geography: Landscape as an Emergent Concept in the Wider Middle East" James Wescoat addresses the historical and geographic bases of a research paradigm of landscape linked with design in the context of the Middle East. Wescoat defines landscape inquiry in three basic fashions: 1) landscape as valued scenery; 2) landscape as functional process; and 3) landscape as social communication. He argues that landscape emerges between the concepts of garden and geography containing cities in between.

Kıvanç Kılınç and Duygu Kaçar, in Chapter 3, "In Pursuit of a European City: Comparing Landscape of Eskisehir's Riverfront," explore the designs of urban parks in the Turkish city of Eskişehir (near Ankara) as being influenced by local municipal politics promoting the Porsuk River and its surroundings as a marker of Eskişehir's European identity as well as a developing center of tourism. They argue that the image of Ankara as a green city can be explained, not merely by the project of having created a garden city in the late 1920s, but also by the persistent efforts to preserve a heritage. Chapter 4, "Inventing the Seashore: The Tel Aviv-Jaffa Promenade," tackles the development of the Tel Aviv-Jaffa promenade, which is a public space completed in 1982, located between the newly established Hebrew city and the sea. Elissa Rosenberg proposes that the expansion of the promenade into a metro waterfront has created a new hybrid leisure culture reflecting both globalized forms and local social patterns. In Chapter 5, "Sculpted Landscape: The Unbuilt Public Square of Islamabad," Farhan Karim provides historical overview of how the production of urban squares and the landscape setting of Islamabad, the new capital of Pakistan established in 1959, are related to deliberate architectural decisions to create a visual metaphor of postcolonial national identity. The Greek firm Doxiadis Associates founded the spatial, infrastructural, and landscape grid of the city. Louis I. Kahn, a US architect, was invited by the government of Pakistan to design the Presidential Complex, the Center of Islamic ideology. Karim argues that Kahn's design for Islamabad shows his desire to create a centralized landscape for the city reflecting the new-nation's state collective objective of nation building.

Kathleen John-Alder, in Chapter 6, "Paradise Reconsidered: The Early Design History of Pardisan Park in Tehran," addresses the global debate concerning the ecological elements impacting the design of the Pardisan Park in Tehran in the 1970s. The Pardisan Park was intended to reflect the interaction between man and nature as the amalgamation of Eastern and Western traditions. However, the Pardisan design, developed by McHarg and his collaborators, was not implemented, rather it was reforested and officially named the Pardisan Forest Park. In Chapter 7, "Aspiring Masonry: Design Thinking and Experimental Vernacularism in Ferdowsi Garden," Hooman Koliji examines the design thinking, involving the multiplicity and complexity of intervening environmental and socio-cultural elements, in the conception and realization of the Ferdowsi Garden in the 1970s, stretching along the northern mountains of Tehran.

Akel Ismail Kahera, in Chapter 8, "Cairo's Urban Parks: Space, Place and Meaning," theoretically and practically explores the relationship between space, place, and meaning in two urban parks in Cairo, namely the Cultural Garden for Children and the Al-Azhar Park. Kahera points out that both the Cultural Garden for Children and the Al-Azhar Park provide a setting for the primordial understanding of space and meaning. Applying Foucault's concept of heterotopia, indicating a single place that encompasses different spaces that are incompatible with one other, Kahera refers to Cairo's City of the Dead, bordering the Al-Azhar Park, as a heterotopia. In Chapter 9 "Beyond Greening: Approaches to the Contemporary Landscape in the United Arab

Emirates," Keven Mitchell expounds contemporary approaches to the landscape in the UAE. Mitchell observes that the focus on the symbolic value of the date palm continues to play a significant role in the public discourse and in urban spaces of UAE. He argues that the rapid expansion of the built environment in the UAE has resulted in a number of challenges that include considerations of the design of the built environment that is manifest in an initiative like the Abu Dhabi Vision 2030. Chapter 10, "Contemporary Landscape as Urbanism: Emergent Ecologies of Doha Corniche" in Qatar, Anna Grichting addresses the concept of "emergence" that highlights the ever-changing and developing urban and natural landscape. Grichting utilizes this concept in the study of the Doha Corniche, a seven-kilometer public landscape that encircles and defines the Doha Bay and serves as an interface between the city and the sea. The emphasis is on the "becoming" of a landscape, not on a fixed identity, so as to investigate the emergent ecologies of the corniche that ties together the esplanades, public spaces, and parks as well as physically connects the city with the sea.

In Chapter 11, "The Sovereign Global City: Omani Post-Traditional Landscape Urbanism," Hala Nassar and Robert Hewitt examine in depth four representative components of Muscat's globalizing urban landscape: 1) the form and structure of Muscat's boarder landscape; 2) the Sultan Qaboos Grand Mosque; 3) Muscat's historic core and Mutrah; and 4) the coastal global venues. They propose that the cities of the Middle East, including Muscat, reflect diverse globalization and modernization trends with multiple trajectories, indicating that tradition and modernity are equally supportive phenomena.

The book's last chapter, "Epilogue: Urban Landscape and Future Sustainable Urban Qualities in Middle Eastern Cities" by Ashraf Salama, provides a critical review of the work stating that the volume examines different cases of cities in the Middle East from evolutionary contextual perspectives within which landscape interventions are developed. He presents reflections on three core interventions to explain the way in which different typologies of contemporary landscapes can contribute to sustainable urban qualities in Middle Eastern cities. In addition to Al Azhar Park in Cairo and the Corniche in Doha, Salama focuses on the Wadi Hanifa Wetlands development, a project in the city of Riyadh that reveals an important aspect relevant to viewing landscape interventions as part of ecological infrastructure strategies. From a comparative perspective, Salama argues that unlike the Doha's Corniche that is not designated as a park and whose surroundings are not well networked, the Al-Azhar Park and the Wadi Hanifa Wetlands appear to address the larger matrix of sustainable urban qualities.

Overall, this scholarly book is a valuable and welcome contribution to Middle East studies, in general, and to the study of urban landscapes of the Middle East, in particular. The book is highly recommended, for it serves specialists and non-specialist alike. ***e-Se-A***

CHRISTIANITY

The Great Knowledge Transcendence: The Rise of Western Science and Technology Reframed

THE GREAT KNOWLEDGE TRANSCENDENCE

Dengjian Jin. New York, NY: Palgrave Macmillan, 2016. 312 pp. ISBN 978-113752793-6.

In this book, Dengjian Jin seeks to address a lingering historiographical problem that has preoccupied historians and sociologists for at least a century. While various revisionist accounts have successfully challenged the Whiggish grand narrative of an inevitable, natural progress for the "rise of the West," its influence still lingers in subsequent historiography. This is because many of the alternative theories employ the concept of "blockages" that afflicted non-Western societies and impeded the development of scientific thought and related emergence of industrialization. Therefore, such narrative constructions imply that the development of scientific thought, and the industrial revolution that it generated in the West somehow evolved "naturally," because Western Europe lacked specific contextual obstacles to it. In Jin's view, this is why the historiographical dilemma cannot be effectively resolved, for the scientific thought that first emerged during the early modern period among groups of European intellectuals was, in fact, the product of a deeply "unnatural" process and was not simply guaranteed to emerge as the sum total of the process of knowledge accumulation over time (p. 2). It instead required an overcoming of the very limitations caused by systemic biases in the human mind and its cognitive systems, and the book aims to explain how this "great knowledge transcendence" occurred.

Jin raises the example of the "Needham Puzzle" as an example of the historiographical dilemma. Emerging out of the studies of the Chinese historian Joseph Needham, it gives a lengthy list of technological advances that the Chinese had developed well in advance of the rest of the world. Yet, despite their pre-eminent place in global history prior to the modern era, the Chinese ultimately did not develop "Amodern science." This anomaly is critical, Jin argues, for while scholars might debate an exact working definition of what constitutes "Amodern science," the consequences of its introduction are indisputable. The failure of non-Western civilizations to generate their own version of the scientific revolution led to the submission of most regions of the world to the Western powers, a situation that persists into the present (p.29). Jin characterizes his own historiographical intervention into assessing these questions by arguing that macro-theories have mostly been abandoned by historians in favor of more localized and contextual explanations aimed at individual cultural contexts and regions. While this literature has made critical contributions to constructing an alternative narrative that does not ground itself in Eurocentrism, historians have not yet tried to draw these variegated perspectives back together into a comparative whole that might allow for new theoretical approaches.

Jin aims to break the historiographical logjam by adopting an interdisciplinary approach that links the discussions of historians together with recent discoveries in the fields of psychology and evolutionary biology. He argues that recent discoveries in these latter fields, which are rarely followed by historians, have direct relevance in addressing the big questions about the reasons for the emergence of science and technology. For example, recent studies have shown that humans have developed, as part of their evolutionary makeup, what is called "core knowledge systems" (CKS) that govern human perceptions of the world and exist in human cognition regardless of a given subject's cultural origin (pp. 57-60). Most pre-modern science or natural philosophy, regardless of cultural context, was a product of conformity with pre-existing CKS biases that governed how humans understood the physical and biological worlds, whether it was the Aristotelian tradition, or the structures that undergirded Chinese medicine. Even in contemporary times, these CKS structures impede the ability of modern college students to learn subjects like physics and evolutionary biology (pp. 61, 63). Furthermore, these CKS are complemented by "knowledge generation systems" (KGS), which are domain-general intelligences that aim to generate knowledge about a world constantly in flux and are based on both CKS and various bodily perceptions (p. 71). Grounded in an enhanced ability for working memory, KGS represents an evolutionary advantage that placed humanity above other species, but it was still subject to fundamental limitations. These include a tendency to default to established patterns of regularity, and a dependence on trial-and-error learning that proved difficult to dislodge. This, in turn, often locked all civilizations and cultures into established patterns of thought that proved difficult to challenge.

Therefore, Jin argues that in order to generate the modern form of science, and the technology it ultimately produced, any given civilization would require a "transcendence" of limitations located within the very cognitive structure of the human mind. Or in other words, the "blockages" that historians normally seek to explain the question of the emergence of modern science are located not in specific contexts in various parts of the world, but in the very structure of human cognition. Therefore, the question then becomes, what made the context of the early modern Europe ultimately conducive to producing such a transcendence of human cognitive limitations, and producing an "unnatural" knowledge of the world, as embodied in the development of modern scientific method?

For Jin, the answer to this question lies in the distinction between what he calls "natural" and "artificial" forms of skepticism. The former is defined by humans readily accepting received knowledge and beliefs, and only questioning them when they receive conflicting information. The latter, on the other hand, is contrary to the functioning of the human cognitive systems Jin has outlined, and "try hard to put as many beliefs as possible into doubt and only accept a knowledge claim after they can find sufficient evidence and rationale for its justification" (p. 194). Whereas "natural" forms of knowledge and societies of "natural knowers" relied heavily on established traditions, the reputation of trusted authorities, and ancient texts to justify their positions, "artificial" knowledge often rejected these foundations as evidence, and demanded objective criteria, procedures and experimentation to escape the limitations of sense-perception and natural language that had undergirded philosophical and natural investigation up to that point.

Jin then seeks to apply this structural framework to the course of human history, starting with the oft-made observation that human history seems to be marked by long periods of stasis, followed by bursts of activity that have led to rapid advancement, such as the appearance of the First Agricultural Revolution in prehistoric times after many millennia in which human groups lived only in hunter-gatherer societies. Since many historians often locate the foundations of modern science in the rapid development of knowledge and new ideas in what Karl Jaspers called the "Axial Age," Jin, however, diverges from Jaspers' interpretation by interrogating these developments in order to separate the knowledge advances of this earlier time frame from the emergence of modern scientific thinking in the early modern period.

For Jin, the advances of the Axial Age are found not in the development of rational modes of thought, growing expressions of self-consciousness, or growing interchange between cultures; these things had been proved to exist in other cultures of the period as well, and did not generate the same outcome. Instead, what characterizes the widely-variegated developments of axial civilizations was a growth in systematic skepticism and disenchantment caused by military, economic, and technological advancement (pp. 89-91). However, the philosophies and systems that these developments fostered ultimately became foundational in their own right, and in Jin's view, they lapsed back into conditions where they became trapped once more by the biases inherent in human cognitive systems. This led to lengthy periods of stasis that simply treated the foundations created by axial thinkers and philosophical systems as an unquestionable given, and intellectual life subsequently aimed at reinforcing the authorities and foundational ideas that undergirded those systems.

Jin recognizes the degree to which the Islamic "golden age" of science and learning is a critical counterfactual that must be taken into account in evaluating his thesis. The obvious superiority of Muslim scientists and natural philosophers over that of Europeans prior to the sixteenth century cannot be denied. So why did Muslims not make the jump to a scientific revolution, whereas Europeans ultimately did (in part by acquiring the legacy of Muslim thinkers over the centuries as an important precondition)? Whereas most scholars have cited various kinds of obstacles or "blockages" as an explanation for the "failure" of Muslim sciences to make the jump, Jin argues that this leads to all kinds of absurdities, such as claiming a rise in mysticism as an obstacle for Muslim sciences, while others make contrary arguments that mysticism played a vital role in the development of European Christian intellectual thought (p. 148).

In Jin's view, what explains the divergence was the fact that most of the civilizations of the eastern hemisphere had well-established systems and a longstanding confidence in them that did not reward an extremely skeptical or challenging approach. While this did not preclude the emergence of individual figures who might make the attempt, the political, social, and intellectual structures of most societies did not allow these figures to proliferate, and they rarely achieved significant influence. The exception, therefore, was European Christianity, which was beset with a need to acquire knowledge from outside (and often hostile) sources who were superior to their own, and inherited religious and philosophical ideas that proved difficult to reconcile with a rapidly-increasing knowledge base (accelerated by the discovery of the Americas, among other things).

One controversial aspect of Jin's theory is an argument that the theological tenets of Christianity were especially counterintuitive. He focuses specifically on the idea of the Trinity, which is especially challenging to basic human understandings of natural categories (and raises questions like how can Father and Son be one and equal, or how can God have both divine and human natures?). For Jin, these counterintuitive doctrines increasingly became combined with the revival of Aristotelian philosophical traditions, which included a principle of non-contradiction as a requirement for the acceptance of ideas. Ultimately, this created a situation where the early modern European thinkers became so mired in unresolvable intellectual conflicts that small but influential groups of intellectuals came to be radically skeptical of all inherited thought and tradition, not just individual aspects of it — a fate which is more radical monotheisms like Islam, which rejected the Trinity, could avoid. When combined with the environment of conflict that surrounded the schisms in Christianity after the Protestant Reformation, this skepticism led to various forms of artificial experimentation that disproved the basis of all human common-sense understandings of the world that had been previously held as part of the Aristotelian tradition, which was mostly congruent with the aforementioned human cognitive biases. Interestingly, the growing scientific revolution largely expanded within the regions that had the most reason to question established religious and political authority, such as England, whereas regions where the Counter-Reformation prevailed proved better able to suppress skeptical thought. Therefore, these regions did not develop a sustained engagement with the new thinking until much later in history — thereby offering a distinctly novel spin on the Weberian idea of a "Protestant ethic" and its impact.

In short, what Jin is arguing in his work is that the Western European breakthrough in developing modern science, and the technological and social advantages that it spawned, occurred not because Western European systems were uniquely superior, or had some special characteristic that allowed them to avoid obstacles to a "natural" evolution. It was instead because their religious, political, and intellectual systems were so weak and contradictory that they forced serious intellectual thinkers to engage in a sustained quest to question the basis of everything, and thereby demand methods of scientific experimentation to generate certain knowledge that ultimately upended the basis of human thought processes. While this process was lengthy and uneven, and marked by attempts to revert to older modes of thought, it ultimately succeeded because of the conditions that allowed it to be sustained, more widely spread among a wider network of thinkers, and broadly accepted.

Ironically, subsequent human historical understandings of this process have obscured its uniqueness. Jin argues that this is because Enlightenment thinkers who helped to establish the growing acceptance of scientific breakthroughs developed a narrative of science and rationality's "natural" progress against the "obstacles" of magical thinking, religious obscurantism, and traditional authority. Furthermore, a general acceptance, until recently, of Locke's idea of the human mind as a "blank slate," rather than an evolutionary organ innately endowed with certain cognitive characteristics, has also come to obscure the "unnatural" origins of scientific thought as modern mankind has come to view scientific methods and ideas as "rational" and "natural" in a context that has become unmoored from previous patterns of thought (p. 228). This has led historians to the anachronistic ideas that, in Jin's view, cannot effectively explain either the abrupt disjuncture marked by the introduction of modern science, or the rise of Western European societies that came to adopt it and made rapid advances, often at the expense of other regions of the world who had previously been far more sophisticated.

This brief outline probably does not do justice to the complexity of Jin's overall theory, which employs a tactic of extensively interrogating already-existing alternative theories to explain why they are insufficient to explain the advent of the modern scientific thought. However, one critique that can be advanced of the work is that it proved a bit repetitive at times, with the same arguments often recurring across different chapters in multiple places. One comes away with the sense that a stronger editorial hand might have been in order here, and that the work could be pared down to a much smaller and more efficient size, which would have the added benefit of making it more accessible to a wider audience.

Furthermore, there is the potential problem of reductionism. As Jin puts it, his approach "does not deny the flexibility of the human mind in creating a diversity of cultures, but it does reveal the inherent limitations of both mind and culture" (p. 53). One might then ask that if the limitations of human cognition are the critical factor for understanding the progress of humanity, what role is there for human agency? Or in psychological terms, does Jin's explanation err too much on the side of "nature" as opposed to "nurture?" Other possible factors explaining the key transitions of the early modern period are therefore reduced to "enabling conditions" — though one notes that these conditions proliferate rather extensively by the latter part of the book, to the point where I struggled to keep track of all the possible permutations. Moreover, the work might encounter the same criticisms leveled against the field of Big History, which some critics suggest downgrades what humans have actually done, and instead posits them as the end product of the random vehicles of environmental and contextual chance — thereby leading to a fundamentally anti-humanist construction of history.

To conclude, there is no question that this will be a controversial work. However, this is not to say that Jin has not made a potentially valuable contribution to the intellectual debate about a major historiographical question that is clearly central to assessing the early modern period of world history.

And to his credit, Jin presents his ideas as a hypothesis, rather than a fully-tested theory, and does not claim to have the special expertise in the multiple geographical regions that he seeks to compare. He fully admits that his thesis will require more rigorous empirical testing in various regional contexts before historians can accept it. But the stakes are high — and not just in regard to historiographical interpretation. For if Jin's hypothesis is correct, there are real implications for other fields, such as education policy. For example, the dynamics in play here may have much to tell us about how the STEM disciplines can be most effectively taught and nurtured (p. 237).

So, despite retaining a number of reservations, this reviewer would argue that Jin's ideas deserve a fair hearing, rather than be dismissed too quickly out of hand. Even if they do not prove as decisive a factor as Jin might suggest, or if they do not fully measure up to the actual historical context of individual regions of the world (which, it should be noted, cannot be fully evaluated or understood strictly through a review of the secondary literature, especially in the case of the Islamic world), they may prove a useful theoretical touchstone by which to more fully assess the questions that are tied to the divergences in the early modern history, which have created the structures and inequalities of the contemporary world. *JJC*

Jesus in History, Legend, Scripture, and Tradition [2 volumes]: A World Encyclopedia

Leslie Houlden & Antone Minard, Eds. Denver, CO: ABC-CLIO/Praeger, 2015. 695 pp. 2 vols. ISBN: 13: 978-1610698030; ISBN: 10: 978-1610698047.

Jesus of Nazareth lived in Palestine in the full light of history in the first century A.D., when the country was ruled by the Romans. His life and teachings were recorded in the gospels of his disciples, Matthew, Mark, Luke, and John. In the writings of no less a personage than the ancient Jewish historian Josephus (37—ca.100 A.D.), he was referred to twice — as "a wise man," "a worker of amazing deeds," and "a teacher of the people," among other things. And yet, over the ages, divergent views of Jesus and his teachings arose, and some of them have continued in Church tradition, sometimes causing ecclesiastical schism, and they have prospered in modern scholarship occasioning diverse interpretations. This two-volume encyclopedia is a good, well-documented survey of them, arranged alphabetically in a variety of topics related to three broad areas: history, thought, and culture; and they are offered in 170 entries written by noted theologians, historians, and other specialists.

Many entries deal with Jesus as he came to be known in the past two thousand years: first, as a man of the first century A.D. preaching in Palestine and winning followers; secondly as the object of later human devotion, the source of ethics, and the crux of theology; and thirdly as an influence and a subject in art, music, and literature. Thus, the entries deal with many aspects of a civilization and a culture that may be called *Christian*, ensuing from the life and teachings of Jesus who was accepted by his followers, according to Hebrew scriptures, as the expected Messiah (meaning the anointed one, in Hebrew), i.e. the Christ (meaning the anointed one, in Greek). [Note that in Arabic, Jesus is called *al-Masi>h}*, derived from the verb *masah'a* , one meaning of which is: to rub with oil, to anoint; hence *al-Masi>h}* denotes the anointed one.]

There is an entry on "Islam and Christianity" and another on "Judaism and Christianity," and another on "Manichaeism;" and there are entries on each of the Christian churches and denominations: "Coptic Christianity," "Armenian Christianity," "Anglicanism," "Nestorianism," "Pentecostalism," "Roman Catholicism," "Orthodox Tradition," and "Reformation and Counter-Reformation," etc. — all explaining their different views of Jesus. And there are interesting and compelling entries on well-known theologians (ancient, medieval, and modern) and what they thought of Jesus: "Origen," "Augustine," "Anselm," "Aquinas," "Calvin," "Bultmann," "Kierkegaard," "Nietzsche," etc. The encyclopedia ends with an important section entitled "Primary Documents" containing 18 primary documents such as the *Didache,* a prayer of St. Francis of Assisi, an excerpt from Martin Luther's polemic, and a selection from Albert Schweitzer's *The Quest of the Historical Jesus.* The Glossary, Bibliography, and Index completing the encyclopedia are very useful for quick reference.

I congratulate the editors and the contributors on their excellent work and know that, for biblical scholars, this encyclopedia will be indispensable. *IJB*

Year of the Sword: The Assyrian Christian Genocide, a History

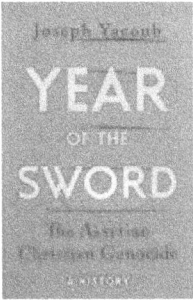

Joseph Yacoub. London, UK: Oxford University Press, 2016. 288 pp. ISBN: 978-0190633462.

This translation of Yacoub's comprehensive history of the 1915 Assyrian Genocide is a timely publication in light of the emergence of Islamic State (IS) in 2014. The violence perpetrated by IS in eastern Syria and northern Iraq, particularly against Christians and Ezidis, has renewed discussions around the recognition of genocide and what the international community can and should do to prevent ethnic or religious cleansing. Both communities have a deep collective consciousness of a bloody history of repeated massacres and displacement. This forms the background to their present suffering and displacement and to the efforts to ensure that the current violence against them is recognized as genocide. This recognition then acts as a mechanism to achieve security for themselves and their culture in the future.

While the Armenian Genocide is perhaps the most well-known example of genocide in the Middle East, current events have highlighted the sad fact that it is not the only example, nor is genocide a phenomenon assigned to the past. As Christians in Iraq contemplate whether they should return to their ancestral homes now that Mosul has been liberated from IS, this book provides important background reading. It points to the impact of such periodical attacks on the diversity that has existed in the region and why it is important that these communities are protected and are helped to remain. Yacoub makes this connection both thoughtfully and forcefully.

Yacoub begins with a succinct but useful introduction to the Assyrian community, which is essential due to continuing debates over the labels used by the community to define itself. Christians from this region place a strong emphasis on their rootedness in the area as inheritors of ancient civilization. The introduction also illustrates that they are based in regions that are disputed. Historically, they were located along the borders of the Ottoman and Persian empires and then along borders that were disputed between modern Turkey and Iraq. They are also neighbors to the Kurds, who have long held their own territorial ambitions. This added complexity to the status of the community as the region transformed from one of empires to one of nation states, largely under mandate to foreign powers after World War 1.

For Assyrian Christians, 1915 is known as *Seyfo*, the year of the sword, which represents the peak of violence against Christians by Turks and Kurds.

But the events of 1915-18 were not unknown to either local or foreign powers. As Yacoub emphasizes, they have been deliberately forgotten. The first chapter shows that there was a wealth of materials and testimonies collected at the time. The violence was widely attested to, as there was a range of witnesses, both local and foreign, and events were reported in the international press. Yet, as the narrative unfolds through the book, there is a sense of the increasing side-lining of the Assyrians in the geopolitics of the post-War formation of the Middle East and the dawn of mandatory rule.

Chapter 2 then tries to explain the background to the events and begins to show why the voices of the Assyrians did not hold the power to ensure their plight was not forgotten. Yacoub argues that persecution is a deeply-rooted experience in the community, beginning with stories of persecution dating back to Roman rule. Much like martyrdom for the Coptic Christian community, persecution is rooted in the collective consciousness of the Assyrians. But for Assyrians, their experience is not simply of persecution but of massacres and displacement. Using a broad range of contemporary accounts, Yacoub, therefore, makes the case that what happened was a "physical, cultural, religious and territorial genocide, geopolitical in nature and deliberately planned, of an ethnic and religious group." (p.145). In Chapter 3, Yacoub further explores this claim that the violence was pre-meditated and deliberately aimed at erasing the community by focusing on the ways in which the strategy of eradication unfolded.

Chapter 4 then seeks to unpack the consequences of the uprooting and fragmentation of the community after 1918. Assyrian Levies took on a central role fighting with British forces in Iraq. They were used against resistance in Kurdish areas and also against Turks, protecting the disputed Iraqi border around Mosul. This only served to set up further tensions with the other communities in Iraq. Assyrians, therefore, relied on British presence for security, leading them to resist Iraqi independence from the British, fearing for their security once the foreign power left. The Assyrians, without a strong political voice, struggled then — as they struggle now — to achieve protection for their community and security of their territories. Then, as now, global powers failed to intervene decisively to prevent bloodshed or displacement. Many Christians in Iraq feel betrayed and abandoned by the international community and this is compounded by their experience in the aftermath of *Seyfo* and the neglect of their security.

In Chapter 5, Yacoub draws together these unresolved challenges faced by Assyrians and asks whether Iraq can provide a homeland or whether it is time to again call on the international community to facilitate a safe haven. The question of an autonomous area seems to split the community. Based on the history presented here, neither the Iraqi nation nor international powers have been able to find a solution to the insecurity experienced by communities like the Assyrians. Consequently, there has been an effort, particularly by Assyrian scholars, to establish more comprehensive research into the Seyfo and producing an English translation of Yacoub's history of the Seyfo is a crucial step that has been complemented by new publications, such as the edited volume *Let Them Not Return*, by David Gaunt, Naures Atto and Soner Barthoma. These authors all draw the terrifying parallels between the events of 1915 and those unfolding now, 100 years later. The value of this book is that it has collected into one place a range of eye-witness accounts and information from primary sources, which are quoted directly in the book. This offers rich insights into events and the way they were perceived and gives a voice to the Assyrians themselves. However, further critical scholarship is needed to build up upon the foundation that Yacoub provides here. ***EM***

CULTURE and LITERATURE

After Tomorrow the Days Disappear: Ghazals and Other Poems

Hasan Sijzi. Rebecca Gould, Trans. Evanston, IL: Northwestern University Press. 144 pp. ISBN: 978-0810132306.

After Tomorrow the Days Disappear: Ghazals and Other Poems explores themes of romantic love, spiritual possession, self and other, being and non-being, the contingencies of mortal life, and the social chaos that ensues when all of these elements are entangled. Ghazal 40, paradigmatic of this thematic versatility, captures this enmeshment and explores its repercussions:

> Lacking the ruby of your lips, my eyes filled with secret pearls.
> Pupil of the eye, cast your glance again.
> Your brow is etched well, as carefully as the mole above.
> Your brows form the letter nun, the mole above is its dot.
> The doctors legislate that the sick ones suffer from pain.
> I will surrender my soul in front of you if you reject this law.
> Oh, Layli, you drive your follower's camels toward the Ka'aba.
> You see how the guardians of the shrine are crazier than Majnun.
> All the while, Hassan, I bring my eyes and heart in front of you.
> My tears are redder than agate. My heart's disposition is a hidden door.

The cry for Layli above draws on the Arabic legend of Layla and Al-Majnun, a love story depicting both the intense desire of young love as well as the mystic's yearning for union with God as the Beloved. This thematic doubling is further complicated by the double-entendre attending the word haram (translated as "shrines"), a space designated for worship in one sense and the space where women live in another. As the translator of the collection, Rebecca Gould, notes, this intermingling of the spiritual with the romantic is not without consequence for both the seeker and the social order in which he lives: "When the poet claims in the fourth distich that the guardians of the shrine are crazier than Majnun, he is therefore claiming that such attraction can overturn the social order, so that even the pious find themselves behold-en to worldly desire" (xix).

This enmeshment of the romantic, the spiritual, the material, the social betokens the genre: the ghazal is a form best suited to explorations of the metaphysical. In this regard, we see the poet's "Sufi convictions, his love of language, and his desire for life itself" (xxiv) reflected throughout the collec-tion, an ethos which we see again in Ghazal 2.

> If the lover does not hold the beloved's hand
> When the beloved is in pain, there's no use for a doctor.
> My pain has crossed the limits of endurance.
> Oh, slave! Arise, and seek the doctor's note.
> Oh, soul, what are the alms of beauty to me?
> Or is my misfortune never to receive alms?
> Send to me a charm inscribed with sorcery
> So that I can bind my rivals' eyes in the city.
> If you go to the temple of faiths in the Friday mosque,
> You'll find a hundred errors in the preacher's speech.
> For the heart that lingers by your door, paradise is only there.
> Strangers don't reside in that person's city.
> Without you, Hasan will find no homeland for his heart.
> Without a flower the world is desolate for the nightingale.

Once again, we see an ambiguity in longing: the lover yearns for the be-loved; he is sick in both body and soul. Here too, however, we also see the spiritual longing of one in search of spiritual fulfillment and wholeness. This longing cannot be fulfilled by the preaching to be found at the Friday mosque, but only through love and beauty — the love and beauty found in the arms of the beloved, but also in the signs of Godly benevolence in the world we call home: "Without a flower the world is desolate for the nightingale."

In the world of Hasan of Delhi, it is also important to note that lyrical poetry (and the emphasis on the ghazal in particular) was central to the revi-talization of the mystical tradition in the subcontinent. The spiritual compo-nent we find in the set is noteworthy in this regard since, historically, we also begin to see a shift in thematic emphasis from the entanglements of political power to "the verse of mystic union" (xi) during Hasan's lifetime.

Material reality and spiritual reality are also brought together in the gener-ic variety offered in this set. The *qasida* or panegyric ode — also of Arabic origin — and the Persian rubiyat are used to remark upon the power shifts taking place at this time: the Mongol invasion, the collapse of the Baghdad caliphate and the proliferation of dynastic orders across the continent, all of which would have implications for the artist.

We cannot leave this set without also remarking upon the collection's Quranic inspiration. The mode of address — the invocation of the slave as one in humble submission to the b/Beloved — recalls God's invocation of Muhammad in Quranic verse, and the interpenetration of the spiritual with the physical we see throughout the collection resonates with the invocation of worldly signs of the divine we find in the *Qur'an*, as in verse 37 of Surat Fusilat:

> Now among His **SIGNS** are the night and the day, as well as the sun and the moon: [hence,] adore not the sun or the moon, but prostrate yourselves in adoration before God, who has created them – if it is Him whom you [really] worship.

As in Hasan's poetry, we see themes of adoration expressed through the body in this verse: The devout will prostrate in worship of God. Invocations of night and day, the sun and the moon call the presence/absence of the Beloved who created the night and day, the sun and the moon, as signs of His power. These kinds of celestial images are echoed throughout this collection, as in the first two distiches of Ghazal 34: "I saw a figure the color of the night inscribed on the moon/ I saw the goal of the heart, and the favor of God." We also find that the lover invoked in the *takhallus* of various ghazals is also variously remarked upon as a "slave," one who is hopeless, bereft, lost, and "heartsick" without the b/Beloved. This, of course, is the pervasive rendering of the human condition without divine guidance we find in Quranic verse.

The collection itself is comprised of 50 ghazals as well as 17 ruba'is or quatrains, 2 qitas or fragments and 1 ode honoring the Shah 'Ala al-Din. The innovation of this collection is the marriage of the ghazal form, written here in the Persian of the Indian subcontinent, with Indian narrative content. While the translator explains her approach to the text, the reader will not be able to assess her linguistic choices since all of the poems in the collection are offered in English. The translator does, however, provide a detailed appendix denoting variations in the translations to the refrains in prior editions. The collection also ends with a glossary of key terms and names as well as a thematically organized list for further reading. *Me-S*

The Book of Khalid: A Critical Edition

Ameen Rihani, Ed. Syracuse, NY: Syracuse University Press, 2016. 530 pp. ISBN: 978-0815634041.

A great service to scholars of Arab American literature has been rendered by Todd Fine with this critical edition of *The Book of Khalid* by Ameen Rihani, originally published by Dodd, Mead and Company in New York in 1911. To commemorate the centennial anniversary, Todd fine was the director of "Project Khalid" that brought together scholars and public figures throughout the year to participate in activities in many American centers of learning in order to promote the life of Ameen Rihani and the relevance of his book to contemporary Arab American relations.

Ameen Rihani (1876-1940) was a writer who wrote in both English and Arabic, and was one of the leading authors of Arab American literature that included his younger friend in New York, Kahlil Gibran (1883-1931). He had immigrated with his uncle to New York as a boy and grew up in the city, revisiting Lebanon, his homeland, as an adult a couple of times, in one of which he wrote his novel *The Book of Khalid,* the first novel in English by an Arab American and the first novel in Arabic literature. It tells us the story of two Arab boys, Khalid and Shakib, who immigrate to New York City from Baalbek, Lebanon, to peddle in its streets and later go on to better things. It also deals with issues that concerned Rihani such as the problem of religious conflict in the Arab world and the necessity of world peace and unity, based on what he believed to be the spirituality of the East and the science and material prosperity of the West.

Dr. Todd Fine's editing of Rihani's book is perceptive as it corrects some minor errors and clarifies the meaning. He gives a list of his emendations on pp. 253-258. An example will suffice (p. 255):

- p. 137: added comma to properly close "therefore"

- *1911 edition:* Let Khalid rest, therefore and ponder these matters in silence.

- *Critical edition:* Let Khalid rest, therefore, and ponder these matters in silence.

Rihani's book contains a number of obscure references and terms, but Dr. Fine does not explain them in footnotes lest he should affect the integrity of the author's text; so he offers his explanation in a glossary that is well-researched (pp. 451-499). An example will suffice (p. 452):

alb: A white garment that comes down to the ankle and is worn by clergy for official services in Catholic and other churches.

Dr. Fine also includes seven drawings, done by Gibran for the 1911 book (for which Gibran had received $50 from the publisher, as is mentioned in one of Gibran's latterly published letters).

But, perhaps the most significant part of Dr. Fine's book is that in which eight scholars in addition to himself offer studies on different aspects of Rihani's book and his other writings. These analytical, historical, and literary studies place Rihani's oeuvre in its contextual perspective. One of these scholars is Ameen Albert Rihani, the nephew of our author, Ameen Rihani, and his study is entitled "The 'Great City' in *ar-Rihaniyyat* and *The Book of Khalid.*" It deals with one of Rihani's major themes, namely, his vision of the great and ideal society based on the spirituality of the East and the material progress of the West, as presented in Rihani's book of essays and in his novel. Another of the scholars is Layla Al Maleh whose study is entitled "The Literary Parentage of *The Book of Khalid:* A Genealogical Study" and it deals, among other things, with how Rihani sought to model his book on Thomas Carlyle's *Sartor Resartus.*

There is no doubt that Dr. Fine's book is a valuable addition to our knowledge of Ameen Rihani, whose life and works need more attention than they have been given in recent years. It provides fresh insights into this man's immense contributions to Arab American literature, and also to his thoughts as one of the earliest Arab nationalists calling for the unity of the Arab world which, in 1922, he toured and got personally acquainted with its kings, rulers and people, and about which he wrote extensively in his interesting travel books. Dr. Todd Fine is to be congratulated on his successful efforts to produce this book on Ameen Rihani, and not least on his fabulous Introduction that sets the scene of what is to follow. ***IJB***

Brains Confounded by the Ode of Abū Shādūf Expounded: Volumes One and Two

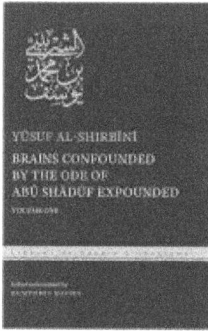

Humphrey Davies & Yūsuf al-Shirbīnī, Eds. Humphrey Davies and Yūsuf al-Shirbīnī, Trans. New York, NY: New York University Press, 2016. 465 pp. ISBN: 978-1479882342; 360 pp. ISBN: 978-1479838905.

Humphrey Davies is a distinguished translator who rendered into English such contemporary Arab novelists as Nobel laureate Naguib Mahfouz, as well as Gamal al-Ghitani, 'Ala' al-Aswani, and Elias Khoury among others; he also edited and translated the nineteenth century masterpiece, *Al-Saq 'ala al-Saq* (*Leg over Leg*) of Ahmad Faris al-Shidyaq. In 1981, he obtained his doctoral degree at Berkeley, his PhD dissertation being a study of the seventeenth century Egyptian colloquial Arabic in the text of the book under review here. He now offers this edition with an English translation.

The book is a sharp satire on seventeenth century Egyptian rural society. It uses the verse-and-commentary genre of literature to produce a hilarious parody of it, and to give us a good example of the Arabic colloquial language of the time in Egypt. Its Arabic title is *Hazz al-Quhuf bi-Sharh Qasid Abi Shaduf*, of which there are ten surviving manuscripts, some of which are incomplete texts. It was first printed in 1858 in Bulaq; other printings followed, but Humphrey Davies's edition, published in 2005, is the best and has the complete edition. The book reviewed here contains this Arabic edition, and is presented with the English translation on opposite pages of the Arabic text.

Brains Confounded (whose full title in Arabic is *Hazz al-quhūf bi-sharh qasīd Abū Shādūf*) is composed in the style of a traditional literary commentary on a 47-line poem which al-Shirbīnī ascribes to a peasant named Abū Shādūf, who is a figment of his imagination.

In Volume I, al-Shirbīnī gives humorous but critical portrayals of three rural types: the peasant cultivator (*fallah*), the village pastor or man-of-religion (*faqih*), and the rural dervish. He offers interesting anecdotes showing their ignorance, their illiteracy, their stupidity, their lack of common sense, and their dirtiness. These qualities are particularly more amusing when rural persons are described visiting the city, in one case needing to relieve themselves and not knowing where to go and what to do.

In Volume II, al-Shirbīnī comments on the poem of Abū Shādūf, using the usual traditional scholarly tools of literary studies, and then he responds to it, ridiculing it and berating its composer. His mock commentary is, however, enriched by digressions that bring in further amusement and by pretense of linguistic sophistry. Nevertheless, his lexicographical knowledge when interpreting meaning is factual and useful.

Dr. Davies' 36-page Introduction is indeed one of the best studies on this amazing seventeenth century text and its author, especially as it highlights the understudied period in the Ottoman history of Egypt and introduces *Hazz al-Quhuf* as an important work particularly useful for the study of pre-modern colloquial Egyptian Arabic, let alone its witty and entertaining narrative elements that pit the coarse rural people of Egypt against the refined city dwellers. Dr. Davies' English translation is an accomplished feat of accuracy and of understanding a text that is difficult in some places and awkward in others that use bawdy and vicious language. Each of the two volumes has its own Index, for which Dr. Davies is to be commended on account of the ease he afforded his readers when searching for a particular fact.

This book is highly recommended to students and scholars of seventeenth century literature and culture in Egypt — it teaches, and it entertains at the same time, it makes readers ponder and it makes them laugh by turns. **IJB**

Cairo Pop: Youth Music in Contemporary Egypt

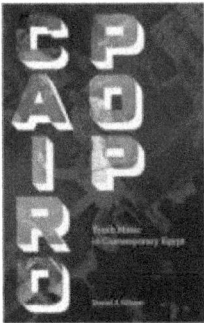

Daniel J. Gilman. Minneapolis, MN: University of Minnesota Press, 2014. 280 pp. ISBN: 978-0816689279.

The study of popular culture as a field worthy of serious consideration has been long in coming. Unfortunately, those who have sought to investigate social, economic, or political phenomena from non-traditional approaches often have also used non-traditional — dare I say, sometimes non-scientific — approaches to match their interests. The results have been less than cogent for those who strongly adhere to more traditional approaches of study, particularly in such conservative strongholds as Middle Eastern Studies, an area long-dominated by die-hard historians and political scientists.

It is, therefore, quite refreshing and exciting to come across a work such as this monograph, which succeeds in bridging the gap between the more staid contributions to our understanding of the region and recent approaches to the scholarship and study of popular culture. Here, Gilman offers a meticulous analysis of the contemporary music scene mostly, though not solely, centered in Cairo. He discusses the role of Cairo's singers, their backgrounds, their songs, their styles, their lyrics and, to a lesser degree, their videos and how these all well correlate with recent socio-economic and political developments throughout Egypt and the region. He does so in such profound detail that only the most cynical of observers could suggest that such analysis of the "commonplace" isn't as relevant — if not more so — than studying the usual machinations of high-level leaders that fill all-too-many volumes these days.

Gilman notes early on what is so evident about research in general, not only in the Middle East, but perhaps in nearly every field: scholarship tends to reflect who we scholars are and what we care about and are, rather than who our interlocutors are and what is important to them (p. 17). It is to this task that Gilman addresses himself, seeking to identify and quantify what music contemporary Cairenes listen to and, more to the point, why they like it. But more to the point, Gilman uses music as a barometer if not a proxy for all that composes Cairene culture today. In short, by undertaking a close reading of the consumption of young Egyptians' musical tastes, Gilman seeks here to analyze the interplay of Egyptian heritage, social issues, and political concerns (p. 58). Here, he sees the society as stratified by a number of factors including race, gender, class, and age — to name only a few.

It is simply impossible to address the level of detail found in this volume. Gilman succeeds in taking on a huge task, parsing out at an exceptional level the relationships found between a variety of musical styles and their fan bases. Indeed, by querying "What is Egyptian music?" he is in truth raising a far greater question, namely: "What is Egypt?" (p. 127).

This volume is not an easy or quick read. It is chock-full of detail, much of it not likely to be of interest to the casual reader or non-specialist. But, Gilman is strongest when addressing the roles of music as they interplay with Arab nationalism, or when showing how the evolving hybridity of the Cairene music scene and Egypt's tenuous relations with the West are virtual mirror images.

That said, the most compelling section of the volume is most certainly the final chapters that concern the rise of the Arab Spring, the revolution, and the fall of the Mubarak regime. Here, Gilman gives us an eyewitness, firsthand perspective of the events of early 2011, how he experienced them, and how popular culture, most especially the music industry, was impacted. Here, his discussion of "martyr pop" (p. 182) and later, the commodification of the revolution as a whole (p. 198) are profound and compelling. Indeed, the development of popular culture, in general, largely hinges upon such issues of "authenticity," commoditization, and similar outcomes associated with the enterprise of early twenty-first century Capitalist accumulation. Thus, discussion of these issues succeeds well in bringing Gilman's fascinating thesis to a conclusion. **SCD**

I Don't Want This Poem to End

Mahmoud Darwish. Mohammad Shaheen, Trans. Northampton, MA: Interlink. 242 pp. ISBN: 978-1566560009.

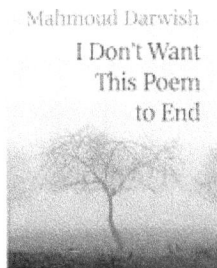

Mahmoud Darwish
I Don't Want
This Poem
to End

For anyone interested in the Palestinian poet, Mahmoud Darwish (1941-2008), and generally in modern Arabic poetry in translation, this book is a valuable addition to the library. It contains three of Darwish's collections totaling about eighty poems, most translated into English for the first time, namely (1) *The End of the Night,* (2) *It is a Song, It is a Song,* and (3) *I Don't Want This Poem to End.* The introduction written by Darwish's friend, the Lebanese novelist Elias Khoury, tells us the interesting story of Darwish's friends who, upon his death in 2008, entered his home in Amman, Jordan, and retrieved poems in manuscript form and other writings of his, some of which appear in this volume. The book also contains a 1965 letter of his to his brother Ahmad from an Israeli prison, as well as a prose essay entitled "On Exile," and an interview with him by Mohammad Shaheen conducted about four years before Darwish's death, and an account of a meeting with him on July 25, 2008, by Faisal Darraj, thirteen days after which, the poet passed away. For all these reasons, the contents of this book contribute enormously to our present knowledge of Darwish and constitute a real addition to the published literature on this Palestinian poet, who is considered one of the great modern Arab poets.

Mahmoud Darwish was the author of more than two dozen volumes of poetry and prose, and the three collections of poetry in this book, though of arbitrary choice, give an excellent view of his poetic development over the years. This is enhanced by the good translation which has succeeded in showing Darwish's move from a lyrical mode at the beginning to an epic one later and then to a dramatic one. He was one of the leading Palestinian poets in Israel, proudly named in the Arab world as 'resistance poets' because of their powerful political poems against the occupation of Palestine by Israel. This coincided with Darwish's lyrical mode, in which his poems were direct in their political themes and wording, and were well received by the Arab people everywhere, painfully chafing under their defeat by Israel in the 1967 war. But, Darwish did not want to be restricted and labeled as a political poet because he knew that poetry was (and is) much wider and deeper than this limitation; hence, his eventual move to other modes of writing poetry, consonant with his artistic talents, his growing personality, and his maturing knowledge of world poetry. The Arab public wanted him to remain expressly political and some may have misunderstood his later poetry. Nevertheless, sophisticated and complex and oblique as his poetry had become, it remained an extended love affair with Palestine, leading him to become a global poet whose poetry was of enchanting beauty and imagination. Yet, the word "Palestine" is not mentioned except once in his collection *I Don't Want This Poem to End* (p. 212) and that is where, speaking of identity, the speaker in the poem says:

> While my passport
>
> Would be just like Palestine, a question that was debatable
>
> And is still debatable! Et cetera …

Even when mentioned in his poetry, Palestine was a debatable question — and still is, with no end in sight — etc.

Mahmoud Darwish died at the age of 67 after heart surgery at Memorial Hermann Hospital in Houston, Texas; his body was brought back to Palestine and buried in Ramallah in a memorable official ceremony followed by three days of national mourning. Dr. Mohammad Shaheen's book is one of the latest and best books about Darwish. **IJB**

An Imperialist Love Story: Desert Romances and the War on Terror

Amira Jarmakani. New York, NY: New York University Press, 2015. 267 pp. ISBN: 978-1479820863.

As indicated by its title, *An Imperialist Love Story: Desert Romances and the War on Terror* investigates the unspoken and unacknowledged beliefs and attachments between desert romances and the war on terror, especially after 9/11, arguing for the relevance of desire and love in the romance industry as a lens through which the war on terror is portrayed. In this book, the writer examines the parallel relationship between the protagonist/sheikh's exotic love story and his activist tendencies toward protection and security, questioning the way hegemonic power and fear conflate with desire that serves as a main engine through which operates the mechanisms of national security.

[The characters are] essentially coherent and recognizable (p.191): the US–Anglo heroine who embodies western modernity, power, beauty, and gift of freedom (p.88), and through whom Arabiastani women are categorized as an indistinct mass of shadowy or silly women (p. 89); and the good alpha–male sheikh much depicted as a primal specimen of nature, usually with mixed ethnic ancestry to justify the horrors of his exotic ferocity, yet nobility and alliance with US–Anglo powers which mark his extreme difference from the other dark desert fellows whom he aims to reform.

This stresses the structured narrative formula of romance novels in general and desert romances in particular, presenting the same old story with new characters in the same desert setting. Accordingly, the writer suggests the so what now? question instead of so what? as an urgent matter to consider while examining representations of Arabiastan in US popular culture, shifting concern from the logic of and ideologies behind the romance industry to the possibility of reading the story [...] in a different way (p. 191).

In the first chapter entitled "To Catch a Sheikh" in the War on Terror, the writer theorizes desert romances as popular narratives of fear and anxieties of late-modern forms of power and, at the same time, as a promoting engine of contemporary imperialism imaginatively implemented through the neo-orientalist sheikh who stands on the very edge of civilization (p. 76), and it is only through his assimilationist union with the heroine and then exceptional alliance with US–Anglo powers that he could civilize his country and protect it from the evil monstrous Arabiastani terrorist (s).

According to the writer, desert romances abide by the rules of ancient romancing tradition based on hierarchical and formulaic taxonomies that imprison romantic sheikhs in their tribal Arab Muslim identities to legitimize the western civilizing mission toward the Arab/ Muslim/ Sheikh/ terrorist character that must be studied, understood, classified, and finally disciplined and normalized into polite, civilized, modern society (p. 75). The stream of love, desire, fear, and terror is much bounded by the in the second chapter entitled "Desert is Just Another Word for Freedom."

In the second chapter, the writer puts into question the fantasy of feminist liberation in desert romances, as the heroine is usually depicted as an independent modern liberal character who criticizes Arabiastani women's oppression and denial of existence either as feminine subjects or even as human beings. This suggests, as the writer stresses, a dialectical relationship between feminism and themes of empowerment in desert romances, constructed within the framework of the imperialist technology of power based on notions of universal exceptionalism. Then, the sheikh can never attain freedom unless he subordinates his nation to the supervision of US–Anglos powers and submits to notions of gender equality and liberation as shaped by western liberal frameworks.

The third chapter entitled "Desiring the Big Bad Blade" discusses racialized formations of Arabs and Muslims in desert romances. This makes the latter the ideal texts for western readers who search for an important lexicon of race related to Arabs, Muslims, and Middle Easterners in general. As the writer claims, desert romances "offer moments of x- ray clarity about the way markers of ethnicity, religion, and culture can be irradiated with racial logic." This makes desert romances highly fetish and paradoxical narratives that heavily abide by the capitalist rules of the romance industry.

As debated in the book's fourth and last chapter entitled "To Make a Woman Happy in bed" desert romances depict micro as well as macro politics of desire, implying simultaneous psychic and social connections between the Middle East as a land of fantasy marked by its known desire for "one's own repression," and the US as an embodiment of power with noble intentions of security and protection, through de-territorializing and re-territorializing terrorized territories. **NM**

Literature and the Islamic Court: Cultural Life under al- Ṣāḥib Ibn 'Abbād

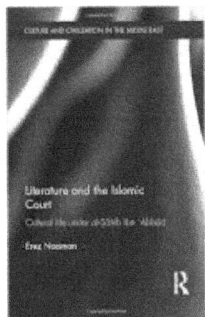

Erez Naaman. New York, NY: Taylor & Francis Group, 2016. 315 pp. ISBN: 978-1138 945258.

This book is based on a Harvard University PhD dissertation completed in 2009 under the advice of professor Wolfhart Heinrichs (d. 2014). As an erudite work of exemplary scholarship, it deals with the court of the vizier al-Ṣāḥib Ibn 'Abbād (938-995 A.D.), who was the agent of the Buyids— the Buwayhid Dynasty of Baghdad, 946-1055 A.D. — in western Iran and who was of Shi'a and Mu'tazili persuasion. The book also deals with the courtiers and the literary activity that the court witnessed, mostly in Arabic, and occasionally in Persian. Since there were no publishing houses in medieval Islamic civilization as in modern times, courts were the ideal place for litterateurs to make public their product and receive an evaluation from a patron and sometimes from peers present at the court, and to get a reward from the patron. Patrons vied with one another to attract the best poets, writers, and other intellectuals of the day to their courts in order to gain prestige and enhance their position and legitimacy, and — understandably — there was competition too among their courtiers.

It may be no exaggeration to say that Erez Naaman, Assistant Professor of Arabic at American University in Washington, DC, left no stone unturned in his effort to study the subject. He had recourse to a large number of primary medieval Arabic sources as well as to numerous modern works in several languages on the literature and the Islamic court, and on al-Ṣāḥib Ibn 'Abbād and related topics. His ample footnotes, often giving additional facts or interesting arguments, as well as his comprehensive bibliography are evidence of his indefatigable endeavor to meet the highest standards of scholarship; furthermore, his commendable acumen in historical and literary criticism is, indeed, remarkable.

From Naaman's research, one learns that the vizier spent more than 100,000 dinars per year on patronage and philanthropy, and during Ramadan, more than in all other months combined. Aside from gifts of money and/or garments, rewards to courtiers for their literary contributions could include profits from the land tax of an estate in the area under his control. The vizier encouraged adherence to the Shi'a and Mu'tazila, but did not require it as a necessity for his courtiers. A poet and prose writer himself, his literary predilections influenced the courtiers seeking his rewards, the court's literary field eventually leaning to his own stylistic preferences — a "natural" style perfected by artifice in poetry, and an "artful/artificial" style in prose. Erez Naaman devotes a large section of the book analyzing, in exquisite detail and with relevant examples, the genres and styles of the poetry and prose used by courtiers in their public recitals at the vizier's court in order to earn his generous rewards.

Professor Naaman explains the dispositions that the courtiers had to have and to develop in order to succeed in the vizier's court. He refers to these dispositions as "habitus," using the term as defined by the sociologist Pierre Bourdieu, although the concept has been known as early as Aristotle; in medieval Arabic philosophical works, it was referred to as *malaka* or *qunya*. Before being accepted at court, the courtiers had to be subjected to screening by the chamberlain and then to auditioning by the knowledgeable vizier himself. For their own advantage, the courtiers had also to differentiate between his formal sessions, when official state matters were the subject, and his informal sessions, in which restrictions were "dimmed" or relaxed, and they were freer to interact with the vizier and the other courtiers.

Several courtiers and their court literary participation are studied by Professor Naaman, some more successful than others in their habitus; but he devotes one whole chapter, Chapter 5, the last in his book, to Abū Ḥayyān al-Tawḥīdī (d. 1023 A.D.), a distinguished essayist and prose writer, who was a courtier for three years at Ibn ʿAbbād's court and earlier at that of his predecessor, Ibn al-ʿAmīd. Al-Tawḥīdī is shown to have been totally out of place at al-Ṣāḥib's court, not having successfully negotiated courtly interaction. Cantankerous as he was, his book *Mathālib al-Wazīrayn: Akhlāq al-Ṣāḥib Ibn ʿAbbād wa Ibn al-ʿAmīd* is a devastating report expressing his view of the two viziers which, with his other works, Professor Naaman used to show al-Tawḥīdī's criticism of the court's literary taste and his aversion to its literary proceedings and its general moral ambience that was not above the scatological sometimes.

I believe that Professor Naaman has admirably described and analyzed the Islamic court as an institution, not only as an indispensable part of political and administrative structure in medieval Islamic life but also as a vital locale for the history of Arabic literature. He has written extensively elsewhere on the concept of habitus and on other Islamic courts, including that of another Ibn ʿAbbād, al-Muʿtamid ibn ʿAbbād, King of Seville (1069-1091). His writings should be consulted by interested students and scholars of Arabic literature, Islamic history, and medieval studies. *IJB*

Oh, Salaam!

Najwa Barakat. Northampton, MA: Interlink Books (an imprint of Interlink Publishing Group), 2015. 207 pp. ISBN: 978-1566569484. ISBN: 978-1566569927.

Najwa Barakat is a well-known Lebanese novelist born in Beirut who has written five novels in Arabic, and one in French. Like her other novels, *Oh, Salaam!* succeeds in gripping the reader with its dark humor and bold realism. First published in Arabic in 1999, it has been translated into Italian and French, and now it has been ably rendered into English by Dr. Luke Leafgren of Harvard University.

Salaam is the name of the main female character. She is unmarried, not beautiful, and she works in the Central Telephone Exchange of an unnamed country bordering on the Mediterranean Sea that has recently come out of a devastating civil war. Luqman and Najeeb are two male characters — the former as an explosive expert and the latter as a sniper — who made a fortune in the civil war and now realize they are no longer needed. They try to survive the arrival of peace, to be wealthy, and to find love. They come to know Salaam, who has money and is afraid of remaining a spinster. Her neighbor Elias, a war-time torturer nicknamed the Albino, loves her, but he dies. So Luqman, his friend, proposes to her after she takes him in to save him from the authorities. However, she becomes interested in Najeeb who, desirous of gainful employment, would rather concentrate on his chemical research to find ways to kill rats. The relationships in the novel are ones in which the characters use and torment each other, having lost all principles of morality as a result of the war. Salaam herself does not feel any ethical remorse after letting her brother Saleem be killed by rats in the basement of her home where she tied him up and abandoned him. She had just recently brought him home from a sanatorium, but she soon realizes that he is a burden on her.

Complicated as the novel's plot sounds, it is effective in portraying "a city that no longer resembles itself," and human beings who have no qualms of conscience. It also captures the horrible effects of civil war on the norms of society.

Najwa Barakat's narrative style in this novel is skillful in her portrayal of antisocial characters. She often uses the stream-of-consciousness style to analyze their aims, their fears, and their desires. The insane and the sane — those in the sanatorium, those at home, in their cars, or in the street — are thus an open book: the reader gets to know their minds by listening to their own words repeated silently in their inner being. Barakat's dialogues, likewise, are replete with insinuations; and the reader remains at all times trying to guess what comes next — until the tragic end. As *Le Monde Diplomatique* said, "…one has the feeling of being caught in the net of a work that is suffocating but enthralling, which fascinates with the resplendence of its images and the clarity of its vision."

If parts of the novel *Oh, Salaam!* suggest cinematic methods by their fast-moving action or intertwined scenes, they reflect Najwa Barakart's training in the theater and the cinema, first in Beirut and then in Paris. In Beirut in 2006, she established *Al-Muhtraf,* a workshop to teach writing novels, and playwriting for the theater and the cinema — now suspended because of insufficient funding. But, in addition to novel-writing, she continues to be a freelance journalist in several Arabic newspapers and magazines, and she contributes radio programs that are produced by Radio France Internationale, the British Broadcasting Corporation, and Al-Jazeera.

Oh, Salaam! is a war novel that will be remembered as one of the best in war literature, not because of its unforgettable descriptions of scenes of violence, but primarily because of its graphic methods of revealing how war affects human beings: civilians, soldiers, mercenaries, and merchants — male and female alike. It is a disturbing novel, but it is well worth reading. **IJB**

Poetry and Politics in the Modern Arab World

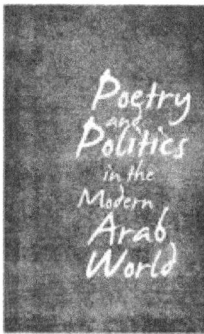

Atef Alshaer. London, UK: C. Hurst, 2016. 256 pp. ISBN: 978-1849043199.

Arabic poetry has been an integral part of Arab culture throughout history and, therefore, an indispensable factor in Arab societal relationships, including those of politics, right from pre-Islamic times in Arabia to our own present days in the larger contemporary Arab world. Dr. Atef Alshaer's book under review here is a timely and good contribution to the understanding of this relationship and to an intelligent comprehension of both poetry and politics in the modern Arab world.

The book consists of three parts. Part One has three chapters and speaks of general trends in modern Arabic poetry in the dominant shadow of the

Ottoman Empire and that of Western colonialism in the Arab world, then it discusses politics in the esthetics of modern Arab poetry. Part Two has three chapters also and deals with the poetry of the Palestinian Mahmoud Darwish, then that of the two main Arab Islamist political movements: the Palestinian Hamas, and the Lebanese Hizbullah. Part Three gives an account of poetry in the enlivening atmosphere of the Arab Spring, and it concludes with an "Afterword."

Lecturer in Arabic language and culture at the University of Westminster, Dr. Alshaer is to be congratulated on this book which is a major achievement that crowns his valuable previous contributions to the field in the form of numerous articles in learned journals and edited books. His profound knowledge of the subject, reflected in his ample notes and references, is coupled with his poetic sensibility and his literary acumen in literary analysis and critical view; he succeeds brilliantly in producing a book that provides a deep understanding of politics in the region and of poetry that is inseparable from it.

It is not surprising that the poetry studied here has themes of resistance and is committed to an assertion of identity and self. It must be remembered that the modern period was one when Arabs were enduring humiliating subjugation to non-Arab rulers: Ottoman Turks, and English, French, and Italian colonizers, and more recently to Israeli ones, let alone despotic Arab overlords almost everywhere. Arab poets, reacting to these resented circumstances, wrote some of the best modern Arab political poetry, and Dr. Alshaer has studied it thoroughly.

His outstanding study of Palestinian poet Mahmoud Darwish is a relevant example. Equally relevant and good is his study of the poets of Hamas: Ibrahim al-Maqadmah (1952-2003) and Abd al-Aziz al-Rantisi (1947-2004) — both leaders of Hamas assassinated by Israel — and Mushir al-Masri (b. 1976). Hamas's ideology is shown to be reflected in their poems interwoven with their personal and political experiences in resisting Israel. As for the Lebanese poets of Hizbullah, their Shi'a beliefs in sacrifice and martyrdom and their references to Shi'a historical people figure eminently in their themes. They earned wide acclaim in the Arab world after Israel was forced to withdraw its forces from the south of Lebanon in 2000 following stiff Shi'a resistance. With regard to the poets of the Arab Spring, Dr. Alshaer shows that they offered an insightful record of their engagement with Arab culture and politics, just as they hailed the Arab people's rise against corrupt leaders whom they condemned. He believes the poetry of the Arab Spring is promising and that it will open up new visions for the future of Arabic poetry.

For its conciseness, precision, and overview, this book is strongly recommended to all readers who need to know about most recent developments in modern Arabic poetry, particularly those interested in its relation to Middle Eastern politics and culture. *IJB*

EDUCATION

Education and the Arab Spring: Resistance, Reform, and Democracy

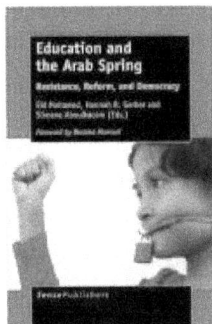

Eid Mohamed, Hannah R. Gerber, & Slimane Aboulkacem. Boston, MA: Sense Publishers, 2016. 188 pp. ISBN: 978-9463004695.

Education and the Arab Spring: Resistance, Reform, and Democracy focuses on the educational system, reforms and needs in the Middle East and North Africa after the Arab spring. Its chapters demonstrate the Arab uprisings and their aspirations toward the educational reforms to obtain the democratic ideals and values of citizenship, social justice, pluralism, and tolerance. The three key issues of this volume are teacher professional development, youth student role in the social change, and reform curriculum.

Dr. Bessma Momani provides a foreword about the crucial turning point in the Arab world and how education is closely tied to bettering their lives, society, and the political institutions throughout the region. To accomplish significant changes in the education system, deeper reforms in educational delivery and the political institution are needed. She concludes with a high recommendation to learn from the findings and suggestions of the authors in this edited volume.

Co-editors Slimane Aboulkacem, Hannah R. Gerber and Eid Mohamed provide an introduction entitled "Education, Democracy, And the Arab Spring" presenting the historical wave of the Arab Spring since 2011. They describe the Les Anciens Regimes as a "colonial oppression, political stagnation, and despotism that continues to rule the Arab world" (p. xix). The Arab Spring came with diverse people hoping to empower the youth, establishing speech and press freedom, and creating a strong educational system. They highlight the challenges facing the protesters who revolted for educational reforms and living democracies in three sections.

The first section, "Classroom Issues and Teacher Professional Development Struggles Post-Arab Spring" includes two chapters focusing on teacher responsibility to prepare students for participation in a democracy, and teacher professional development to perform this important role. Abdullah F. Alrebh and Radhi Al-Mabuk analyzed the educational reforms in general and pedagogical reformation in particular in the Arab World by addressing four areas: the pedagogical approaches, the impact of the teacher in change, transformative pedagogies to promote democracy, and challenges and opportunities for teaching for democracy in the Arab World. They examined the role that teachers' assumptions and beliefs play on how they teach; "Teachers must deliberately seek to cultivate virtues and ideals of citizenship, social justice and pluralism in the minds, heart, and souls of their students" (p. 9). Nahed Abdelrahman and Beverly J. Irby focused on the influence of Arab Spring on in-service teacher education in Egypt. They explored in-service teachers' perceptions on teacher professional development programs provided to them before and after the Arab Spring in Egypt. The teachers responded that their dissatisfaction grew after the Arab Spring because the Egyptian Ministry of Education neglected teacher professional development. The chapter concludes by recommending that the Egyptian Ministry of Education has to collaborate with international universities and organizations to provide virtual professional development.

The second section, "Youth Education and the Seeds of Social Change" features three chapters on the youth's role in the revolution and change. Ahmed Abd Rabou discussed how student unions at high education institutions have struggled for change in Egypt. He explored the relationship between higher education and democracy with a focus on Egypt's student unions and movements both before and after the revolution in an attempt to understand why the hoped-for change did not occur in this densely populated country, and why the military eventually intervened to oust the country's first-ever democratically elected president. Student activism in Egypt has been negatively affected by the deteriorating political environment and "Most of the political gains achieved by student unions between 2011 and 2013 were lost due to the ongoing violence" (p. 64). Fadwa Bouguerra and Slimane Aboulkacem explored the fragility of the Tunisian education system before and after the Revolution. They discussed various issues such as equal access to education, private and public education, and inequality between rural and urban areas. However, they argue that the revolution introduced significant educational reforms, but it seemed Tunisia needed to establish a new educational system that would guarantee access to education and jobs for all. Waleed F. Mahdi and Abdulghani A. Al-Hattami focused on the youth's demands to reform higher education in Yemen. They investigate three policy-oriented dimensions in current higher education establishments: admission policy, teaching methodology, and campus politicization. The urgency arises for a serious educational reform in the higher education system to grant the Yemeni youth the opportunity to learn and innovate.

The final section of the text, "Ideologies, Religion, and Education after the Arab Spring" includes three chapters focusing on ideological and religion education. Bader M. Al-Saif and Haneen S. Ghabra examined the identity construction and ideologies of domination in higher education in the State of Kuwait through the example of the American University of Kuwait (AUK) after the Arab Spring. They conducted an ideological rhetorical discourse analysis of AUK respondents that consist of students, faculties, and staffs. The study was an attempt to bring about a balance between resisting and conforming to dominant ideologies. They made an attempt to trace ideologies as they investigate curricula and classroom practice. Hence, they end up with the policy recommendation that "AUK's administration will empower its students further when it frees itself from the Whiteness and hegemony that it exercises on itself before exercising it on its student" (p. 110). Hyun J. Ha's chapter concerns the non-Muslim students and religious education in Egyptian's classrooms. The chapter discussed how school education can contribute to mutual respect and recognition among Egyptians instead of marginalizing non-Muslim students in the classroom. He argues that the current religious education divides students on the basis of religion and further deepens the gap between Muslim and non-Muslim students, negatively impacting amicable relationships among Egyptian students. Said Hassan's chapter reviews the attempts to reform al-Azhar religious education system during the period before and after the 25th January Revolution era. He examines how al-Azhar gained its status in the modern world, what role it played in the past and is expected to play in Egyptian's society. Thus, he examined the question of reforming al-Azhar's current religious curriculum in the post 25th January Revolution era. There are certain positive changes; especially, from the perspective of content structure and pedagogy, but still, there is "some ambiguity in the overall objectives of an Azhar syllabus" (p. 146).

Generally, the book provides an in-depth analysis of the educational system in the Middle East and North Africa post-Arab Spring. It provides a deeper understanding of the role of education in post-Arab Spring states and societies. Indeed, it may be considered a required reading for those who are interested in the Arab educational reforms. It is considered highly informative for Arab decision-makers in policy, academia, and public institutions to work toward affecting a flourishing democracy in the Arab region. *SA*

Islamic Education in Britain: New Pluralist Paradigms

ISLAMIC
EDUCATION
IN BRITAIN

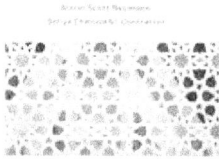

Alison Scott-Baumann; Sariya Cheruvallil-Contractor. London, UK: Bloomsbury Academic, 240 pp. ISBN: 978-1472569387.

The discussions in the book titled "Islamic Education in Britain: New Pluralist Paradigms" (2016) are based on four publicly funded research projects. It explores the nature of faith — based on educational needs within several groups of British Muslims, including Sunni and Shi'a, the two main sects of the Islamic faith. The authors focus on the Islamic education in Britain by addressing crucial issues, including training the Imam (leader), learning the Arabic language, the role of women, and collaborative partnership between universities and Muslim institutions.

The book contains six chapters, each of which focuses on a specific issue. The first chapter, titled "British Islam and Islamic Education: Two Approaches," compares Islamic theology, which is taught in seminaries, and Islamic studies, which is taught in British universities. It seeks to contextualize certain trends in both disciplines in order to look at the nature of the relationship that Islam in Britain has with the education sector.

The second chapter titled "Mapping Islamic Studies Provision in Britain," which focuses on the provision of Islamic Studies in Britain. "Yet there is very little provision that takes into account both the Britishness and Musilimness of British Muslims, and collaborative partnerships between Muslim institutions remain few" (p.55). It asserts that efforts to initiate further partnerships are often met with suspicion and barriers that prevent their success.

The third chapter, titled "More than Imam: New Narratives of Muslim Faith Leadership" the authors discuss the meaning of "Imam" and many other terms, roles and forms of relegations, and community leadership which exist within the Muslim community. They also describe the new faith leaders as vitally important for creating the imagination for modern-day Islam that supports Britons, whatever their belief system, to lead morally good lives and address the challenges of both pluralism and particularism.

The fourth chapter, titled "Arabic: The Centrality of a Living World Language" focuses on the Arabic language. Arabic has great importance in many different ways for all Muslims and is a modern language that could be of great value to non-Muslims. The authors deal with: Arabic in British higher education, Arabic learning and identity, Arabic as a bridge to bring people together, and language as paradigm for tolerance. British Muslims "seek to develop modern understanding of Islam, which requires that they are fluent in Arabic: then they can read the Quran and attend texts such as the Hadith for themselves in Arabic and interpret them for themselves" (p.103).

The fifth chapter, titled "Muslim Women's Voices, Feminisms and Theologies" focuses on the role of the alimah (women scholar) in the community. Muslim women are making important contributions to British Muslim society as mothers of the future generation and in myriad other roles as chaplains, community workers, and British citizens. Muslim women want to train in their faith and they also want validation for their courses and become a great voice for women.

The sixth chapter, titled "Universities and Muslim Colleges: 'Collaborative Partnerships' in Higher Education" deals with the benefits of collaborative partnerships between British universities and Muslim institutions. Active collaboration can indeed improve community cohesion, for offering a broader, more vibrant higher education for all and for validating Islamic theology courses within the UK quality assurance system. This partnership will create opportunities to "shape the future of young British Muslim citizens as they live, work and contribute to pluralist Britain, and have as much influence upon young non-Muslim Britons who wish to explore alternative approaches" (p.158).

Overall, the book presents an interesting collection of topics that contributes to our understanding of the Islamic education in Britain. It embraces various disciplines in its six chapters in order to create bridge and permeable membranes between Muslim communities and their pluralist societies living in the West, particularly in Britain. However, there is dissatisfaction among many young Muslim men and women with the theological/secular split and express their desire for courses that provide combinations of these two strands of their life experience as Muslim British citizens. *SA*

Middle East Studies for the New Millennium: Infrastructures of Knowledge

Seteney Shami & Cynthia Miller-Idriss, Eds. New York, NY: New York University Press. 512 pp. ISBN: 978-1479827787.

Area studies has been a project study by the Social Science Research Council (SSRC) for the past fifteen years. The collective effort of the Council's research and participants at various levels of academia have resulted in this published effort focusing on the general notion of area studies and more particularly on the study of "the Middle East." How one studies any region of the world can be sliced according to discipline, cultural affiliation, or a myriad of cross-disciplinary approaches. With regard to the Middle East, the study of this geographic region by western scholars has recently come under attack as "orientalism," a cultural approach indexed by western values and perceptions. A serious deterrent to the study of this area is the lack of appreciation by virtue of the lack of familiarity with the relevant languages of the region, Arabic, Persian, Turkish, and Hebrew, along with subsidiary ones, Kurdish and others spoken by the various minorities.

Under the able editorial work of Seteni Shami, the SSRC's Director of the Arab Council, and Cynthia Miller-Idris, an education and sociologist specialist at The American University, they bring together a wealth of perspective and a sober reflection on how past and present social scientists have formed their craft in higher education. The report is broken down into three distinct parts, initially focusing on standard academic disciplines, the relationship of the university and the region, and the last one covering the influence of political designs by domestic forces on area study.

Interest in the Middle East emerges periodically with the eruption of inter-state armed conflict, revolutionary activity, and of course, Islamic-based terrorism. A great deal of attention is paid to the institutional structure of these organizations and their particularly goals in the region. Discipline-oriented studies continue to search for how the combinations with area studies best fit. One example potentially complicating the relationship is the prevalent focus of political scientists whose efforts are heavily on methodology. A single chapter is devoted to the history of the role of sociology and how the academic approach today services the ends of understanding Middle Eastern societies, followed by an obvious commentary on the importance of the study of the Middle East and the weak connection to economics. Even the description of the "Middle East" reflects greatly on the role of geography and an inter-disciplinary opportunity to study. Part two examines education as a product of universities, beginning with a trend to introduce study abroad programs, supplemented by data of foreign students found in universities in the United States. Arabic language interest, it is noted, has increased significantly after the tragedy of 9/11. A review of graduate study emphases, determined by the production of doctoral dissertations, is surveyed. There is also a chapter outlining the extent of Islamic studies across many universities in the United States. Part three delves into the controversial element of the study of politics, relevant to the region, and its many faceted impact on how academic study organizations side with on group or another. In the post-9/11 era, sensitivities can run raw and can have possible complicating results on area studies themselves. Historiography, it is shown, has made methodological improvements to "orientalist" approaches. The role of the media in a democratic society comes under review, examining the issues of events preceding the war in Iraq and, of course, the Arab–Israeli conflict. A concluding chapter is instruction to wit: As social scientists, we do not necessarily study a region, we study elements we can observe in the region.

This is a contribution to all those interested in the multi-faceted and varying levels of society in what we know as the Middle East. It is also a tome that should find interest in administrations in institutions of higher learning who have programs dedicated to the study of the region or in which are in the process of contemplating introducing a serious effort for its study. In addition to the erudition found in the essays themselves, the review contains a valuable asset found appended to each essay with reference material and a wealth of collected data dealing with education and the region. *SRS*

Researching Biology and Evolution in the Gulf States: Networks of Science in the Middle East

Jörg Matthias Determann. London, UK: I.B. Tauris, 2015. 234 pp. ISBN: 978-1784531560.

Jörg Matthias Determann, author of *Researching Biology and Evolution in the Gulf States: Networks of Science in the Middle East* (London: I.B.Tauris, 2015), received his Ph.D. in History from the School of Oriental and African Studies (SOAS) in the University of London and is currently Assistant Professor at Virginia Commonwealth University in Qatar.

I was eager to review this book as I, myself, am a faculty member of a university in the Gulf and have encountered both certain religious limitations on academic freedoms and have witnessed students' reactions to the theory of Natural Selection and evolution. As such, Determann's work was an interesting read; it focuses on the study of and research output on the subject of evolutionary biology by Westerners and, periodically, local academics in the Gulf. In so doing, he uses the research methods of interview and other anecdotal evidence to a high degree because, like the shifting sands, an academic's grasp of hard data and statistics here is often tenuous — sometimes this evidence is not available, other times it is redacted. This should not be read as a critique, as it is simply a reality of doing research in a place with such a lack of access to public information.

Following a discussion of opponents of the subject — these being the usual suspects of Islamists — Determann proceeds to his discussion of the dilemma of Gulf governments, which, on one hand gain legitimacy through religiosity, but on the other, need to utilize evolutionary biology to develop agriculture and prevent the extinction of indigenous species. Determann focuses much of his discussion on these two large divisions of biology: plants and animals. Beginning with plants, he discusses the desire of Gulf governments in the study of evolution and adaptation as related to plants for practical, economic purposes: "greenifying" the desert. Projects with this aim are very costly and require academic and practical understanding of plant adaptation in order to select trees, grasses, and agricultural crops that will survive and thrive in the extreme conditions of the Gulf. One example of success of this policy is that the Kingdom of Saudi Arabia has been an exporter of wheat since 1984.

On the subject of animals, the focus is different. Research in animal adaptation began with the species that hold a significant place in Gulf tradition and/or culture. This included the oryx, which is important in the Gulf psyche as evidenced by the fact that it is a popular name for girls (Maha); and it is prominent in the logo of Qatar Airways. One of the early successes that Determann describes is that scholars were able to bring an overhunted oryx herd back from extinction in Oman. The research into animal adaptation continued and was largely through the non-governmental funding from members of royal families, with gazelles and the houbara bustard, which is the key prey for falcons — falconry being a significant traditional form of hunting in the region that is still practiced today. Successes in these efforts have brought the study of animal adaptation to a much greater number of species up to and including insects.

Determann analyzes the difficulties present in this research that come in the forms of fluctuating oil prices, the rentier mentality and its effect on scholarship, and the high turnover of Western scientists, which is in many ways a function of the previous two.

Determann also includes a discussion of a phenomenon that aided the research and study of evolution in the Gulf: a differential access to this research. By this, he means that a greater proportion of the research carried out in the Gulf was published in international, not local, journals and other publications. The decreased access to this research among the local population meant a decrease in possible opposition.

Overall, I found this book to be quite interesting and informative, and I think that it would be valued by students and scholars of Gulf studies, history, history of science, and biology. In addition, this text is written in such a way that it would be both informative and entertaining for the lay person or people with a casual interest in the region. **DCM**

The Teaching and Learning of Arabic in Early Modern Europe

Jan Loop, Alastair Hamilton, & Charles Burnett, Eds.
Leiden, NL: Brill, 2017. 366 pp. ISBN: 978-9004328143.

Jan Loop, Alastair Hamilton, and Charles Burnett have brought together an impressive group of scholars and leading experts in the history of European Oriental Studies within the pages of *The Teaching and Learning of Arabic in Early Modern Europe.* The book is wide-ranging, rich in data and sources. This diversity of data and sources is matched by the diversity of views expressed in the book and the diverse background of the participating authors. The book is divided into 13 chapters, beginning with an introduction which lays out the main themes and outline of the 13 chapters. Generally, the articles in this book shed light on how and for what purposes the Arabic language was learned and taught by European scholars, theologians, merchants, and diplomats in early modern Europe covering a wide geographical area from Southern to Northern Europe.

Beginning the discussion of Arabic studies in the Netherlands, Arnoud Vrolijk reports the achievements of many outstanding scholars that the Leiden School of Arabic has produced. The article is a critical consideration of the political and religious ideologies that shaped the teaching and learning of Arabic in the Netherlands. Vrolijk clearly shows that the Dutch Arabists could not escape from the constraints of their own scholarly culture. They are fairly characterized as merely pawns in the play of politics and religion. They remained staunchly anti-Islamic. A rather tolerant approach of Islam and Arabic culture can be detected in the works of Thomas Erpenius and Adriaan Reland, who debunked the medieval myths about Islam and called for a rational approach. Michael Jan de Goeje was also inspired by the Arabs and their culture. The essay clearly provides an enormous amount of information on how Dutch scholars observed and studied a culture that was not theirs. Vrolijk makes a convincing case that Arabic studies in the Netherlands have always been, and still are, more about the Netherlands than the Arab world.

The second chapter focuses on learning Arabic in early Modern England. Mordechai Feingold investigates the learning of Arabic beyond the constitutional history of Arabic studies. The author investigates the private instruction. He argues that most English scholars studied Arabic independently with the occasional recourse to native or visiting experts such as Solomon Negri, who taught Arabic all over Europe to several European scholars. Feingold explains that the supply of private teachers became steadier in the course of the eighteenth century, so did the availability of visiting speakers of Arabic who offered instruction for free or in return for hospitality.

The third chapter by Asaph Ben-Tov is about Johann Zechendorff and Arabic studies at Zwickau's Latin school. It examines the spread of Arabic studies in Latin schools in the Roman Empire during the seventeenth century. Ben-Tov explains how the teaching of Arabic was completely dependent on the efforts of Johann Zechendorff and ceased with his departure. Another most important aspect of Ben Tov's article is the scarcity of books in teaching and learning Arabic. The sole reference text was the *Qur'an*. This led

Zechendorff to translate the entire *Qur'an* into Latin and add his own refutation claiming that the *Qur'an* was a collection of fables. Ben-Tov explains that it comes as no surprise that Zechendorff made several mistakes in translating the *Qur'an* without the use of a dictionary.

In his essay "Arabia in the Light of Midnight Sun: Arabic Studies in Sweden between Gustaf Peringer Lillieblad and Jonas Hallenberg" in Chapter 3, Bernd Roling points out that the study of Arabic was developed by drawing on Sweden's own models of national supremacy in the seventeenth century. Arabic, considered to be derived from Hebrew, was needed to spread the truth of the Gospel in Arabia. Roling points out that the privileged role of Arabic was the incentive to establish Arabic studies in Sweden. Sweden orientalism had a national character for which Peringer himself is partly responsible. Hellenberg himself saw that all languages shared a substrate and that they should be studied by showing their relationships. Arabic studies in Sweden did not differ from other countries of central Europe. Despite the autonomy of the discipline and its subjects of study, this national motive was still influencing Arabic studies in Sweden into the early nineteenth century.

In Chapter 5, Mercedes García-Arenal and Fernando Rodríguez Mediano describe the attempts to de-Islamize the Arabic language in Spain. Arabic was conceived as a Christian language that could become a legitimate object of study. Scholars linked the Arabic of Andalusia with the evangelization of Granada, especially after the famous forgery known as the "Lead Books." The authors also illustrate that the institutional teaching and learning of the Arabic language in Spain was driven and legitimized mainly because of its proximity to Hebrew. The Arabic language in Spain was identified with Morisco Islam. It was a forbidden language and its prohibition was enforced with the population of Muslim origin. The restrictions on Arabic were supposed to uproot the Morisco's apparently persistent belief in Islam and to complete their conversion to Christianity. García-Arenal and Mediano make a convincing case that, unlike other European countries where Islam did not form part of the historical narrative, the identification of Arabic with Islam in Spain was long and deep, and there is no doubt that this was one of the reasons why books were not printed in Arabic in Spain until very late.

The sixth chapter examines how different universities tried to institutionalize the teaching of Arabic in the Iberian Peninsula. Nuria Martínez de Castilla Muñoz also investigates the teaching of Arabic, particularly in the city of Salamanca and shows how the attempts to institutionalize the teaching of Arabic in Salamanca were hampered by the lack of qualified teachers and teaching materials.

Chapter 7 explores the teaching and learning of Arabic in early modern Rome and the political promotion of Arabic in the pontifical capital. Aurélien Girard argues that the teaching of Arabic in Rome was shaped by the need to prepare missionaries to converse with Arabic-speaking Christians and Muslims in the Middle East. Many books were produced for this purpose, including textbooks for the teaching of Arabic. The missionary orientation attempted to Christianize Arabic and intentionally remove Islamic terminology. Eastern Christians were invited to teach their native language, but it was not a success. The difficulty in recruiting good teachers and the low level of students also show its limitations.

Chapter 8 deals with the *Qur'an* as an important resource in learning and teaching Arabic. Alastair Hamilton views the *Qur'an* as chrestomathy in early modern Europe since the knowledge of Arabic literature was highly limited. Similarly, Jan Loop in Chapter 9, examines the use of Arabic poetry in early modern textbooks and grammars and shows its important role in teaching and practicing Arabic. Arabic scholars of the eighteenth and nineteenth centuries were mainly interested in the grammatical, lexicological, and formal aspects of Arabic poetry.

Chapter 10 explores the languages spoken outside Catholic and Protestant territories, mainly in the Ottoman Empire, North African cities, and in the Safavid Empire. Sonja Brentjes points out that anyone trying to learn Arabic often learned at least one of the local languages. Users of such language tools were missionaries, merchants, private travelers, and prisoners, who brought their notes and manuscripts with them. A case in point is Pétis de la Croix's version of Arabic that he acquired during his stay in the Ottoman and Safavid Empires. This explains the difficulties that he encountered due to the cultural, economic, and religious differences.

Simon Mills' essay in Chapter 11 examines the practical utility of studying Arabic in light of Europe's growing diplomatic relations with the Arabic-speaking world. Although English merchants and diplomats relied on interpreters or on Italian as the lingua franca of the Eastern Mediterranean, interest in Arabic was present in trading factories and embassies in the Middle East.

Maurits H. Van den Boogert's essay "Learning Oriental Languages in the Ottoman Empire: Johannes Heyman (1667-1737) between Izmir and Damascus" in Chapter 12, examines the no-academic motives that constantly shaped the teaching and learning of Arabic. Boogert documents the achievements of Johannes Heyman, the Chaplain to the Dutch Council at Izmir, who used his period of the diplomatic proficiency through private lessons in order to take up the professorship of oriental languages at the University of

Leiden. In a similar vein, Chapter 13 talks about alternative ways in teaching Arabic. John-Paul Ghobrial's essay looks beyond the institutional history of Arabic studies. He reports the different modes and practices of teaching and learning Arabic by Solomon Negri. Solomon Negri from Damascus taught Arabic all over Europe and his experience points to the importance and significance of the private teaching of Arabic.

The number of chapters included suggests the complexity of issues involved in this book. Although the chapters are readable and accurate, they differ in length and complexity. Some chapters are longer and densely footnoted than the others. The events reported in chapters 2, 3, and 13, for example, are entirely long, condensed, and confusing to the reader. The shortcoming of these chapters could have been remedied if the authors divided the chapters into sections and subsections, and list the events in a chronology, a sequence of earliest to latest. The organization of the chapters is also confusing and the transition from one chapter to the other is not smooth. It would also have been more helpful to group the contributions according to the major themes addressed in the book. Hence, the book should be divided into different parts, each reflecting a key and dominant theme of Arabic learning and teaching. The content of each chapter should have been confined to the key sectional theme. This would have led to a more inclusive book, which incorporates a range of very diverse views and perspectives about Arabic teaching and learning. Although the book is readable, it is not clear to tell the target audience of this work. The title of the book *The Teaching and Learning of Arabic in Early Modern Europe* does not give a better picture of the book's content. It leads us to think of it as a book expected to cover designing curricula, theory and methods, testing, and research in order to help teachers and students improve their teaching and learning of Arabic as a foreign language, but this is not the case. Instead, we find detailed analysis of Arabic theology, orientalism, Arabic as a missionary language, and the de-Islamization of Arabic.

The minor objections raised in this review are not meant to undermine or question the merits of the book under review. The book makes a significant contribution to the field of Arabic studies. It contains a wealth of information and stimulating analyses. It is certainly worth reading for anybody who is interested in the political and religious ideologies that shaped Arabic teaching and learning in early modern Europe. **AZ**

Youth and Education in the Middle East: Shaping Identity and Politics in Jordan

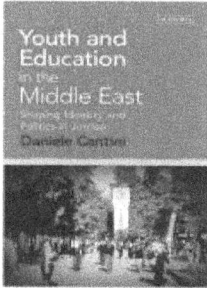

Daniele Cantini. New York, NY: I.B. Tauris, 2016. 240 pp. ISBN: 978-1784532475.

Youth and Education in the Middle East: Shaping Identity and Politics in Jordan is a theoretically sophisticated ethnography of higher education in the Middle East and its contradictions. It focuses on the University of Jordan as a site for modernity by addressing crucial issues, including global policy initiatives, student lives, campus activism, and the gendered challenge of the labor market.

Daniele Cantini provides an introduction entitled "Youth and Education in Jordan," where he describes the link between youth and higher education in a variety of ways that range from the actual structure of the university, the changes in policies, social and political lives of students, and the entrance into the labor market in Jordan. The author mentions that "the country's university system has long played an important role in the political socialization of Jordanians" (p.21). In addition, he highlights the Palestinian Arabs and refugees' status and the government's efforts at building the nation as a complex intermingling on Jordan — particularly, state bureaucracies and religious establishments and their effects on politics and social issues.

Chapter 1 introduces the early history of higher education in Jordan, its birth and development, its philosophical foundations; additionally, it discusses its political and social relevance. The author reports that on September 1962, law no. 34 was the first law which authorized the establishment of the Jordan State University. However, "Teaching at the university started on December 15, 1962, with only 167 students" (p.27). Later economic development in the region reinforced the emphasis on higher education. Now "Jordan is ranked 18th in the world and first in the Arab world by UNESCO" (p.29). The remainder of the chapter discusses Jordan State University's concrete function in two particularly relevant ways: admission policies, and differences between teaching methodologies in different faculties by analyzing two lessons in the faculties of Shari'a and literature, as examples.

Chapter 2 discusses the crisis of universities in Jordan, describing some of main reforms that have taken place during the last 25 years, such as privatization and budget cuts, as well as the language in which these reforms are wrapped. The second part of this chapter deals more specifically with policies, including an in-depth analysis of the HERfKE (Higher Educational Reform for Knowledge Economy) program, sponsored by the World Bank, as "the project, officially approved in 2009, aims to support the development of a higher education system" (p.74). The final section of this chapter deals with yet another set of policies enacted by international agencies such as the European Union through its TEMPUS "promoting cooperation in higher education between the European and 29 partner countries" (p.79), including Jordan.

Chapter 3 expounds upon how university students live their years on campus, trying to observe their everyday experiences in the context of attendance at the university as a foundational moment in their lives. However, most students tend to spend the entire day on campus, rarely engaged in study-related activities; more often they are "engaged in conversations with peers, in walks to neighboring faculties to meet friends and ongoing attempts at setting up some flirtatious to meet with members of the opposite sex" (p. 90).

Chapter 4 deals with the contradictory character of universities as organized spaces of political dissent. The chapter discusses the history of student movements in Jordan, and how they integrate with the political development in the country. The chapter asserts that the protests on campus are limited to "national and international political events and to student elections" (p.126), and focusing on the broader relationship between education, citizenship, and stability in Jordan. The chapter moves to describing the main clashes that occurred on different campuses as a result of unresolved tensions at the university level, as well as at the social and political levels.

The concluding chapter investigates the relationship between the university and the labor market. The chapter presents the varying trajectories of students after graduation with reference to the "most fundamental conceptual tools of social analysis, such as class differences, and social and economic background, while always bearing in mind individual orientations" (p.136). In addition, the chapter discusses the gender paradox situation as a result of cultural and political factors.

Generally, the book provides a balanced combination of ethnography and literature about the contradictions of the higher educational system in the Middle East. Indeed, the importance of this book is in its theoretically sophisticated ethnography and contribution to the anthropology of higher education in the Middle East by examining the University of Jordan as an example. It may be considered required reading for those interested in the higher educational reforms in the Middle East, especially in issues of university structure, the change in policies, social and political lives of students, and their entry into the labor market. *SA*

GENDER ISSUES

Modern Woman in the Kingdom of Saudi Arabia: Rights, Challenges and Achievements

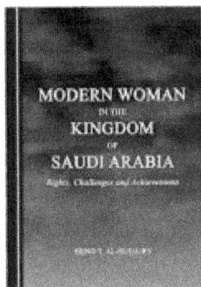

Hend T. Al-Sudairy. Newcastle, U.K.: Cambridge Scholars. 150 pp. ISBN: 978-1443872812.

Modern Woman in the Kingdom of Saudi Arabia: Rights, Challenges and Achievements is a book written by Hend T. Al-Sudairy and published by Cambridge Scholars Publishing in 2017. The book documents a Saudi woman's phases of life, achievements and challenges, notably shaped by Saudi conservative traditions and social structures that have restricted her opportunities and played a major role in making her unfamiliar with the world.

Divided into six chapters, this book portrays this Saudi woman's life's journey from the nineteenth century to the present time, scrutinizing the way she has been situated within her family, society and nation in general, and thus, highlighting the major empowering governmental policies and the social changes which have contributed to her progress and development.

According to the book, the twenty-first century Saudi woman is much more than the mystery stereotypically represented to the masses as either an ignorant oppressed woman or an extravagant and luxurious creature. She revolts against social destructive traditions that inhibit her success, yet honorably embraces others. The Saudi woman is an active pioneering subject in her society, taking on national and international roles.

The book's first chapter focuses on the Saudi woman's history, describing aspects of her social and economic life and contributions to her community that differed according to geographical limitations as well as social strata. It is an attempt to unveil the Saudi woman's life facets described by the writer as "aspects […] of pride, while others were gloomy and hectic" (p. 22), especially amid the change and development of the country advocated by the Saudi government in the last 100 years to allow much more socio-economic space for female citizens who, according to the writer, have " always had [their] status given within [their] home and among [their] family" (p. 2), yet not equally "granted a role outside it" (p. 2).

In the second chapter, the writer tackles the issue of the Saudi woman's early education and compares it to the modern era, and affirms that education problem has been worldwide and not a dilemma that has existed only in the area that would become known in the early nineteenth century as Saudi Arabia, asserting that "the early women's education problem is not confined to Saudi Arabia only, as education is one of the most important paths towards the empowerment of women everywhere. It is also an area where discrimination against women exists everywhere" (p. 27). This chapter describes the progress of the Saudi woman's education and its modalities throughout history, as well as the role education has played in developing Saudi women's critical thinking and thus attitudes towards themselves, traditions, rights and demands.

The flow of the Saudi woman's personal, social, and economic development would be widely examined in the third chapter that depicts the way Saudi women have abandoned their traditional role for a more successful and assertive one, though heavily challenged by a variety of obstacles.

In the fourth and fifth chapters, the writer provides a general view of Saudi women's early and contemporary writings, drawing major lines of conversion in writing conditions and then interests and tones, as early women writers used to "exemplify an anxiety in many different periods of their writing journey, and an awareness of their status, rights, struggle, and the social pressures upon them" (p. 55), and hence, documented Saudi women's personal development as well as political, economic and social awareness, whereas contemporary writings are stronger and more liberal in their modes of expression, "seeking social reform, criticizing the social laws regarding women or simply attempting to climb the fame ladder through stepping on forbidden territories" (p. 69). According to the writer, contemporary novels are an optimistic female response toward a powerful writing tradition that reflects Saudi women's consciousness of their own existence. A selection of contemporary Saudi women's novels, such as *Malamah* (*Features*) by Zainab Hufni, *Jahliah* (*Pre-Islamic Era*) by Layla Aljahni, and *Alwarfah* (*the Lush Tree*) by Omaimah Al-Khamis, is studied in the fifth chapter to familiarize readers with their themes and artistic values.

The book's sixth chapter is devoted to examining the Saudi woman's achievements in the fields of education, politics, sports, and mass media, as well as the impediments she is still facing, some of which are "not limited to Saudi women but are shared by other women worldwide" (p. 123). The chapter stresses the fact that Saudi women have had major leading roles as social and political decision makers, and that they have always been active subjects in their society, yet in the modern era, their active political role "has entered a hibernation period for social and custom-related reasons" (p. 113). **NM**

Pious Fashion: How Muslim Women Dress

Elizabeth Bucar. Cambridge, MA: Harvard University Press. 248 pp. ISBN: 978-0674976160.

The subjects of veiling, hijab, and modesty dress have all become increasingly prevalent in recent years. Given the rise in Muslim orthodoxy across the world, it is no wonder that women are donning burkas and hijabs like never before. Social media only further reflects this trend; "hijabbers" now communicate across the digital spectrum and #hijabfashion is a major trending topic of shared discussion.

How timely then, that Elizabeth Bucar has written this engaging, beautifully researched and illustrated this monograph concerning pious fashion. From the outset, she explains that the subject at hand is not merely about modesty; pious dress, she contends, is an inclusive category which comprises an entire montage of styles, colors, accessories, and habits. When combined, these all allow the wearer to express values true to their Muslim ideals.

But further, as she repeats throughout the text, pious dress should not be viewed as a "problem." Rather, if there is any problem here, it is in women having to make too many choices each day concerning what to wear, how to wear it, when to wear it, where to wear it, and so on. Pious dress provides a panoply of daily choices. As Bucar explains, the occasional faux pas is inevitable, resulting in, for example, "bad hijab," (p. 50) a term she teases out at length, but which means, at its most basic level, failing to dress "correctly" for a given time, place or circumstance.

Indeed, the text is written in an accessible style which easily draws the reader in, imagining the challenges and embarrassments which the author's young interlocutors must experience each day. As a man with a college-aged daughter, I could only guess at how much more vexing, (albeit fulfilling), it is for the women Bucar encounters to present themselves in highly pious, yet highly fashionable garb as they interact with one another and with the communities around them.

Most of the volume is based upon a decade of participant-observation and focus group analysis at three sites: Iran, Indonesia, and Turkey. Notably, none is an Arab-majority country but all three are, of course, Muslim-majority. In each, Bucar is able to compare and contrast not only "pious fashion across cultures" (p. 171), but further, how history, political systems, local context, national identity, and personal preferences each are negotiated, formed, and performed through one's clothing choices and styles. Her own personal experiences at each site only further enrich what is already an engrossing, first-person narrative.

Like any text emphasizing the world of women's fashion, the cases here do tend to be somewhat skewed. The women under discussion are, for the most part, both urban and, more to the point, urbane. There is little mention, in other words, of how women from villages, for example, or of the lower classes — who also seek to dress piously — will, or can, make choices comparable to those made by the women encountered in these pages. As but one example, Bucar describes the esthetic of one of designers she encounters as a combination of "layering, pockets, straps, seams, and buckles" which accompany "bonnets topped with twisted fabrics, embroidery, broché, lace, and crystals…spotlighted [with] airy whites and creams, some pastels, and multiple layers of gauzy fabrics" (p. 113). One cannot help but wonder how anyone but a woman of means could afford such materials.

That what one wears is a distinct marker of social class is a consistent thread which runs throughout this study. As for economic class, this issue is understated. Bucar suggests here that "fashion itself is the maker of and the means to piety" (p. 91). While this brilliantly researched and written examination of women's fashion well addresses this contention, I am left hopeful that while it may be *one means,* consuming one's way to piety — as Bucar herself rightly points out by way of conclusion (pp. 182-83) — is surely not the only way for pious women of all classes and socioeconomic levels to express honor and modesty in the twenty-first century context. **SCD**

The Politics of Female Circumcision in Egypt: Gender, Sexuality and the Construction of Identity

Maria Frederika Malmström. New York, NY: I.B. Tauris, 256 pp. ISBN: 978-1784531577.

Few topics strike at the heart of the Western psyche as does the subject of this monograph. It, like "honor killings" and similar practices found predominantly (though certainly not solely) in the Muslim world, are offered today by media and politicians alike as but further evidence of the extent to which the "Clash of Civilizations" between the developed nations and the traditional East continues unabated.

Malstrom's work is a beautifully crafted corrective to just such contentions. Her style and approach are engaging; her narratives seem to bring the reader into the discussion, offering access to the views of women who, quite clearly, few of us might encounter on our own. And were we to, our conversations would not likely take us where Malstrom seeks to go.

In short, this work enters realms very rarely touched upon by modern scholars. In part, this is due to the fact that most buy into the "Western interventionist discourse" (pp. 2, 191) when it comes to this very sensitive topic — that is, female circumcision is "mutilation," a primitive affront to women's right which must be stopped at all costs.

Refreshingly, Malstrom avoids taking this tack. Rather, she interrogates the issue from an entirely different perspective, namely that of those who have undergone the procedure. She seeks here to better understand how and why this practice persists, and what it means not to those who wish to attack it, but rather, those who embrace and perpetuate it.

Her findings are profound and are respectfully narrated here. Influences on what is obviously a very private, personal practice are reflected, she contends, are not only local, but are found at the political and economic levels. She suggests that aspects of Egyptian identity can be traced directly to the national level have their roots in family relations — including, control over women's reproductive organs (pp. 56-57).

Just as "Westernism" and modernization might be conflated, if not misconstrued, as one and the same thing, so too might these, in turn, be seen as forces which act concomitant with colonialist or Orientalist mentalities. Thus, Malstrom seeks here to "give a nuanced picture of Egyptian women living [in] lower income areas, specifically in relation to Islam, sexuality, gender and agency against a background of growing mistrust in the West of Islam and its values" (p. 68). In other words, an attack on the practices of the body and the body politic are difficult if not impossible to distinguish. Cairo is the *Mother of the World*, after all. Her body is hers alone, not open to the Western judgement or gaze.

Perhaps the most sensitive and gentle discussion in the entire volume is to be found in Chapter 3. Here, Malstrom gives voice to Egyptian women, young and old, who describe the role of circumcision in their marriages and sexual lives. They offer an open discussion of their feelings and experiences in incredible detail. The chapter is written beautifully, with an understanding of both subject and reader sensibilities, which I found admirable. The material is rich; rarely do I recall reading such detailed personal material (which I know is difficult to access) in such a respectful, open, yet uncensored manner.

The book's strengths do not stop here. I also found the discussion of the "hygiene narrative," (p. 182) of particular interest. Purity, cleanliness, femininity, and control of the body/self are all interwoven here, along with female circumcision, presenting a picture marked by remarkable complexity. Such issues have been addressed within a robust literature which far surpasses the black/white, right/wrong mindset so often utilized by feminists, human rights organizations, and the media (p. 27).

It is for this reason that the volume concludes where it must. For if scholars are to understand others, they must begin with the concept of agency. To assume everyone (women, minorities) is a victim of external powers is, in fact, to remove further the agency that those actors actually do hold. The women of Egypt are actors in their own lives, not passive receptacles or victims of circumstance (p. 206). The sooner we in the West realize that not everyone needs saving, the better off we'll all be. **SCD**

Resistance, Revolt, & Gender Justice in Egypt

Mariz Tadros. Syracuse, NY: Syracuse University Press, 2016. 360 pp. ISBN: 978-0815634508.

Mariz Tadros's *Resistance, Revolt, & Gender Justice in Egypt* tells us the story of women in modern Egypt and of their struggle for gender justice. The book recounts the mobilization and organizational initiatives of Egyptian women in the last 35 years: the Mubarak regime, the trials and tribulations of the 2011 revolution, the brief military rule of the Supreme

Council of Armed Forces under Field Marshal Tantawy, the democratic presidential elections, the Muslim Brotherhood government of Mohamed Morsi,
and its ousting in 2014, which led to the military government of General
Abdel Fattah el-Sisi. Tadros discusses the social and organizational developments, especially as they pertain to women, in their political and historical
context.

The book is the outcome of extensive research, which includes numerous
case studies, interviews, and a thorough study of official documents, Egyptian media, autobiographies, and literature on gender issues and feminism.
The author is an Egyptian feminist, whose knowledge and understanding are
enriched both by her personal involvement and her professional research.
Having taken part in, or personally witnessed some of the events and initiatives that she describes in her role as activist and journalist, Tadros is very
well informed on the inner forces that shaped the turbulent times of the years
after Mubarak's rule. The result is a far-reaching analysis of the struggle toward gender equality and gender justice in Egypt.

Tadros begins the book with a discussion of the *red line* — a reminiscent
of the catch-cry of the participants of the woman-led uprising of 2011, who
protested against police brutality and sexual harassment of female protesters
by security officers. The author states that Egypt presents a particularly good
case study for examining citizen-state-society relations under "shifting red
lines." The author discusses the challenges faced by feminist movements in
an authoritarian regime and a patriarchal society that is hostile to women's
rights. In Egypt, as in other countries in the region, there is no separation
between state and religion, and the Personal Status Law is predominantly determined by religious law, which is inherently discriminatory toward wom-
en. Another problem facing women's activism is the establishment of institutions that seem independent of the government, but in fact are controlled
by it. These organizations did not enjoy political autonomy from the ruling
regime. Some were headed by the first lady, were answerable to the prime
minister, and were used to redirect funds from foreign donors away from civil
society initiatives and feminist organizations.

The relationship between feminism, women's agency and empowerment
and gender equality is an overarching analytical thread throughout the book.
The process of Islamization has resulted in a shift in the discourse of women's
organization towards a less secular framework and one which is more compatible with the precepts of Islam. In response to this difficulty of continuing the struggle for gender equity in a religious conservative society, secular
feminists began accommodating for Islamization by framing their discourse
in religious terms, in an attempt to encourage the engagement of different

political actors and forces. The author delineates the subtle and nuanced similarities and differences between various actors, strategies, and agendas.

A whole chapter is devoted to the activities of the coalition against female genital mutilation (FGM) and the difficulty it encountered with Islamists' decrees sanctioning the practice, the willingness of medical professionals to perform it, and the reluctance of the population to abandon it. Subsequent chapters tell us the gains and backlashes of women's movements in the period following the ousting of President Mubarak and during the governments of Morsi and el-Sisi, up to the end of 2014. The author compares and contrasts the various articles in the constitutions that are related to women's rights that were amended following the political changes in those years.

The book is not an easy read. The breadth of erudition invested in the work is both a strength and a weakness, as the author is so well versed in the intricate details of the subject matter, she often seems to forget that most readers may not be so well informed. Information that could make the book much more "reader friendly" is often missing. A minor and trivial example of this is the failure to indicate a year next to a date. For example, the first sentence of Chapter 10: "The mass uprising against Morsi's rule that erupted around June 30th and the much smaller but highly visible protests in support of the president marked the second major rupture in Egypt's history, both of which occurred within the same two years." Another minor hindrance to the reader is the myriad acronyms and abbreviations, found on almost every page, some of which may not be familiar to a reader who is not acquainted with Egyptian politics. These shortcomings, however, do not diminish the substance and purport of the book.

The importance of this book is in its contribution to the understanding of the recent dramatic events in Egypt, as well as to the study of feminist movements in Muslim and other conservative societies, and the complex relationships between civil rights, women's rights, authoritarian regimes, and religion. The volume concludes with a glossary of terms in Arabic, a rich bibliography, and an extensive and detailed index. **MLA**

Vulnerability in Resistance

**Judith Butler, Zeynep Gambetti, & Leticia Sabsay,
Eds.** Durham, NC: Duke University Press, 2016. 352
pp. ISBN: 978-0822362906.

A collaborative effort resulting from a workshop the
theme of which was the "Rethinking Vulnerability
and Resistance: Feminism and Social Change" held
at Columbia University's Global Center in Istanbul,
Turkey in 2013. There are 13 essays representing a
number of nationalities, but principally Turkish and
Greek participants, with a sprinkling of American, British, French, Belgian,
and Palestinians. The editors are professors of comparative literature (Butler), political theory (Gambetti), and gender studies (Sabsay).

The general focus is a feminist social theoretical approach and understanding of how women become vulnerable under a variety of circumstances and
offer strategies within a self-designed concept of power. There is an overall
concern for how vulnerability is found in neoliberal societies. Vulnerability,
the contributors here argue, is the product of a paternalistically-dominated
social system using its hegemony to control the disenfranchised elements in
society. Women, by their physical nature, are subject to abuse by virtue of
their perceived physical weakness vi-à-vis males whose dominance is often
in evidence. The emphasis of all the essayists certainly is concentrated on
gender attribution. There is also a strong concern evinced on active participation in opposition to institutionalized governing systems especially ridiculing Turkey and Greece, but also to a lesser extent, the Israeli occupation
forces on the West Bank. The theoretical approach relies heavily, but not
entirely, on the opuses of Hannah Arendt and Judith Butler. The contributors
seek to explore the many manners available, particularly to women, not only
to object, but also to resist the many forms of subjugation that form the basis
of the perception of vulnerability to such degradation. The understanding
of vulnerability here clearly reflects a gender sensitivity, rather than a public
policy approach which takes into consideration a system that creates the potential for harm without the character of risk involved in any single incident.

The initial essay is by Judith Butler, who introduces the idea that vulnerability is a socially induced phenomenon within which resistance is a response
in effect to vulnerability and is understood by it as well. The next installment
is by Zeynep Gambetti, whose experience with the Occupy Gezi Park protest in Turkey in 2013 as a form of performance that serves to educate one's

self. A similar focus is found in the contribution by Başak Ertür, who views the human barricades become a political symbol — again the Gezi demonstration — as the embodiment of unworthy resistance to state-initiated violence. Moving on with Sarah Bracke, the character of resilience to the nature of inequality and injustice leads to a willingness to cope with the precarity [sic] of her life. It becomes the essential responsibility of the individual themselves to deal with the question of social difficulties imposed by the system. Marianne Hirsch, an artist, argues that her colleagues link vulnerability to trauma and memory and must, therefore, think about alternatives to events they have been forced to which to contend. Elena Loizidou sees resistance as the basis of a link between sensual responses and exigent political action. Elena Tzelepis reacts to the work of Mona Hatoum whose interest is the fate of Palestinians and whose art emphasizes the disfiguration of bodies as representative of the vulnerability faced. Again, with Palestine taking center stage, Rema Hammami requires a connection of an informal network that would bring about greater gender solidarity. The Turkish Kurds are the subject tackled by Nükhet Sirman, who focuses on the living conditions of this minority population. Battered women is the subject of Meltem Ahiska, who argues that humanizing them makes them victims. Faced with this condition, therefore, when faced with a forced gender identification, violence is then linked to sexuality. Moving on to the debate in France over [Muslim] women wearing the traditional Islamic veil forces women to be subject to hypersensitivity and unnecessary surveillance. Women in violent-infused Serbia serve as the subject of Athena Athanasiou, who notes that the common feature of mourning is a form of resistance. Leticia Sabsay writes a theoretical essay rethinking the nature of subjectivity when one views themselves within the context of the world.

The composite work is certainly a worthy one, a positive contribution to a number of subjects: gender studies, social status, political opposition efforts, comparative politics, all of which are supplemented by an extensive bibliography. There is a great deal to appreciate by reviewing the cross-cultural examination of a single condition that women have faced in space and time. There may be some difficulty in absorbing the erudition presented because of the abstruse rhetoric that can only be appreciated by readers familiar with feminist political philosophy. Nevertheless, this is a book for anyone interested in feminist political theory or an understanding of the nature of political opposition movements. **SRS**

Women's Movements in Post-"Arab Spring" North Africa

Fatima Sadiqi, Ed. New York, NY: Palgrave Macmillan (1ˢᵗ ed.), 2016. 325 pp. ISBN: 978-1137520470.

Women's Movements in Post-"Arab Spring" North Africa, a collection of essays edited by Fatima Sadiqi, tears across the cultural, economic, legal, and political history of the region during the post-colonial era, presenting an exploration of how relatively static political images of male-female relations define the limitations of a revolution's ambition. The most vivid essays in the collection demonstrate how the patriarchy finds a way to co-opt, not only tradition, but modernity in North African societies. Women remain trapped in complimentary status — if not to males, then to male conceptions of modernity. As Rachida Kerkech summarizes in her contribution on cultural challenges facing Moroccan women: "women's development might be accepted, but only as long as it does not impinge on men's absolute power" (p. 277). Rachid Tlemçani, examining Algeria, writes "modernization has been stronger than modernity in Muslim countries, and as a result, women have been marginalized in modern state-building" (p. 238).

In highlighting feminist involvement and interpretations of revolution in this volume, Miriam Cooke discusses "The Algerian Lesson" from that country's revolution, in which women called on to join the fight were shunted back to traditional roles when hostilities ceased. Dina Wahba observes in her piece on gender in the Egyptian revolution that providing only limited, abstract political concessions regarding women's rights rather than altering longstanding socio-economic patterns is a method for the patriarchy to re-establish itself, strengthening its foundation even as its elaborate structures splinter in the storm of revolution. The principle of establishing a "new normal" (Margot Badran's phrasing in her essay on the Egyptian experience) regarding male-female relationships is the most difficult phase of social transformation; if it cannot occur in the ideologically-latent Algerian War, what hope for the patchwork of revolutions twisting across North Africa in recent years?

This volume also addresses the willingness of regimes that otherwise espouse modernist principles to rely on sexual violence or the threat of it to secure themselves during the rebellion. Cooke describes Muammar Qadhaafi's alleged use of mass rape as a tool to salvage his rule, and Wahba the crumbling Mubarak regime's attempts to degrade female activists as impious or debauched. Wahba further discusses the crucial role of women in helping to combat regime propaganda aimed at portraying Egyptian protestors as simply masses of angry young men, easily dismissed by international media as dangerous or radical. The very presence of unintimidated women in the crowd on television screens is a powerful disruptor of this narrative.

The often-facile attempts of modernist regimes to deal with women's rights on a meaningful level, in part, explain the tendency of Libyan and Tunisian society to revert to Islamist or traditional practices once "secular" leaders are removed. Such regimes have also shown a willingness to take retrograde stands on women's issues as it suits their needs. Tlemçani observes how, in 1980, the Benjadid regime in Algeria passed legislation prohibiting women from traveling without permission from a male guardian. It was incumbent on women to protest this law, which they did in a successful effort to have it canceled, in part due to the negative attention the regime garnered internationally.

Some essays explore the history of women's activism in the region, whether in resistance to the colonial patriarchy or the masculinist, secular dictatorships, and juntas to follow. Sondra Hale writes about how Sudanese women continue to see the struggle for their rights in terms other than ideological, substituting the new term "activist" for terms such as "Islamist" or "communist," which may immerse women's causes in broader pantheons of political objectives.

Moha Ennaji's sweeping regional scope allows her chapter to serve as a bridge between the earlier contextual chapters and later, focus on individual countries. It taps into the most stirring thematic concept of the collection, that the future of freedom in the region is absolutely tied to the future of women's emancipation (addressing this fundamental point more clearly than does even the volume's introduction). This principle, so clearly understood and articulated in anti-colonial struggles, is often forgotten in the absence of a state-level threat. Ennaji writes of how male leaders of the Islah Islamic organization advocated for women's emancipation during the colonial era across the Maghreb. The connection of women's rights to broader political freedom and development was understood by modernists, both Islamist and secular. But the lack of consideration of women's rights as an *inherent* good rather than simply a benchmark for supposedly weightier political and economic policies is the crucial question Ennaji underscores.

The essays which analyze post-2011 developments in context with earlier history are welcome additions. Moushira Khattab reviews Egypt's constitutional history and new challenges to women's freedom, like the 2012 repeal of FGM laws by the Islamist-controlled parliament. Ellen McLarney discusses the tactical importance of women's rights to Egypt's autocratic rulers, in both symbolism and black-and-white constitutional guarantees. Her review of legal protections and considerations in Egypt's various constitutions is perhaps the best integration of history with recent events in this collection. The compromises Sadat and others made regarding the role of Shari'a as it relates to women are reviewed in this insightful essay, as is the ostentatious advocacy of women's issues by Jihan Sadat and Suzanne Mubarak. Many women's advocates believed the control of the few legal women's organizations by these autocrats' wives tarnished the women's movement among broad sectors of the public. Soumia Boutkhil includes Leila Trabelsi among these figures of "state feminism," and explains how their lack of commitment to freedom made them part of the problem, not the solution (p. 256).

Even when male leaders advocate for women's rights in the region, a disconnect remains between regime promotion and public demands. Khadija Arfaoui observes that Bourguiba's 1956 Code of Personal Status, providing significant individual freedoms for Tunisian women unknown elsewhere in the Arab world, was not the result of a demand by those women; it was a personal "gift" from the president in accordance with his preferences. Perhaps the most exaggerated example is put forward by Amanda Rogers, who writes that while Qadhaafi heralded his own role in improving the lot of Libyan women with respect to the previous monarchy, his official Green Book philosophy still held them as subordinate to men in accordance with natural order. His regime had a role for the objectification of women and possibly even sexual violence when it found itself threatened. Nabila Hamza demonstrates how the mission of Tunisia's Islamist Al-Nahda Party to justify women's roles in society in "complementary" terms to men's roles creates a tension with its need to be seen as a champion of democracy in the birthplace of the Arab uprisings (p. 217). Like Islamist parties before it (e.g., Sudan's National Islamic Front in the 1980s), Al-Nahda has learned the symbolic and constitutional value of having strong female representation in legislative assemblies; the vast majority of female parliamentarians elected in 2014 were Al-Nahda members.

"Balance" is a term modernists may choose to reconcile a vision of a modern future with one in which women remain bound to "special" roles that they and only they can fill. Tlemçani quotes Prime Minister Recep Erdogan in 2008 describing the status of women in Turkey: "Our religion [Islam] has defined a position for women: motherhood. Some people can understand this, while others can't" (p. 247). Boutkhil's chapter ventures an idea on how patriarchy and conservatism feed on global conflicts and tensions to create the conditions of what the chapter refers to as women's transitional, "liminal" citizenship. In the Moroccan context, she writes that "tradition and moderni-ty" is a narrative to promote the country as a balance between two concepts seen as at odds elsewhere. In Morocco, the contrast with the rest of the re-gion's turmoil is meant to lead to a natural confidence in the establishment.

Highlighting another theme of this volume, Névine El Nossery cites Leila Ahmed's caution against the tendency of treating women as "oppressed" as a rule in Middle East rather than viewing them as articulate agents of their own will, free to put forward narratives that may contradict those of their supposed benefactors in the West (p. 148). Abdellatif Zaki argues that mass involvement of women in protests and revolution allows them to become even more aware of "the limitations of the scope of the discourse on issues related to their status and rights" (p. 308).

In conclusion, though the theme of the "Arab Spring" is certainly constant in this book, it seems to me the focus on this period unintentionally down-plays the scope of what is covered. The book's primary theme is the role of women in expanding and progressing concepts of what constitutes "moder-nity". The events of December 2010 onward are important, but only one of the latest transitions in this ongoing struggle, as the rich history reviewed in much of this work attests. *JDL*

GULF STATES

Gateways to the World: Port Cities in the Persian Gulf

Mehran Kamrava, Ed. Oxford, UK: Oxford University Press, 2016. 282 pp. ISBN: 978-0190499372.

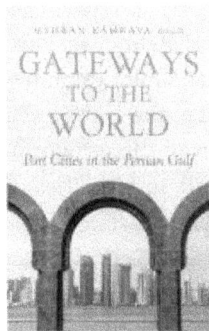

In *Gateways to the World* Mehran Kamrava, a widely published Middle East scholar and Director of the International and Regional Studies Center at Georgetown's School of Foreign Service in Qatar, and a group of scholars and practitioners specializing in the Persian Gulf, have joined to examine the evolution of the region's port cities with an emphasis on the modern era beginning in the 1980s. These decades witnessed the entry of larger, technologically advanced ships into the market, and a general decline in oil incomes. These factors saw governments steadily increasing their involvement in urban planning in a rush to develop their infrastructures, update their port facilities, and diversify from the carrying trade to become commercial and information hubs. The move to fewer and larger ports resulted in a dichotomy between those, such as Kuwait, Manama, Doha, Abu Dhabi, and Dubai that successfully diversified and integrated; and those, like Basra, Bandar Abbas, and Bushehr that have not been so successful. However, a major theme of this collection is how, even for those who have been successful, these "encounters with modernity" have brought significant challenges and have often come at a loss of identity and sense of place.

The analysis begins with Arang Keshavarzian's "From Port Cities to Cities with Ports" in which the author describes how "containerization" and the development of airports resulted in a "retreat of the waterfront" so that many Persian Gulf cities are now physically detached from their ports, and have become more unequal and hierarchical, as the most technologically advanced sites are able to concentrate commercial activity in a transoceanic rather than Persian Gulf network. Editor Kamrava's contribution, "Contemporary Port Cities in the Persian Gulf," picks up on this hierarchy by identifying a three-tier division of the region's cities into company towns (Abadan), secondary port cities (Basra, Bushehr Bandar Abbas, Dammam), and aspiring global cities (Kuwait, Manama, Doha, Dubai, Abu Dhabi). Stephen Ramos'

"An Historical Examination of Territory and Infrastructure in the Trucial States" surveys the resolution of boundaries and the defining of territory between and among the Trucial States and they evolved into the United Arab Emirates and adds a few words about competing infrastructure projects, most notably airports. "Gulf Urbanism," by Ahmed Kanna does not really address specific examples of the topic but, instead, takes a semantic approach to the "Gulf urbanism discourse" and questions the relevance of the notions of "city" or "urban" to Persian Gulf localities.

Thereafter, the articles become more specific in focus. Ashraf Salama's "The Emerging Urban Landscapes in the Southern Persian Gulf" examines architectural development, arguing that "global flows," i.e. the movement of people, capital, information, and knowledge, have driven the growth of Doha, Dubai, and Abu Dhabi in what she terms multiple modernities as they struggle to establish a sustainable local identity. In "Real Estate Liberalization as Catalyst of Urban Transformation in the Persian Gulf," Florian Wiedmann examines Manama and Dubai to argue that property ownership and real estate construction projects promote economic growth through increasing land prices while also reinventing urban identities with new forms of government, and, due to extensive immigrant labor, a demographic transformation — unfortunately not in particularly positive ways. Remah Gharib et al. focus on Masdar City, a private sector "smart" city urban development project in Abu Dhabi as an example of neoliberal — i.e. greater emphasis on market forces and much less government monitoring — urban development. The final two articles, "Urban Dynamics in Iranian Port Cities," and "Residential Satisfaction and Place Identity in a Traditional Neighborhood," examine two less successful settings, Bandar Abbas and Mutrah, Oman. For Pooya Alaedini and Mehrdad Javaheripour, Bandar Abbas demonstrates the negative impact of rapid urbanization with the proliferation of unplanned, under-serviced, poverty-stricken neighborhoods. Marike Bontenbal's research comes away with a somewhat more positive result showing that, despite rapid urbanization, localities with stable, albeit diverse, populations can still enjoy a high quality of life and have a strong sense of identity despite low standards of living and poor housing conditions.

The Persian Gulf is one of the most rapidly urbanizing regions of the world, with Bahrain, Qatar, Kuwait, and the UAE all exceeding or nearing 90%, and there is no dearth of literature addressing the development of the city-states of the region. This does, however, raise the issue of what is meant by city and urbanization within the Persian Gulf context, a topic interestingly addressed by Ahmed Kanna who asks what we mean spatially, politically, culturally, even intellectually by "city" and, more broadly, how do these all relate to the Anthropocene? An even broader semantic issue relates to "global city," the term coined by Saskia Sassen in 1991, in reference to cities which exhibit overwhelming political, economic, communications, cultural, intellectual, etc. influences and are centers of innovation. While most authors seem willing to accept that one or more Persian Gulf ports have attained the status, Kamrava is much closer to target by limiting their status to "aspiring" and observing that Gulf ports might possess world-class architecture, museums, airports, and all of the other symbols of global city status, they remain simply consumers rather than the producers, conveyers, and innovators of urban development.

While successfully documenting the major developments of free trade zones, world-class cultural, educational, and finance infrastructure, the iconic land reclamation projects, and new urban areas such as Masdar "smart" city, the authors have done an excellent job or balancing with the down side of rapid urbanization with its erosion of sense of place and identity. Kamrava sets the tone with his descriptions of how the "imaginary Arabia" style has dominated development, and the articles on Bandar Abbas and Mutrah approach these issues directly, although from the perspective of ports that have not so successfully integrated.

But each of the authors, in turn, points out these problems, with Salama describing the social segregation resulting from "cities within the cities" and the struggle for an architectural identity, and Wiedmann reinforcing the social segregation impact and adding the problem of the physical deterioration of older urban areas due to the emphasis on newer, showier projects. *Gateways to the World…* is an important work and a valuable addition to the literature on urban development in the Persian Gulf. Kamarava and his colleagues have done an excellent job of describing the unprecedented rapid modernization of the Persian Gulf ports during the past four decades while not ignoring the serious social and cultural consequences. **CHA**

The Gulf Monarchies and Climate Change: Abu Dhabi and Qatar in an Era of Natural Unsustainability

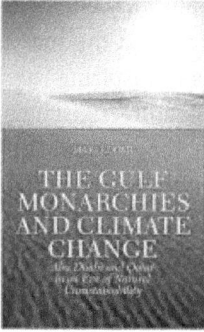

Mari Luomi. New York, NY: Oxford University Press, 2014 (1ˢᵗ ed.). 301 pp. ISBN: 978-0199387526.

In the introduction of her book, *The Gulf Monarchies and Climate Change*, Mari Luomi asks whether the Gulf States will survive the "ongoing century of climate change" (p. 9) and the short answer is a qualified "no." The sale of oil and gas is the main source of wealth for the Gulf monarchies, and their global consumption is a contributing factor to climate change. Luomi states that this may play a role in their potential collapse, as portions of the Middle East, according to a recent climate study, will "experience temperature levels that are intolerable to humans" by the end of the century. Using Abu Dhabi and Qatar as case studies, she analyzes their policy choices, priorities, and politics that circulate around the issue of climate change.

Based on the rapid rates of resource consumption (i.e., water and energy) for economic development and comfortable styles, Luomi argues that the political economies of the Gulf States are fundamentally unsustainable in the long term. She makes this argument based on her concept of "natural sustainability," which is defined as "the valuable natural assets of a state, both renewable and non-renewable, [that] are consumed in a way that allows for the prosperity of both present and future generations while achieving a balanced relationship with the surrounding environment" (p. 9). This is not the case of the Gulf where, as Luomi writes, it would take five to seven earths to maintain the type of economic growth and the middle-class lifestyle to which Gulf societies have now grown accustomed. Also, not unexpectedly, these developments have damaged the local marine and desert environments of the Gulf region.

The dynamics of this "unsustainability," Luomi writes, is to be found in the economies and authoritarian political structures that have emerged around oil. These have created social contracts that are economically wasteful and environmentally harmful because they are maintained by the welfare systems that are resource intensive. For example, low rates for water and energy use, which are heavily subsidized, give the "illusion of abundance" (p. 4) and encourage careless use. However, she proposes "rentier structures do not inevitably create natural resource and environmental challenges" (p. 20) and government responses to them are not mechanical. She points out the importance of (elite) human agency in working out possible solutions. At the heart of unsustainability are three overlapping features: energy, water, and human resources. The profusion of energy resources has encouraged rampant consumption in both residential and industrial sectors, enabled by inefficient subsidy regimes. Water is characterized by its scarcity in the area, but the promotion of desalination technologies as a techno-solution fosters overuse. Lastly, Luomi asserts that "most of the Gulf monarchies' population simply does not think about the environmental consequences of their life-styles and everyday choices" (p. 23), encouraged by western consumerism, patterns of population growth (e.g., labor migration), and the economic mis-match of skills in the national labor force.

The policy responses of Abu Dhabi have largely focused on the Masdar initiative for green technologies and the creation of a civilian nuclear pro-gram. While Masdar suffered issues early on from technical, financial, and personnel issues, it, nevertheless, enjoys elite patronage, given the role it plays for both international and domestic audiences in terms of economic development, regime legitimacy, and state branding. The role of nuclear en-ergy as a renewable resource is also discussed as part of the Emirati strategy of energy security. Qatar's response is more "conservative" in comparison to Abu Dhabi's and has mostly focused on securing prestigious conferences such as the COP18 in 2012. Luomi also details the work of Qatari institu-tions such as the Qatar foundation and the Qatar science and technology park that work on sustainability issues. In addition, both countries engage in isolated public relations campaigns such as beach clean-ups. Luomi rightly critiques these activities as green-washing as they have no measurable im-pact on environmental sustainability issues that both states are facing. The final section explores the evolution of the GCC states position vis-à-vis the international climate change agenda, following Saudi Arabia's lead against it. It also charts the development of independent positions on climate change by Abu Dhabi and Qatar from Saudi Arabia.

Luomi's choice of Abu Dhabi and Qatar as case studies for her work is well founded. Both states share similar economic, demographic, political pro-files and concrete policies related to sustainability and climate change more broadly. Additionally, her work highlights the important role of personal pol-itics and elite networks in forming policy in the Gulf States. Returning to the original question, Luomi's answer is a pessimistic and paradoxical one. With-out *substantial* political and economic reform that will render wasteful rent-ier bargains unnecessary, the Gulf States will probably not survive in their current political form. However, this potential transformation depends on a political leadership that is materially invested in maintaining their position, which begs the question, where will the change come from?

Many of the issues that Luomi brings up in her work are presented as technical problems that have technocratic solutions. For example, the overuse of water can be solved through better management. However, these issues are much more complex, have political undertones, and demand overarching solutions. She hints at that but does not develop this line of argument thoroughly. Moreover, Luomi gives the impression that Gulf political economies are internal to the region and leaves out their global histories of British and American imperialism and their implication in global capitalist circuits. These entanglements complicate her narrative, question the technocratic solutions proffered in the book, and the idea of natural (un)sustainability located strictly in local economies and not in the global capitalist system. Finally, though the rentier state paradigm has provided many insights and remains useful in many contexts, it cannot account for all kinds of political activity. New works on the Gulf such as *Joyriding in Riyadh* ably demonstrate that politics can take unconventional forms and unfold in different spaces.

Despite these minor criticisms, this is a very readable and well-researched book on a topic that is unfortunately overlooked in the region that is facing seemingly insurmountable problems. I would recommend this book for courses related to international relations, political economy, Middle East/ Gulf Studies, and environmental politics. **FK**

HAMAS and HEZBULLAH

Hamas, Jihad and Popular Legitimacy: Reinterpreting Resistance in Palestine

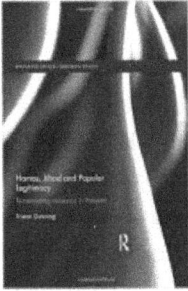

Tristan Dunning. New York, NY: Routledge. 236 pp. ISBN: 978-1138937291.

Since the attacks of September 11th, the problem of political violence has taken center stage in world affairs. This is not because political violence is new, nor because contemporary political violence is itself particularly unique. The history of the twentieth century attests to the endurance of this problem. Rather, contemporary political violence has assumed a new identity and so the narrative about it has changed. Terrorism, particularly Islamic terrorism, has become the problem that wars once were as the military aggressions of prior eras have been replaced by non-state actors. The battle field, the scene of historic national epics, has been virtualized as war itself has become a fully technologized endeavor fought with drones and laser-guided precision strikes. These changes are consequential not only to technological advancements in military weaponry. They are also reflective of a new kind of enemy and a new way of thinking about violence itself–the global terrorist organization, state and non-state militias, secret cells, and the lone wolf who values nothing more than his cause, including his own life. While the scale of today's violence continues to be great, the threat itself is constituted at the level of the quotidian. Violence seems possible anywhere, at any time and the aggressor could be anyone and everyone. Terror is not simply an act, but an objective condition.

Tristan Dunning's *Hamas, Jihad and Popular Legitimacy: Reinterpreting Resistance in Palestine* injects itself into this narrative. It does so, however, by looking at the discourse of terror from the inside and asking about the subject of its violence. Taking Hamas as his object of analysis, Dunning reconceputalizes "terror" through the Palestinian struggle for independence undertaken by Hamas. Moving away from dominant narratives of terror associated with global jihadi groups such as Al-Qaida, Dunning attempts to reframe understandings of political violence through an analysis of Hamas' polyvalent conceptualization of "resistance." Dunning argues throughout the text that the assimilation of Hamas to "terror" obscures the organization's strategic use of violence as well as the group's broader reconceptuatialization of resistance as a polyvalent means of struggle encompassing political action, institution building, community service and religious obligation, including charity-giving, prayer, and acts of patience. Because, Dunning writes, Hamas has been described as "an implacably violent and regressive Islamist 'terrorist' organization," opportunities for brokered negotiations in the ongoing Palestinian-Israeli conflict have been missed. Dunning's purpose in the text is thus twofold: to uncouple Hamas from the larger narrative of global terror which has framed analyses of the organization and to contextualize Hamas' ideology, policies, institutions as well as its violence within the immanent frame of the ongoing Israeli occupation to show why and how it has gained popular legitimacy. In this way, Dunning hopes to open the channels of discourse which might lead to lasting peace in the region.

The project itself is "conceptualized as a subaltern socio-political ethnography" privileging "the largely unheard human voice of the Palestinian community," "in particular Hamas supporters and sympathizers" (p. 5). The "intent is to humanize the movement" and add a new perspective to an area of scholarship dominated by security oriented-approaches (p. 5). Dunning's method is, therefore, interdisciplinary and draws on established research as well as Dunning's own fieldwork. Dunning supplements personal interviews with 131 anonymous surveys conducted at universities in Nablus, Beirzeit and Abu Dis as well as official opinion polls. Dunning shows the connections between Hamas rise' and its ability to meet the material, psychological, and spiritual needs of Palestinians. Dunning redefines Hamas as a "militant socio-political Islamist movement deeply embedded in the Palestinian community" (p. 2) and demonstrates the group's formation and ongoing reformation in the context of its communities' evolving needs as well as the changing political dynamics on the ground. **Me-S**

Hezbollah: From Islamic Resistance to Government

James Worrall, Simon Mabon, & Gordon Clubb.
Santa Barbara, CA: ABC-CLIO/Praeger, 2016. 200
pp. ISBN: 978-1440831348.

Hezbollah has long become the subject of near fascination by both adversaries and supporters, all relating,
whether supportively or not, of its achievements in becoming a key factor in Lebanese politics and standing
up to Israel. A book coolly, neutrally, and factually analyzing this group was long overdue, but no more.
Worrall, Mabon, and Clubb provide us with a very condensed, interesting and well-written and researched book about the Shi'a movement. Shi'a?
Not Lebanese? Well, this is a question rightly and properly dealt with in this
book, which starts (ix) with the speech by Hassan Nasrallah, the elusive leader of Hezbollah — hiding almost all the time since 2006 in a bunker, fearing
an Israeli attack, while claiming to be the victor in the war of that year —
ahead of the Hezbollah attack on Syrian Sunni Muslim rebels in the strategic
Qalamoun barrens in Syria.

So far as I can see, the involvement of Hezbollah in the Syrian civil war
brought to the fore again, the main problem which is at the root of the chronic instability in the Fertile Crescent in general, and in Lebanon and Syria in
particular; the sectarian divide, the clash between communal and state loyalties. In a nutshell, who are we?

This is for the parties concerned to answer in the first place, but observers of
Lebanon could and should answer as well. For me, it is sectarianism, Shi'ism,
but not Lebanonism. Our writers are less definitive, claiming that the conflict
in Syria and its outcome mark a significant point in the continued evolution of
Hezbollah and raises questions about its future trajectories, both in Lebanon
and across the region. Its involvement in … Sunni-Shi'a divide … might suggest a return closer to its older identity, but this underplays Hezbollah's adapt-
ability and it roots within Lebanon (p.152). So, while I, for one, may differ
with the writers on this key question, I still applaud the fact, that they delved
seriously and objectively into the minefield of dealing with sectarianism in
Lebanon, a subject of high intensity , not just intellectual, but also emotional.

But this is just one example of their ability to look at Hezbollah through
the lenses of realism, rather than romanticism. So is the case, when they refer
to the 2006 with Israel, and their seeming successes there, as well as their
miscalculations, which resulted in heavy losses and inability to capitalize on

its victory since then (pp. 56-57), the writers went here against the current in Lebanon, the Arab world, and even in Israel, where the war of 2006 was deemed a resounding success for Hezbollah. Little attention was paid then and afterward to the fact, that Nasrallh himself admitted, that had he known what the results of the war would be, he would not have started it.

The book is at its best dealing with two important issues; first, the emergence of Hezbollah, and second, Hezbollah as socio-political actor. Starting with the second, it is always a question to be asked about terror groups like Hezbollah and Hamas and their ilk: terrorists only, or also political, social, communal sources of identity and loyalty. A question easily turned political, terrorists, or freedom fighters, bad or good guys is well dealt with here. They correctly write, asking how far Hezbollah has moved from its Islamic fundamentalist and terrorist roots, and to what extent it has been socialized into the complex realities of Lebanon's sectarian structure is a perennial yet still vital question with partisans on each side of the debate; clearly, though, both narratives have some merits (pp.110-111). Sure, and this is one of the gems of this book. I was also intrigued and fascinated by their dealing with the emergence of Hezbollah, shying away from the superficial and common reference to Israel's invasion of 1982 as being the one most significant factor. Clearly, it was one of the factors, but the writers rightly define that, when trying to explain what causes militant groups to emerge, clearly, there is no single factor at play, and the case of Hezbollah is keeping with this tendency (pp.39-40). Israel is not even mentioned in their conclusion remarks of this subject. Altogether, this is a useful, easily readable, and well-documented book; a must read. *JO*

Hezbollah: The Political Economy of Lebanon's Party of God

Joseph Daher. London, UK: Pluto Press, 2016. 248 pp. ISBN: 978-0745336893.

Founded officially in 1985, though its roots date back to earlier in the 1980s, the Lebanese Shi'a Islamist party and militant organization Hezbollah today is arguably the most powerful group actor in the country's politics. Based and invested in Shi'a neighborhoods in Beirut and the Shi'a-majority south as well as around the eastern city of Ba'albek, Hezbollah is also presently

heavily engaged militarily in neighboring Syria on the side of that country's Ba'ath Party government under Bashar al-Assad. Hundreds, if not thousands, of Hezbollah fighters are active alongside Syrian regime forces and Iranian-coordinated Shi'a militias, many of them from neighboring Iraq, but some, such as the Iranian Revolutionary Guards'-controlled Fatimiyyun and Zaynabiyyun brigades, manned by Iranian, Afghan, and Pakistani foreign fighters. At the same time, Hezbollah also seeks to maintain significant military and security capabilities inside Lebanon in order to ward off both potential domestic opponents and Israel along the southern border. Dedicated to the Iranian Islamist revolutionary creed of *wilayat al-faqih* (guardianship of the jurist), Hezbollah, as an organization, is at its heart a revolutionary movement, though it has tempered, at least outwardly, its revolutionary fervor since the end of the Lebanese Civil War in the early 1990s. There is an extensive set of academic and policy studies on the organization's ideology and "axis of resistance" self-identity, political and military structures, and on-and-off-again conflict with Israel. Joseph Daher's book fills a gap in the literature concerning Hezbollah's economic activities and policies as well as the political economy of its organizational success within Lebanon and the wider Middle East. Drawing upon extensive archival research, including examinations of party publications, and interviews, Daher has written an important study on the political economy of Hezbollah in Lebanon, calling into question the party's much-promoted self-identity as a movement for the "oppressed and downtrodden." Instead of espousing true social justice and economic equality, Hezbollah, he argues, is an integral participant in the country's neoliberalism. Its leaders endorse free-market capitalism and operate so as to ensure the party's interests are protected rather than to truly be representative of the common people.

Beginning with a brief history of sectarianism in Lebanon (Chapter 1), beginning in 1920 under the French Mandate and continuing up to the end of the Lebanese Civil War in 1990, Daher discusses the social, political, and economic milieu in which Hezbollah was formed and rose to prominence. Sectarianism, he argues, was a tool used by communal elites in the country to control and manage the general population by keeping them loyal to their particular "sect" by promoting a rigid sense of identity rather than a unified national identity. Hezbollah benefited financially and drew ideologically from post-Pahlavi Iran, first under Ayatollah Ruhollah Khomeini and then his successor, Ali Khamenei, supplanting AMAL as the premier Lebanese Shi'a Islamist actor. Through Iran, Khomeinist ideas were transferred through Hezbollah to larger numbers of Lebanese Sh'a, reinforcing sectarian identity. The Lebanese state, for its part, contributed strongly to the maintenance of sectarian identification by organizing the electoral process and marriage and divorce laws according to confessional group, mandating, for example, a set number/percentage of seats for different confessional communities and requiring citizens to abide by the personal status laws of their respective sect. The Ta'if Accord, which ended the civil war, also reified the sectarian political system rather than delivering a new way to organize municipal and national politics. By promoting a sectarian "Shi'a" identity Hezbollah is attempting to manage the contradiction between socioeconomic class shifts among the country's Shi'a before, during, and after the civil war as well as its attempts to build bases of support among the Shi'a poor, middle class, and wealthy segments of the Lebanese diaspora.

Neoliberalism in Lebanon, covered in chapters 2 and 3, dramatically expanded under the leadership of Rafiq al-Hariri, a wealthy Sunni businessman with significant business ties to Saudi Arabia who served as prime minister from 1992 to 1998, and again, from 2000 to 2004. Parts of Beirut, in particular, were rebuilt following the civil war as neoliberal economic centers far removed from the daily realities of poorer segments of Lebanese society such as the southern suburbs (*al-dahiyya*) of Beirut, a stronghold of Hezbollah. The Shi'a Party, though it represented itself as the champion of the poor, has, with few exceptions, followed a neoliberal path in post-civil war politics. It endorses a privatization of public spaces as part of urban renewal programs, to the detriment of the long-term residents in certain neighborhoods and has failed to back up its rhetorical support for the poor into political action against the increasing neo-liberalization of the country. In parliament, its MPs have regularly sided with wealthy business interests when it comes to issues such as economic and rental regulations, further harming a large segment of its support base.

As detailed in Chapter 5, Hezbollah has also prevented the cross-communal growth of trade unions by restricting membership in its own unions to the Shi'a, further promoting an ingrained sectarian identity in society. To overcome these contradictions, Hezbollah leaders emphasize a sectarian Shi'ite identity as the primary means the country's Shi'a should self-identity. To be "Shi'ite" is to be a supporter of Hezbollah, they say. They promote this idea heavily through their extensive social service networks and routine missionary (*da'wa*) and political proselytization activities in Shi'a communities across the country. Through these activities, the party seeks to create a particular type of civil society in which it is able to dominate the everyday life and self-identities of Shi'a generally (Chapter 4).

Best known for its military activities against Israel, Hezbollah emphasizes its militant *jihadi* "resistance" identity heavily in a bid to maintain popular support among Shi'a generally as well as among allies from other sects (Chapter 6). The party's position against Israel and Zionism, however, is not solely political and anti-imperial/anti-colonial, but is also expressed in religious and civilizational terms. The party's guiding ideology is not only opposed to Zionism as a political project. It casts Jews generally, whether adherents to Zionism or not, as enemies of Islam and Muslims. In the late 1990s and early 2000s Hezbollah, despite its Shi'a identity and promotion of sectarianism domestically, attempted to garner support from in the wider Muslim-majority world by emphasizing its "Islamic" identity vis-à-vis Israel, winning a significant amount of support among Sunnis in many countries, including even in Saudi Arabia to the chagrin of that country's Salafi *'ulama*. Much less publicized, certainly by the party, is Hezbollah's use of coercion and threats and actual use of violence to suppress criticisms of it from Lebanese Shi'a.

In Chapter 7, Daher traces Hezbollah's reactions to the "Arab Spring" uprisings, which changed over time in line with the party's interests as well as those of its main allies, Iran, and Ba'athist Syria. Despite heralding the Tunisian and Egyptian mass protests in 2010 and 2011, which the party's leadership, in line with the Iranian government, claimed were "inspired," albeit three decades late, by the Iranian Revolution, Hezbollah quickly changed its tune when mass protests broke out in Syria. As demonstrations in Syria grew against the al-Assad regime, Hezbollah adopted a conspiratorial outlook on the uprisings, alleging that they were an "imperial-Zionist plot" against Islam and Muslims. The party's rhetorical support for its ally al-Assad expanded to military support in 2012 and 2013 as an increasing number of Hezbollah militants crossed the border, ostensibly to "defend" Lebanon from *"takfiri"* terrorists, referring to the practice by some Sunni militants of declaring Shi'a and other Muslim opponents to be "non-Muslims." Despite its claims of ecumenism, Hezbollah has adopted a broad sectarianized outlook with regard to the Syrian civil war, alleging that all of the political and armed opposition is "Wahhabi-*takfiri*" and "terrorists," rhetoric also used, not coincidentally, by the Iranian state. As Daher sums it up, Hezbollah's international relations and decision-making have little to do with supporting oppressed populations and everything to do with the party's own interests.

Daher's book is a significant contribution to the literature on Hezbollah as well as studies on political Islam more broadly. He argues convincingly that Islamist movements and parties operate generally according to their own self-interests, which are determined by a combination of social, political, and economic dynamics, and cannot be understood solely or even primarily through their espoused ideology because they often deviate in action from their rhetoric. **CA**

IRAN

The Baluch, Sunnism and the State in Iran: From Tribal to Global

Stéphane A. Dudoignon. New York, NY: Oxford University Press, 2017. 405 pp. ISBN: 978-0190655914.

The Baluch, a transnational ethnic group spread historically across what is now parts of Iran, Pakistan, and Afghanistan, make up a significant ethnic minority in both Pakistan and Iran, with estimates putting their numbers at around eight million and one-and-a-half million, respectively. In Iran, the Baluch are concentrated in the southeastern province of Sistan-Baluchistan on the country's shared borders with Pakistan and Afghanistan and parts of Khurasan province. Unlike the majority of Iran's population, who are Twelver Shi'ite Muslims, the Iranian Baluch are Sunni Muslims who follow the Hanafi School of Islamic jurisprudence. Traditionally divided along tribal lines, the Baluch in Iran have more recently been the target of recruitment and ideological wooing by militant Sunni Islamist organizations including Al-Qaeda, Islamic State, and various Pakistani Taliban factions. Islamic State has successfully recruited a number of Iranian foreign fighters from among the country's Sunni Baluch, Kurdish, and Ahvazi Arab communities, using them in its sophisticated propaganda campaign, and to carry out some attacks, the most notable being the storming of the Iranian parliament building and the shrine of the late Ayatullah Ruhollah Khomeini in June 2017. The emergence of militant, virulently sectarian Sunni Islamism among segments of the Iranian Baluch is the latest development in their relationship with the centralized Iranian state.

It is the history of the place of the Baluch in Iranian history that is the subject of the book under review by Stéphane A. Dudoignon, a researcher at the Center for Turkish, Ottoman, Balkan, and Central Asian Studies (Centre d'Études Turques, Ottomanes, Balkaniques et Centrasiatiques) in Paris, a study that places analytical focus on an important but understudied subject. Comprehensive in its coverage and empirical and analytical detail, the book is based on extensive field work, diplomatic and other archival documents, and primary and secondary sources in Persian, English, and French.

Dudoignon lays out the history of the Iranian Baluch, their sociopolitical and religious institutions and practices, the role of Islam in their society, and their changing relationship with the Iranian state.

Located in between Iran and Pakistan, the Baluch have long been influenced by the Deobandi school of Hanafi Sunnism that was founded in British India during the nineteenth century as a revivalist movement, which Dudoignon documents in Chapter One. Seeking to reconnect the region's Muslims with what they saw as more historically and theologically authentic practices while sweeping away problematic accretions to Islam, the Deobandi *'ulama* founded influential seminaries and other schools through which to proselytize, train, and shape future generations of the Subcontinent's Sunni Muslims. Deobandi and Ahl-i Hadith interpretations of Sunnism also benefited during the twentieth century from Pakistani state patronage under the military regime of General Zia-ul Haqq in the 1970s, which used Deobandism to try and penetrate Pakistan's own restive Baluchistan region. The transnational nature of Deobandi religious networks also influenced the influence of the concept of *jihad* among the region's Muslims, particularly during the anti-Soviet *jihad* in Afghanistan during the 1970s until 1989. Deobandi religious scholars have been active, as the author documents, in Sistan-Baluchistan for many decades, since before the Second World War, where they have been viewed with suspicion by Iranian governments that have sought to establish their own bridgeheads among Iranian Sunnis in the province.

The book argues that despite the religious differences between the Iranian state after the revolution of 1978-1979, virulently anti-Shi'a sectarian violence has only recently emerged among the Iranian Baluch relatively recently in the twenty-first century. Even today, Baluch *jihadi*-insurgent groups, such as Jaysh al-'Adl, Ansar al-Furqan, and, formerly, Jundullah, remain small rather than widespread; and Baluch ethno-nationalism in neighboring Pakistan has not adopted similar religious extremism or identity politics, perhaps because of the different environment there. Radical religious voices among Iran's Baluch remain, despite increasing security attention to them, quite limited in their influence an ability to mobilize. Baluch society has been profoundly impacted by post-Second World War changes to the role of tribes, tribal confederations, tribal leaders (*sardars*), and religious networks in the region brought on by the advent of the expanded power of the centralized, bureaucratic Iranian state, covered in Chapters Three and Four.

The Pahlavi monarchy and Islamic Republic both sought to expand the state's influence among the Baluch through patronage politics and the co-option of Baluch community leaders such as tribal chiefs and Sunni *'ulama.*

Unlike the Pahlavis, the Shi'a Islamist system ushered in by Khomeini and his followers included a significantly more pronounced sectarian identity but also an interest among the new revolutionary elite to forge ties to Sunni communities both inside and outside of Iran in an attempt to both solidify power domestically and expand Iran's regional influence. By the 1960s and 1970s, Baluch *'ulama* and other religious leaders began to enjoy greater autonomy from the traditional tribal chiefs and it was through religious institutions and figures that the Iranian government was able to negotiate and cooperate with Baluch notables. In later decades, Baluch religious leaders were recognized even by Iranian Shi'a Islamist politicians and officials as important influencers and organizers of the vote during election cycles. Shifts in Iranian government policies toward the Baluch and within Iranian Baluch society itself are covered in Chapters Four, Five, and Six.

Iran's Baluch *'ulama* have benefited from the desire of the Islamic Republic's desire to both extend its Sunni "soft power" and further legitimize itself through everyday politics and political processes such as semi-democratic elections, particularly since 1993. Like their Shi'a counterparts, the Baluch Sunni *'ulama* have participated in what the author dubs "republican Islam," that is, an Islam that is used to forge links between the state and religion and religious communities. The government and the religious classes each support one another based on mutual benefit with state recognition further institutionalizing the religious class and the support of the *'ulama* providing the state with increased legitimacy and, as in the case of the Iranian Baluch, deeper societal penetration. The Iranian Baluch *'ulama* have been, in effect, agents of Iranian nationalism rather than sectarian dividers, despite the existing religious differences between themselves and the ruling political and social order under Khomeini's successors.

The book is extensively researched and includes copious end notes and, thankfully, a stand-alone bibliography. The writing is often dense, and the sheer amount of information provided by the author can be daunting to even academic readers but is well worth the effort. One of Dudoignon's most important contributions, in addition to producing one of the only detailed scholarly studies of Iranian Baluch society and religion, is to successfully contest simplistic narratives about sectarianism and Sunni-Shi'a relations in the modern period. **CA**

The Emergence of Iranian Nationalism: Race and the Politics of Dislocation

Reza Zia- Ebrahimi. New York, NY: Columbia University Press, 2016. 312 pp. ISBN: 978-0231175760.

Iran usually is perceived with its actual political feature — as a Muslim country; nevertheless, if an Iranian abroad is asked where she/he is from, it is highly possible that the answer focuses on her/his pre-Islamic dimension of Iranian identity. It is likely to hear "I am a Persian" rather than "I am a revolutionary" or "I am a Muslim Iranian." This example is a very approximate example of everyday life of Iranians abroad; it cannot be generalized to the self-perception of all them. But, it is an important point to think which dimension of Iranian identity is crucially a hit, nowadays. Reza Zia-Ebrahimi's *The Emergence of Iranian Nationalism: Race and the Politics of Dislocation*, gives a very deep analysis of Iranian identity, in addition to other interesting facts; for instance, naming Iranian-owned restaurants and businesses across the world under names such as "Persepolis," which was the ceremonial capital of the Achaemenid Empire, referring to pre-Islamic time. In this book, he argues a specific type of Iranian nationalism, "dislocative" nationalism — according to analysis, the writings of two Iranian intellectuals, Fath'ali Akhundzadeh and Mirza Abolhossein Kermani, who lived in the late nineteenth century.

The idea that Iranians are willing to identify themselves as "Persian" and "Aryan heritage," rooted in an ideology which is directed by "dislocative nationalism" as Zia-Ebrahimi discusses. In his view, this ideology is based on a number of core ideas: "First, Iran is a primordial nation that has been in uninterrupted existence for about 2500 years… Second Iran's essence and glory is to be found in its pre-Islamic golden age. Third, Iran's shortcomings and decadence must be blamed on Islam, which Arabs imposed upon Iranians at the point of the sword. And fourth, Iranians are part of the Aryan race, thus akin to Europeans and racially quite distinct from Arabs…." (pp. 2-3). This specific type of nationalism is "dislocative," not in relevance with diasporic studies, but in the context of being dislodged from its empirical reality as a majority-Muslim society which is located in the East, and being positioned in the European context, due to its Aryan origins, along with Europeans (p. 5). It is of particular importance that the book does not analyze the "dislocative" nationalism as the only form of nationalism in Iran. Zia-Ebrahimi argues that there is a multiplicity of nationalisms which concern the same nation; for instance, nationalisms which are influenced by the Constitutional Revolution (1906-1911), Mohammad Mossadegh (1882-1976), and the Islamic Revolution of Iran (1979). But according to Zia-Ebrahimi, none of these nationalisms has had the degree of ideological relevance as "dislocative" nationalism.

This "dislocative" nationalism, not only has illustrated itself in everyday behavior of most of Iranians, but also has often been demonstrated in the political culture of Iranian society. As Zia-Ebrahmi argues, it became the most conventional ideological form of secular opposition to the Islamic Republic. Even some of Iranian officials have used the same discourse to create a patriotic support of Iranian people. An example would be the diplomatic team of Mahmoud Ahmadinejad, the former Iranian president, discussing the shared Aryan heritage in meeting with Europeans. Having said that, the idea of "dialogue among civilizations" of Mohammd Khatami, the ex-President of Iran, can also be considered a similar discourse.

But, here a question arises why and when such a nationalism emerged. The book claims that "dislocative" nationalism is a modern ideology which emerged in the Qjar period between 1860s and 1890s and then it integrated into the official ideology of the Pahlavi state during the years between 1925 and 1979. It is the contention of the author that the ideas of Fath'ali Akhundzadeh and Mirza Abolhossein Kermani, who are intended in their writings, had a considerable role in constructing the ideology of "dislocative" nationalism. Akhundzadeh was an author, playwright, and intellectual who "was deeply affected by Iran's encounter with the European imperialism" (p. 43). Akhundzadeh's initial period of intellectual career is renowned for his plays and other works of literature. Later, his nationalist thoughts took shape and appeared in his books, such as *Maktubāt*. The ideas of Akhundzadeh were promoted by other intellectuals. One of those intellectuals was Kermani, whose texts were also analyzed by Zia-Ebrahimi in this current book. Kermani was also an author and intellectual reformer whose ideas, it is believed, played an important role in the Constitutional Revolution of Iran in 1906. Kermani revived Akhundzadhe's thoughts in two books of *Seh maktub* and *sad Khatābeh* and complemented them with his additions. He used them to form a project of reform and adaption of the Iranian nation to modernity. This nationalist doctrine shaped a predominantly discursive and historic ideology. Objectives of this ideology presented a traumatic encounter with Europe and encouraged Iran's "backwardness."

"Dislocative" nationalism had ideological aspects of pre-Islamic archaism (in Chapter 3), Arab-hatred (in Chapter 4), and a hybridized-despotic approach to European modernity/Europeanization (in Chapter 5). According to Zia-Ebrahimi, these ideological aspects are found in the writings of Akhoundzadeh and, in a sharper and radicalized way, in the writings of Kermani. Nevertheless, these objectives are not based on logicical facts. Zia-Ebrahimi used this point to discuss that, for instance, Kermani's vision of pre-Islamic Iran and his hostility toward Arabs and Islam pursued a particular objective which was the creation of an ideology, which is appealing enough to sway mass conversion. "He does not aim to provide his readership with facts or as compendium of scientific discoveries. His aim is to promote dislocative nationalism, and he makes this aim abundantly clear in the concluding of *Seh maktub* when he announces that his wish is to awaken Iranians' patriotism, to strip them off their 'Semitic' nature and through a *changement subit* (French for "sudden change") revitalize this 'buried alive lot'" (p. 71). Putting main objectives of these texts in the historic context, Zia-Ebrahimi argues that they created an ideology which addresses, not only needs of Qajar's intellectuals, but also the authorities of Pahlavi.

Zia-Ebrahimi concludes his discussion (in Chapter 8) with this point that ideas of Akhundzadeh and Kermani failed to close the gap with the nations of the West or generate the modern state and society that most Iranians aspired to, for two reasons: first because the outlook of the "dislocative" nationalism is exclusively romantic; and second, because the "dislocative" nationalism has some despotic tendencies.

Reviewing this book, it is important to mention three points:

First, the discussion of this book opens new doors to identify specific types of nationalism in Iranian nationalism and focus the light on some of its dark and gloomy dimensions. Many Iranians are familiar with clichés about Arabs such as "lizard eaters," but discussing their roots and analyzing them in the context of "dislocative" nationalism is a pretty fascinating new issue. This makes reading this book even more necessary for Western readers who are, not only familiar with these insider clichés, but also have rare access to texts and ideas of Iranian intellectuals who diffused or kept alive those clichés to shape "dislocative" nationalism.

The second point is that although "the failure of 'dislocative' nationalism" is presented, it seems that the criteria for failure or success of an ideal nationalism or ideology is not discussed by the writer. It is easy to follow the objectives of "dislocative" nationalism in the analyzed texts, and why these objectives are challengeable and based on weak or no facts. Moreover, chapters of book on officialdom (in Chapter 7) and triumph (in Chapter 8) seem to attempt to explain how "dislocative" nationalism has been applied (or not applied) by different Iranian states and intellectuals to shape the Iranian nation. Nevertheless, these discussions present no criteria to determine how "dislocative" nationalism can be considered as a failure or a success. Furthermore, the analysis of the book can convince a reader that the outlook of "dislocative" nationalism was "romantic" and had some "despotic tendencies." But, these two characteristics can be common in other nationalisms as well — nationalism is an imaginary process, "dislocative" or otherwise. Being romantic and being formed by some despotic tendencies cannot convince a reader about failure of a nationalism.

The third point is that it would be great to continue the discussion of this book and argue how the "dislocative" nationalism connects itself to recent times, to the behavior of Iranians abroad, to discussions of secular opposition to the Islamic Republic, and finally to political discourses of Iranian officials. These points are mentioned by Zia-Ebrahimi at the beginning of the book. It would be also quite interesting to know how "dislocative" nationalism has been continued and kept alive along with other types of Iranian nationalisms, for instance the nationalism which is rooted in Constitutional Revolution and Islamic Republic of Iran.

Regardless of these minor objections, this book is highly recommended to everyone who is interested in understanding different aspects of nationalism, generally, and the construction of multiplicity of identities and nationalisms in the Iranian society, particularly. **FKC**

Gender and Dance in Modern Iran, Biopolitics on Stage

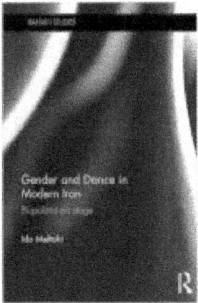

Ida Meftahi. New York, NY: Routledge, Taylor & Francis Group, 2016. 200 pp. ISBN: 978-1138804043.

Ida Meftahi's book *Gender and Dance in Modern Iran, Biopolitics on Stage* skillfully explores the historiographical accounts and transformation of staged dancing bodies over a span of ninety-years during twentieth century modern Iran. Meftahi takes on the challenging topic of dance (*raqs*), dancing bodies, and other forms of performances that are understudied in modern Iranian history and cultural studies (p. 5). She artfully explores the topic from a trans-disciplinary, multi-layered, and contextual perspective.

Meftahi researches Iranian socio-historical accounts of dance and performance over three genres and eras: 1) the "national dance" (*raqs-e melli*) of
Pahlavi era (1925-79) under governmental influence; 2) cabaret dancing
between 1940 and 1979 that appeared on stage and screen under the private
industry's influence; and 3) post-revolutionary (1979-present) "rhythmic
movements" (*harekat-e meezoon*) regulated under the post-revolutionary
Islamic government of Iran. Meftahi colorfully explores each of these genres
and analyzes them through socio-cultural, ethical, and political lenses. Her
focus is on the gender binary, sexual anxieties, and the construction of
modern femininity as it is reflected on stage and through the dancing bodies.
The vagueness of the concept of dance (*raqs*) in different time, space, and
place in Iran adds another layer of complexity to her research.

The author focuses on the esthetics and ethics of staged dancing bodies
and dance (*raqs*) as an artifact that is examined through time, space, and
place within a modern Iranian socio-political context. "The transformation
of the staged dancing body, its space of performance, and its spectatorial cultural ideology" (p. 1) become the core of the author's analysis. Collecting
data presented a challenge that required someone with Meftahi's skills and
training. She has a background in dance education and Middle East studies
and is well versed in Iranian society, culture, cultural cues, and language with
native connections to Iran. Her data collection based on mixed methodology and multi-method includes: 1) interviews – conducted with artists and
performers ranging from pre- to post-revolutionary Iran; 2) archival – au-
diovisual sources such as cinematic productions, video footage of dances; 3)
participant observation – conducted in dance classes, rehearsals, and performances; and 4) cultural artifacts and motifs – analyses of literature, symbolism, mysticism, rituals, and folklore.

Meftahi's starting point is the *Mutrebi* troupe (early musicians who often performed in cafes, tea houses, and private settings accompanied by the
cross-dressing male performer (*zanpush*), or the transvestite child dancer
(*bachcheh-raqqas*), and the Lalehzar district. The Lalehzar district was a social gathering place and a product of Tehran's urban modernity. It became the
center of performing arts, cinema, dancing performances, and entertainment
in Tehran during the late nineteenth and early twentieth century and continued up until the 1979 revolution.

In the aftermath of the Iranian constitutional revolution (1905-09) and
the Russian revolution of 1917, Russians disbursed to Iran (among other
factors) and influenced Tehran's artistic scene by developing performing arts
(e.g. opera, ballet) and introducing foreign female dancers on stage (mainly from the Caucasus and Poland). As Meftahi puts it, female performers

replaced and consequently eliminated the cross-dressing male performer and the transvestite child dancer from the "national stage" of the late Qajar, early Pahlavi era and the *mutrebi* troupe (p. 18).

Meftahi explores the transformation of the national dances (*raqs-e melli*) and the "invented ideal female subject" (p. 42) in theatrical performances during this era which is reflected in the dancer's clothing and movement, the themes and music, and emphasizes regulated and graceful feminine charm as she performs narratives of the nation (e.g. Persian classical literature) for her audiences to "witness and to emulate" (p. 42). These performances were often played in Rudaki Hall (*talar-e roudaki*) in Tehran. The hall was state-owned and operated and was considered part of Iran's modern high culture and prestigious Persian cultural heritage. A female dancer of the national dance company portrayed femininity, chastity, and charm in her performances (often in groups, or sometimes solo) distancing her character from the vague sexuality of the transvestite child dancer and the cross-dressing male performers of the earlier era. Meftahi explains this transition from vague to more polished femininity on stage: "Iranian dance required a departure from its immediate past: it was in that process that on the national stage, the female national dancer with a controlled femininity emerged to replace the *bachcheh-raqqas* of the *mutrebi* scene, whose performance combined hyper-sexuality and homoeroticism" (p. 49).

During the 1940s and 1950s, the Lalehzar district became more affordable and accessible to everyone. Cabaret performances and female dancers (*raqqasah kabareh*) along with Iranian cinema productions (*film-e farsi*) featuring female performers became the main attraction of the entertainment industry and "these venues gradually became dominated by male audiences from range of backgrounds" (p. 9). This is where Meftahi gives life and voice to the cabaret dancer (*raqqasah kabareh*) that has been dismissed, ignored, and omitted in historical analyses and cultural studies. As Meftahi remarks, the cabaret dancer is a dominant and visible character of twentieth century Iran. She is featured in novels and periodicals, and in pre-revolutionary cabaret and commercial cinema, she plays leading female roles. As visible as she is in different mediums, she is also regarded as the "other" and her "otherness" spills over to the view of her character as morally corrupt (often viewed as a dancer/prostitute/loose woman) and an unworthy character. She is often dismissed, marginalized, and represented as vulgar and over-sexualized. The cabaret dancer became the main attraction of the commercialized Iranian cinema (*film-e farsi*) where she was a fundamental part of the cinema industry's business strategy to attract male audiences and at some point, to save the industry from collapsing and bankruptcy. The popularity of the cabaret

dancer as a movie attraction was so lucrative that short clips of her dancing and singing were inserted in Western cowboy movies that were shown in
movies theatres (dubbed in Persian).

Meftahi's narrative continues to the post 1979 revolutionary era when
a range of performance forms went underground for a few years until they
reappeared, renamed, and relabeled as "rhythmic movements" (*harekat-e
meezoon*) and "professional aerobics" (*arobik-e herfeh'i*). The "rhythmic
movement" performances returned to theatres with religious and mystical
themes (pp. 10, 164). The "desexualized and controlled" performer became
the main subject of the dance scene reinforcing the image of the proper Muslim with the expression of purity, chastity, and spirituality (p.165). Meftahi
connects this new genre of performance to the Islamic government where it
"has deployed movement-based performance as part of its ideological state
apparatus, particularly useful for fostering its domestic and foreign policies"
(p.165). Ironically, since the 1979 revolution, dance has taken on a life of
its own. Private educational venues have multiplied, and educational dance
videos led by male instructors teaching international trends such as break
dancing, salsa, and hip hop — renamed and relabeled as professional aerobics (*arobik-e herfeh'i*) — are extremely popular (p.11).

Meftahi has made an invaluable contribution to the ever-expanding literature on Iranian studies, Middle East studies, the politics of gender and sexuality, historiography, and ethnographic studies of modern Iran, media and
cultural studies of the Middle East and Iran. Meftahi's book opens up a whole
array of scholarly opportunities that will engender further contributions to
the critical and objective study of the twentieth century modernizing and
urbanizing Iranian society. *EH*

Iran: A Modern History

Abbas Amanat. New Haven, CT: Yale University Press,
2017. 979 pp. ISBN: 978-0300112542.

Building upon a lifetime of study, writing, and scholarship
on Iranian and Central Asian history and religious movements, Shi'a Islam, and apocalyptic religious thought,
Abbas Amanat has produced a magisterial social, cultural,
and political history of Iran beginning with the advent of

the Safavid imperial dynasty under the boy-king Isma'il I in 1501 up to the contemporary period under the post-revolution and post-Khomeini Islamic Republic of Iran. Drawing upon a range of historical sources including political, religious, and literary sources, and diplomatic cables and reports, the book paints a vivid, living picture of Iranian history in addition to tracing the multiple histories of different Iranian ethic groups and social classes. Historically, comprehensive in its coverage, the book is also geared, in part, toward an interested, but not necessarily a specialist or academic audience, though Amanat does presuppose some, and arguably a good deal, of prior knowledge on the part of the reader.

Amanat's book begins by tracing the history of ancient Iran, that of the Achaemenid Empire and its constituent peoples who are primarily understood through the lens of their enemies, the writings of the ancient Greeks who viewed them as an alien, exotic, and strange culture. Orientalist images of ancient Iran and Eastern and Asian societies generally continue up to the present day through both pundits and popular culture in graphic novels and blockbuster Hollywood films such as *300*. A recurring theme in Iranian history, according to Amanat, has been the concept of a charismatic monarch who claims an aura of divinely-given authority to govern, represented in historical Iranian notions of the "king of kings" (*shahan shah*) and of the monarch as the "shadow of God on Earth." The Achaemenid and Sasanian emperors, the Safavid *shahs*, up to the Pahlavi dynasty and the Shi'a clerical ruling order based on the concept of the comprehensive authority of the supreme jurisprudent (*vilayat-e mutlaqeh-ye faqih*). The "divine right" claimed by different Iranian monarchs has infused Iranian history with a charismatic, quasi-religious aura not all that different from the monarchical histories of other societies in Europe and other parts of the Middle East and Asia where rulers have claimed that their authority comes from a "higher authority."

The book is subsequently divided into four main parts. The first covers the years 1501 to 1797 and traces the rise, decline, and eventual fall of the Safavid dynasty, whose main lasting contribution to Iranian society was the introduction and spread of Twelver Shi'ism in what previously had been a predominantly Sunni region. This section also covers the invasion of what is now modern-day Iran by disgruntled Afghan tribes and the short-lived monarchy of the peculiar Nadir Shah from 1736 to 1747.

The rest of the book is focused on the nineteenth, twentieth, and twenty-first centuries or the period of modern Iranian national and nationalist history. The second section covers the Qajar period up to the Constitutional Revolution and period of 1905-1911 when the power of the Qajar monarchs was limited by popular demand, social movement activism, and even the support of key clerical and juridical voices including Mirza Muhammad Tabataba'i and Mirza Muhammad Hasan Shirazi. These figures, backed by the merchant class, implemented constitutional limitations on the power of the Qajar kings.

The third section is dedicated to the Pahlavi dynasty founded by the gruff Reza Khan and inherited by his flamboyant son and the "king of kings," Muhammad Reza Pahlavi. Under the father, Iran underwent sustained campaigns of modernization, forced settling of nomadic peoples and tribes, and restrictions on public religion. This modernization campaign was continued under the son who introduced the "White Revolution" in the 1960s to further develop Iran's industry, introduce land reforms, and expand its influence and power as a regional power. Dissenters and protestors were ruthlessly suppressed, imprisoned, tortured, and even killed. Muhammad Reza Pahlavi's policies, while they expanded Iranian power, also created new waves of protest including among the powerful religious clerical class. The latter was soon represented by a previously obscure cleric, Ayatollah Ruhollah Khomeini, who railed against the Pahlavi regime's business deals with Western companies regarding Iran's oil resources and taking advantage of growing discontent among many segments of the Iranian population including secular Marxists and progressive democrats as well as more conservative religious groups and hybrid groups and intellectuals such as Ali Shari'ati. The fourth and final section of the book covers the massive shifts in Iranian society, politics, religion, and history during and after the Iranian Revolution of 1978-1979 and the establishment of an Islamic republic governed by *vilayat-e faqih*. Though the focus of many previous works, Khomeini's career and ideology and the political activism of his supporters are both adeptly and succinctly covered by the author here.

Amanat tells us the engaging story of how the young Isma'il I, who inherited control of a Sufi order and was backed by fierce Turkic tribal warriors, the Qizilbash, who held him to be quasi-divine. The Safavid dynasty profoundly changed Iran over two centuries, gradually converting the majority of its population from Sunni to Shi'a Islam, and fusing together aspects of pre-Islamic and early Islamic Iranian and Central Asian notions of kingship with the two main schools of thought within Twelver Shi'ism during different periods, the traditionist Akhbaris and the eventually triumphant Usulis. Even Khomeini, who, like other Shi'a religious scholars (*'ulama*) rejected the legitimacy of hereditary monarchy in Islam, drew upon concepts of charismatic ruling authority in his formulation of *vilayat-e faqih* and, shortly before his death in 1989, the "comprehensive authority" of the supreme jurisconsult (*vilayat-e mutlaqeh-ye faqih*). The adoption of the honorific title "Imam" for Khomeini by his followers broke with centuries of Shi'a precedent which reserved the title solely for the line of successors to the Prophet Muhammad, beginning with Ali ibn Abi Talib, who are considered to be legitimate by Twelver Shi'ites, ending with the twelfth Imam, the "Mahdi," Muhammad ibn Hasan, who is believed by them to now be in a mystical occultation (*al-ghayba al-kubra*, the "Greater Occultation") but who will return at a divinely-appointed time. Iranian historical conceptions of the charismatic ruler continued through the Qajar period up to the Pahlavis and the Islamic Republic.

The book is not only a political history of Iran, in its broader historical sense as well as, geographically, in its modern nation-state form, but also a sociocultural and literary history. Amanat has included numerous examples and translated passages from Persian literature and poetry, bringing the importance of these modes of expression in Iranian history to the forefront. Although it regrettably lacks a true bibliography and includes very few end notes for a book its size and scope, which will annoy academic readers, the book includes an extensive "Further Reading" section where the author highlights major studies and works on different aspects of Iranian history, culture, and society. The book, unsurprisingly, also includes a number of typos and can be in places a bit confusing or overly detailed in his descriptions, but these minor errors do not mar what is otherwise a substantial and laudatory contribution to existing histories of modern Iran. **CA**

Iranian Jews in Israel: Between Persian Cultural Identity and Israeli Nationalism

Alessandra Cecolin. New York, NY: I.B. Tauris, 2016, 320 pp. ISBN: 978-1784533113.

Alessandra Cecolin's book, *Iranian Jews in Israel: Between Persian Cultural Identity and Israeli Nationalism,* is a socio-political analysis of two waves of emigration of Iranian Jews, and the challenges of their integration in Israeli society.

The first wave of Jewish immigrants left Iran and came to Israel in the late 1940s and the early 1950s, shortly after the establishment of the state. The second wave was a reaction to the Islamic revolution of 1979, when Iran severed its diplomatic relations with the Jewish state.

Cecolin's study helps us understand the significance of these emigrations in shaping the identities of Iranian immigrants in Israel, as it underscores the significance of the time and circumstance of each of these emigration waves in fashioning identities as Jewish or as Iranian.

In the first chapter, "Zionism and the birth of Israel," Cecolin gives a thorough review of the Zionist movement, from its inception in the nineteenth century until the declaration of independence of the State of Israel in 1948. Chapter 2 is devoted to the history of Jews in Iran, their education, and their social status. Chapter 3 tells us the story of the rise of political Zionism in Iran, and the difficulty it encountered penetrating Iranian Jewry. This was due to the isolation of Iranian Jews from the rest of the Jewish world, and the conservative nature of the community, which clashed with the predominantly secular and socialist Zionist movement and its representatives in Iran. Chapter 4 describes the international influences that triggered the two waves of emigration. In Chapter 5, Cecolin discusses domestic factors, and explains what motivated the two waves of Jewish emigration from Iran; in Chapter 6, she describes the process of emigration and the integration of Iranian Jews into Israeli society.

Cecolin writes that the first wave of immigration of Iranian Jews to Israel was characterized by their relative low socioeconomic status and their traditional values. These immigrants were not Zionists, and like other non-Ashkenazi groups, they were marginalized in the young evolving Israeli society with its predominant "melting pot" ideology. However, this particular group experienced difficulties over and above those encountered by other non-Ashkenazi immigrations. Having arrived not fluent in either Hebrew, Arabic, or any European language put them at a disadvantage compared to other non-Ashkenazi groups. The Iranian Jewry consisted of scattered groups of people without leadership. Their lack of ideological motivation and their traditional characteristics were ill-fitted with the ideals of Zionism and social-democracy. In order to assimilate into Israeli society, they had to forgo much of their cultural heritage and traditions. The second wave of emigration from Iran was differently motivated, and this time Iranian heritage figured heavily in the process of integration. The immigrants came to a different Israel, amenable to the revival of many Iranian customs, festivities, and food traditions.

The book is clearly the fruit of painstaking research into the history of Iranian Jewry; it demonstrates the author's thorough familiarity with the subject matter. A relatively small fraction of the book is devoted to the main topic of the book, as is suggested by its title. The bulk of the book is devoted to the history of Iranian Jewry, including ancient history and biblical accounts, the relevance of which to the main thesis of the book is not always evident.

Albeit short, this chapter features vivid anecdotes and a thorough analysis of the challenges and the difficulties that Iranian Jews encountered when they arrived in Israel. Not least of these was the social structure endemic to Iranian Jewry and the absence of community leadership. Reading Cecolin's account of the education of Iranian Jews throughout history, I was left with some unanswered questions: What was the degree of overall literacy in the community? In particular, what was the percentage of female literacy, a significant factor in the social mobility of subsequent generations? Another interesting issue that receives only a sketchy and marginal treatment in the book is the situation of Jewish women in Iran, and after immigration — in Israel.

Another minor shortcoming is the way sources are presented. The thorough research invested in the book notwithstanding, the bibliography is far from reader-friendly and references are often difficult to track. An example of this is the author's way of citing a quotation by referencing only the catalogue number of the source in an archive. The reader has no way of knowing what the source is or who said or wrote what is reported.

However, these drawbacks do not diminish the substance of the book. Issues of nationality versus cultural and religious identity are increasingly pertinent, and Cecolin's book is a welcome addition to the literature on immigration in general, and Jewish immigration in particular.

The book concludes with a glossary of social and political terms, mostly in Hebrew and some in Farsi, an index, and a rich bibliography. The sources include personal interviews, a myriad of archival documents, and secondary sources such as scholarly books and articles as well as newspaper articles. *MLA*

The Revolutionary Guards in Iranian Politics: Elites and Shifting Relations

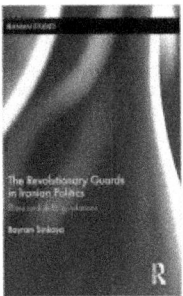

Bayram Sinkaya. New York, NY: Routledge, 2016. 234 pp. ISBN: 978-1138853645.

The Iranian Revolutionary Guards Corps (IRGC) has long been one of Iran's preeminent and most powerful military organizations, tasked with safeguarding the country's "Islamic revolution" and revolutionary republic from enemies both at home and abroad. Founded in late 1979 by the order of Ayatollah Ruhollah Khomeini, the

IRGC provides the Iranian government with a capable external operations network through the Quds Force, currently commanded by General Qasim Soleimani, and internal security apparatus together with the official paramilitary organization, the Basij. It is through the Quds Force and IRGC that militant organizations allied to the Iranian state such as Lebanon's Hizbullah and a network of Iraqi Shi'a Islamist parties and militias, including 'Asa'ib Ahl al-Haqq and the Badr Organization, are supported financially and militarily. More recently, the Houthi movement in Yemen has also reportedly received logistical and military support from the IRGC to help fuel the ongoing civil war in that country that pits the Iran and Hizbullah-backed Houthis against a coalition of Arab Gulf states led by Saudi Arabia and backed by the United States. The IRGC's role, however, has gradually expanded in recent years into the political and business/economic spheres with current and retired Guards officers playing an increasingly important role in both. The support of the IRGC has also had a significant impact on Iranian domestic politics, particularly during the two presidential terms of Mahmoud Ahmadinejad, whose two administrations included numerous members who were former Guards officers. The IRGC also continues to play a major role in Iran's involvement in the Syrian civil war and ongoing conflict in Iraq through the Quds Force, financing, training, and equipping militia forces to fight to uphold Iranian interests in the Middle East.

In the book under review, Bayram Sinkaya provides an in-depth look at the IRGC as a major political force in Iranian politics, both domestically and internationally, that traces the organization's involvement in the political sphere since its inception. Rather than being politicized later, the IRGC, from its inception, was conceived of as a revolutionary political entity, one that was tasked with protecting the Islamization of Iran's broad-based revolution by Khomeini and his supporters. The trajectory of the IRGC's participation and reaction to politics is determined, Sinkaya argues, by two sets of variables: first, the organization's ideological outlook and corporate characteristics, and second, changes in Iranian political dynamics since the revolution including the ideological positions of the ruling elite and cohesion and division among its different and sometimes competing segments. Comparing the Iranian case with revolutions and revolutionary armies in France (1789), Bolshevik Russia (1917), and Maoist/Communist China (1949), he pinpoints three critical variables that influence the relationship of revolutionary armies with politics: first, the balance between the "corporateness" and ideological commitments of the revolutionary army; second, the relationship between the ideological outlook of the army and the political elite; and third, the power of the political leadership vis-à-vis the military

leadership. Shifts in any of these areas has an impact on civil-military relations. When faced with liberal or weak political leaderships, ideological-
ly-committed revolutionary armies, Sinkaya argues, tend to see intervention
in the political sphere as both increasingly possible and necessary.

Constitutionally backed, the IRGC has been since its founding a primarily
ideological driven force. Its very identity, according to the new post-revolution constitution, was to be a military defender of the ideological principles
of the Iranian revolution and specifically its "Khomeini-zation" following the
ouster of more moderate political and religious voices in the aftermath of the
flight of Muhammad Reza Pahlavi and the return of Khomeini from exile. A
volunteer force, the IRGC attracted ideological recruits, but the organization's membership still included individuals with a variety of sometimes differing ideological views beyond being supportive of the "Islamic" revolution.
Ideological uniformity was aided by the utilization of Shi'i Islam, specifically
important concepts such as martyrdom and self-sacrifice, that were reformu-
lated to encourage striving and sacrifice for the revolutionary Islamic republic. IRGC members are encouraged to see themselves as participants in a cos-
mic conflict between "good" and "evil," between belief and unbelief (*kufr*),
beliefs that encourage ideological commitment. Differing views on what the
organization's specific goals and duties should be have allowed IRGC commanders to gradually expand the realm of the Guards' involvement in Iranian
society to the political, economic/business, and social spheres, thus expanding the IRGC's influence and power. The ongoing turmoil in the Middle East
has also enabled the IRGC to play a major role in regional affairs by acting
to prop up the faltering Syrian Ba'ath Party government and support allied
groups such as Hizbullah and the Houthi movement.

The increasingly broad-based nature of the IRGC's involvement in Iranian daily life became most apparent during the two presidential terms of the
neo-conservative Mahmoud Ahmadinejad. After his election in 2005, however, Ahmadinejad and Iran's neo-conservatives began to face competition
from traditional conservatives and were thus forced to seek the blessing of
the supreme leader, Ali Khamenei, or engage in compromises with the traditional conservatives. Khamenei and the traditional clerical conservatives
also tightened their ideological influence over the IRGC by establishing a
close relationship between the organization and a set of clerics appointed to
serve as ideological advisers and officials in the Guards and the Basij. Rising
threats in the early 2000s, such as the rumbling of war drums among American neo-conservatives and the presidential administrations of George W.
Bush, also enabled IRGC commanders to increase their political clout. The
Syrian and Iraqi conflicts, joined later by the re-sparking of a "hot war" in

2006 between Hezbollah and Israel, and Yemen, have also allowed the IRGC to maintain a role at the forefront of the Iranian state's foreign policy. The organization is heavily involved in both Syria and Iraq, providing military advice along with funding and military supplies to an array of armed Shiʻa Islamist militias and political factions in both countries and losing an increasing number of officers from both the IRGC and Basij as military casualties, including a number of generals and other senior officers. The highest thus far has been Brigadier General Hossein Hamedani, who was instrumental in forming the Syrian government's "National Defense Forces," which was modeled after the Basij.

Sinkaya's book places the IRGC in a broader historical framework within modern Iranian history as well as the literature on revolutionary militaries and states. Drawing from previous studies of revolutionary states and militaries in France, Russia, and China, the book traces the evolution of the IRGC's involvement in Iranian domestic politics and foreign policy with a careful attention to detail and the specifics of changes on the ground inside Iran since 1979. The book is a welcome addition to the literatures on modern Iranian politics, modern Middle East history, revolutions and revolutionary politics, and military affairs. **CA**

Social Media in Iran: Politics and Society After 2009

David M. Faris, & Babak Rahimi, Eds. Albany, NY: State University of New York (SUNY) Press, 2015. 334 pp. ISBN: 978-1438458830.

Given its accepted network role, what is the state of social media in Iran? David Faris and Babak Rahimi brought together a diverse group of contributors to address that question with attention to the 2009 presidential elections. Not anticipating the promotion of collective action, the editors are sanguine about the social media facilitating dissent — what Nancy Fraser called "counterpublics." Focusing on the experiential and networking processes, Faris and Rahimi explore three theoretical perspectives: globalization, networked communities, and communications. The edited book, with original contributions, is divided into three parts: societal, politics, and culture. The societal segment discusses Facebook, gender, gays, and the disabled. The politics section is the centerpiece and covers online journalism, blogs, Facebook election campaigns, web protests, contested Persian language space, government counter-strategy, political memorialization, and a comparative study. The culture portion gives a glimpse of cinema and video art.

Jari Eloranta, Hossein Kermani, and Rahimi focus on Facebook in Chapter 1 in addressing social capital formation, which is associated with democracy promotion through the twin elements of trust and connectivity. Distinguishing it from the internal relations of "bonding," the key to social capital for the Internet is the external relations of "bridging" in establishing new contacts — a point also noted by Mohammad Esfahlani.

Chapters 2, 3 and 4 focus on gender, gays, and the disabled, respectively. In a textual analysis of Persian-language Facebook pages and blogs, Elham Gheytanchi finds that the uprising of 2009 led to the creation of a politically vocal Internet group, the Mothers of Park Laleh (originally called the Mourning Mothers of Iran). Abouzar Nasirzadeh holds that the gay community falls into three categories of Internet users: socializers, information disseminators, and bridge makers. Those in the third category have taken to online political activism in three ways: developing Farsi language alternative to Western words, increasing visibility and humanity of gay individuals, and countering homophobia. What is noteworthy for Nasirzadeh is the absence of lesbians in the online social media. Kobra Elahifar notes that the Internet social media empowerment of the disabled is at the individual level given the continued stigmatization by the society. In contrast to the extroverted "rich become richer" hypothesis (Patti Valkenberg and Jochen Peter), Elahifar finds support for the introverted "social compensation" hypothesis (Katelyn McKenna and John Bargh). In addition, there is a gender differentiation for both the gay community and the disabled.

With the 2005 rise to power by Mahmoud Ahmadinejad there were censorship of Internet blogging and persecution of journalists. These policies were countered by a growth of online journalism outside government control, observes Marcus Michaelsen in Chapter 5. He gives interesting insight into reformist online activities and counter-moves by the government. *Mosharekat* (Participation Front) and *Mojahedin-e Enqelab-e Eslami* (Warriors of the Islamic Revolution) newspapers moved online in the face of press censorship. Likewise, reformist *Shargh* (East) daily newspaper in 2006 reappeared as *Shahr-e Farda* (City of Tomorrow) website. When judicial authorities closed down *Baztab* (Reflection) website in 2007, *Tabnak* (Shining) website appeared soon thereafter. Iranian journalists in exile in 2005 founded *Rooz* (Day) online newspaper. *Keyhan* (Cosmos) hardline print newspaper accused *Emrouz* (Today) website of being a tool of the West. *Yek Khabar* (A Message) and Efsha (Disclosure) conservative websites targeted reformist politicians. *Gooyaa* conservative website was launched to counter the popular *Gooya* (Rational) reformist website.

In Chapter 6, Arash Falasiri and Nazanin Ghanavizi examine dissent in the blogosphere, which they view as a public realm in citing Hannah Arendt. They hold that Internet blogging in Iran is facilitated by four factors: high speed, low cost, high literacy, and high unemployment. Along with communication, deliberation, and exchange of ideas, the blogosphere plays an important role in promoting public awareness. Whereas Twitter is useful for fast updates, Facebook blogging has been paramount for three reasons: control, security, and networks.

Esfahlani elaborates on conflict within the ruling elite in Chapter 7. During the 1985, power struggle between conservative President Syed Ali Khamenei and moderate Prime Minister Mir-Hossein Mousavi, Ayatollah Ruhollah Khomeini intervened to preserve Mousavi in office. The 1997 election of President Mohammad Khatami ushered a reformist era. However, the reformist camp was ousted following the 2005 election of President Ahmadinejad — and privileged the power of the Islamic Revolutionary Guard Corps (IRGC), adds Samira Rajabi. The 2009 campaign by Mousavi led to the Green Wave, which was transformed into the Green Movement following the presidential election results. The social capital accumulated helped the 2013 election of reformist President Hassan Rouhani. Contrary to the skepticism in the introduction by Faris and Rahimi (pp. 4-6), Esfahlani argues with impressive graphs of Mousavi's Facebook page that collective action is "central" to social movements in drawing attention to three types of "framing": diagnostic, prognostic, and motivational. The contribution by Esfahlani is the most insightful in the book.

The June 2009 post-election protests marked a "trans-spatial" collective action by activists at home and in the diaspora for political reform in Iran, argues Reza Nejad in Chapter 8. The Web 2.0 social media (Facebook, Twitter, You Tube, and wikis) facilitated crowd-sourcing in allowing activists to simultaneously be the audience and content creators. In a case study of Balatarin, a Persian language online blogging site, Rahimi and Nima Rassooli examine the politics of gatekeeping in Chapter 9. The Green Movement activists became unofficial gatekeepers in undermining impartiality. Not only religiously blasphemous posts were banned by site administrators for fear of government retaliation, but also rights for Kurd and Azeri ethnic minorities were downplayed in an online voting process.

Faris provides a useful comparative framework of three regime types in Chapter 10 for understanding authoritarian governance of the Internet social media: response, control, and cordon. In categorizing Egypt as a response regime under Hosni Mubarak during the Arab Spring, he views Iran as a cordon regime during the 2009 elections upheaval. The post-2009 elections "soft war" by the Islamic Republic is distinct from the "soft power" concept by Joseph Nye in two ways, argues Niki Akhavan in Chapter 11: narrower focus of preserving moral fabric of the society and couching state counter-offensive as public safety (national security and criminal) issues. The author notes the 2011 establishment of *Polic-e Fazay-e Toleed va Tabadeel Etellaat* (The Police for the Sphere of the Production and Exchange of Information, FATA), the cyber police. Other attempts were the *Gerdab* (Whirlpool) Project by IRGC and *Sazmaan-e Zanan-e Enghelab-e Eslami* (Organization of the Women of the Islamic Republic) website. In Chapter 12, Rajabi argues that the cultivation of *shahid* (martyrdom) as a state policy since the 1980-1988 Iran-Iraq War was the context that transformed Neda Agha-Soltan from a "referential" to an "iconic" image. In transitioning from a collective memory to a political memory, her death itself became the driving force for the reform movement.

Chapters 13-14 deal with culture. Michelle Langford holds that cinema and the social media are converging in promoting "collective intelligence." She credits the Internet with distribution of Iranian films banned by the authorities. However, video-based social medium has been undermined by government-imposed filtering and speed restrictions. With attention to the virtual museum Vimeo, Staci Scheiwiller discusses video art as an artistic medium for rebellion. Noting the preference for Vimeo platform by Iranian artists for its avant-garde display, she is concerned that uninformed buyers may be procuring low-quality artwork for profit motive. Langford and Scheiwiller open an interesting window into Iranian films and videos.

The societal and culture parts seem grafted on to the politics section. The book would have been better served in being limited to politics. Also, the broader framework of the social media facilitating dissent in Iran could have been better articulated in the introduction. While Michaelson mentioned "fragmented authoritarianism" involving hardline and conservative factions within the ruling elite (p. 105), furthermore, he left the reader waiting for insight into that dynamics. In addition, Rajabi did not clarify how Agha-Soltan being an active participant was related to the transformative process discussed (p. 234). Finally, a separate conclusion that tied together the various contributing chapters to the theoretical framework of globalization, networked communities, and communications would have been helpful. Nevertheless, those in communications studies will enjoy a fascinating glimpse into the social media in Iran. In particular, non-Farsi speaking readers will find useful information. Those interested in the 2009 presidential elections and the subsequent protest movement will benefit from the essays. **RGM**

ISLAM

Arguing Islam after the Revival of Arab Politics

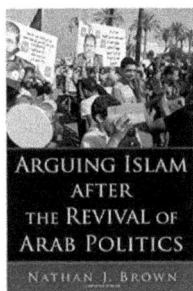

Nathan J. Brown. Oxford, UK: Oxford: Oxford University Press, 2016, 296 pp. ISBN: 978-0190619459.

This book is original and timely. I think it has almost everything a modern book on Middle East politics following the Arab Spring should have — a reliance on both fieldwork and narrative techniques; an openness to new theories of public space, sociology, anthropology, and political science that promise better outcomes, illustrations with real data sets that show the cultural and political perspectives and specificities of this region of the world. The book raises useful questions with step-by-step answers that help the reader work out how to understand the challenges facing Arab politics and society in countries like Egypt, Jordan, Syria, Kuwait, and Saudi Arabic in the post-Arab Spring era. It is a sophisticated book that truly provides an elegant and useful analysis of the interaction of religion and politics in the region.

This is a book for readers and researchers who are already familiar with theories of politics and public sphere, but who may not know the complexities of Arab and Muslim societies. The title of the book and the introduction seem to indicate that this book is suitable for those who are interested in Islam and the Islamic movement in the Middle East and North Africa and who want to know how political discourse, activism, and religion impact on policy-making and democratizing the region.

What is interesting about this book is that it focuses on several types of public sphere and analyzes how they interact. It investigates political conversations in small groups in public and private circles, debates in public squares and mosques, discussions that take place in social and regular media, and debates in institutions like parliaments, especially the political discussions and clashes that take place between opposing parliamentary groups before agreeing or voting on legislation.

However, I have two major concerns about this book. First, it gives the impression that religion and politics can go together, and that people should overcome their fear of religion. However, we know for a fact that one of the reasons for the violence and civil wars in the region is the overwhelming power of Islam and its utilization in politics as "the main language of public debate," as the author states. Religion has its own discourse and perspective, and it is actually problematic for public life and for human rights. The Middle East would do better if it could separate religion and politics.

Second, although the book discusses amply the role of religion in advancing political debate and democracy, it does not refer to jihadist groups systematically, perhaps because they are violent or are situated outside recognized official institutions. But, I think one cannot discuss religion in politics without include jihadism and jihadists who use religion for political ends and who have their conversations displayed mainly in social media. They also aim at transforming society and at changing policy and the nature of politics. Moreover, they do have an impact on political debate and policy in many Muslim countries.

While the book focuses on religion, it develops a comprehensive approach to understanding the revival of Arab politics which has a significant impact on policy, and how Arab peoples assess their political systems and governance structures. The book also argues that there is much variability in religious debate and the revival of politics in Arab countries.

The book describes the various facets of the ideology crisis in the Arab world and the revival of the public's interest in politics despite the failure of the Arab Spring and the restrictions of public freedoms imposed by authoritarian regimes. The book explores the numerous strategies used by politicians, religious groups, activists, and media to surmount these difficulties and to increase their chances of influencing policy-makers. It reveals the remarkable influence of political and religious conflicts and conflicts of interests, and the role they play in youth's integration, participation, and achievement. The book also nicely reveals how the government uses the political argument to silence public voices and shut out the opposition in this region. The book also thoroughly analyzes what happens when politics becomes a public issue, and people discuss it and argue about it in public.

The book is divided into three major parts. Part I begins by defining and explaining concepts such as "politics," "publicity," and "argument," and then turns to discuss publicity, religion, and the revival of politics (Chapter 1). The reader is slowly and clearly led through how Arab societies are struggling to achieve democratic rights by showing concern for political matters and by using religious discourse, wavering between tradition and modernity (Chapter 2).

Part II discusses a number of arguments used in the public and private spheres to describe and deal with political and social problems, in relation to the state's cultural and political perspectives and governance (Chapter 3). It investigates the various features of spaces where politics is discussed in the Middle East, and how these spaces interact with each other, and how Islam and the Islamic law (shari'a) are used and argued in the public debate (Chapter 4 and 5).

In Part III, the author describes Arab constitutions and the multitude of voices of the public sphere, tracing the socio-cultural ramifications of public politics for policy outcomes. He analyzes how politics and religion are discussed in the contentious public sphere leading a remarkable argument about religion (Chapter 6). In Chapter 7, the author focuses on the family law, showing a strong separation between the law as it is practiced and the law as it is understood and debated. He argues that such arguments which are divorced from reality are rarely taken in account in policy-making.

The book also researches the more practical issue of textbooks in schools and universities. It shows that the political and religious arguments operate in these textbooks, and provoke heated discussions and disagreements, thus "sharpening divisions" and widening the gap between different social and religious groups in society. However, these divisions do not have a significant impact on policy (Chapter 8).

The book ends by a reflection on the political revival of the Arab world in post-Arab Spring, illustrating that this political dynamism, which gave rise to powerful public debates, has been reduced by challenging political realities and structures (Chapter 9).

In sum, while the book brings out the deep-seated tensions and contradictions in the socio-cultural fabric of Arab societies, it underlines how Islam functions, impacts and integrates the political arena of the Arab world today. As such, the book is a significant contribution to understanding the Middle East politics and society, and the role of Islamic traditions and the ramifications for policy outcomes and governance across the region.

Reference

Ennaji, Moha, Ed. (2014). *Multiculturalism and Democracy in North Africa: Aftermath of the Arab Spring.* New York, NY: Routledge. **ME**

Beyond Shariati: Modernity, Cosmopolitanism, and Islam in Iranian Political Thought

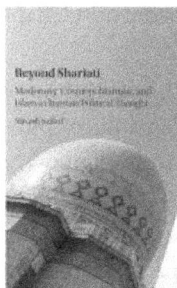

Siavash Saffari. London, UK: Cambridge University Press. 256 pp. ISBN: 978-1107164161.

Questions pertaining to the conceptual relationship between Islam and modernity — and therefore between cultural relativism and (hegemonic) universalism — continue to occupy the minds of scholars of contemporary/modern Islam and/or Muslim societies. The book under review examines the thought and legacy of Ali Shari'ati (d.1977), famously dubbed an "ideologue of the Iranian Revolution" and what are broadly termed "neo-Shari'atis" (i.e. Shariati's intellectual interlocutors) through this broad theoretical lens. In essence, in many ways, the book under review wishes to problematize the preponderant view of Islam's (supposed) incompatibility with modernity by examining the ideas of Ali Shari'ati and how they have been interpreted by neo-Shariatis (p. 4-5). Saffari identifies that the main argument of the book is to present the ideas of Shari'ati and neo-Shari'atis as a simultaneous critique of Eurocentric conceptualizations of modernity as well as essentialist understandings of Islam. This is achieved by their espousal of "socio-politically progressive discourse of indigenous modernity that engages freely and creatively with a wide range of emancipatory projects in the modern world" (p. 5), thereby forging a distinct third way, discursively speaking, between hegemonic universalism and essentialist particularism. This third way, in turn, is conceptualized as a form of non-western post-colonial cosmopolitanism which is informed by and imbued in local systems of knowledge.

While there are many existing studies on the ideas and legacy of Shari'ati and the debates surrounding Islam and modernity, Saffdari considers that his approach is unique insofar as it focuses on the arguments of Shariati's intellectual followers in the context of the debates on Islam and modernity briefly alluded to above as well as its "dialogical" approach which is also conceptualized as a methodological tool the book adopts (p. 14).

The book consists of an introduction, five chapters, and a conclusion. In the introduction, the main concepts, methodological cum theoretical framework are presented. In this respect, it is noteworthy that the author does not see the main aim of the book to be evaluative in nature, but seeks to place the ideas of Shariati and neo-Shariatis in "conversation with some other responses to European Enlightenment and colonial modernity in Islamic thought, postcolonial thought, and Western normative thought along the axis of four major themes: the genealogy of modernity, the Islam/modernity binary, colonial legacy and Eurocentrism , and identity and identitarianism" (p.18). Also, a useful, albeit brief biography of Shariati and his legacy as a "radical Islamic thinker" is included in the introduction.

The first two chapters seek to contextualize the ideas of Shariati and neo-Shariatis by examining a (too narrow) range of modern Muslim scholars' responses to the manifold challenges the modern condition poses to the Islamic tradition. A particular focus is placed on Muslims scholars such as Abu Zayd, Arkoun and Soroush, who, while remaining within an "authentic" approach to reform of the Islamic tradition are considered not to have not fallen into the Islam/modernity binary conceptual trap (in contrast to Islamists like S.Qutb, Maududi and Khomeini who have).

The other three chapters are much more original and are designed "to reveal the ways in which Shariati's thought finds common ground with a wide range of global discourses that treat Europe's Enlightenment modernity, its metanarratives of modernization and secularization, and it's associated socio-political and socio-economic formatives (i.e. nation-state structures and capitalist economics) as objects of reform and critique" (p. 15). In this respect, Saffari's comparative approach brings into conversation Shari'ati's view of religiously mediated indigenous modernity with J. Casanova's concept of public religion and that of N. Eisenstadt's multiple modernities construct (Chapter 3); ch. Taylor's idea of communitarian thought, Cornel West's liberation theology, and F. Dallmayr's Gadamerian phenomenology (Chapter 4). Chapter 5 theorizes the relationship between universalism and "nativism" from the conceptual perspective of a "civilizational framework" as espoused in the thought of Shariati and neo-Shariatis. The author engages primarily with the scholarship of Edward Saeed, Hamid Dabashi, and Fred Dallmayr when wresting with the question of the conceptual relationship between Islam and modernity, East and West, colonial and postcolonial, nativist and cosmopolitan, Universalist and particular. In this respect, the author's main argument is that "For neo-Shariatis, Shariati's idea of an indigenous modernity, with its overall civilizational framework , represents neither a total rejection of modernity nor the total embrace of the native self" and call instead for "a critical and selective approach toward both the local sources of identity and the global condition of modernity, one based on the recognition of cultural flux and hybridity" which "seeks to transcend the prevailing oppositional binaries of tradition/modernity, Islam/West, and East/West" (p.1610). Ultimately, the aim is to establish a new dialogical

relationship between these binaries which conceptualize them as "co-consti-
tutive," "unfinished projects," and complementary "existential orientations"
(pp.156-162).

In the conclusion titled "Toward a Postcolonial Cosmopolitanism," Saffari
focuses primarily on outlining arguments about the discursive or intellectual
advantages neo-Shariatism has — over competing form of Islamic reform-
ism — in the context of post Islamism — as defined by Asef Bayat — with
respect to solving the main conundrum that book has addressed, namely the
conceptual relationship between Islam and modernity. One such argument
is that only neo-Shariatism is in a position to simultaneously develop "religiously mediated and contextually grounded accounts of secularism and
democracy," yet maintain a critical posture toward "western-style, liberal democracy" which is by many Muslims associated with legacies of imperialism
and western hegemony. Another identified advantage of neo-Shariatism is its
insistence on non-banishment of religion from the public sphere and its privatization and the recognition of its emancipatory potential as an anti-dote
to religious conservatism and fundamentalism. Other purported advantages
include the role neo-Shariati thought can play with respect to facilitation of
social welfare, socio-economic development and gender equality in Muslim
majority contexts (pp.173-177). Finally, Saffari argues that neo-Shariatism
offers a plausible venue for the process of indigenization of modernity in
universalist terms by being a socially and grass roots-oriented process that
is premised on what I have elsewhere in the context of defining progressive
Muslim thought (Duderija, 2011, 2017) termed epistemological openness
and methodological fluidity and that is not purely intellectual in disposition
but is based on "social hermeneutics" (Duderija 2017).

This reviewer is not an expert on Shariati and my views of the book primarily focus on its conceptual rigorousness and how neo-Shariantism fits
into the larger framework of contemporary Islamic intellectual currents, especially progressive Muslim thought (Duderija, 2007, 2011, 2013, 2017).

One of the main strengths of the book is its acute attention to the conceptual, methodological, and conceptual difficulties in maintaining an essentialist and binary conceptual relationship between concepts such as tradition/
Islam-modernity and East/Islam–West. Another important theoretical intervention of the book is its balanced, multiple critique of both Orientalist and
Occidentalist tendencies in scholarship when approaching the same conundrum. The book's conceptual rigorousness is somewhat diminished by inadequate theorizing of the concepts of progress in the context of the book's
main aim, namely the efforts of Shari'ati and neo-Shariaties in advancing a
contextually grounded discourse of progressive social and political change

by means of indigenization of modernity. While Saffari repeatedly states that the Western-centric, European Enlightenment concept of progress as conceptualized by Hegel and Fukuyama, for example, is not the progress that neo-Shariatism accepts no alternative definition of progress is offered. This is despite the fact that existing scholarship on this very concept of progressive does exist on which this reviewer has been publishing since 2007 in the context of theorizing progressive Muslim thought (Duderija, 2007, 2011, 2017).

Moreover, the concept of authenticity should have been much more problematized. Saffari uses it to basically denote a process of return to Islamic nativism and cultural relativism, which is what some readers of Shariati have ascribed to him as being an advocate of (which is, according to Saffari an erroneous reading of Shariati). But, the process of authenticity in the context of theorizing the Islamic intellectual and cultural heritage (*turath*) can also be conceptualized as a critical, creative one too (Duderija, 2011). More generally speaking insufficient, if any, attention, was given to the very concept of turath itself.

Finally, the purported advantages of neo-Shariantism and its worldview outlined above very much mirror the ideals, values, and objectives that underpin progressive Muslim thought and its *weltanschauung* (Duderija, 2007, 2011, 2017). From that perspective, neo-Shariantism, especially its more cosmopolitan manifestations, should be considered as part of a progressive Muslim thought whose theoretical framework in terms of both its conceptualizations of turath and late modernity episteme has found fruitful answers to the main question the book under review addresses. I would recommend this book to postgraduate students and academics working in the broad field of contemporary Islamic Studies.

References

Duderija, A. (2007). Islamic groups and their worldviews: The case of progressive Muslims and neo-traditional Salafis," *Arab Law Quarterly, 21* (4), 341-363.

Duderija, A. (2011). Constructing religiously ideal 'Believer' and 'Muslim woman' concepts: Neo-Traditional Salafi and progressive Muslim methods of interpretation (Manahij). New York, NY: Palgrave.

Duderija, A. (2013). Critical progressive Muslim thought: Reflections on its political ramifications. *Review of Faith and International Affairs, 11* (3), 69-79.

Duderija, A. (2017). *Thei of progressive Islam.* New York, NY: Routledge. **AD**

Brand Islam: The Marketing and Commodification of Piety

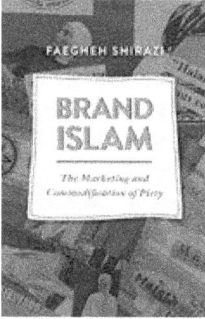

Faegheh Shirazi. Austin, TX: University of Texas Press, 2016. 294 pp. ISBN: 978-1477309469.

To say that this volume surprises and delights is an understatement. For the very notion of the "commercialization of Islam" (p. 7) seems, prima facie, to be a contradiction of sorts. Is piety not by its very definition a response — if not a corrective — to the capitalist global economy which now seeks to envelop every aspect of our lives? And yet, as Shirazi beautifully reveals in this slim but powerful text, the use of Muslim ideas, ideals, values, and attitudes as marketing tools has, in recent years, grown into a multi-billion-dollar phenomenon.

The book begins with what at first appears to be a brief, albeit timely, diversion into Islamophobia discourse. And yet, this is no diversion at all. Shirazi argues, in effect, that the embracing of "all things Muslim" is, to a degree, a response to a response; that is, as Muslims around the world in both Muslim-majority and diasporic communities increasingly are being pressed to the social margins, identity cohesion has become crucial and with it, the embracing of Muslim identity markers that reify a sense of difference amidst a sea of non-believers has been heightened.

Chapters 2 and 3 take this argument where many Western observers might expect. If you are what you eat, then the rapidly growing halal food industry well represents this growth in Islamic commercialism. Still, this industry has mushroomed in a relatively short period of time into something far larger than many might realize, having entered, for example, numerous non-traditional venues such as the fast-food chain industry as well as a variety of packaged foods not usually associated with the Muslim world (Campbell's Soup Company, for example (p. 60).

And yet, as Shirazi points out repeatedly, what is and is not "halal" must be taken with a dash of salt, for certification has become "big business" (p. 64) — not unlike the kosher food industry one might add — and the use/abuse of certification increasingly has as much to do with power, market manipulation, and profits as it does with what one is actually consuming at the dinner table. And like any big business, new challenges may arise. "Muslim consumers select halal food items based almost exclusively on label information....

Because halal products can command high prices and generate impressive profits, there is always the danger of fraud" (p. 80).

For those following any dietary restrictions today, the first half of this volume may sound all too familiar. But what adds further heft and relevance to this already cogent argument is the second half of the volume. Here, Shirazi turns to a variety of other aspects of commercialization which may be situated under the single heading of "commoditized modesty." From "appropriate" toys to makeup to fashion and dress, Shirazi shows in these chapters that what one consumes internally is only part of the narrative. One must also wear (literally and figuratively) one's "Muslimness" in a way that is pious, yes, but also conspicuously so.

In this regard, numerous examples are documented, many with helpful images, to illustrate this growing phenomenon of how female modesty and gendered space have now entered the global marketplace with a vengeance. Such products include "Islamically"-sanctioned dolls, cosmetics, sportswear, and even lingerie. What is notable here is that in the case of such products, what makes them "halal" is not necessarily what they are made of (as in the case of food), but in what they symbolize, harken, or represent — both to wearer and observer alike. While halal cosmetics, like vegan products, must not contain animal byproducts, such concerns clearly do not apply in the same way to the fashion industry. Here, "halal" takes on new meaning, referring to design, style, and a variety of cultural reference-points. Such accoutrements are no small thing: notably, the global Islamic fashion industry took in nearly $3.0 billion in 2010 alone (p. 144).

In short, the book is chock-full of examples of this growing and significant global trend. As Shirazi concludes, this is a movement that is likely to grow and expand exponentially in the years ahead, and academics and consumers alike would be wise to give due attention. Thus, I highly recommend *Brand Islam* .... It is quite readable, well-documented, and can easily be adopted for use in a classroom setting. **SCD**

A Brief Introduction to Qur'anic Exegesis

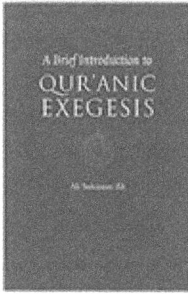

Ali Suleiman Ali. Herndon, VA: The International Institute of Islamic Thought, 2017. 177 pp. ISBN: 978-1565646889.

Qur'an exegesis (tafsir al-Qur'an) is one of the most important Islamic sciences. In various forms and modalities, initially oral and later in books, it has been practiced throughout Islamic history, from the time of the Prophet Muhammad to modern times. Its aim of understanding the meaning of the Holy Book of Islam has always been at the center of the concerns of scholars; and as time went by, methodologies of comprehending the sacred book developed in accordance with changing circumstances related to the growth of linguistic knowledge, theological traditions, sectarian visions, and even political interests.

At 177 pages, Professor Ali's book is really a brief introduction to this science, especially when one knows that works of Qur'an exegesis normally consists of large volumes of close arguments and intricate explanations. In seven chapters and a conclusion, he has been able to present the history of the science in a clear and well-written manner with rich and up-to-date documentation; he followed this science's development into methodological schools across the ages and ended with a good account of its trends in modern times.

Professor Ali begins with a useful historical overview and then, in the following chapters, he goes into the details of Qur'an exegesis developments. His masterful account of tafsir in the third and fourth centuries A.H. leads to an insightful study of the two emerging methodologies, namely, (1) al-tafsir bi al-ma'thur [exegesis based on tradition] as received from the Prophet, his Companions, and their Successors; and (2) al-tafsir bi al-ra'y [exegesis based on opinion] as received from Muslim scholars who depended on their own understanding of the Qur'anic text, as far as its language and its revelation circumstances. Works of the first kind include books like Jami' al-Bayan by al-Tabari; and works of the second kind include books like al-Tafsir al-Kabir by al-Razi. The two major methodologies are analyzed by Professor Ali in dozens of works of Qur'an exegesis throughout Islamic history, and examples are shown from them how and to what extent their particular interpretation was affected by theological principles and by sectarian and political interests.

Coming to modern times in his last chapter, Professor Ali takes into consideration the cultural and political influences of the West in Muslim life, and the attempt of Muslims to stem them and strengthen their own identity. Their revivalist and reformist stance affected their writings on Qur'an exegesis as is shown by him in works like Tafsir al- Qur'an al-Hakim (known as Tafsir al-Manar) of Muhammad Abduh, continued after the latter's death by his student Muhammad Rashid Rida, and like Al-Jawahir fi Tafsir al-Qur'an al-Karim by Jawhar Tantawi who offered an understanding of the *Qur'an* in the light of modern science. But, there were other modern trends like the rhetorical-literary one of Sayyid Qutb in his Fi Zilal al-Qur'an and the philological-historical one of Bint al-Shati' in her Tafsir al-Bayan li-al-Qur'an al-Karim.

I believe Professor Ali's book is a good historical conspectus of the Islamic science of Qur'an exegesis and is a very useful introduction for graduate students and others who, from it, can go to more detailed studies in Arabic and other languages. It has a good and up-to-date bibliography, but the book could have been improved by an index. The contributions of Orientalists to Qur'an exegesis studies are mentioned summarily in the course of the book, but these contributions might have needed a separate chapter devoted to them showing their positive and negative aspects. And yet, Professor Ali is to be congratulated on a well-written book that should be welcome in the field of Qur'an exegesis studies. *IJB*

Confronting Political Islam: Six Lessons from the West's Past

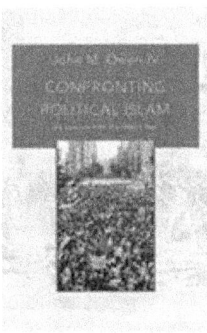

John M. Owen, IV. Princeton, NJ: Princeton University Press, 2015. 216 pp. ISBN: 978-0691163147.

It is difficult to know quite what to make of this intriguing, but ambiguous, and sometimes, even off-putting volume. The author is a Professor of Politics at the University of Virginia who wrote a notably impressive 2010 book, *The Clash of Ideas in World Politics: Transnational Networks, States, and Regime Change 1510-2010* (Princeton University Press, 2010). Therein, Owen had ranged across a broad terrain of comparative global political history, in exploring how "transnational ideological struggles" (p. 270) from early modern Europe to the contemporary Islamic world have informed contending visions of how to best structure regimes. In key respects, *Confronting Political Islam*... continues, and carries up through to the Arab uprisings, and present-day Turkey and Iran, the prior book's undeniably welcome "ideas matter" (*The Clash of Ideas in World Politics*... , p. 9) approach to the history of international relations; also carried forth is the specific historical comparison between intra-Islamic and intra-Western struggles over ideology and political legitimacy. Thus, in *Confronting Political Islam*..., Owen seeks to compare how the contemporary *"legitimacy crisis,"* that is, the *"contest over the best way to order society"* that has been wracking *"the Middle East"*... *"for at least a century"* (p. 5, italics Owen's), bears resemblances to contestations that have occurred within the history of Western societies, from Reformation-era Europe, to post-Enlightenment settings in Europe as well as the Americas.

On the one hand, the reader admires Owen's seeming effort at countering reductionist portrayals of the supposed face-off between "Islamists and secularists" embroiling today's Islamic world. As he cautions, centuries of bloody enmity among (depending on the era) Catholics and Protestants, monarchists and republicans, and communists, liberals, and fascists should preclude Western pretenses to civilizational superiority. Yet, the overall feel of the book leads one to wonder whether it protests too much. There is, first of all, its — well, confrontational — title. In addition, Owen resorts, withal, to the dichotomous portrayal of "Islamists and secularists" (even as he cautions that such "ideologies are (usually) not monolithic" (p. 46), and particularly in the conclusion, presents an implicitly triumphal depiction of "America" as the privileged vantage point from which "Political Islam" must be warily assessed and contained.

The central flow of *Confronting Political Islam*...'s argument opens as follows: there is, within the Islamic world today, a spectrum of perspectives lying between the "ideal types" of "Islamism and secularism" (p. 9). (It is telling that, more often than not, the book tends to elide distinctions between the Middle East and the Islamic world, as a whole; while there is some treatment given to Pakistan, and less to Indonesia, a country like Malaysia does not arise, nor does the currently salient matter of "Islamism" within the "Western" world appear to factor significantly). Therefore, while Owen allows that the two categories are internally varied, and sometimes overlap with one another in differing configurations, the "fundamental line...between *secularists* and *Islamists*" hinges on: ...who or what is sovereign in society, and the chief sign of this is the source and content of the law. Islamists insist that law must be Shari'a, derived from the sacred texts of Islam.... Secularists counter that law should derive from human reason and experience, not from Islam (or, for moderate secularists, not from Islam alone) (p. 7).

Owen does not purport to be writing a detailed treatise on *Shari'a*, but even so, foregrounding, as he does in an unexamined epigram, the notoriously tendentious Nonie Darwish's claim that "Sharia leaves no room for democracy" (p. 110) can only detract from the book's line of reasoning. To be fair, Darwish's quote is juxtaposed with an outtake from Turkey's now-President Recep Tayyip Erdoğan suggesting that Islam and democracy are indeed compatible, and Owen goes on to take Erdoğan seriously as a populist leader with whom one must reckon. Moreover, elsewhere in the book, Owen cites Darwish's kindred intellectual spirit Robert Spencer as an example of "those who blame the problems of the Middle East on the religion of Islam itself" (p. 20), a viewpoint that Owen seems to disfavor. However, the ultimate effect of including such fringe figures as Darwish and Spencer is jarring and tends to leave the reader somewhat confused about where Owen himself stands.

As *Confronting Political Islam...* unfolds, Owen structures his presentation around "Six Lessons." First, there is "Don't Sell Islamism Short" (p. 26), which reads as a kind of "know thy enemy" account. Its central motif — that those secularists who declare Islamism to be a spent force are as self-deluding as, say, Cold War liberal capitalists who could not acknowledge genuine support for communism within the Western world — is sure to resonate in the age of ISIS. However, the matter of whether a diverse and antagonistic array of 'Islamists' ranging from Turkey's Justice and Development Party, to the Iranian regime, to al-Qaeda (one imagines that ISIS was not quite yet salient when Owen sent the book to press) warrants being grouped together, as Owen does in this chapter, is precisely the questionable point.

After Lesson 2, the previously-mentioned one about ideologies not necessarily being monolithic, there comes the well-argued and well-taken Lesson 3, "Foreign Interventions Are Normal" (p. 67). The latter tenet certainly rings true at a time when Middle East powers like Turkey, Iran, Saudi Arabia, and Qatar view regional tumult as an opportunity for manipulating proxy wars to their own perceived strategic advantage. However, even here, Owen's peculiar selection of examples evinces, perhaps, a kind of 'comparing apples and oranges' reasoning. Because, Ottoman interference within a sixteenth-century Europe wracked by interdenominational wars, and the United States' 1940s Truman Doctrine, are scenarios whose dynamics of contending imperial ambitions — especially in the pre-Westphalian state instance of the Ottomans — are radically different from a late-modern era of disintegrating states. Indeed, the fact that Islamism is defined, in significant measure, by its being a quintessentially modern form of reaction to modernity, exemplifies why there may be overbroad leaps of historical logic in comparing Islamist ideologies with early-modern, or pre-modern circumstances.

Lesson 4, "A State May Be Rational and Ideological at the Same Time" (p. 86), is a welcome rejoinder to arch-realist theories of international relations, and caricatures of Islamism's supposed irrationality, alike. Owen counsels that, from the strategically savvy, once-Catholic German Palatinate state, "zeal [ously]…convert[ed]" (p. 91) to Lutheranism in the mid-1500s, to the Soviet Union, to the Islamic Republic of Iran, a *"state may… be a rational ideologue"* (p. 103, italics Owen's). Lesson 5, "The Winner May Be 'None of the Above'" (p. 110), is an intriguing chapter, likening a possibly foreseeable Islamist/secularist hybrid to forms of modern Western consilience between monarchism and republicanism.

Not least, Lesson 6, "Watch Turkey and Iran" (p. 130), demonstrates begrudging respect for those two formidable practitioners of conjoined, twenty-first century Islamism and power politics. In the end, it is this sort of sentiment that exemplifies *Confronting Political…* Islam's basic posture: a good part of the book's logic appears valid, so far as it goes (notwithstanding some arguably problematic dimensions, such as the historical comparisons between late-modern and early-modern eras), and its range of examples is admirably (if, again, perhaps not always aptly) capacious. However, there is the disconcerting sense that, even as it seeks to call into question too-facile assumptions about a supposed clash of civilizations, *Confronting Political…* actually serves to re-inscribe them. **AMW**

Contemporary Issues in Islam

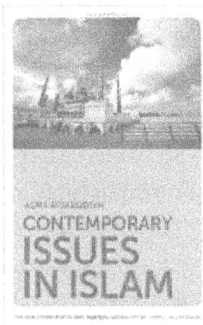

Asma Afsaruddin. Edinburgh, UK: Edinburgh University Press, 2015. 288 pp. ISBN: 978-0748632763. ISBN: 978-048632770.

As its title indicates, this book tackles "key 'hot button' contemporary issues in Islam." Finding it essential at the outset to insist that there is no one understanding of modernity, Afsaruddin argues that "multiple modernities" may better reflect the diversity of the modern world. Noting that modernity was introduced in Muslim societies in tandem with colonization, she briefly discusses early attempts to "indigenize" it in these societies since the late nineteenth and early twentieth centuries at the hands of the "fathers of Islamic modernism," such as Jamal alDin alAfghani, Muhammad Abduh, Sayyid Ahmad Khan, and Muhammad Iqbal. These called for and practiced *ijtihad* to make Islam in tune with the modern age. How they and later "reformists" have been doing that is part of most subsequent chapters of this book.

In Chapter 2, "Engaging the Sharia: Rereading the Quran and Hadith," Afsaruddin emphasizes a (modern) distinction between Shari'a and *fiqh* according to which the former is "more accurately understood as referring to a wide-ranging moral and behavioral code and broad ethical principles of divine origin which are interpreted by humans to yield specific legal rulings (*ahkam*) and moral prescription," whereas *fiqh* is a human intellectual activity and, by definition, leads to fallible and changeable results" (p. 25). In dealing with the *Qur'an*, she argues that although Muslims have regarded it as God's infallible word, they still accepted various interpretations of it. Engaging with interpretations of the Quran that arose in specific historical milieu (in medieval Islamic history) and led to the "subversion" of some Quranic values and even texts, "reformist" Muslims have undertaken the task of offering new interpretations of the *Qur'an* that demonstrate that it does not prevent Muslims from modernizing. They are also critical of the blind reliance on Hadith, taking issue with the traditional method of examining the reliability of traditions (many of which were transmitted by individual transmitters, *ahad*), and engaging in renewed scrutiny of Hadith in light of the *Qur'an* as the ultimate authoritative arbiter on ethical and legal matters.

Next, Afsaruddin proceeds to discuss specific issues, starting with "Islam and politics" in chapter three. According to this, some Muslims and non-Muslims tend to believe that the *Qur'an* prescribes a certain kind of government that is generally assumed to be characteristically despotic. This belief is used to explain dictatorship in Muslim countries, ignoring the fact that opinion polls have consistently demonstrated that the majority of Muslims support democratic rule (results that the "Arab Spring" has confirmed, Afsaruddin argues). Here, she presents at length the views of the Egyptian scholar 'Ali 'Abd alRaziq (d. 1966) on governance in Islam and the uproar that they caused in Egypt and the rest of the Muslim world at that time. This is followed by the views of two critics of 'Abd alRaziq who relied on and advocated the "politicized understanding of the *Qur'an* and Sunna" imposed by medieval Muslim scholars on these texts. Later, she discusses the views of Abu alA'la alMawdudi and Sayyid Qutb and their *jahiliyya* and *hakimiyya*. As opposed to these, she argues, "'Abd alRaziq's position in favor of a separation between religion and politics resonates strongly among modernists as an accurate reflection of the traditional bifurcation between religious and political authority already characteristic of Islam's formative period" (p. 71).

In Chapter 4, "Islam, gender and feminist hermeneutics," Afsaruddin argues that the perception that Islam discriminates against women contradicts reports about their participation in public life at the time of the Prophet Muhammad and engagement with the Quran which stresses that "men and women have equal moral agency" (p. 87). Discussing the exegetical history of Q. 9:71, she concludes that failing to distinguish "the general or universal commandments of the *Qur'an* and the particular, contextualized applications of them" (p. 107), medieval scholars were "not capable of extrapolating from this verse a larger scriptural mandate for men and women to work together companionably and on an equal footing in all spheres of life" (p. 91). In contrast, modern Muslim feminist hermeneutics seeks to "retrieve the original egalitarian élan of the *Qur'an*" (p. 101) by offering new interpretations. For example, whereas Q. 4:34 was and is generally understood to permit men to beat their wives, this new hermeneutics suggests that, through a "slight change in orthography," the word *idribuhunna* in the verse could mean either "have intercourse with them," or "depart from them/leave them alone" (p. 104), the latter interpretation being popular among feminist exegetes.

The next, equally thorny issue, is "war and peacemaking" in Islam. Afsaruddin argues that whereas the "original" message of the *Qur'an* is irenic, some "hawkish" early and medieval Muslim scholars used abrogation (*naskh*) to render irrelevant many Quranic verses that advocate peace and highlight others that, out of context, sound aggressive and belligerent. They also privileged military or physical *jihad* (the lesser *jihad*, according to a Prophetic tradition) over the greater and true jihad, namely, the spiritual striving for "selfimprovement." Afsaruddin makes reference here to some incidents from the time of the Prophet Muhammad and to some medieval interpretations of verses relevant to the subject. These demonstrate clearly, in her view, that "[i]n addition to laying down a specific protocol for conducting a justified war, the *Qur'an* also establishes an explicit ethic for refraining from fighting and for making peace" (p. 119). In this authentic Quranic view, war in Islam is only defensive and proportional, a fact that is disregarded by both Islamist militants and Western Islamophobes who agree on asserting that verses such as Q. 9:5 (known as the "sword verse") abrogates all peace-promoting verses and thus represents the true essence of Islam's teachings on the relationship with non-Muslims.

Chapter 6 takes on the issue of the Muslim community in the US and the challenges that face it. According to Afsaruddin, the events of 11 September 2001 were a turning point in the history of Islam and Muslims in the

US and "appeared to end the possibility of normality from that point on for American Muslims" (p. 143). She argues against a minority, but nonetheless vocal and powerful views, that Islam's teachings are incompatible with the "American way of life." Next, she discusses the development of the so-called jurisprudence of minorities (*fiqh alaqalliyat*) for the purpose of negotiating Muslims' position in the modern, secular nation state. This new jurisprudence, rejected by some scholars on either religious or practical grounds, is based on the principles of *da'wa, maslaha,* and *darura,* all of which seek to facilitate the integration of Muslims in western societies. Historically, she points out, there have been positive and negative encounters between Muslims and non-Muslims, selection from which encounters have led to either Islamophobia that manifests itself in various ways in the US, or to creative initiatives to enhance Muslim integration in American society.

The last chapter tackles the issues of "religious dialogue and interfaith relations," ideas which Afsaruddin argues are firmly grounded on Quranic statements. She points out that whereas the potentials of these statements for establishing courteous relationships with non-Muslims were undermined by some early and medieval Muslim scholars, they recently led to the establishment of concrete initiatives encouraging interfaith dialogue. Furthermore, contrary to the insistence of "conservative traditionalists and hardline Islamists" that Islam is the only way of salvation and that it is the duty of Muslims to conquer the entire world and convert it to Islam, modernist Muslims seek to establish equal rights for non-Muslim minorities in Muslim societies by promoting Islam's authentic egalitarian and pluralist vision. In a short epilogue, "Looking to the future," Afsaruddin is optimistic that Muslims will gradually come to terms with others, noting, however, that this requires efforts by them, but also by others whose actions can be seen to be targeting Islam and Muslims.

The major issue that informed readers will have with this book is the unmistakable inclinations of its author toward certain, 'modernist,' views, which is likely due to the fact that she herself is part of the controversies that she discusses in it. (Uninformed readers will probably go away thinking that medieval Muslims have deliberately distorted the obvious and beautiful meanings of their religious texts, which meanings modernist Muslims currently salvage.) Expecting to read an objective analysis of the views of the diverse groups and individuals in the modern Muslim world on key issues, they would have to struggle to sift these from the author's own views. In other words, whereas they may expect to read a secondary source on these key issues, this book will strike them as a primary source where the author makes strong generalizations and value judgments, and at times even derogatory comments (such as calling some medieval scholars "hawkish," or using "not surprisingly" excessively and obviously derogatorily in the particular context of critiquing some medieval or "Islamist" views — and here Islamists are lumped together as if no variations existed among them, a belief that one hoped recent scholarship and political events had laid to rest). This is not to say that the author's views and value judgments are of no value; but it is to say that this particular book, with its title that suggests a more objective content, may not be the proper place for them.

Consequently, informed readers will inevitably be bogged down in engaging with views that the author presents rather apodictically. For example, trying to show how interpretation of the Quran has changed over time, Afsaruddin mentions the case of Q. 4:59. Here, one is struck by her insistence that in the first three centuries of Islamic history, *uli alamr* in the verse was generally, or perhaps exclusively, taken to mean "the scholars," or those who possessed knowledge, a reading that she obviously supports. Afsaruddin dismisses as anachronistic an interpretation attributed to Ubayy ibn Ka'b according to which uli alamr referred to rulers, a reading that alTabari (d. 310 H.) favored (Afsaruddin mentions the views that alTabari mentions, but not his own view). Be this as it may, it is indeed difficult to believe that, given the uses of the word *amr* in the *Qur'an*, only a few people in early Islam entertained Ubayy's alleged reading. (And one could argue that, semantically, the "first meaning" of *amr* would be "authority," in the "political" sense of the word. One could also wonder, if God meant "knowledge" by the word *amr*, why did He choose a word that is ambiguous (that is, a word that has multiple meanings) rather than the straightforward word for knowledge, *'ilm*? This question is obviously more theological than linguistic or jurisprudential, and it is the kind of question that one might have hoped to see in this book.)

But, what is really intriguing here is Afsaruddin's belief that the interpretation that she likes is "nonpolitical," whereas Ubayy's (which, she contends, developed later in medieval Islam and is now adopted by "Islamists" — who are all obedient to their rulers?) is "politicized" (p. 37). Here, one has to wonder which view is more politicized: a view that, perhaps purposefully, does not allow rulers to use the *Qur'an* to command absolute obedience on the part of their people, or the view that preaches obedience to rulers but also emphasizes their absolute responsibility before God? Additionally, one would imagine that Afsaruddin is trying to militate here against the idea of "absolute obedience." What she does, however, is replacing the rulers with the scholars, which means that the *Qur'an*, according to her, does not preach obedience to rulers, but does preach obedience to scholars. Well, in the traditional Sunni view that Afsaruddin critiques, Muslim rulers are supposed to be possessors of knowledge indeed.

In all this, Afsaruddin is not actually demonstrating the "polyvalence" of the *Qur'an* as she promises to do; she is primarily showing how some readings of the *Qur'an* are 'distortive' of its real message and others are 'correct.' Specifically, whereas some traditional and Islamist views have distorted the "original" message of Islam, Muslim "modernists," "reformists," and "liberals" are working to recover that original message from centuries old distortions. And although our understanding of the religious texts must, in this modernist approach, be tuned to modern situations, the "Quranic" rules of warfare can stay the same. According to these rules, Muslims are allowed to fight only if they are attacked and only to the same degree as the aggression. Accordingly, if an enemy threatens to attack a Muslim country today with modern weapons of mass destruction, to be truly Muslim, this country has to endure the first strike first before it —if it still exists — can respond in kind. It is not clear why these specific rules do not need to take the nature of modern warfare into account, whereas all other rules have to adjust to modern conditions. Neither is it clear why the author has chosen not to engage the claim of many "jihadists" — a claim that she does allude to — that their terrorist attacks are indeed part of a defensive war against powers that are already engaging in aggression against Muslims in various parts of the Muslim world.

Afsaruddin is most likely able to respond to this critique, but this does not invalidate the point that a book of this title should not be an occasion to propound the author's own views. As it promises on its back cover, the book seeks to reveal "multiple interpretations and contested applications" of the issues that it discusses. Readers would expect this to be done as objectively as possible. The failure to heed this subtle difference between presenting an objective analysis and propounding certain personal views has undermined many parts of the book. In addition to the cases mentioned above, when discussing Hadith, for example, readers would need to know that whereas the traditional Hadith criticism focused solely on examining the chains of transmitters (*isnads*), recent trends have called for critiquing their contents (*matns*), too. This Afsaruddin does mention (p. 106), but in a context that deals with an issue other than Hadith. One also would have liked to see an objective discussion of the debate over Abu Hurayra in a way that does not imply that attacks on his character are too compelling to need more than a brief mention (p. 40). Furthermore, on talking about democracy, readers would need to learn that the main issue that most Islamists have with democracy is not the process of choosing rulers and holding them accountable, but that it gives parliaments the right to legislate laws that could contradict Islamic law (as, of course, they understand it).

In brief, the author's failure to put aside her personal views in the process of writing this book has colored, indeed marred, most of her discussions and dictated which views should be discussed in which ways. Perhaps this would be taken into account in the second edition of the book. Finally, the book ignores some major issues that the vast majority of Muslims today face daily and which some Muslim intellectuals do address. These include poverty and the lack of social welfare, education, and security, as well as what Muslim societies can do about these issues in the particular world order in which they live. *AO*

Everyday Piety: Islam and Economy in Jordan

Sarah A. Tobin. Ithaca, NY: Cornell University/ Ithaca Press, 2016. 248 pp. ISBN: 978-1501700460. ISBN: 978-1501700453.

Sarah Tobin's *Everyday Piety: Islam and Economy in Jordan* combines ethnographic artistry with astute theoretical analysis. Tobin observes as a bank teller in Jordan's Islamic banks, she studies at Jordanian universities, and she socializes with Jordanian women in the modern shopping malls and cafes of West Amman. Throughout her book, she seeks answers to the question that was omnipresent among the cosmopolitan Ammanis with whom she conducted this research: "What is the *real* Islam?"

In Chapter 1, Tobin begins with an ethnographic vignette focused on a middle-class, middle-aged Ammani woman named Asma who recalls a trip she made as a young woman to a Las Vegas casino. The vignette reveals the ways in which Asma and a growing movement of Muslims are practicing — and "economizing" — Islam in a new way that is shaped by neo-liberalism. Unlike the past, where Muslims self-identified as Muslim, but whose practice and intention are now considered inadequate, contemporary Muslims are investing in the practices of piety in ways guaranteed by scripture to increase heavenly reward. Tobin's ethnography is ideal for use in courses on gender,

Islam, and the Middle East for students whose preconceived ideas of Islamic societies need to be rebuilt on a foundation of class, gender, and the economics of globalization.

Tobin uses a tripartite model to conceptualize belief in practice that allows for understanding of the malleability of belief and practice that neoliberal piety necessitates. This tripartite model includes the public performance of religious activities and rituals, doctrinal beliefs that command societal consensus, and finally the orthodoxy of individually-held belief. Tobin argues that there is a dialectics between the orthopraxy and orthodoxy that is core to the neoliberal piety construction.

Tobin's focus is West Amman, the wealthier part of the city, and not East Amman, where the working classes live. This focus has implications for her findings. There are many participants who are from East Amman, with whom Tobin socializes in West Amman. These people aspire to be middle class, as can be seen by their consumption practices and their espoused ideals. Those in East Amman do not even know what Starbuck's is, as one of Tobin's informants disparagingly describes (p. 37).

In Chapter 2, Tobin describes the history of Amman in terms of what makes Amman different from other Orientalist depictions of urban Islamic cities of the Middle East and North Africa (MENA). Amman is far from a typical urban Islamic ancient city. It was a Circassian fishing village until relatively recently, as well as a stop on trade routes for people headed for "more important" places. Contemporary Amman is a place shaped by the regional circumstances of the last century, especially in the period between 1946 and the Civil War of the 1970s, and the peace treaty with Israel of 1993. Tobin also contextualizes contemporary ethnic and class differentiations in their historic circumstances. She emphasizes the ways in which Jordan's imagined community negotiates the ethnic divides of "Jordanian-Palestinian" versus "Jordanian-Jordanian," and the religious diversity of the nation, while making a compelling case for the centrality of class, especially middle-classiness, as the central distinguishing difference in contemporary Amman.

In Chapter 3, Tobin's use of ethnographic vignettes serves to elucidate the ways in which Islam is experienced individually, and how it is regulated by the Jordanian State through law. She also describes the ways in which religious minorities who do not follow the Ramadan fast experience Ramadan, and how Muslims experience the non-Muslims in their midst. Tobin's excellence as an ethnographic researcher is clear. She captures the reflections of Jordanian Christians who sometimes rebel against restrictions on their behavior during the month of Ramadan, such as a Christian woman who smacks her gum more loudly in the supermarket during daylight hours once she notices fasting Muslims staring at her with disapproval. She also captures the very different perspectives of Jordanian Muslims, who tend to report that Christians are happy with the Ramadan rules.

Ammani Muslims' economizing of Islam and Islamizing the economy are explored by Tobin, who describes some of the ways in which promoting virtue and preventing vice among the Ammani public can be illiberal. The reader of this ethnography will see that Tobin was troubled by the strictness of these forms of social control. Especially intense is her description of a taxi driver who becomes so irate that he swerves off the road when she drinks water in his cab during the Ramadan fast. However, Tobin overcomes stereotypes of the Muslim Middle East through the diversity of people with whom she conducts this research. For example, she describes a strange Ammani Muslim who describes the many benefits of doing Ramadan fast (including as a "detox"), as economizers of Islamic practice in similar ways to others of Amman's middle class.

Tobin's description of the economizing of Islam that happens through *Laylat Al-Qadr*, the most religious night of Ramadan, the night when all prayers and good deeds are multiplied many times over, is especially fascinating. Tobin recounts her attendance at two weddings that happened near and on *Laylat Al-Qadr*, and interviewed the brides concerning the significance of multiplying blessings and serving *Iftar* dinner as a wedding dinner as double-dipping the spiritual reward.

While Ramadan is described in Holy Scripture as a time for egalitarianism, Tobin finds that Jordanian society is rife with "competitions for moral correctness" (p. 72). Her discussion of the ways in which class distinction complicates the Islamic principle of egalitarian offers a way for university students to study Islam against Orientalist depictions of Islam as a timeless and unchanging religion. In our current political climate, this is an urgent educational necessity.

Tobin finds that the social status of men — if below women — such as male servers at a women's party or event, does not compel women to cover in front of these men. Tobin describes that their "status as men" becomes "marginalized," with little further analysis. This was an opportunity for some class analysis, but also more analysis on the special context of weddings, where oftentimes gender boundaries and the boundary between men and women soften. Was it really that these men's very "status as men" was marginalized or was it that their masculinity was mitigated by their working-class status to render them beneath female deference. The analysis at this same wedding, where women danced in a driveway without the hijab or with a "downsized" hijab unimpeded by the male neighbors who might be looking downward from their balconies at them as not mattering because they weren't at women's sight lines also seems unsatisfactory. This only seemed to happen at weddings, so again, there is more of a need for understanding of what cultural aspects of weddings are.

In Chapter 4, those of us who teach gender in Muslim societies will find the nuance we need in Tobin's depiction of Muslim Ammani women who wear, do not wear, or once wore, a hijab. The complexity of decision-making compels elevated class discussion around this practice. The hijab is not just a personal spiritual choice, but a part of orthopraxis that is purported to prevent *fitna*. Furthermore, Tobin describes the ways in which women who do not wear the veil are likely to be perceived as not yet "ready" to wear it, or as ignorant. This second category again links the hijab with class, cultural capital, and modernity. Tobin's description of the few women who choose to stop wearing the hijab reveal the value of ethnographic research based on friendship and trust. For students who are studying ethnographic research methods, this book will be formative.

Yet, the consequences for women who make the unlikely choice to remove the hijab are dismal. Since they cannot be considered merely ignorant of the Islamic rationale for wearing the hijab, they are the subjects of gossip and condemned as in moral decline. Of note is the story of a woman who stopped wearing the hijab after leaving her abusive husband and immigrating to the USA. Many of this woman's social circle on Facebook condemned her posts of herself without the hijab. Tobin's etic analysis of the ways in which women's maturity is denied in a decision to not wear or stop wearing the hijab is eloquent. However, if Marwa had down-veiled, but she had NOT exerted agency over her marriage plans, or had a goal to travel abroad to work, would her family would have ostracized her? If Marwa had continued to wear the socially accepted hijab and abaya, but had continued to exert agency over her marriage plans and still planned to travel abroad, would her family still have ostracized her (p. 90)? Is it possible that her assertion of her own goals to travel abroad to work and to marry for love rather than by arrangement were really what troubled her family?

In Chapters 5 and 6, Tobin delves into the Islamic banks. She illustrates the complexities of making a bank "Islamic" in Jordan's capitalist economy. She conducts participant observation research as a bank employee, as a teller, and in other positions that tend to be held by young, college-educated Jordanian women. In a rare feat, she combines the intricate artistry of her ethnographic story with astute political economic analysis of the Jordanian capitalist consumerist culture in which these banks exist.

Tobin shows that the Islamic banks exist in a precarious place in society. There is much debate and frustration over what makes an Islamic bank Islamic. For example, when an Islamic bank advertises a new product, an "Islamic Credit Card," the bank line is flooded with calls from people who ask if the credit cards that they already hold are forbidden. Furthermore, the bank's Shari'a Committee is composed of Islamic scholars, who must be convinced by the bankers to get on board with the economic practices that will make the bank successful.

She describes the ways in which Ammanis' assertion of what makes for the "real Islam" are debates about adequation. Her synopsis of the history of Shari'a and Islamic economics, the complications, technicalities, and justifications for Islamic banking and finance in a complex node in the global capitalist economy are sometimes seemingly contradictory. How can the principles of Shari'a economics be reconciled with the brutalities of capitalism?

In Chapter 7, Tobin describes the confusion many Muslim Ammanis feel when trying to figure out what makes an Islamic bank different from a bank that is not labeled as such. Here, Tobin employs the psychological concept of affect (interpretations, judgments, and feelings) to analyze the uncertainty Ammanis feel about Islamic banking, and banking in the non-Islamic banks as well. Many of her informants describe not feeling anything different when entering the Islamic banks, and therefore choosing not to bank there. The pressures of orthopraxy also compel some Ammanis to open accounts; however, many keep accounts at the regular banks simultaneously. Indeed, many informants felt that the bank was only Islamic in name and doubted that there could be no interest accrued. Thus, many of her informants seemed resigned to orthopraxy, without having much actual faith in the Islamic banks.

Tobin then analyzes the ways in which consensus among Ammani Muslims surrounding Shari'a norms informs decisions to bank or not to bank with the Islamic banks. While affect influences the choice, higher-level reasoning is also employed in the decision. While there is consensus that Shari'a is the best source of guidelines for living one's life, the interpretations are quite varied. Much of the interpretation that would lead Ammanis not to bank at Islamic banks comes from outside education, especially university courses. Thus, social class is central to the decision. Similarly, those who advocate that Ammani Muslims should be customers in Islamic banks also appeal to intellectual, higher-order thinking, rather than affect or orthopraxy. This emphasis on intellectual logic is an expression of the hegemony of modernity. The complexity of people's perceptions of the Islamic banks is well depicted through Tobin's use of a profile of a woman who chooses to be a customer at an Islamic bank. Tobin makes clear that just having the name "Islamic" in it will draw only limited numbers of new customers. Customers need to feel Islam and modernity simultaneously when they enter the bank.

In Chapter 8, Tobin concludes her ethnography with a focus on the political economic reasons that there was not a successful Arab Spring in Jordan. Middle-class ideals trump ethnic divides, and political Islam is aligned with the Hachemites, rather than in political opposition groups. As Tobin shows through her ethnography, the Jordanian middle class calculates risk and benefit in their Islamic and economic practice, and they used a similar calculative strategy in weighing the risks versus the benefits of an Arab Spring.

Tobin also tells the story of Jordan's 2011 bid to join the Gulf Cooperation Council (GCC). In this bid, that happened at the time of the Arab Spring in several countries, there can be seen a political economic strategy for maintaining personal wealth through the patronage of the wealthier Gulf countries. Tobin analyzes Jordanian people's online responses to their government's bid to join the GCC. She finds that many chose to sarcastically and aggressively compare and contrast Jordanian "real Islam" with the Salafist Islam associated with the Gulf countries. Many online writers expressed sarcasm at their government's move to align with the Gulf, emphasizing Jordan's diversity and democracy in comparison to the Gulf countries. The Hashemites maintain power through fomenting notions of middle-class diversity in Jordanian society's institutions. Tobin ends her final chapter with a fascinating discussion of Islamic branding. Branding Islam is already being done, and the link between a comfortably Islamic, modern consumerism and the promotion of good through proper forms of consumption is likely to compel a continued emphasis on Islamic diversity in urban Jordan. Tobin offers rare and vital insight into Jordan's future that not only is a testament to the value of anthropological ethnography, but to what this work can do to inform political science of the region. **CO-P**

Inside the Muslim Brotherhood: Religion, Identity, and Politics

Khalil al-Anani. New York, NY: Oxford University Press, 2016. 224 pp. ISBN: 978-0190279738.

The Muslim Brotherhood is the originator, in many ways, of the modern mainstream Sunni Islamist movement in the Arab world; it has played a profound role in influencing the formation of other Sunni Islamist parties in the wider Muslim-majority world, including in countries such as Pakistan, India, Bangladesh, Somalia, and Indonesia. Since its founding by Egyptian schoolteacher Hasan al-Banna in 1928, the Muslim Brotherhood organizational model and style of grassroots activism have been adapted by other groups of Islamist activists to fit local dynamics. There is, thus, a significant deal of country-specific differences that distinguish different incarnations of the Muslim Brotherhood in different countries. Historically, for example, the Jordanian Muslim Brotherhood and its political wing, the Islamic Action Front, have followed a more moderate political program within a monarchical system, though the Jordanian Brotherhood has more recently experienced internal divisions following an increase in government interference. In contrast, the Yemeni Brotherhood, which for years has been a part of the al-Islah party umbrella, has been much less moderate in its political platform because it has had to operate in a very different political and social environment. The different Brotherhood groups, sometimes referred to as "branches," though this makes them appear as unified under a central transnational leadership, which they are not. Despite significant differences from country to country, the different Brotherhood organizations also have much in common and particularly with regard to their organizational principles. Khalil al-Anani provides an in-depth look at these principles and, though his book is focused on the Egyptian Brotherhood, there is much in it that is relevant to readers interested in other Brotherhood groups in different countries.

The book is a timely addition to the academic literature on the history, political organization, and possible future trajectories of the Brotherhood groups in the aftermath of the "Arab Spring" revolts and the crackdown on Brotherhood activists in countries such as Egypt and Jordan and amidst ongoing civil wars in Yemen and Syria. As the oldest and largest Brotherhood group, the Egyptian Muslim Brotherhood is of key importance to the future possible paths for the organization since it is still seen by many as the epitome of the group. It was in Egypt that the Brotherhood movement came to hold the reins of political power, albeit briefly, before its ouster by mass protests and the country's military under current autocratic president Abd al-Fattah al-Sisi in June 2013. The organizational and ideological core of the Brotherhood as a hierarchical social and political organization and mass movement were set in Egypt and thus an understanding of the original Brotherhood in the country is necessary for a fuller understanding of Brotherhood groups in other places. Al-Anani focuses here on the internal organizational principles and identity of the Brotherhood rather than on its external political decision-making and operational history, topics that are covered amply in the work of other scholars including Carrie Rosefsky Wickham, Nathan J. Brown, Mona El-Ghobashy, Quintan Wiktorowicz, Raphaël Lefèvre, Jillian Schwedler, and Steven Brooke, and Marc Lynch.

The central identity espoused by the Brotherhood is that of the collective community (*al-jama'a*), a form of group identity that is collectively and interactively formed through, not only ideology, but also through experiences during processes of activism, negotiation, bargain, conflict, and exchange. Using Alberto Melucci's concept of collective identity as the process in which different actors develop common cognitive frameworks, al-Anani sees the shaping of the Brotherhood's group identity as being the result of a dynamic interplay between ideological core principles and its experience as a living, ever-changing social movement. Through its recruitment, indoctrination, and self-identification processes, the Brotherhood forms a collective, socially constructed identity ("Ikhwanism") that in turn is one of the main drivers of its activism. The Brotherhood has proved to be so resilient in the face of significant state repression in Egypt because of how it incorporates its identity with its organizational hierarchy, recruitment, and management of supports and members at different levels. In order to advance in the organization, al-Anani shows, individual activists had to demonstrate their willingness to engage in different forms of activism for the group, undergoing increasing levels of risk, while also adhering to Brotherhood ideational principles.

As al-Anani demonstrates in Chapter 3, the movement solidifies the collective ties between individual members by carrying out continuous sets of activities ranging from study circles to physical training camps and political study courses that are aimed at continually reinforcing the *jama'a* paradigm and thus ensuring loyalty to the group. This is necessary in order to unify many different, diverse, individual personalities in a common direction so as to move forward toward achieving the Brotherhood's organizational goals. Drawing upon the original inspiration of al-Banna, whose key founding role is covered in Chapter 4, the contemporary Egyptian Brotherhood seeks to create and activate a collective Islamic social identity that inspires and drives its members and supporters toward a common goal. Brotherhood leaders do this by seeking to instill deeply a set of Islamic frames based on shared religious beliefs and sacred history, rich in the symbols and idioms of an idealized Islamic past and future, so as to further invest individual members into the collective identity and set of goals.

Because Brotherhood recruiters and leaders seek to incorporate individuals from different social and economic backgrounds, the need to develop a unifying socialization process that instills a strongly-held group identity becomes all the more necessary for organizational success. In Chapter 5, al-Anani details the Brotherhood's recruitment model. Rather than being an open organization, the Brotherhood is highly selective and often secretive, requiring individuals who wish to become members and rise in the ranks to fulfill certain tasks, often with increasing levels of personal risk in the autocratic systems in which the Brotherhood groups operate, as a way of proving their reliability and group loyalty. This is a social movement process that is not unique to the Brotherhood or Islamist movements and can be found in other activist movements that operate in high risk environments, such as in countries where autocratic regimes severely repress opposition movements. In order to ensure that individual recruits become intensely loyal to the *"jama'a,"* the Brotherhood requires its members to undergo a lengthy and intensive education/indoctrination (*tarbiyya*) process during which the group's principles and identity is instilled. This process, covered in Chapter 6, is designed to ensure the loyalty and dedication of individual members so that they are willing to carry out activities of high risk for the good of the collectivity.

In Chapter 8, al-Anani details how the Brotherhood's bureaucratic organizational structure is designed to further this process of *tarbiyya* and grow the support and membership base of the social movement. He demonstrates how both the vertical leadership and horizontal departmental structures within the Brotherhood operate and how the movement operates at neighborhood, district, and upper levels of group organization and command-and-control structures. Though senior Brotherhood leaders and executive bodies determine organizational policy, the implementation of it is left to middle- and lower-level managers and members who have a significant deal of autonomy in deciding how best to achieve the movement's larger goals. In other words, the senior leadership does not micromanage implementation though it does provide a centralized, hierarchical form of decision-making for the movement, as a whole.

The Brotherhood, despite its remarkable resilience in the face of state repression and relative cohesion, has experienced internal divisions, which are discussed in Chapter 9. The movement's leaders have attempted to manage internal divisions by doubling down on group identity. The movement has come under increasing strain since the military coup in June 2013 that over-threw President Muhammad Mursi, with segments of it separating as many senior Brotherhood leaders have been arrested by the state. Disagreements over a turn to political violence and survival strategies divide Brotherhood members and there is a danger, for the movement, that a prolonged period of state repression will ultimately lead to the break-up of what has, up to this point, proved to be one of the most durable forms of Islamist activism and group identity formation in modern times.

Al-Anani's book is a significant contribution to the literature on the Broth-erhood, filling in a significant gap by closely examining and explaining the organizational role of ideology and group identity in the movement's activ-ism, organization, and decision-making. Though focused on the Egyptian Brotherhood, the book includes many relevant discussions to readers inter-ested in Brotherhood groups in other countries as well as political Islam and Islamist movements more broadly. Theoretically sophisticated, it is written in clear prose and will be of great use and interest to students and researchers in Middle East politics, Islamic studies, and social movements. CA

Islam and Competing Nationalisms in the Middle East, 1876-1926

Kamal Soleimani. New York, NY: Palgrave Macmil-lan, 2016. 312 pp. ISBN: 978-1137601292.

One of the fine contributions of this book, perhaps unintentionally, is to point out what appears to be two separate and parallel, evolutionary socio-political de-velopments, on-going diachronically. In the West, the concept of the nation-state emerged from the Treaties of Westphalia as a western European, Christian com-ponent of a regional cultural setting allowing for the establishment of a peoples' governing system. In the East, Islam, as pro-pounded by the Prophet was deeply involved with the identity of the prima-ry social unit, the tribe and, in this case, the Quraish, and characterized by the Arabic *qawmiyah*. There was no equivalent expression in Arabic for the western-developed "state," save for the famed Arab historian's *Muqadamah* (1377) by Ibn Khaldun who introduced not necessarily as analysis, a word to recognize the equivalent of a political organization, *dawla*. As students of Islam are well aware, the significant difference between it and western Christianity is the latter's emphasis on separating religion from the state — at least in some form — whereas in Islam there is an all-inclusive, comprehensive weaving of institutions that guide the believers' life. Rather than emulating a prototypic model, the Islamic world molded its own political structure and supporting institutions to comport to an idiosyncratic mode. Notably, the classic Sunni theologian Ibn Taymiya, in his *al-Kitab al-siyasi al-sharia* (1314), argued that religion could not be practiced without state power and returning to Ibn Khaldun who wrote that according to *asabiya*, the state and religious sentiments were mutually beneficial. Soleimani, here, similarly takes issue with those who argue that religion and nationalism represent mutually exclusive themes. Rather, he argues that both phenomena serve as overlays that interact and reinforce one another. The study is divided into three parts, initially, the focus is on Islamic political theory, what is meant by "nationalism" in an Islamic context, the role of the caliph (*al-Khalifah*) in Islam's diffuse rule and evolution, and Ottoman Turkish nationalism. This is then followed by an extensive discussion Kurdish nationalism and the interaction this ethnic group has with Islam.

The author, an independent Turkish scholar, trained at Columbia University, has made extensive use of Turkish (both Ottoman and modern), Arabic, Persian, Kurdish sources, and British archival materials in which he displays a high degree of comfort in handling, as well as a wide range of secondary sources. Densely written language is supplemented by the insertion of Arabic and Ottoman Turkish terms that might not be adequately translated into English. There is on display, furthermore, a heavy emphasis on the scholarly, theoretical literature on the topics presented and appropriately recorded.

In his discussion of the caliphate (*khalifah*), Soleimani notes that there is no single Islamic authority on whether the basis for the role is lineage connected to the Quraish, thus allowing even non-Arab folk, in this case, the Turks, to assume that function. The geographical extent of the Ottoman Empire necessarily encompassed multiple ethnic groups certainly to include non-Arabs, allowing or maybe forcing the Turks to concentrate on prioritizing Turkish nationality. The author's posturing on Abdülhamid II's interest in supporting a pan-Islamic ideology across the Empire was not merely a reformist goal, but also positioning the Empire to protect its culture against any possible encroachment by European colonialism and how

Turkish nationalism came to dominate, particularly under the leadership of Abdülhamid II. For Soleimani, nationalism extends beyond any ethnic community's self-reference; it is a far more inclusive set of social and behavioral characteristics. He employs critical discourse analysis to set straight how and why the Ottoman rulers sought to add a thing to the official language of the Empire, adding to the attempt to unify and centralize its authority while simultaneously diminishing the legitimacy of non-Turkish minorities who were seeking their own self-determination.

The author examines the nationalist sentiment of the Ottomans followed by the efforts of the Kemalists and the Community for Progress and Unity and then the secularists in the Republican period, to obstruct the pressure being brought to bear on the role of Islam in Turkey. Here, Soleimani carefully traces the transition Turkey seeks to make in maintaining an Islamic character while emulating a wester style state system.

Those who have but a rudimentary appreciation of Kurdish political dynamics and aspirations can have their repertoire enhanced by the thorough description of the activities of Naqshbandi Sheikh Ubeydullah of Nehri, who led a Kurdish uprising against the Ottomans in 1880. His oeuvres reflect in a basic manner the connection within the Kurdish community its reliance on Islam for a national identification. It was *sheikh* Ubeydullah's belief that Kurdish national spirit was a means to bring about a "true Islamic" rule. His view of nationalism was decidedly liberal, allowing for the toleration of other peoples' existence and expression of cultural self-group expression. There is then brought into the fold, the Kurdish *mullah* Bediüzzaman Said Kurdi. In support of the role of Islam in government, *mullah* Said strongly objected to what was thought to be the western attempt to influence the Ottomans to refine the caliphate and the *Sheikh al-Islam*, instead seeking to reform the institutions, fitting a more modern form.

The quality of this fine addition to an understanding of the relationship between religious beliefs and politics, well-supported and argued and based upon solid research could only be enhanced by the efforts of a copy editor. **SRS**

Islam and Popular Culture

Karin van Nieuwkerk, Mark LeVine, Martin Stokes, Eds. Austin, TX: University of Texas Press, 2016. 404 pp. | ISBN: 978-1477309049.

ISLAM AND POPULAR CULTURE *Islam and Popular Culture* is a text that has been edited by three scholars who have published extensively on the subject of culture and Islam: Karin van Niuwkerk (Professor of contemporary Islam in Europe and the Middle East at Radboud University Nijmegen in the Netherlands), Mark Levine (Professor of modern Middle East History, University of California, Irvine) —whose *Heavy Metal Islam* is a book this reviewer both reviewed and enjoyed, and Martin Stokes (King Edward Professor of Music at King's College, London). The editors begin this work with an excellent introduction in which they problematize the terms, introduce the related theory, and analyze the nuances that this type of study is able to bring to light with regard to Islam. They themselves state their aim for this book as one that "demonstrates the variety, and the importance of the contemporary processes in the Middle East, the larger Muslim world, and the Muslim diaspora communities which can be studied from the vantage point of Islam and popular culture" (p. 2).

The individual contributors to this text have produced chapters that have been categorized into parts that include "Popular Culture: Aesthetics, Sound, and Theatre Performance in the Muslim World," which analyses esthetics and performance of Sufis in France, Islamic music in Turkey, and performance activism and the Arab Uprisings; "Artistic Protest and the Arab Uprisings," which addresses music, art, and poetry and protest in North Africa, "Islam: Religious Discourses and Pious Ethics," which contrasts Sunni and Shiʻa discourses on art and music, and art education and cultural production in Egypt, next comes "Cultural Politics and Body Politics," which focuses on television, music and dance in Syria and Iran, and finally, "Global Flows of Popular Culture in the Muslim World," which compares performance Islam in the Indian Ocean (Oman and Indonesia), music and tolerance in Egypt and Ghana, music festivals in Pakistan and England, and Moroccan hip-hop. In this way, in a total of eighteen chapters, the text does a fairly complete job of accomplishing its stated goal of addressing "the Middle East, the larger Muslim world, and the Muslim diaspora communities."

This is a thought-provoking work that does an excellent job of emphasizing the historiographical significance of art and architecture. Some of the chapters also accommodate references from social media, which I think is a potentially problematic source, but when used properly can be quite current and provide excellent insight into prevalent opinions. I have one word of caution, however, and that is with regard to the number of chapters that address the concept of Islamism. Perhaps because the contributors are addressing the subject through the lens of popular culture, perhaps for other reasons; nevertheless, there seems to be a de-emphasizing of the threat of Islamism. Organizations, whether they are political or artistic, that have links to the Muslim Brotherhood, for example, need to be assessed with the ideologies of Sayyid Qutb in mind. At the core, these ideas promote violence and that must not be glossed over or trivialized. Thankfully, in his chapter, Jonas Otterbeck reminds the reader of this when he writes that Islamists today "always have at least two issues on their agenda: first, to restrict women's freedom of dress and movement; and second, to censor and quell with violence if necessary, musical expressions, musicians, and musical listening" (p. 164). This, of course, is intended to focus on the political leadership, but Islamist artistic and musical groups, who may produce art and music, may still promote potentially oppressive ideas.

Overall, this is a valuable collection addressing an understudied field in Islamic studies. It will be a valuable addition for university libraries and students of religion, history, and political science of the Muslim world (in particular the Middle East). **DCM**

Islam and the Future of Tolerance: a Dialogue

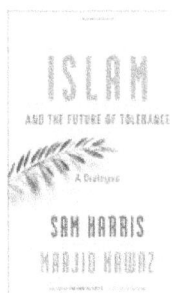

Sam Harris & Maajid Nawaz. Cambridge, MA: Harvard University Press, 2015. 144 pp. ISBN: 978-0674088702.

The terse volume *Islam and the Future of Tolerance: A Dialogue* is a discussion on contemporary Islam between a liberal Muslim and a liberal atheist. The dialogue starts with Maajid Nawaz's clarification substantiating his earlier contention that Islam is a religion of peace, which, to Sam Harris, is nothing but pretense, its impossibility, inevitable. Nawaz, kind of structuralists way, argues, "my honest view is that Islam is not religion of war or peace- it's a religion. Religion doesn't inherently speak for itself; no scripture, no book, no peace of writing has its own voice. Scripture exists; human beings interpret it" (p. 5). He further holds that if Islam is only what its adherents interpret, it is a religion of peace as a majority of the Muslims today do not subscribe to its being a religion of war.

Then, while locating the root of extremism in Islam, Harris hinted toward internal substances of Islam saying that "religion is that it creates in-group loyalty and out-group hostility" (p. 26), Nawaz maintains, not religion, but two constituents fundamentally contribute to extremism: grievances Islamists experience because of mainstream societies' racist, othering behavior to them, and the ideological dogma of charismatic recruiters that frames their world view.

After that, the conversation advances on elucidating the terms used in the contemporary literature on Islam, which often puzzles people. To Nawaz, "Islamism" means the desire to impose any given interpretation of Islam/ its scriptures on society, "Political Islam" that seeks to impose its views through the ballot box, biding their time until they can infiltrate the institutions of society from within, "revolutionary Islamism" seeks change from outside the system in one clean sweep, and finally "Militant Islam" or "Jihadism" uses force to spread Islamism. He is not comfortable with the term "moderate" Muslim because the term is so relative — juxtaposed against increasingly worst atrocities — that it has become meaningless. It does not tell which values the person in question holds as Islamic State or even al-Qaeda can claim to be "moderate".

Next, Nawaz argues that motivation for Islamism, Jihadism, communism, or any other ideological recruitment primarily originates from four fundamental factors: a grievance narrative; an identity crisis; a charismatic recruiter; and ideological dogma (p. 63). All the ideologies seek for societal transformation whether change comes from direct action and conflict. Unlike other ideologies, Nawaz maintains, Jihadists believe in taking direct action for change and he further argues that Islamic State (IS) has originated from the ashes of power vacuum created because of the West's abandoning Middle East. While discussing the role of religious conviction on fundamentalism/ Jihadism, though Harris stressed that religious ideology is sufficient to motivate the Jihadists, Nawaz points out that only religious conviction is not enough to understand difference between Islamism and Jihadism, one need to consider all four factors he outlined.

In the following discussion, Nawaz harshly criticizes the western liberals calling them "regressive leftiests," which are reverse racists. They are culturally deterministic, and in the name of "cultural authenticity," or to satisfy their orientalist fetish, they rightly question every aspect of their own western culture in the name of progress, but censure liberal Muslims who attempt to do so within Islam. In fact, in the name of liberalism, communal rights have been prioritized over individual autonomy within minority groups and consequently, minorities within minorities — feminist Muslims, gay Muslims, ex-Muslims — suffer the most. Harris agrees with Nawaz and adds that liberals don't see that they've abandoned women, gays, freethinkers, public intellectuals, and other powerless people in the Muslim world to a cauldron of violence and intolerance. Rather than supporting the women and girls not to live as slave, Harris argues, western liberals support the right of theocrats to treat their wives and daughters however they want.

The debate proceeds on discussing the role of religious scripture on fundamentalism in general, Islamic scripture in particular. Hence, Harris held that all the practices in Muslim world, including the ghastly method of murder, find explicit support in scripture and therefore, Islamic scripture instigates Jihadism. But, Nawaz replies that the problem does not lie in scripture, but the interpretation of it. Going beyond literal interpretation of texts what he calls "vacuous literalism," he — similar to Quentin Skinner of the Cambridge School — agrees that there is no true reading of texts. While reading texts, we simply impose certain values and judgements from our own vantage points. Nawaz supports the idea that we should popularize the premise that all conclusions from scripture are but interpretations, and that all variant readings of a holy book would become a matter of differing human perspectives.

Finally, the authors discuss some possible ways to abolish the present conundrum of the Islamic world. Among these, first of all, the idea that any given text has multiple interpretations, which demonstrate that there is no correct one. If we can understand that, then we arrive at a respect for difference, which leads to tolerance and then pluralism, which in turn leads to democracy, secularism and human rights (p. 86). Secondly, it has been suggested that fatwa should persist because otherwise, young would-be recruits to the IS would read the silence of Islamic scholars as a form of consent to the heinous crimes of that group and it reassures the mainstream Islamists. Thirdly, to escape from the Islamic polarization established over the years, a complete overhaul of cultural identity is required. The Islamic concept of Ummah, or people must be reappraised here, that would comprise not the Muslims alone, but the entire humanity. Finally, it has been recommended that to defeat the militant groups — both militarily and culturally — not only the group has to be neutralized, but the ideology has to be discredited. For these, we need to facilitate a genuine grassroots movement to popularize alternative narratives that can compete with the Islamists, Khudi in Pakistan, for example.

From my personal experience, being a part of Muslim majority society, it seems that the biggest cause of fundamentalism is identity crisis of the Islamists. It is evident that the number of people seriously practicing the fundamental pillars of Islam has been shrinking, while the number of religious institutions and cultural Muslims (people only saying prayers once on Friday and participate in Islamic festivals) is increasing. Therefore, a group of Muslims have started believing that if it continues, their existence in the world would be seriously threatened, as they regard religion as their only identity of existence. Therefore, they search for enemy and oftentimes find western culture and thoughts on one hand, and liberal thinkers of their own countries on the other as responsible for the diminishment of religiosity. It leads them toward sort of an identity crisis, and ultimately, they initiate fighting against these perceived enemies for survival. *MR*

The Islamophobia Industry: How the Right Manufactures Hatred of Muslims

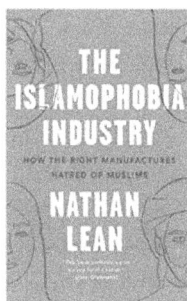

Nathan Lean. London, UK: Pluto Press, 2017 (2nd ed.). 242 pp. ISBN: 978-074533717. Pbk: 978-074533716.

Islamophobia, much like anti-Semitism, and xenophobia, flourishes in a politically charged nationalistic environment that caters to the worst elements in human nature. Advocates of hate groups can use a myriad of excuses and incidents to fan the flames of hate and bigotry and divide families and nations.

America's divide and the negative attitudes towards Muslims and Islam became evident in the aftermath of the tragic events of 9/11. Advocates of hate and Muslim-bashing crawled out of their dark dungeons and found receptive ears among certain opportunists and elected officials, and media moguls, speakers for hire, talk show hosts, and even comedians and unprincipled preachers. Like anti-Semitism and racism, Islamophobia can linger on in American society and must be strongly faced with unrelenting forces of good against evil.

Nathan Lean has penned an excellent and articulate argument against the forces of hate and evil in our American society. He took advocates of hate and Muslim bashing to task by listing and then refuting their old tired hateful arguments against Islam and Muslims.

First published in 2012, Nathan Lean's *The Islamophobia Industry* brings the book's readers up-to-date from the times of the "war on terror" to the current events surrounding the Trump Administration and an increasingly divided nation. The book's introduction, titled "Islamophobia from the War on Terror to the Age of Trump" gives an accurate survey of events that illustrate how hate — sometimes deadly violent crimes against Muslims in America — is rising and even being instigated.

The aim of the author is to "correct" what the author sees as "unfair and imbalanced representation of Islam and Muslims by calling attention to the small band of hucksters who benefit from the pain of others" (p. 20). He presents his case against Islamophobia in the eight carefully written chapters which are rich in cited sources and references chapters.

In Chapter 2, he addresses the growing expressions of hate speech and expressions of prejudice against Muslims and Islam, as they are spreading on the Internet and social media targeting Muslims. He points to growing anti-Muslim networks that rely on sensationalism, use of fabricated or falsified stories, and images that are even cited by the current American president, Donald Trump. Other fake images and news are being spread by anti-Muslim figures, who use the media and the Internet to spread their anti-Muslim venom. Among them Jihad Watch, American Freedom Defense Initiative (FDI), and others.

In Chapter 3, the author gives due attention to the mainstream media and its mutually beneficial relationship "where ideologies and political proclivities converge to advance the same agenda" (p. 84). Fox news is singled out as major source of shamefully spreading misinformation about Islam.

Attention is given in Chapter 4 to the "Christian Right's battle for Muslim Souls," by detailing the war of words directed against Islam and Muslims by right wing Florida-based Evangelists like Bill Keller, and other Muslim-bashers like him who proclaim that "Islam is not…a religion of peace…" (p. 102).

In Chapter 5, Lean addresses the influence of the pro-Israel lobby and the connection between Religious Zionists and anti-Muslim groups, citing the example of David Yerushalmi.

The rise of liberal Islamophobia is treated in Chapter 6, as the author introduces and refutes the arguments of Islamophobia-enablers such as Sam Harris, Asra Nomani, Ayan Hirshi Ali, and their ilk. He also exposed Bill Maher, as a Muslim-hater.

In Chapter 7, "Politicizing and Legislating Fear of Muslims," the author cites the 2016 American presidential campaign during which candidate Trump fanned anti-Muslim-bashing and legitimized the anti-Muslim hate mongering. True to his rhetoric and attempts to appeal to the worst elements in our society, Trump signed presidential orders to ban certain Muslim nationals from entering the United States, much to the delight and support of racists like David Duke, and in spite of objections from a number of state courts.

In the final Chapter 8, the author describes the equally Islamophobic hysteria in Europe and the hateful acts of European terrorists like Anders Behring Brevik, who underscore the falsehood of the standard-bearers of Muslim-bashing, like ex-Fox host Bill O'Reilly, Robert Spencer, Pamela Geller, Brigitt Gabriel, Geert Wilders, The English Defence League (BDL) and others who are quick to point at Muslims, and shame themselves when the identity of Brevik, the White European terrorist, was revealed.

This highly recommended book is well written, well researched, and documented. The author managed to expose individuals and groups that make their living from bashing Muslims and promoting fears of Muslims among the few who are eager to find someone to hate and fear. *MMA*

Islamic Exceptionalism: How the Struggle over Islam is Reshaping the World

Shadi Hamid. New York, NY: St. Martin's Press, 2017. 320 pp. ISBN: 978-1250061010.

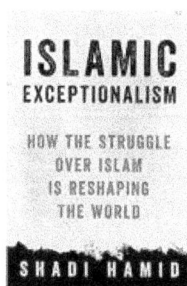

Shadi Hamid's *Islamic Exceptionalism: How the Struggle over Islam is Reshaping the World* argues that Islam plays an exceptional role in Muslim societies and cannot be reconciled with the liberal ideals of modern government. The text not only explains why secularism hasn't taken hold in the vast majority of Muslim societies, it also explains why it *had* to take hold in the vast majority of western ones. Following the Protestant Reformation, a cacophony of voices emerged: "Lutherans and Calvinists — but also Anglicans, Anabaptists, Mennonites" — suggesting alternatives to Catholicism (p. 59). These groups not only disagreed with the doctrine and practices of the Church, but also disagreed with one another, including on matters of doctrine, leading to a situation in which theological questions proliferated and basic doctrine had come into doubt. In this context, Hamid writes: "Reason, science and secular approaches to knowledge came to be seen as offering more clarity and consistency on the animating questions of man's relationship to the world around him" (p. 60).

By contrast, the Islamic tradition from its inception provided the conceptual and practical resources for dealing with such questions. Notions of Islamic faith were in this way intrinsically tied to political questions of governance; Islam as a tradition is comprised not simply of what people believe, but of what they do as a matter of abiding by Islamic law. Thus, where secularism thrived in the West, it did so because the available alternatives in Christianity had failed to provide the necessary means for the structuration of communal life. Islamic societies never faced the same problems since the notions of "politics" and "faith" were never distinct; the impulse to turn toward a secular worldview was therefore never present in the Muslim world to any considerable extent because there was no need: "Where a political Christianity had failed, a political — and politicized — Islam could succeed" (p. 67).

The thrust of the author's thesis comes across in chapter three where Islamic tradition comes up against the modern state. Remarking on the late nineteenth-century attempts to modernize Islam and reconcile it with the state, the author notes that from the modernist point of view:

This made enough intuitive sense: If the *Qur'an* was a book for all times, then its laws and principles should be appropriate for the modern era just as they were for seventh-century Arabia. If God in his wisdom had revealed Islam as a complete and comprehensive religion that could only mean that the text and the tradition had an inherent power to renew themselves, even if it meant going where Islam hadn't quite gone before. And this is where they went (p. 77).

According to the author, modernists were attempting to "reconcile the irreconcilable" (p. 78): Islamic law and the modern state. The author echoes the thesis of Wael Hallaq's *The Impossible State*, a work cited in the text, but does not pursue Hallaq's method of interrogating the moral limitations of the modern state. Instead, the author pursues the limitations of "Islam" in the state: "And this is where our story of modernists and modernism leads to the Middle East's present predicament" (p. 79) — a reference to the political chaos which has ensued in the wake of the Arab Spring.

At this juncture, the author introduces Hassan Al-Banna, the founder of the Muslim Brotherhood, as a prelude to unfolding the Middle East's "present predicament." At the same time, Hamid peculiarly omits details of the events and forces to which Muslim modernists like Al-Banna were reacting, namely, the policies of European colonialism in the Muslim world. Instead, the focus is on how "religions become religious ideologies" (p. 80), the author's reference to "Islamism" vaguely defined as a movement where it is thought that "Islamic law should play a central role in political life" (p. 6). Such a wide-ranging definition produces a number of questions throughout the text: How is "religion" is being thought? Relatedly, what distinguishes an "Islamist" from any other pious Muslim given the interrelatedness of the political with the spiritual in Islamic tradition, an interrelatedness the author himself recognizes early in the text? The failure to address these questions results in confusion about what makes "Islam" exceptional — is it exceptional in comparison to other religions or in comparison to other political ideologies?

The author also seems to contradict his argument at many points, with the thrust of the problems facing the Middle East shifting from Islam to the state itself. This is illustrated in the analysis of Turkey where Islam appears to be a problem not because of its inadequacy as a system of governance — the author provides powerful historical examples of stable governance under Sharia — but the opposite; Islam, as such, emerges as a problem only because the state insists on displacing it. "Until 2013," the author notes in reference to Turkey's paternalism, "children would start their day at school with a pledge of allegiance: 'I love my country more than myself... I offer my existence to the Turkish nation as a gift.' The state, rather than religion, was something to die for, reflecting a sort of secular 'martyrdom' with Turkey assuming the pose of the omniscient deity" (p. 161). If this is so, then it would appear that Islam, even in its "extremist" forms, is not at all exceptional but akin to other sensibilities, such as those of citizenship.

In sum, it would appear that the paradoxes peppering the text are the consequence of an unrecognized assumption: liberalism is preferable to any other system of governance and that Islamists or Islam should be modified to accommodate the demands of liberal ideology. The problem with Islamists is that "all Islamist parties, by definition, are least somewhat illiberal" (p. 19). The text's central questions produce answers that are consequential to the text's approach. **Me-S**

Islamism: Contested Perspectives on Political Islam

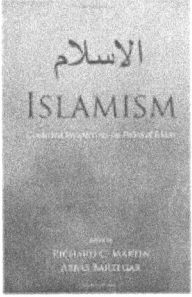

Richard C. Martin, & Abbas Barzegar, Eds. Stanford,
CA: Stanford University Press, 2009. 200 pp. ISBN-13-
978-0804768863.

Islamism: Contested Perspectives on Political Islam presents itself as a meditation on the very term "Islamism",
reviewing the baggage and restrictions said to be associated with the word in order to determine what alternatives may be available for describing the political dimensions of Islam. Donald K. Emmerson and Daniel M. Varisco are the principal
essayists and their arguments — in favor of and against usage of the term
respectively — dominate the book's content and form its first section. These
opening essays are followed with a series of critical discussions of the topic
comprising the large middle section of the book. To conclude, Emmerson
and Varisco return to discuss the responses to their initial essays.

As Varisco and others explain, the modern history of "Islamism" as a
common term begins with Fazlur Rahman's attempts in 1970 to distinguish
right-leaning writers on Islam and governance such as Sayyid Qutb and Abul
Ala Mawdudi from those on the left end of the spectrum. The dilemma some
authors pose with the term is the associations it has developed with extremism. Amir Hussein considers the term problematic in that, by its very name,
it allows a connotation between extremism and mainstream Islam that is a
disservice to Muslims worldwide.

In addition, it is submitted that "Islamism" does little to clarify many contemporary conflicts within Islam. Feisal Abdul Rauf notes that the term mud-
dies the water regarding ideological debates within the Muslim World; in the
rivalries of Ahmedinejad and Khatami in Iran, Saudi Arabia and Al Qaeda on
the Arab Peninsula, and Sunni and Shi'a militias in Iraq, Islamists are to be
found on all sides. Nadia Yassine also argues against the conflation of nonviolent modern Islamists with Islamic clerics, and terrorists. Bruce Lawrence
cites Sudanese-American scholar Abdullahi An-Na'im's caution against using
language to create false dichotomies. Graham E. Fuller hits similar notes in
his article stressing that terms should not be used to denote "good guys" and
"bad guys".

Other authors in the collection put forth a case for keeping the term in
usage. As Ziba Mir-Hosseini and Richard Tapper explain in their article,
Varisco's shirking of the term allows ideological critics of Islam (political
or otherwise) such as Daniel Pipes to define how terms are used, thereby

ceding to them control over the conversation. Anouar Majid provides some perspective with the observation that these debates are more the concerns of academics rather than the average Muslim looking to proceed with their own lives. Hillel Fradkin explains that Rahman initially devised the term to *distinguish* radical Salafi writers from mainstream Islam.

While "academic word games" (the title of Fradkin's essay) is perhaps too much, the potentially esoteric premise of the book has the potential to make it of limited interest to those not fully prepared to wade into a debate over se- mantics. The best pieces in this collection use the semantic premise as an op- portunity to explore the history of "Islamism" as a concept rather than simply a term. Rauf's essay expands to discuss the nature of and debates within the earliest Muslim community. Angel Rabasa's substantive, rewarding contribu- tion traces the history of modern political Islam from relatively liberal mod- ernists of the 1800s such as Jamal Al-Din Al-Afghani and Mohammed Abduh to their more conservative twentieth century counterparts such as Rashid Rida and Hassan Al-Banna.

The unwillingness to engage the issue of political Islam beyond the nar- row question being asked can hinder some efforts. Hassan Hanafi's dismissal of the debate as one between orientalists comes off as incurious if not in- different. Syed Farid Alatas's warning that Muslims should be treated less as "objects of study" than purveyors of ideas worthy of study is a much more thoughtful approach to the same perspective. Alata notes that Islamism is really a variant of modernism, disregarding the traditions and ambiguities of Islam in favor of a perceived precision untainted by actual human history.

While the concerns of many writers that use of "Islamism" may unfair- ly draw a connection between Islam and violence have merit, Emmerson's submission of a revised definition of the term by James Piscatori demon- strates that good faith efforts to preserve it for academic and popular usage can be achieved. Piscatori defines Islamists as "Muslims who are commit- ted to political action (Emmerson substitutes "public action") to implement what they regard as an Islamic agenda". While such common-sense solutions are ideal, Varisco's argument rightly demonstrates that the power of words and their potential association with negative, inaccurate characteristics are a constant. Zuhdi Jasser effectively proves Varisco's point when he defines Islamism in terms of transnational objectives synonymous with the work of Hassan Al-Banna and Sayyid Qutb, therein seeming to argue against the pos- sibility of an Islamist having more constrained political objectives. However, Jasser's point that the term is necessary in order to allow Muslim liberals and secularists more space to actually have the debate about the role of religion is intriguing. Ultimately, this collection, edited by Richard C. Martin and

Abbas Barzegar, elevates itself above the topic at hand to examine issues of political Islam from a wide range of perspectives. *JDL*

The Oxford Handbook of American Islam

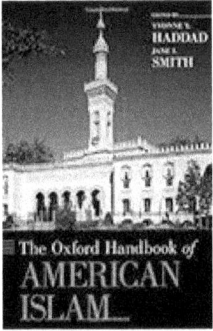

Yvonne Y. Haddad, & Jane I. Smith, Eds. Oxford, UK: Oxford University Press, 2014. 560 pp. ISBN: 978-0199862634.

As Muslims in America are growing in number and becoming more organized, their political and societal impact is increasing, and general interest in their history and culture is deepening accordingly. The two editors of this volume, who have earlier devoted much of their scholarship to this issue, now offer readers a virtually comprehensive book on the subject to meet the continuing and undiminished public interest.

After an introduction by the editors, the volume is divided into three parts, logically presented to cover the history of the Muslims in America and to give an analysis of their culture and organization. The articles in the parts are written by thirty-one scholars, including the two editors. Part I is entitled "Formation of the Muslim Community in North America," Part II "Institutionalization of Islam in North America," and Part III "Integration and Assimilation of Muslims."

While there is some inevitable though innocuous duplication of information in the articles because each is independently conceived, the editors are to be complimented on having successfully brought together an encyclopedic amount of knowledge in this book, which is one of the *Oxford Handbooks* series offering authoritative and state-of-the-art surveys of current thinking and research in particular subjects.

The reader learns that from the arrival of the earliest Muslims brought to America from West Africa as slaves, to the formation of the "Nation of Islam" under Elijah Mohammed (1897-1975) in the 1930s, and from the continuing immigration to America of Muslims from various regions of the vast Islamic world in Asia and Africa, to the conversion of Blacks and other Americans to Islam — the religion of Islam has been a continuous part of

American history. Despite their different ethnic origins and languages, and despite their sometimes-conflicting interests, American Muslims eventually institutionalized themselves by building mosques, creating regional gatherings, and national organizations and publications. Each of the articles in this book deals at some length with one aspect or another of this long process which has, in the end, led to the assimilation of Muslims and their integration in American society.

The process has not been easy or harmonious, and Muslims were often thought of as a "fifth column" (p. 188) in certain circles of American society. Political events in the Muslim world reflected themselves variously on their attitudes and actions, and on their relations with the general American public. After 9/11 in particular, there was a strong feeling of unease about the presence of Muslims in America. Even American Muslims themselves debated to what extent they should assimilate or remain fully faithful to their original traditions, just as they had been debating this issue throughout their history in America. The chapters of this volume deal with many of these dilemmas and uncertainties, and give a clear picture of the state of Muslim affairs today in America.

In 2011, there were about seven million Muslims in America (p. 75) according to the estimates of the Council on American-Islamic Relations (CAIR), which is the largest Islamic advocacy organization in America; it documents cases of bias against Muslims, encourages an understanding of Islam, and helps educate American Muslims about their legal rights and responsibilities. There are many other Muslim organizations in America having other purposes, such as the Islamic Society of North America (ISNA), the Fiqh Council of North America (FCNA) that issues *fatwas* (i.e., legal rulings) on religious questions arising in the novel conditions of Muslims in America, the Islamic Circle of North America (ICNA) concerned with religious learning and character-building; and other professional organizations like the Association of Muslim Social Scientists (AMSS), the Islamic Medical Association of North America (IMANA), the Association of Muslim Scientists and Engineers (AMSE), the Muslim Students Association of US and Canada (MSA), and others.

Some articles of this book deal with specific Muslim groups in America like Sunnis, Shi'a, Sufis, Blacks, and Ahmadiyya; others deal with specific topics concerning Muslims in America like Shari'a, youth, women, marriage, and prisons; and still others deal with politics, Muslim-Christian relations, filmmaking, art, and architecture. Article 29 is about the effects on American Muslims of the recent war on terror, and article 30 — the last in the book — is about Islamophobia and anti-Muslim sentiment in the US. The book starts with a question: "Could a Muslim become president of the United States?" and, although Thomas Jefferson thought so, it seems that most Americans believe this question to be of great concern.

... *American Islam* is an important and timely book for Americans and all others interested in reading. It is well-planned, well-written, and well-documented; and it has a good index that makes it easy to refer to particulars in the book's encyclopedic content. Fraught with controversial issues that some of its topics entail, the book offers objective scholarship; the two editors and the contributing scholars are to be congratulated on a job well done. One slight error has to be corrected, however, and it is related to Muhammad 'Abduh on page 177, where it is wrongly said that he died in 1902 and he had been rector of al-Azhar University and a "prominent Egyptian intellectual of the late eighteenth century." In point of fact, he was the Mufti of Egypt, but was never rector of al-Azhar, nor did he live in the eighteenth century — he was born in 1849 and died in 1905. Other references to Muhammad 'Abduh in the book are correct.

This book is highly recommended to scholars and students of modern Islam, and particularly to those interested in Islam in the USA and Canada. I daresay that it is indispensable and opens new vistas for further new research. *IJB*

The Oxford Handbook of European Islam

Jocelyne Cesari, Ed. Oxford. UK: Oxford University Press, 2016. 869 pp. ISBN: 978-0199607976. ISBN: 978-0198779322.

This book is essential reading for all those interested in Islam and Muslims in Europe. Written by twenty-five impressively knowledgeable contributors, including the editor, it is divided into five parts. Part I (with five chapters) deals with Islam as a postcolonial, post-second world war religion in Europe; Part II (with four chapters) deals with the arrival of Islam in Europe as a post-1974 migration of Muslims; Part III (with four chapters) is a consideration of the old, historical lands of Islam in Europe; Part IV (with three chapters) studies Islam and Muslims in the influential presence of European secularism and modernity; and Part V (with two chapters and a Conclusion) presents Islam and European politics.

Each of the chapters has a distinctly large and multi-language bibliography of many pages that is, indeed, a very helpful resource to scholars needing further research.

Not that Islam was unknown in Europe in earlier times, for Europe experienced the very rise of Islam and its expansion from Arabia across North Africa into Spain in the eighth century, and it sustained the expansion of the Ottomans in the sixteenth century into Eastern Europe, resulting in the continuing presence of Muslims in the Balkans — Albania, Bosnia, and Herzegovina — and in Bulgaria and Russia. These facts are detailed in Part III of the book. However, the more engaging presence of Islam in Western Europe today is mostly the outgrowth of earlier European colonization of parts of the Muslim world, and the result of Muslim migration into Europe after World War II and after 1974, as explained in Parts II and IV of the book.

How these Muslims were received in Europe by Europeans and how they reacted to European culture and life conditions is, I think, the most important contribution of this book. Islamophobia, on the part of some Europeans, and reluctant integration, on the part of some Muslims, played into the hands of European politicians and lawmakers as well as into those of Muslim leaders in Europe. There is no doubt that Europe has changed with the presence of Muslims in it, and that Muslims have changed after they came to live in Europe. Moreover, this book is a good record of this change, and a good presentiment of things to come. *IJB*

Saudi Clerics and Shi'a Islam

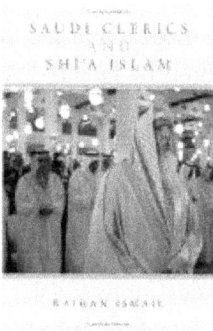

Raihan Ismail. New York, NY: Oxford University Press, 2016. 328 pp. ISBN: 978-010233310.

The theological disputes over "true Islam" between Salafi Sunnis and Shi'a Muslims, once an obscure issue of interest only to specialists and academics, has entered the mainstream consciousness of Western media and general audiences, thanks in large part to the ongoing conflicts in Iraq and Syria. The 2003 US and British-led coalition invasion and subsequent

occupation of Iraq, following the toppling of the Iraqi Ba'ath Party government of Saddam Hussein, marked the beginning of Western fascination and
often, misunderstanding, of this increasingly bitter set of disputes between
competing groups among the global Muslim population. At the forefront
of this conflict are Saudi Salafi religious scholars (*'ulama*), who represent
arguably the most vocal and influential segment of anti-Shi'a Sunnis today,
and their Twelver Shi'a clerical opponents, some of them independent and
others aligned with the Iranian Shi'a Islamist state. Neither group, however,
represent a unified front, nor are they divided into a number of sub-groups
or intellectual/ideological currents. Disputes between Salafi Sunni and Shi'a
clerics and scholars are also often shaped by current events and contemporary politics as well as medieval theological disputation and the clash of historical narratives. In the book under review, Raihan Ismail provides a major
contribution to the scholarship on both Salafi, and specifically Saudi Salafi,
Islam and historical and contemporary ideological differences and conflicts
between Salafi and Shi'a Muslim theologians and *'ulama*. She does this, however, with a careful eye to how modern politics impact how these seemingly
obscure theological disputes.

Ismail utilizes an extensive array of primary sources including audio and
video recordings of sermons and lectures, written publicans, and juridical
opinions (*fatawa*) and rulings (*ahkam*) from Saudi Salafi *'ulama* related to
their positions on Shi'ism and modern conflicts in places such as Yemen,
Iraq, and Bahrain. She examines materials not only from mainstream *'ulama*
aligned or even employed by the Saudi state but also materials produced by
a diverse group of Saudi Salafi religious scholars including more moderate
voices, such as that of *Shaykh* Salman al-Awda, and more extreme anti- Shi'a
voices, such as that of *Shaykh* Nasir al-'Umar. This second group include *'ulama* from the non-establishment clerical elite, a collective that is loosely referred to generally as the Sahwa or "Awakening" movement, though it is not
a single organization but rather an intellectual/ideological current of *'ulama*
not employed by the state and who are willing to sometimes criticize the
monarchy when it fails to, in their eyes, maintain proper Islamic positions on
a range of issues.

Beginning with a brief historical overview of the Saudi Salafi *'ulama* and
their relationship with the Al-Sa'ud family, Ismail details how the *'ulama*, particularly the state-aligned clergy, became institutionalized within the modern Saudi state. Understanding this relationship is critical to understanding
the ways in which state *'ulama* both use and are used by the monarchy and
how dissident and non-establishment Sahwa *'ulama* see themselves as being
separate from the state-sanctioned clergy. Many of the Sahwa clergy were

influenced not only by the Najdi Salafism of Muhammad ibn Abd al-Wahhab and his clerical descendants but also by aspects of the political thought of the Muslim Brotherhood organizations in Egypt and Syria through ideologues such as Muhammad Qutb, the brother of Sayyid Qutb, many of whom fled their home countries to escape government persecution and were allowed to settle and work in Saudi Arabia in the 1970s. Some Saudi *'ulama* therefore draw not only from a particular form of Salafism, but also from political aspects of the Muslim Brotherhood.

In the book's second chapter, Ismail provides a historical overview of the division and differences between what would become Sunni and Shi'a Islam. The origins of the theological/doctrinal disputes between Sunnism and Shi'ism, such as the debates over the Prophet Muhammad's decision (or not) to name a specific successor as leader of the Muslim community and the status of his companions (*Sahaba*), are discussed in detail. Criticisms of Shi'ism from Sunni *'ulama*, though today often blamed solely on "Wahhabis"/Salafi, have been made historically, as Ismail shows, by many mainstream Sunni scholars, many of them predating the emergence of Salafism, broadly speaking, as a recognizable intellectual current within revivalist Sunnism in the eighteenth and nineteenth centuries. These include Malik ibn Anas, one of the founders of the four surviving schools of Sunni jurisprudence, the famous *hadith* compiler and commentator al-Bukhari, and the medieval Syrian Hanbali jurist Taqi al-Din ibn Taymiyya, though the latter is now often accused of being a sort of "Wahhabi"/Salafi godfather figure. Ismail also discusses the more accommodating views of more modern Sunni *'ulama* such as Mahmoud Shaltut, the grand rector of Al-Azhar mosque and seminary in Cairo between 1958 and 1963 and the Egyptian Muslim Brotherhood-affiliated Yusuf al-Qaradawi based in Qatar. Shaltut accepted the Ja'fari school of jurisprudence as a legitimate legal school of thought and al-Qaradawi has generally taken a more inclusive view of Shi'a Muslims, though his views have hardened since the execution of Saddam Hussein in Iraq and even more so since the sectarianization of Syria's ongoing civil war.

Moving beyond the theological and creedal disputations of Saudi Salafi *'ulama* with Shi'ism, which she covers in great detail in chapter three, Ismail also recognizes the role of politics and social competition as drivers of anti-Shi'a sectarianism. Saudi Shi'a, who make up a significant and even majority of the populations in the oil-rich Eastern Province of al-Ahsa, spark demographic fears of an internal "enemy" among many Saudi Salafis, both *'ulama* and non-clerics. The history of anti- Shi'a discrimination in the Saudi state from its founding in 1925-26 is long and continues to this day, despite a relative loosening under the late King Abdullah (2005-2015). Though

Abdullah was relatively more tolerant toward the kingdom's Shiʻa citizens, there remained certain limits imposed on Saudi Shiʻa social and political activism, employment discrimination, and public denigration of Shiʻism by state *ulama*. Ongoing conflicts in Iraq and Syria, both beset with mounting levels of violent sectarianism, also had an adverse effect on Saudi Shiʻa. In addition, even relatively more moderate Saudi Salafi *ulama*, such as al-Awda, still do not accept the legitimacy of Shiʻa theology and creed, thus limiting the nature of any acceptance of Shʻism by a Saudi Salafi religious scholar.

Saudi Shiʻa are also negatively affected by the state's geopolitical rivalry with Shiʻa Islamist Iran. They are seen by many Sunnis as a potential "fifth column" of Iran in the domestic space. Iranian involvement in conflicts in Lebanon, Bahrain, Syria, Iraq, and Yemen is seen by Saudi *ulama* and many Saudi Sunnis and Sunnis in the Arab Gulf states as being a part of a broader attempt to spread Shiʻism in Sunni majority countries. Thus, the Saudi state has harnessed the official Salafi religious establishment as yet another tool to use against Iran. Through financial support for religious institutions, building projects, *da'wa* (missionary propagation) campaigns, and political actors across the globe, the Saudi state is engaged in a sustained anti-Iran campaign designed to counter Iranian state interests and attempts to broaden its popularity among the world's Muslims. The Saudi state form of Salafism has thus been able to spread through official and semi-official Saudi religious institutions to Sunni communities from North America to Indonesia. Modern political disputes often shape the nature of Saudi Salafi *ulama* criticisms of Shiʻism and Shiʻa actors, but Ismail argues that it is primarily Salafi objections to Shiʻa theology, creed, and ritual practices, such as mourning rituals during Muharram and Arba'in, that form the basis of the former's anti-Shiʻism. The intensity, timing, and specific parameters of anti-Shiʻa sectarian discourse, however, is influenced significantly by geopolitics.

Ismail's book fills a gap in the literature on Saudi Salafism and Salafi- Shiʻa theological disputes and also makes a significant contribution to the understanding of the utilization and contours of sectarianism in modern conflicts in the Middle East. It is thoroughly sourced and includes many fascinating details while remaining clarity and highly readable prose. **CA**

Scapegoating Islam, Intolerance, Security, and the American Muslim

Jeffery L. Thomas. Santa Barbara, CA: ABC-CLIO/ Praeger, 2015. 272 pp. ISBN: 978-1440830990.

In the book, *Scapegoating Islam, Intolerance, Security, and the American Muslim*, the author argues that American policies toward Muslims and Muslim countries have been largely shaped by the history of the relationship between Europe and both the Arab world and the Muslim world. Most of the negative perceptions and attitudes about Muslims which can be found in the US are the legacy of inherited European hate and fear from Muslims, the European ancestors carried with them their perceptions about Muslims and unfortunately those perceptions remained alive for centuries. The author also argues that the American governments have failed to recognize the Muslims who live within the American society since the slave trade and consequently failed as well to protect this unrecognized element of the American society. The policy failure of the governments has extended to a failure in adopting an efficient homeland security policy that relies on the cooperation and engagement of all members of the society, Muslims included.

This book is written to shed light on, and to explain how history affects contemporary relationships between American Muslims and their government, society, and law enforcement agencies. The author utilizes qualitative approach using historical analysis and policy-based analyses to clarify how and why things happen within American society in regard to Muslims. Although the book addresses the issue of Muslims in the US, it indeed discusses American domestic as well as foreign policies in the realm of Islam and Muslims because these policies often overlap.

The topics of the book are covered in six chapters in addition to an epilogue and timeline of policies and actions affecting Muslims in America. In the first chapter, titled "America's Evolving Perspectives on Islam: From Threat Abroad to Challenge at Home," the author provides an excellent typology of the milestones of the relationship between the American government and Muslims. The author summarizes five hundred years of wars, peace, literature, and perceptions to conclude that the relationship is complex and cannot be understood without properly examining the historical relationships between Europe and the Muslim world. In the second chapter titled "9/11 and the New Homeland Security Paradigm," the author examines the events and policies that followed the catastrophe of September 11 and in doing so he discusses important issues such as the government's targeting of Muslims' charities and organizations. In this chapter, as in many other sections in the book, local affairs come closer to global affairs when the invasions of foreign countries affect the domestic policies in the US. The government's coercive and intrusive measures, the author concludes, caused damage to the government's ability to protect the society. In chapter three titled "Homeland Security and the Muslim Experience at the State and Local Levels," the author discusses several experiences of law enforcement agencies when they have encountered Muslims and how appearances and stereotypes have influenced the decisions and actions of public employees. Lack of understanding Islam has often resulted in the infringement of Muslims' ability to live normal lives within their country. Chapter four is titled "Climate of Fear" and the author outlines here the changing positions toward Muslims in the media as well as in public policies after 9/11. The chapter discusses the role of fear in shaping the image as well as the policies in America post 9/11. In chapter five titled "Hate Crimes and Anti-Muslim Violence," the author documents the many attacks on Muslims and on their organizations. The violence against Muslims in the US took many forms, but all was driven by fear and hostility which the government did not necessarily create but failed to properly prevent. In the last chapter, number six, the author discusses the bright side of government's success in tackling the issue of the relationship with Muslims. "Muslim Americans and the Homeland Security Enterprise" explains how the success of homeland security cannot be achieved without a successful engagement of Muslims themselves in cooperating to realizing the goals of security policies. The successful examples of voluntary cooperation of Muslims in securing their own communities provide a promising future of the Muslims in America.

Although the author makes a clear effort to objectively discuss the various subjects in his book, his analyses remain influenced by the same bias and Euro-centric conceptions of Muslims. Some readers, especially those from the Muslim world, may find this as a significant flaw. For example, on page 164, the author discusses the 9/11 incident and how it impacted Muslims in the country. Yet, he discusses the success in avoiding civic clashes in cities like Dearborn, Michigan by giving the credit of such success to the government alone; thus, he under-evaluates the role which Muslims themselves paid to prevent inevitable unrest. Moreover, while the author tells stories and describes incidents, he rarely presents perspectives and interpretations other than his own (see, for example, his elaboration on the Islamic charities and the non-profit organization, pp. 148-150).

Some readers may have preferred that the book had included statistics about important facts, such as numbers of Muslims in America, their racial and age distribution, size of their nonprofit enterprises, size of trade between the U.S. and Muslim countries, number of prominent American Muslim officials and scholar, and so forth. Statistics if included would have supported the narrations and conclusions of the author. In addition, as the author makes his overarching argument to victimize Muslims and clarify the misconceptions about their culture and religion, his argument would have been strengthened if he had included a chapter on Islam, Islamic, values, Islamic civilizations, and the role of Muslims in today's economic, scientific, medical, philosophical, organizational, and industrial developments among many other contributions of Muslims in the US. The sacrifices and patriotism of American Muslims have not been highlighted in the book despite the positive discussion that uncovered the violations and discrimination against Muslims. The author seems shy when he, on page 174, speaks about the patriotic Muslims who protected their fellow Americans and secured their communities, despite the fact that he defended the civil rights of the Muslims and their overlooked role in assisting the government in homeland security matters. Overall, this is an excellent book that documents the sufferings and as well as the successes of Muslims in America and their civic role in today's America. *AY*

ISRAEL AND PALESTINE

The Ambiguous Foreign Policy of the United States toward the Muslim World: More than a Handshake

David S. Oualaalou. Lanham, MD: Lexington Books, 2016. 200 pp. ISBN: 978-1498508971.

At a time when the US grapples with the problems in the Middle East region, David S. Oualaalou's book *The Ambiguous Foreign Policy of the United States toward the Muslim World: More than a Handshake* analyses where the US has gone wrong. The self-explanatory title of the book suggests the author knows the Muslim World more than just in the passing. Written in good faith, the book urges the US to completely overhaul its policies because, as a major player in the region, its policies have a bearing on the lives of millions of people in the region. Though the title implies dealing with the Muslim World, his discussions focus on the Middle East region. The author draws upon his personal experience and other resources and frequently cites experts across the book.

The book is divided into eight chapters and an introduction. Despite lacking a balance in terms of the length of the chapters, with some chapters longer than the others, the common theme running through these chapters is the foreign policy of the US in the region. Oualaalou is highly critical of the foreign policy of the US, and rightly so. The US, he believes, lacks vision, clarity, and decisiveness and therefore, unable to take on the new challenges in the region. He suggests developing a clear, systematic, pragmatic, long-term strategy based on a thorough understanding of the social, cultural, and political dynamics of the region. The book is very prescriptive as it provides a list of do's and don'ts for the US. The burning question 'to intervene or not to intervene' has no simple answer where both courses have implications. He forbids use of force and another military venture as it would sign a death knell for the US and the region.

Despite the criticism, Oualaalou does not want the US to take a back seat, asking it to play its part in order to secure its vital interests. He discusses in great detail the ingress made by both Russia and China in recent years under the pretext of economic interests. China has earned itself a favorable status due to its non-interference in domestic affairs of the country. Russia's cooperation with Iran and Syria — coincidentally two countries that happen to oppose the US — is based on pragmatism, yet seems to be working quite well. Taking a realistic perspective on the situation, he does not approve of it and fears that this may harm US interests. He advises the US to win over the support of the people and leaders in the region before China and Russia firmly entrench themselves. He sees the situation in zero-sum terms still considering the US as the sole power in the region. However, toward the end of the book, he mentions the US is taking a reality check and adjusting to the multipolar world.

The book has its strengths and shortcomings. Oualaalou shows a good understanding of certain issues, particularly democracy and the role of Islam in the region. For some reason, he has treated the Arab Spring as a critical juncture in the Middle Eastern politics where the people have demanded social justice and freedom. Unfortunately, the outcome was not acceptable to the US as it became nervous with the rise of Islamist parties in the elections. The US stood by when the elected government in Egypt was thrown over in total disrespect of the wishes of the people, thus, exposing the double standards of the US on democracy. He notes that it is hard for the US, and also the West, to get its head around the fact that, given the choice between democracy patterned on western style or religious interpretation, Muslim societies would opt for the latter. It is because they lack an understanding of the local culture and beliefs. He states that the basic principles of western-patterned democracy (i.e., freedom of religion, equality, justice and fairness) are emphasized in the *Qur'an*. The US must acknowledge that democracy is a long and tedious process, requiring a multidimensional approach, especially more so when the regional countries are not ready to embrace it as yet.

True to a current affairs analysis, the author sees things in broad perspective as he discusses strategic interests and concerns of major regional and extra-regional players in the region and also their inter-relationship. He deliberates upon Iran and Saudi Arabia and the power play between them. He briefly recaptures American policies under various administrations beginning with President Wilson's era, and explains foreign policy compulsions as well as its failures over the years — most notably, the failure to constrain Israel on many occasions. In recent years, the two outstanding blunders made by the US are: invasion of Iraq and inaction in Syria.

In terms of shortcomings, the author's linkage between Islam and tribalism lacks sophistication. Tribalism is not true for all countries across the Muslim World. Loyalty is not confined to the tribe, but can be patterned along ethnic, linguistic, and sectarian lines. Typical to a current affairs analysis where the developments outpace the writings, the developments have made the analysis seem a bit dated — for instance, when he states Turkey could serve as a model for all countries in the region. The layout of the book is confusing, as Chapter 5 provides a brief background of the countries — Saudi Arabia, Jordan, Bahrain, Egypt, Turkey, and Iraq. Had this chapter come in the beginning, it would have provided background information on these countries that are discussed throughout the book.

The take-away from this book is there cannot be any quick fixes. The situation is complex, and any solution will need time. The US must match its words with its actions and must deliver what it promises. The onus, however, does not lie with the US alone. Much needs to be done by the Muslim societies, as no meaningful change cannot come unless it originates from within the region. Muslims need to be educated in order to discredit militancy. **MS**

Extraordinary Rendition: American Writers on Palestine

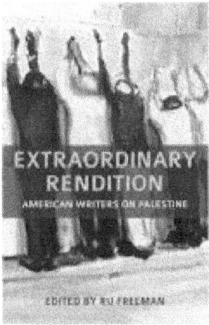

Ru Freeman, Ed. Northampton, MA: Olive Branch Press, 2016. 452 pp. ISBN: 978-1566560603.

A most disappointing book unless the reader is a literati familiar with a humanistic approach to understanding and appreciating history and politics through the devices of literature. The adage that you can't tell a book by its cover is most *apropos* here with the painting "Against the Wall" by the artist Marlene Dumas serving this function. In fact, Dumas is one of the 65 American contributors to this anthology, divided essentially in half with novelists and poets. There is scant attention to the difficult subject matter as is evidenced by the dearth of the words Palestine or Palestinians in this 400 plus-page tome. The editor, herself is a Sri Lankan novelist and activist, has taken it upon herself to bring together a group of writers who, in their own way, express their concerns for human rights and the plight of the Palestinians living under Israeli occupation but do so in a most opaque manner. Again, without an ability to appreciate a humanist's approach to a political problem, this book will be a loss. **SRS**

The Gaza Strip: The Political Economy of De-Development

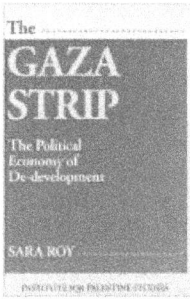

Sara Roy. Washington, DC: Institute for Palestine Studies, 2016. (3ʳᵈ ed.). 511 pp. ISBN: 978-0887283215.

Sara Roy is definitely the leading expert on the Gaza Strip economy, an expertise which she acquired through hard field work, not at a desk somewhere in the comfort of an American city. This is not being said with the inevitable "but", or with the expectation of reading now what is so bad about her book. It is a statement of respect and appreciation, and these stay with me, even though I happen to have major exceptions to some of her main points. It is the Middle East that we review in this book, a region of conflict, a region of opposing narratives, a region whose research – confronts both the researcher and reviewer with the inevitable challenge of maintaining the utmost level of objectivity. Some (including this reviewer) will argue that total objectivity under these circumstances is near an impossibility. Sara Roy is not a-once-in-a-time visitor in Gaza, but a continuing visitor there, and someone who wants to bring the case of the Gazans to the world. She does it with grace, professionalism, and expertise, but she still leaves the reader with a very strong sense of partisanship, and it is in this context that I am reviewing this important book.

To begin, it is beyond a doubt that there is de-development in Gaza, and it has political roots. Roy tells us a lot about what preceded 1967, and surely a lot about the period afterward, mostly under Israeli occupation. It is here, where I find myself surprised by Roy's failure to address in much greater detail and nuance, the complete Israeli withdrawal in 2005 from Gaza, lock, stock, and barrel. According to Roy (p. xxxvi), "with its 2005 disengagement, Israel claims that it no more occupies Gaza". Claim? Well, Israel really does not occupy Gaza. Then, she goes on to talk about "Israel's hostile relationship with Hamas". (p. xxxvi). Here again, a "little" deviation from reality. Hamas declared Jihad against Israel, and refuses to accept any Jewish state, under any borders, in so-called Palestine. So, no relationships here, at least not as we understand relationships to be. And it is becoming a greater issue, when Roy does not even mention the Green Houses story, the story of the 14 million $ US paid to the removed Israeli settlers in Gaza, in order for them to give the houses with their advanced technology to the Gazans, to create at least the beginning of modern agriculture, as a contribution to the Gazan economy. Hamas destroyed and burnt the Green Houses. It is a defining situation, as it touches exactly on the main theme of the book, the politics of de-development. What Hamas did was political, and it contributed to the de-development of Gaza. A strong case can be made, that the story of Gaza after 2005 with the repeated clashes with Israel and Egypt, should get its due attention in this book. It did not strangely enough, as the book was closed in August 2014, and Roy had all the time in the world to add a good, hefty chapter (only pages 395-412).

Roy concludes that "de-development is a process, shaped by a vision of denial and renunciation that was articulated early in the occupation and which remained fundamentally and substantively unchanged ever since" (p. 413). So, if it is only the occupation by Israel which caused the very tragic abysmal state of affairs in Gaza, then Roy has a problem with another of her own observations, which is that "Gazans are victims, but they are also actors" (p.413). If they are actors, where is Roy's description and analysis of their responsibility to their predicament, whether by what they did, or by what they did not do. And alongside the Gazans, one has to include also the other Palestinians, as of the Oslo Agreements, the Palestinian Authority (PA), and Arab countries.

That said, I read with interest the reference to the implications of the war of 1948-9 on Gaza, especially the establishment of the All-Palestine Government there by the Grand Mufti of Jerusalem (in September-October 1948), whom Roy describes as "unpopular", and the ensuing conflict with Jordan and Egypt (pp.65-101). This was a formative period, mostly with Gaza under Egyptian occupation for nearly 18 years, (with the short exception of the brief Israeli occupation in 1956) without Egypt allowing the Palestinians the opportunity to have their independence, but also because it was a long enough period in which the governing Egyptians could and should do much more for the sake of the welfare of the Gazans, for the Gazan economy altogether. In her own conclusions for this chapter, Roy argues, "the imbalance between Gaza's wealth of human resources and dearth of natural and material resources could not be corrected." A realistic conclusion, but then what about it being used also in order to explain the difficulties of overcoming that same problem when referring to the Israeli occupation? A good question to ask when we turn now to the Israeli occupation and its implications, the lion's share of the book, and for obvious reasons.

This question of responsibility and predetermined intentions which goes throughout the book, with the finger pointing to an Israeli policy of intensifying and perpetuating the de-development of Gaza, is interestingly addressed by a Palestinian Human Rights activist, Bassam 'Eid, who wrote after the 2014 fighting and after the closure of the book the following: "3281 trucks carrying 131, 240 tons of cement.; 353 trucks carrying 12,355 tons of steel.; 3,380 trucks carrying 135, 200 tons of gravel.; 276 trucks carrying 11,040 tons of cement for the Qatari projects.; 19, 628 trucks carrying 785, 120 tons of gravel for the Qatari projects". And altogether, it was his conclusion, that the Gazans would welcome Israel back. (Israel Hayom, August 5, 2015). Why I included this — although it was written after the closure of the book — is, first because this is not a description different than the descriptions of similar situations following the rise of Hamas to power in Gaza in 2006-7 and the imposition of the so-called Israeli siege, which in reality, is only the attempt to prevent introduction of arms for the Jihad of Hamas. Secondly, it could be a good way with which to conclude the book, as Roy writes, (p.413), "Gazans are desperate for a connection with the outside world". They have one offered to them, but that can be done only if there is no Jihad in the background. Roy does recognize that, arguing, that "economic change cannot occur without political change" (p.376). She is right, but discussing what political change, will stretch to the impossible, the idea of an important, solid book.

This is an important, solid book. I recommend it, for what it contains with regard to the wealth of data, and less recommend it for the political connotations. But intelligent, unbiased readers will sift through and still learn a lot! What is, after all, the baggage that a reader should take from a book, if not the ability to ask good questions, and get answers that can still be different than the ones offered by the writer. *JO*

The Hebrew Republic: Israel's Return to History

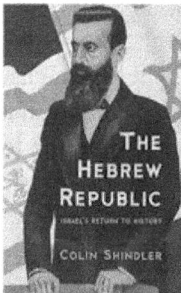

Colin Shindler. Lanham, MD: Rowman & Littlefield. 392 pp. ISBN: 978-1442265967.

Colin Shindler is a well-known historian of Zionism, particularly of Nationalist Zionism, the Revisionist movement established by Ze'ev Jabotinsky; his previous books positioned him as a senior researcher and analyst of this important wing of the Zionist movement. It was an important wing before the establishment of Israel, and it is so much more important these days, considering the dominant role of the Likud Party in Israeli politics since 1977. It is arguably the case, that the purist among Jabotinsky followers — he died at the age of 60 in 1940 — have a good many reasons to doubt the sincerity of the Likud claim to be the ideological successors of Jabotinsky. However, the party keeps saying it, his picture hangs conspicuously in their national meetings alongside that of Menachem Begin, the Jabotinsky disciple who was the first non-Labor Prime Minister of Israel, so there is no way to dismiss their claim out of hand. Being a historian who specialized in the Revisionist movement is, in itself, a great plus to Shindler as a historian, as most of the other noted Jewish Zionist historians come from the Zionist Left Wing, and those who know one or two things about the ferocity of the debates between Zionist historians can appreciate Shindler's unique contribution to the study of Zionism. Shindler however — and justifiably so — largely emphasized the role of the Labor movement in the historic process leading to the establishment of Israel.

The most important contribution of Shindler this time is with the combination of a flowing and highly readable descriptive narrative with a good deal of analysis, something which put it all in a proper historic context. Shindler refers to Israel's return to history, a clear reminder of the ancient connection between the Jewish people and its old, historic homeland, but I personally would have liked to see this important point being highlighted in the book with a special chapter.

The reason for that is the fact that modern day critics of Zionism and Israel — and there are so many of them, and among them are Jews — tend to portray the Zionist movement as a late nineteenth century political movement, whose emergence coincided with the rise and expansion of Western imperialism in the Middle East, hence the association of Zionism with colonialism. The fact is, that the political/organizational expression of Zionism, starting with Theodor Herzl in the First Zionist Congress in 1897, reflected thousands of years of an unstoppable connection of Jews to their homeland, as the Jews are the indigenous population of the land.

Shindler may be recommended to add this to the next edition, as he is the right person to do it. That said, there is little that I can offer as criticism of the book. Among the few which stand out, is the lack of sociological/demographic analysis of the Labor movement political decline in Israel, as well as the rise of the "Right wing". The electoral coalition which brought Begin and Likud to power in 1977 is a combination of the political and economic "haves not" in Israel, the Jews from Arab and Muslim countries (the Mizrachim), the Religious Zionist community and, as of the late 1980s, the immigrants from the former Soviet Union. It is also important to draw a line between the Religious Zionists and the more secular Nationalist Likud. They may come to the same political conclusions on issues like settlements, but they differ on other issues. In Likud, there is a very strong Populist wing, which somewhat defies the classic definitions of Right and Left in Israel. The

American reader will be surprised to know that a vast majority of the poor in Israel vote Right, not Left.

Some weaknesses notwithstanding, the strengths of the book by far outweigh them. I was greatly impressed with the description and analysis of the attitudes toward and connections between the Zionist movement and Nationalist movements in other parts of the world (pp.44-65), as well as the references of world history makers to Zionism (pp.88-108). Also, Shindler's honest description of the relations between Israel and "Pariah regimes" (pp.141-165) and the Evangelical Christians (pp. 165-177), a situation which is a cause of friction between Israel and many diaspora Jews, particularly in the US. In this context, it is also noteworthy, that Shindler widely covers the long-standing phenomenon of Jewish anti-Zionism and anti-Israel feelings (pp.288-304). He refers to this issue in connection with the disputes over the Palestinian issue but refrained from falling into the trap of devoting most of his book to a discussion of this issue. For him, history did not start with either the war of 1948, nor with that of 1967. I also liked the extensive coverage of British attitudes toward Zionism and Israel, something which has to do with Shindler's being from England, but also with the British role.

I, for one, would have expected a more critical view by Shindler of the White Paper of 1939, which was a major betrayal by Britain of the Jewish people in its greatest time of need, just on the eve of the Second World War and the Holocaust (pp.70-71).

Altogether, this is an indispensable book, a great source for understanding Israel of today, its roots, ideological background, policies, and internal politics. I wholeheartedly recommend it. *JO*

Israel's Colonial Project in Palestine: Brutal Pursuit

Elia Zureik. New York, NY: Routledge, 2016. 298 pp. ISBN: 978-0415836104.

Zureik, a well-established Palestinian affairs advocate, and sociologist, now head of the department of sociology and anthropology at the Doha Institute for Graduate Studies in Qatar, focuses his attention on Israel as a colonial power — actually, a settler colonial regime — repressing and oppressing Palestinians, not only in the Occupied Territories, but in Israel itself. Without noting any kind of a paradigmatic shift in held values between the era of European imperial dominance and the subsequent period when colonies became independent states, Zureik assumes in a clear mean-spirited fashion an ignominious characterization of the first British and Zionist policies in what Britain created and nominally titled as Palestine. Scant attention is paid to what Britain had done with its prize as a victor in World War I in gaining territory in the eastern Mediterranean then in addition to what perhaps was a set of clumsy diplomatic measures, not only acceded to Zionist designs, but also in 1922, bifurcated its mandate over Palestine by creating a purely Arab state of Transjordan.

Zureik's study is premised on the major argument that from the latter time in the nineteenth century, European Jews fueled by a politically-oriented Zionist ideology, entertained a policy with a European urbanized notion of cultural superiority, to create a Jewish community in historic Palestine. Undoubtedly wedded to the western understanding of the "state" as a sedentary folk attached to territory, it was to be superimposed on a native eastern population whose connection was to its residential land. Hence, imperialism required colonialism, a political policy during which few critics were in evidence to decry British and French efforts in the near and Middle East, Italy and France in North Africa, Belgium in sub-Sarahan Africa and the Dutch in Oceana. Only in the post-World War II period and the onset of national liberation movements and the action of the universal recognition of human rights did colonialism earn a mark of opprobrium. Nevertheless, the study of peoples being dominated (and by extension, subjugated) by major political forces has continually gained academic recognition in the form of colonialism studies, to which Zureik's work has provided a serious addition.

The current study under review goes to the belly of the beast in the form of a value judgment framing Zionism and Israeli policies toward the Palestinian Arab population as a colonial movement bent on dispossessing an indigenous folk, necessarily through the use of violence, and once Israel was created using the official ability of legislation, marginalizing still further its Arabs. It is, of course, from the perspective of all anti-Zionists that of intent to rid the Promised Land of its indigenous Arab population. Never is there a consideration that a western folk with a cultural affinity to institutions necessary for the establishment of a (western) state would use its leverage to overwhelm a Palestinian society rife with familial strife and an eastern lack of state building evidence, marked by some as Orientalism. Whatever social fragmentation existed in the Palestinian community that has continued is for Zureik laid at the Israeli doorstep as a product of its colonial project. Even though it is widely recognized that the central authority of the state is to provide protection for its citizens, it must also ensure domestic stability and order. Relying heavily on the thought of French political philosopher Michel Foucault, the concept of colonialism, characterized by racism and a tendency to control what is perceived to be potentially disloyal elements within the state, surveillance of those social elements, becomes a major contributory element to this study. With this as context, censuses and the benefits of cartography are all a part of a dark design with insidious intent to favor Israel's control of its Palestinians. This set of factors is what Foucault refers to as "biopolitics" which Zureik accepts uncritically. It is with this theoretical framework in place, that Israel's policy toward the Palestinians in the Occupied Territories leads to the seizure of Palestinian land for what is claimed purposes of national security, privatizing communal territory allowing of Jewish Zionists to create "settlements," all of which realizes dispossession of Palestinians' land.

Following the insertion of Foucault, Israeli attitude toward the Palestinians combines biopolitics with the disproportionate fertility rates of Palestinians versus that of the Israelis, which is then added to Israeli security concerns and its geopolitical concerns with the West Bank certainly wedged between prime Israeli urban centers and neighboring Jordan. Zureik is aware of the distinctive nature of the Occupied Territories and although the Palestinians have a semblance of self-government, it is structured in a wide oppositional manner with the West Bank under the leadership of *Fatah* while the separated Gaza Strip is controlled by the more violently active *Hamas*. In turn, while *Hamas* engaged in, depending on the orientation of the observer, terrorist or armed resistance to Israeli occupation, Gazans were subject to Israeli retaliatory attacks during the years 2006 and 2014, with West Bank residents reduced to the unwitting role of "helpless spectators."

Zureik's meta-analysis of the prevailing literature, and to the author's credit quite an extensive survey of Palestine and related colonial studies, makes this book a major contribution for the student and researcher. *JO*

Mapping My Return: A Palestinian Memoir

Salman Abu Sitta. Cairo, EG: The American University in Cairo Press. 332 pp. ISBN: 978-9774167300.

Salman Abu Sitta has a plan to return home after a long journey. His initial journey away from home began in al-Ma'an in May 1938 when Zionist forces attacked and drove his family from their home. Then a boy of ten, he fled with his elder brother on the back of a horse to Khan Yunis, and eventually to Egypt where he was able to enroll in school. Salman Abu Sitta became a refugee at age ten. He was from a prominent landowning family with connections throughout southern Palestine and Egypt. Through his own efforts and some luck, he was able to complete his degree in engineering, gain professional work in Kuwait, and eventually immigrate to Canada where he established himself and raised his family.

He skillfully fuses the story of his life with well-known historical events to bring to life the Nakba, the Palestinian resistance, and his growing conviction of what must be done to bring a measure of justice to the tragedies he had lived through. He did extensive archival research to understand who had taken his land. He joined leading Palestinian organizations and founded others. He became active in Canadian politics. He sought out and met with Israelis who had attacked and displaced his family. His story echoes that of many Palestinians. His narrative joins the growing genre of accomplished and illuminating Palestinian memoirs. He juxtaposes world-shaking and very personal events in an accessible, well-researched account.

In 1995, he was able to visit his homeland for the first time since 1948. He visited a Palestinian family in Acre and learned that the family was not allowed to repair their house or to make changes to it. The Israeli authorities would eventually class it "uncared for." If an Israeli purchased it, he would be allowed to repair or change it as he wished. In another instance, in a deserted area of al-Ma'an, he and his daughter followed a sign to an ancient synagogue that he had not remembered being there. He found the ruins of a Byzantine church with its typical mosaic floor. His daughter found that a menorah had been inserted into the floor but with stones that had been painted.

His goal is the return of Palestinians to their land despite its reconstitution into a Jewish majority state and society. He founded and headed organizations devoted to the return of Palestinians. He attended conferences and became close friends with leading Palestinians like Edward Said and Ibrahim

Abu Lughod. He opposed Oslo and other peace plans because they did not address the question of return.

He knows how difficult any sort of return will be. In one telling episode, he had dinner with Uri Avnery, the noted Israeli peace activist. He asked Avnery if he would accept him as a neighbor. Anviery firmly replied, "No."

Abu Sitta's great discovery, however, was that Palestinians might be able to return to their land without living next to Israelis. Most of their destroyed villages are in areas that are nearly uninhabited. The vast majority of the Israeli population lives along the coast or in large urban areas. Palestinians who wish to return could resettle in their lands and still be far removed from the dominant society. They would have to work in light industry or other non-farming pursuits, he realizes, but investment is available and development possible.

In the last chapter of his fascinating book, the author details his final journey. He hopes to be buried in Amman, in his family cemetery, next to his brothers. He then wants to be taken to the Gaza Strip, one mile from his birthplace to be interred facing al-Ma'an. He then wants to be brought to al-Ma'an, accompanied by family and friends, be interred on the spot where he was born. **NG**

Occupied Lives: Maintaining Integrity in a Palestinian Refugee Camp in the West Bank

Nina Gren. Cairo, EG: The American University in Cairo Press, 2015. 288 pp. ISBN: 978-9774166952.

The Palestinian refugee camp studied in this book is the Dheisheh camp, just south of Bethlehem. It is one of 59 Palestinian refugee camps administered by UNRWA (the United Nations Relief and Work Agency) in the West Bank, the Gaza strip, Jordan, Lebanon, and Syria. It houses about 9,000 inhabitants at present. During the first years of its existence, it has consisted of tents pitched for displaced Palestinians on land leased by UNRWA. Today, it is a built-up area looking very much like a city slum in a "Third-World" country and is virtually a society of its own.

The author of this study, Dr. Nina Gren, is a Swedish social anthropologist who is a researcher at Lund University and an external lecturer at the University of Copenhagen. She conducted extensive fieldwork inside the Dheisheh camp and, meanwhile, lived for a whole year in it with a Palestinian family. Her study covers the social, political, and economic conditions of those living in the camp — it even deals with their psychological and moral stances vis-a-vis their situation and the Palestinian-Israeli conflict. It is one of the few studies of its kind and is invaluable to anyone interested in the region, let alone specialists in anthropology, sociology, international relations, and refugee studies.

It is particularly interesting because it looks into the everyday life of the people in the camp and gives an account of their ways of trying to cope with the Israeli occupation. It becomes really engaging when it delves into the means that the Palestinian refugees devise to maintain their integrity as a community of human beings who have been forcibly dispossessed of their homes and lands, and deprived of their rights and social worth. Nina Gren's account records the refugees' stance in 2000 during the second Palestinian uprising, the so-called Al-Aqsa Intifada with its more militarized struggle for statehood.

With no solution to their predicament in sight, the Palestinian refugees — as Dr. Gren argues — have concentrated on upholding 'normal life', social continuity, and morality based on usual family life and the obligations of kinship. They have established new households by building houses, by marrying, and by having children and thus by creating continuing bonds that had been broken by the 1948 Nakba and recent violence — they have consequently maintained their moral supremacy over Israelis and their intentions. They have sustained the links between *resilience* and *resistance* in their life, and they have shown that politics is about *existence* itself. This existential emphasis is the foundation of all Palestinian nexus to the intrusive Israeli occupiers encroaching on Palestinian rights.

Dr. Gren's approach is an insightful vision of the Palestinian predicament as seen in Dheisheh and certainly replicated in other places. It is inspired as much by sound anthropological theory as by sharp observation of facts, and it is documented by a vast relevant bibliography. Her book is an invaluable addition to the many studies on the Palestinian-Israeli problem. *ISB*

The Palestinian Deception, 1915-1923:
The McMagon-Hussein Correspondence, the Balfour Declaration, and the Jewish National Home

J.M.N. Jeffries. William M. Mathew, Ed. Washington, D.C.: Institute for Palestine Studies, 2014. 194 pp. ISBN: 978-0887283208.

As I sat and thought about what is being written by William M. Mathew my mind flew to the epic film, Lawrence of Arabia (1962). The scene is the return of Major Lawrence to Cairo and his decision to leave Arabia, but there he finds Prince Faisal as well General Allenby and:

Faisal: Aurens! Or is it Major Lawrence? Ah. Well I will leave you, General. Major Lawrence doubtless has reports to make about my people; and their weakness, and the need to keep them weak in the British interest. The French interest too of course, we mustn't forget the French now.

Allenby: I've told you sir; no such treaty exists!

Faisal: Yes, General, you have lied most bravely, but not convincingly. I know this treaty does exist.

Lawrence: Treaty, sir?

Faisal: He does it better than you, General. Bu then of course, he's almost an Arab... (Faisal exits.)

Dryden: You really don't know?

Allenby: Then what the devil is this?

Lawrence: It's y(our) request for release from Arabia, sir.

Allenby: For what reason!?! Are you sure you haven't heard of the Sykes-Picot Treaty?

Lawrence: No. I can guess.

Allenby: Don't guess. Tell him.

Dryden: Well now, Mr. Sykes is an English Civil Servant and Monsieur Picot is a French Civil Servant. Mr. Sykes and Monsieur Picot met, and they agreed that after the war, France and England should share the Turkish Empire; Including Arabia. They signed an agreement... not a treaty, sir; an agreement, tothat effect.

This cinematic masterpiece captures the early struggle of the Arab peoples in their attempt to create a national consciousness in the midst of tribal divisions. The Arab Revolt and the Arab National Council had come to an end by 1920 and the ANC disbanded in the 1930s. Lawrence's dream for an independent Arabia had come to an end, and now there were issues with the provision and agreements that had been made between the Arabs and the British. Essentially of course, the British were no longer willing to follow the provisions they had set forth for their Arab allies.

The Palestine Deception, 1915-1923… is a compilation of the works of J.M.N. Jefferies and is edited by William M. Mathew. The book itself does not provide an answer for the question of Palestine; however, it shows a portion of the historical background of the Palestinian issue. This book is very much recommended for anyone doing a serious study of Palestinian scholarship, and anyone attempting to understand the rise of the Palestinian Question; it also serves as a good companion book to scholars, professors, and students reading primary documents written by Jeffries.

Mathews offers his own thoughts on the works of Jeffries and does a wonderful job in keeping the language simple so that anyone interested in the book may be able to read it. Although its content is expansive in the range of years it covers, the letters that are referred to in this book date only in the months of January and February of 1923. This book is well organized and would be a great asset to anyone who enjoys learning about the Palestinian Question. *MS*

Palestinians in Jerusalem and Jaffa, 1948: A Tale of Two Cities

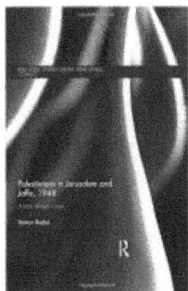

Itamar Radai. New York, NY: Routledge/Taylor & Francis Group, 2016. 211 pp. ISBN: 978-1138946538.

The year 1948 was a crucial one in the history of modern Palestine, for in it the *Nakba* (Catastrophe) occurred. The State of Israel was created on the 15th of May, 1948 at the end of the British Mandate over Palestine, and its creation resulted in dispossessing Palestinians of their homes and lands in a major part of the country and making them refugees. In this book, Dr. Itamar Radai of Tel Aviv University focuses particularly on Palestinians in Jerusalem and Jaffa during this crucial and tragic year, and he succeeds in producing one of the few books in English dealing with the actual fighting between Palestinian Arabs and Jews, resulting in the defeat of the former.

Conflict between the Palestinian Arabs and the Jewish community of Palestine raged as of the 29th of November 1947, mostly in the form of reciprocal terrorist acts and retaliatory operations — even before the British left the country in mid-May 1948. It gradually became a full-fledged communal war. Dr. Radai concentrates on the fighting in Jerusalem and Jaffa as focal points in the conflict because of their centrality, size, and symbolic importance. His book has two parts: Part I is on Jerusalem and Part II on Jaffa, with three chapters in each, and it ends with a twelve-page Conclusion.

Dr. Radai's book is documented by valuable archival material from Israel and England, and also by contemporaneous Arabic and Hebrew press reports, and by about 200 published books in Arabic, Hebrew, and English — some of which are memoirs and eye-witness accounts of the events. All this documentation gives his book credibility as he follows the fighting in Jerusalem and Jaffa from day to day, sometimes from hour to hour, describing its happenings, its heroes and victims, and giving names of commanders and their strategies, and explaining the viewpoints and aims of politicians. His book is a good example of microhistory.

Dr. Radai tries to explain the causes of the social collapse of the Palestinian Arab communities in Jerusalem and Jaffa, and the flight of the inhabitants from their homes despite the pleas of their leaders to stay. He believes that the Palestinian people were alienated from the leadership because, during the British mandate, the rise of the middle class, the migration from rural areas to the cities, and the shift from agriculture to wage labor changed the nature of Palestinian Arab society but no effective institutions were created to make it cohesive. The social collapse eventually led to the military defeat.

Not all scholars would agree with this explanation, of course, but it is a view that has to be explored further. At any rate, this book is useful to all those interested in the Arab-Israeli conflict and in Palestinian studies. **IJB**

The Rise and Fall of a Palestinian Dynasty: The Husaynis 1700-1948

Ilan Pappe. London, UK: Saqi Books, 2017. 450 pp. ISBN: 978-0863564536.

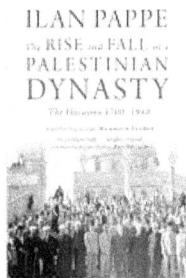

A comprehensive, descriptive narrative providing a genealogical portrait of one of the more prominent mandarins of Palestinian society. The author's focus is on the Jerusalemite elitist al-Husayni family, but for the reader seeking to place this family's role in mandatory Palestinian politics, one should look to Victor Kattan, From *Coexistence to Conquest: International Law and the Arab-Israeli Conflict*[1] for a general political history of Palestine. Pappe's presentation is the product of a professional whose interest in Palestine has been well established. His approach is basically chronological, delineating the al-Husayni family history back to the 18th century and the al-Ghudayya clan and ultimately and more significantly to a direct line to the Prophet. The tale ends with the establishment of Israel in 1948 and the formal trouncing of a Palestinian nationalistic policy. Hence following the establishment of the family structure, the history is given over to its role as an Islamic leader in Jerusalem and the Muslim sanctuary in the *Haram al-Sharif* and generally political control over Palestinian affairs.

Establishing recognition in the outlying regions of the Ottoman Empire centered on the urban areas and those families that registered wealth by virtue of property ownership, extensive familial relationships and displayed religious piety. The al-Husayni family was not the only notable Jerusalemite clan (a peculiar referent here would be *ḥamula*) but one of several that vied for attention and conspicuous public award. Thus, at various points in time, one member of the family or the other would be considered a *mufti* of Jerusalem, *sheikh al-haram* in Jerusalem, and *naqib al-ashraf*. As the author points out, coveted positions of social dominance were not always achieved politely, but occasionally through violence, covered with great detail here. It was after World War I that the phenomenon of Arab nationalism really emerged within the Ottoman Empire so that there erupted a sense of not only Arabism in response to Ottomanism but also some form of Palestinian nationality as an element within the social arena in which the al-Husaynis sought their dominant role.

Interest in the West on Palestine was probably no greater than when Britain created it as a political subject within the context of a Mandate under the

auspices of the League of Nations following World War I. Political developments that followed including the artificial creation of Transjordan by excis-
ing the territory west of the Jordan River and placing a Hashemite in charge,
setting up a non-Palestinian contender for leadership and tension with the
al-Husaynis, as if they didn't have enough competition from other Jerusalemite families. Here Pappe brings together a wealth of information that goes
to the heart of the institutionalization of a Palestinian political development
or lack thereof. Much of contemporary Palestinian history revolves around
the persona and leadership of Haj Amin al-Husayni. Haj Amin, as is pointed
out was a strong advocate for Palestinian statehood, advanced along with an-
ti-British sentiment during the Mandate period and above all virulent anti-Zionism. Certainly, Pappe discusses the Haj Amin's notorious relationship with
Nazi Germany but tends to balance this aspect of his activities by an overall
respect for his attempt to serve as a leader of the Palestinian community.

As exhaustive as Pappe's treatment is, there are a number of issues that
require nitpicking and need to be addressed. While an erstwhile propo-
nent of the Palestinian cause, Pappe squandered the opportunity to expli-
cate the context of Palestine as an amorphous geopolitical entity (e.g. al-ki-
yan al-filastini)[2] distinguishing between *qawm* and *watan* and indicating the
impulse for its evolution. While meticulously researched with an ability to
work with multiple relevant languages and searching a number of national
archives, Pappe could have earned considerably more detailed information
on Palestinian notables and institutions by mining OSS (Office of Strategic Services) materials from the U.S. National Archives.[3] There then is the
question revolving around the title of *"Grand Mufti,"* and to whom should
the originating honor be given. On a number of occasions, Pappe mugs many
of his former Israeli academic historians' interpretations which fit his biases
characterizing Zionist goals as a colonialist project and conducting ethnic
cleansing of the native Palestinian folk.

All criticism aside, there can be no denying that anyone interested in the
affairs of contemporary Palestine, whether it be history, politics, or sociology, must consult *The Rise and Fall of a Palestinian Dynasty.* **SRS**

References

[1] London and New York: Pluto Press, 2009.

[2] For general background see Louis Feldman, "Some Observations on the
Name of Palestine, *Hebrew Union College Annual,* 61 (1990), 1-23.

[3] U.S. National Archives and Records Service, Record Group 226 and
Washington National Records Center, Record Groups 226 and 227.

The Routledge Handbook on the Israeli-Palestinian Conflict

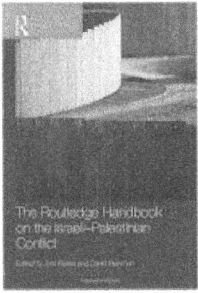

Joel Peters, David Newman, Eds. New York, NY: Routledge, 2013. 496 pp. ISBN: 978-1138925373.

Routledge should be highly praised for this project, a handbook on one of the most significant political conflicts of the world in the last century. In fact, the publisher deserves a big *Mabruk* for assigning the editing to two scholars.

Who has Israeli connections? Not a mean feat in a world where there is a sustained campaign to boycott Israeli academics and universities, a campaign endorsed by many who claim to advance this effort in the name of peace. How can people advance peace between two parties to a conflict, when they boycott one of them, is one of the more folkloristic aspects of modern-day Middle Eastern studies. But the subject on hand is so important and serious, and the project could not have had two better balanced, serious and ethical editors than Peters and Newman.

The desire to maintain evenhandedness is so clear, and the results are so obvious. This is a serious academic book, not a propaganda pamphlet. Not Israeli Hasbara (euphemism for propaganda....) and not Palestinian textbook. Still, there could be more balance, and here are some examples. The chapter on Palestinian refugees, which is important (pp. 109-121), but without a chapter about Jewish refugees from Arab countries, the overall discussion about refugees is lacking. This group of Jews — nearly 50% of the Israeli Jewish population — suffered a lot and is today and has been for a long while, the backbone of the right wing electoral Likud coalition in Israel. Other chapters which lack proper balance, are the one on the peace plans by Galia Golan (pp. 92-107), and the chapters by Newman (pp. 256-267) and Chazan (pp. 267-278) on the settler movement and Israeli peace movements (respectively). There is nothing on a Palestinian peace movement and if it does not exist, why? If it does, where is it? There is nothing about the center right and center left of Israeli politics. Finally, the chapter by Waxman on the Jewish diaspora and the pro-Israel lobby (pp. 346-357) — as much as the settlers and the peace movements are important — they are secondary in importance to Likud and Labor. Maybe the politics of Israel could be better presented through a more general analysis of what is Right and what is Left in Israeli politics, and the impact of demographic changes in Israeli society on the politics of the country. On the same token, I would have liked to see a chapter on Palestinian society, a chapter leading us to a better understanding of current Palestinian politics, and a chapter on the Palestinian diaspora, perhaps one relating to the BDS movement, as the proPalestinian equivalent of the pro-Israel lobby.

That said, what is there in the book by far surpass in importance, substance and context what is missing. This is a book which should be in every good library, to be in the required reading list of every good and serious course on the conflict. Books like this restore my own belief that there still is a good future to the discipline of Middle East Studies in the US. Highly Recommended. *JO*

Young Palestinians Speak: Living under Occupation

Anthony Robinson, and Annemarie Young. Northampton, MA: Interlink, 2017. 118 pp. ISBN: 978-1566560153.

Young Palestinians Speak... is a conjuncture of personal narratives of youth living in occupied Israel. It is the voices of witnesses to the gruesome treatment of Palestinians in the hands of Israelis and their military. These are children who live in despair and in a situation from which the world turns its face.

Children are possibly the most essential part of our society. They are not only the future, but the present as well. Their development and growth will mold them into the adults that they will become and their experiences will either make them or break them.

As parents we will always seek what is best for our children. We hope to see them grow emotionally, psychologically and physically healthy. However, is this really the case everywhere? What if you are not able to raise your child in a land where their wellbeing is possible? Such is the conundrum of the Palestinian peoples. Ten-year-old Yara of Ramallah states:

> We should be able to live and be happy with our lives. I am from Gaza, but our family is not allowed to return. The Israelis won't give us permits. My father lived in Ramallah before, so the family came here, but now we are not allowed to go back.

Palestinian Arabs have been losing their homeland since 1946. Following the United Nations Partition Plan of 1947, the Six Day War in 1967, and the illegal Israeli settlements in the West Bank, Palestinians have lost almost all their lands. Some of us can only imagine what it is to suffer loss of homes, family heirlooms, stability, jobs, and at times, family. Nour, a 14-year-old from Gaza says that living in Occupied Palestine is not living.

> We survive. Some families are separated and might never see each other again. It's too crowded here. There is no space and not enough housing for families. Everybody gets tense, fights start. We are prisoners and have no control over our lives.

Many of these children see more than what they should and live through more than what they can. Lina, a 10-year-old from Sebastiya stated that her cousin was arrested for two days without being told why. He was returned at 2am and will not speak of the incident. What could have happened? What could he have gone through? Is there no sense of justice?

The land continues to be stripped from Palestinians, at times even desecrated. Ahmed of Sebastiya states that settlers constantly uproot their olive trees and in 2012 they began to pump raw sewage into Palestinian olive and apricot groves. How disgusting is that?

These are just some of the situations that Palestinians go through. This book is not a book to be interpreted. This book is filled with the hopes and dreams as well as the live nightmares of many young Palestinians from Jenin, Nabulus, Qattana, Sebastiya, Gaza, Beit Ur, Hebron, Ramallah, and East Jerusalem. Do not seek to read this book if you are prejudice. Read this book to learn what the youth of Palestine go through on a daily basis. Through many of these quotes you can see what life they live. **MS**

LEBANON

Citizen Hariri: Lebanon's Neoliberal Reconstruction

Baumann, Hannes. New Delhi: Oxford University Press, 2016. 256 pp. ISBN: 978-0190687168.

While many books consider Lebanon's history broadly, Baumann offers an account that focuses on Rafiq Hariri's life story and the neoliberal transformation that emerges under his leadership. This work shows how Hariri's economic fortunes and the insight gained as a contractor manifested themselves in national policy when he became the head of state. Hariri gained his wealth as a developer in Saudi Arabia and ultimately became Riyadh's representative in Lebanon. The history also shows that Hariri employed neoliberal economic policies that increased sectarian divisions and transferred national wealth to organizations he controlled and unduly benefited Sunni populations. Hariri remained faithful to Riyadh and even when international tensions grew between Syria, the United States, and Saudi Arabia, he failed to adjust his policies, thus provoking his own downfall.

Hannes Baumann is a lecturer at the University of Liverpool in the Department of Politics where he teaches courses on comparative politics, the international political economy, and Middle East politics. He is well-suited to offer a theoretically-informed chronology focusing on Hariri's neoliberal orientation and relies on previously published work as well as interviews to build an original narrative. Prior to this book, Baumann had published a journal article and two book chapters on Lebanese politics.

Baumann presents the case of Rafiq Hariri as a neo-liberal reformer whose policies brought about an economic transformation but not development. Lebanon's governmental policies reflected the Gulf contactor's interests and sought to introduce luxury housing that would be available to affluent foreigners. Hariri was an extraordinarily wealthy leader who created policies that disproportionately benefited the well-to-do and increased the difficulties for most Lebanese families — particularly those from other religious communities. Since Hariri's economic policies were derived from his time as a Saudi developer, he sought to reproduce those plans in Lebanon. To carry this out, he reassigned property rights and established the Council for Development and Reconstruction (CDR) to manage and coordinate his endeavors. The main project was to introduce luxury condominiums in central Beirut to attract further investment from wealthy Gulf clients. In retrospect, Hariri was good at reproducing the elements that made him prosperous, but this did not trickle down to improve the economic life for the wider Lebanese population.

Rafiq Hariri was an effective, pragmatic contractor and not an economic theorist; Baumann traces the policies Hariri employed to show that they follow the neo-liberal paradigm. One key element was that the Lebanese pound was tied to the US dollar and this required the Lebanese Central Bank to spend vast reserves to maintain its stability. Prior to Hariri's leadership, the pound floated, but was able to preserve its value in international markets. David Harvey has shown that one feature of neo-liberal economic policies is to curb inflation so that the wealthy can maintain their financial power and Baumann successfully shows that Hariri followed this path. The idea is that inflation reduces purchasing power and thereby weakens the ability to use profits to gain more income or to further consolidate wealth. Hariri was also able to personally benefit from this policy as his bank profited from charging the state high interest rates and guaranteed his earnings by preventing inflation. It would be hard to argue that preserving the purchasing power for the richest segment of the population would benefit Lebanese families or communities. Hariri's wealth increased through this policy, but economic growth did not follow; instead, inequality and poverty grew, thus creating pressures to further destabilize the sectarian political system.

While Baumann presents a case study focusing on the leading Sunni politician who was particularly important following the civil war, the work provides additional insight into Saudi Arabia's foreign policy and interference in Lebanese politics. Rafik Hariri was Saudi Arabia's man in Lebanon and he ushered in the transition from Christian to Sunni rule. The policies he enacted would disproportionately serve his religious community and would generate new sectarian divisions rather than serve the cause of unity. Riyadh brokered the treaty that ended the civil war and ushered in the transformation that led to Hariri's leadership. The outcome was not ultimately pleasing to the Saudis, as the Lebanese political complexity prevented Hariri from consolidating Sunni control.

There was a tension between Saudi Arabia's goals and Lebanon's ethnic divisions and the Syrian occupation of the Beeka Valley that gave Damascus more influence in Beirut than Riyadh wanted. These geopolitical pressures placed constraints on Hariri that he failed to comprehend. When a country is occupied, there are real limits on the actual power wielded by the head-of-state. Hariri did not recognize how the Syrian occupation and de facto control of Lebanon affected his leadership. Hariri would grow more problematic to Damascus over time; these problems would peak when Washington threatened Syria with regime changes after the 2003 Iraq invasion. Assad was willing to tolerate Hariri's economic policies as long as they did not interfere or threaten Syria's influence within Lebanon. While the external circumstances changed, Hariri did not perceive how Damascus would respond to his challenge to their influence and this, unfortunately, led to his death.

This work covers an important gap in Lebanese history and Baumann is able to support his arguments and conclusions with in-depth research and factual evidence. There are a couple weaknesses that should be noted: first, by being a chronology of Hariri's career and leadership, the book limits its analysis to the historical record, thus omitting a discussion of Hariri's internal thought and intellectual development. Baumann also underestimates the importance of geopolitics in this narrative and does not adequately account for the religious tensions present within Lebanese society. As in all published works, there are some elements that the author could have better developed. Even with these limitations, the text is methodologically and logically sound.

This book has some importance to me as I worked on European international development projects in Lebanon during the time of Hariri's leadership. The NGO sought to bring agricultural and economic improvements in the predominantly Christian regions that were some of the poorest areas in the country following the Civil War. Ultimately, Hariri's neo-liberal policies were a much greater force than the small introduction of development aid, and while there was some success in the projects, poverty and inequality increased nonetheless. My experience in Lebanon corresponds to and supports Baumann's conclusions.

Hariri was an important player within Lebanon, but his economic policies, in retrospect, were a failure. Baumann's work is not a biography, but a chronology that provides insight on Sunni leadership between the Civil War and the Cedar Revolution. As such, this is an invaluable historical account of Hariri's leadership in an era of Sunni dominance within Lebanon. **GDD**

A History of Stability and Change in Lebanon: Foreign Interventions and International Relations

Joseph Bayeh. New York, NY: I. B. Tauris. 256 pp. ISBN: 978-1784530976.

Domestic politics and foreign interventions are at the very core of Lebanese politics. One cannot go without the other, and in this regard, a book which sets out to examine this phenomenon is always timely. When such a book is published, it is bound to be relevant, that is to say, coming at a time when this connection is so obvious, and so it is in this case. In an amazing move, even by the bizarre criteria of Lebanese politics, Sa'ad Hariri, the PM, announced his resignation in Saudi Arabia, not in his native Lebanon, pointing the finger at Iran and their Lebanese stooges, Hezbollah, accusing them of a plot to assassinate him, and then stayed over in Saudi Arabia. There can be no more dramatic evidence of the symbiotic connection between domestic politics and foreign policy in Lebanon; Saudi Arabia itself has traditionally played a part in this Middle East political game. In 1943, a critical year in the political history of Lebanon, the year of the National Covenant, King Ibn Saud grudgingly expressed support for the establishment of an independent Christian-oriented Lebanon, because he objected to the Hashemite ambitions to establish Greater Syria with Lebanon as part of it. This year and its implications is mentioned in Professor Bayeh's book, though the Saudi role was really ignored.

This, however, may be only a minor weakness in the book, as Saudi Arabia of 1943 was not as important as Saudi Arabia of today. The book of Professor Bayeh is devoted to the close, inseparable connection between domestic politics and international relations so far as Lebanon is concerned. A tragic reminder of the consequences of this connection is provided by the great Lebanese poet, Said Aql, quoted by Bayeh, saying that "From this small country, we travel the World, people and countries, and we build wherever we want a Lebanon" (p. 198). The tragedy is that the Lebanese, while building Lebanon wherever they want, have failed to do it in Lebanon itself — in their homeland. Bayeh blames the "Muslim Community" for the Lebanese instability, which led to civil wars and massive emigration, arguing that the Muslims "found it very difficult to acquiesce to an independent Lebanon," quoting situations involving the Sunni Muslim community (p.203). The focus on the Sunnis is surprising, because the Shi'a community, which is larger than the Sunnis, has been for a few decades under the yoke of Hezbollah, which is an Iranian-led movement, though claiming to be Lebanese, and basically is showing loyalty to Iran rather than to their own country. Clearly, the Shi'a under Hezbollah preferred communal interests over Lebanese statehood, as can be seen by their intervention in the Syrian civil war, as well as in other regional conflicts involving Shi'a. The truth is, that segments of Christian communities, such as the Greek Orthodox, have also preferred to serve regional, mostly Arab nationalist causes, rather than Lebanese independence and distinctiveness as a mixed Muslim-Christian state. The famous Lebanese diplomat and scholar, the late Charles H. Malik, himself a Greek Orthodox Christian, referred to it, arguing that the Christians themselves are still looking for their place in the world around them. ("Beirut-crossroads of cultures," in *Crossroads of Cultures*, p.210). The sectarian divide, by far, is the main stumbling block to internal stability in Lebanon, and it is true, as Bayeh argues, that "whenever a major change in the structure of the international system has occurred… a subsequent change in the structure of Lebanon has generally accompanied it" (p.199). Could, however, this international influence be so effective, had it not been to the chronic inability of the Lebanese communities to decide among themselves about the identity of their state? Bayeh very eloquently describes the various stages of the political evolution in the last few centuries, and repeatedly emphasizes his main theme, about the impact of regional and international involvements about Lebanese politics, but the fact is, that throughout the book, there is not enough focus on the root domestic causes of Lebanese strife and civil war. Somehow, the reader is left with the sense, that if it was just in the hands of the Lebanese, if somehow Lebanon was on its own, the Lebanese would have found the magical formula to coexist harmoniously. This is not really the case, but to the credit of Bayeh, I should make it clear, that he presents his case with ample supportive documentation, and it is all well-written and thus, creates the feeling that his argumentation makes the overall Lebanese situation less complicated than what it really is.

This is one narrative of a troubled country, one of many possible. The great Lebanese historian, the late Kamal Salibi wrote about these complications, that "should the Lebanese attics one day be properly swept, there would be no end to the ways in which the history of Lebanon could be reinterpreted-for the good of Lebanon, and also for the welfare of the Arab world" (Kamal Salibi, *A House of Many Mansions: The History of Lebanon Reconsidered*, p.234). I also believe that professor Bayeh can agree with that, and surely his interesting book is one such valuable interpretation. It is for this reason, that I warmly recommend this book. *JO*

Spheres of Intervention: Foreign Policy and
the Collapse of Lebanon, 1967-1976

James R. Stocker. Ithaca, NY: Cornell University Press, 2016. 296 pp. ISBN: 978-1501700774.

James R. Stocker's *Spheres of Intervention: U.S. Foreign Policy and the Collapse of Lebanon, 1967-1976*, is a welcome addition to the literature concerning Lebanese politics during a turbulent time in the Middle East. Within this carefully research and balanced text the reader is presented not only with a detailed examination of Lebanon's domestic politics, but also how various non-Lebanese actors (Israel, the Palestinians, Syria and the United States) that influenced Lebanon's internal affairs.

Lebanon has always been a fragile state, possessing a complex political system based upon balancing various confessional and ethnic groups. Identity politics is diverse, for it involves not only an individual being the member of a particular confessional and ethnic group, but also entails the sense of being Lebanese. Left to its own devices, Lebanon no doubt would have made its own way during the period Stocker considers. Unfortunately, as this work clearly points out Lebanon is rarely left alone.

Although Stocker's primary focus is on the relationship between the United States and Lebanon between 1967 and 1976, from the beginning, it is clear that the Washington-Beirut connection is not simply bilateral. Rather it is one tested by events largely outside of the control of either the United States or Lebanon. The easy connections of the past are no longer relevant.

Historically the United States and Lebanon have had a pleasant relationship. The good works of American missionaries in the nineteenth and twentieth centuries in Beirut created fond feelings for Americans among the Lebanese people. Yet, Stocker is quick to point out that his work is no nostalgia trip. Rather, the focus is Lebanese politics from 1967 to 1976. This time period involved two wars between Israel and its Arab neighbors as well as Lebanon's own decay into Civil War.

Washington's policy toward Lebanon must be seen within the context of three issues: first, the Cold War between the United States and the former Soviet Union and their respective competition for influence in the Middle East; second, the need to secure Western access to the oil resources of the Middle East; and third, the Arab-Israeli conflict. As Stocker tells his story it is the first and third factors (the Cold War and greater Arab-Israeli Conflict) that occupy the majority of Washington's efforts in Lebanon. The second issue, access to oil reserves, has little relevance to the Washington-Beirut connection. Although the United States will welcome the flow of petrodollars from wealthy Persian Gulf States into Lebanon, this issue is largely outside Stocker's concern. It is the Cold War and the Arab-Israeli Conflict that dominate the analysis.

This point is clearly brought to mind when Stocker examines the impact of both the Six Day War in June 1967 and the October War of 1973 upon Lebanon. These conflicts showed the overall weakness of the Lebanese military, exposed Beirut's political structure to stresses between opposing elites in the country and laid bare the critical importance of the Palestinian refugees and the various groups associated with the Palestinians (Fatah and Popular Front for the Liberation of Palestine, for example). Of course, above all this floated the United States, first during the waning days of the Johnson Administration, and then under the Nixon and Ford Administrations, with Henry Kissinger first as National Security Advisor and then as Secretary of State guiding Washington's policy in the region.

That policy revolved around the major combatants of the region (Egypt, Syria, and Israel) and when possible, reducing the influence of the Soviet Union. Kissinger's "Shuttle Diplomacy" and resulting Disengagement Agreements between ignored Beirut. Lebanon was viewed as a side show within this context. The United States, of course, wanted a peaceful and stable Lebanon. Washington did provide limited military and political assistance when needed, and tried to bring a measure of peace to the country when the Lebanese Civil War broke out. An example of these efforts at peace-making involved the mission of Special Envoy L. Dean Brown in 1976, which Stocker devoted a significant part of Chapter 7 to examining.

Washington also served as a useful go-between for Lebanon and Israel as well as Israel and Syria throughout the period under examination. This communication channel did much to prevent direct conflict between Damascus and Tel Aviv, especially when the former moved forces into Lebanon in 1976. Never though did the United States address the key factor of the Palestinians, in terms of their impact upon Lebanese politics or the larger Middle East peace process.

As Stocker notes in his insightful *Epilogue*, the end of his analysis does not mean an end to Lebanon's woes, nor Washington's involvement in this country. The United States will return to Lebanon again during the Reagan Administration and have as little to show for its efforts as it did between 1967 and 1976. This reviewer hopes that Professor Stocker will bring his insightful analysis to the post-1976 period of Lebanese politics in the future. **WLR**

War Is Coming: Between Past and Future Violence in Lebanon

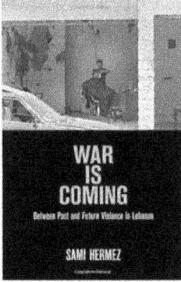

Sami Hermez. Philadelphia, PA: University of Pennsylvania Press, 2017. 280 pp. ISBN: 978-0812248869.

The political eruption engulfing the Middle East since late 2010, known as the Arab Spring spared, to a large part, and up to now (December 2017), a country whose history, stretching for centuries, has been characterized by frequent bloodshed, large scale violence — in fact, terrible civil wars. This is Lebanon. It is arguably the case that predictions of many pundits and experts, including many Lebanese, were that the eruption would strike Lebanon like an unstoppable hurricane, but that did not happen, and the analysis of why it did not, is beyond the scope of this review. What is not beyond the scope of the review is the fact that the prospect of Lebanon being engulfed in yet another round of mayhem is still very tangible, and this is, in fact, the underlying assumption of the book — that such a scenario is nearly inevitable.

This book is an important and valuable contribution to our understanding of this turbulent country. Most importantly, it is so because, unlike a lot of the literature about Lebanon, it does not attempt to beautify or romanticize the Lebanese situation by portraying a picture much rosier and more optimistic than what is the actual situation. The central thesis is simple: that the Lebanese themselves are living in the shadow of the grim realization that "something" is imminent, and "something" means bad news. It does not mean a political misunderstanding between different factions, it means war because political differences in Lebanon usually are being contested and resolved through bloodshed. The book covers three years of research, 2006-2009, but the writer, being connected to Lebanon, tells us that "every year since (2009); however, I have returned for several months in the summer and again in the winter. Invariably, with every return there have been conversations about the coming war and, by extension, memories of past political violence" (p.193). Indeed, a very sad state of affairs — it is so also because, if not almost entirely due to the memories of the past, not just the waiting for the troubles of the future. As Hermez so artfully tells us, what happened in Lebanon since the end of the great civil war of 1975-1990, "was a power struggle between different players in society over how to interpret the war and who had the rights to a process of history making" (p.192). In fact, in a way, Lebanon has healed in an impressive way from the horrors of the 15-year civil war, and it reconstructed its political institutions, though their level and quality of functioning is so far off what we expect to have in a real functioning democracy. Yet, rebuilding political institutions, even with differences from the past, is one thing, but rebuilding society, rebuilding the human aspect, the relationships which were destroyed, the life shattered, is something else altogether. So, with that in mind, Hermez leaves us with the inevitable conclusion, that as civil society "being unable to deal with the war's causes, [it] facilitated war's anticipation into the future" (p.192).

What makes this book a really memorable contribution to the research of the question which is the basis of the discussion, is the fact that the writer focuses his thesis on the experience of talking to ordinary Lebanese, and clearly such discussions are about everyday life, and it is here where the conclusions of the book as mentioned above are so valid and significant. They reflect the overriding sense of people, not the polished, political-oriented, points-scoring statements and testimonies of leaders. Hermez deals a lot with the question of political amnesty for crimes committed during the war, and we all know how horrific this war was. In 1991, the Lebanese government passed an amnesty law, and in itself was not a novelty in the war-torn country, and Hermez refers to this somewhat cynically, when observing, that "rather than write a history of war, it is useful to recount the history of amnesties" (p.174). Clearly, writing one history of the war is impossible, because then, the question is whose history? The famous Lebanese novelist Elias Khoury, is quoted by Hermez with his answer to this question. "We make a choice what to remember and what to forget but the unsaid in history must be said" (p.173). So, time and again, we are confronted with Hermez's basic assumption: war is on the minds of the Lebanese because the problems which beset their society and polity continue to be open and big wounds. With that in mind, it is important to explain why this review does not get into the details of political events which occurred in Lebanon in the period researched by Hermez — for example, the list of actual and attempted political assassinations (p.40) — as this data can be found elsewhere. The explanation and context of all that is what makes the Hermez book so important. It is, however, my sense that what is missing in the book is a description and analysis of the impact of the civil war in neighboring Syria over the Lebanese situation. Not a long chapter, but an insightful reference to the role of Hezbollah in this war, and how and why it has been a deterrent for a full-scale Lebanese civil war. I wholly recommend this book. There is no way to fully grasp the complicated realities of Lebanon without reading it. *JO*

MEDIA

Arab TV-Audiences: Negotiating Religion and Identity

Ehab Galal, Ed. Frankfurt am Main, DE: Peter Lang, 2014. 151 pp. ISBN: 978-3631656112.

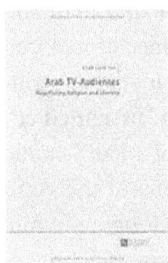

Arab TV-Audiences: Negotiating Religion and Identity examines the way Arab Muslim and Christian audiences react to the omnipresence of religious, cultural and political discourses in Arab media. The book focuses on the transnational and global impact of mediated religion on Arabic-speaking audiences, investigating the way it forms their identities and conceptualizations of belief and belonging. The volume presents six case studies examined by six scholars with different affiliations, basing their research on qualitative culturalist and mediatization approaches.

The two key questions of this volume are 'how' and 'why,' as its general interest is to understand the way Arab audiences can choose what to watch amid a quite plural and fragmented network of media outlets, and to depict the reasons that shape their choices.

The book begins with a prelude by the editor Ehab Galal entitled "Where has the authority gone? New imperatives and audience research" in which he introduces three main points: 1) the influence of satellite TV on the emergence of new religious channels and programming, examined in the first four chapters; 2) the major attention religious discourse has gained in popular media genres such as drama series and cinema, explored in the last two chapters; and 3) the active participation of audiences in the critical interpretation of media messages and the way they ascribe authority to mediated religious discourses, debated in all the chapters.

In the first chapter entitled "Audience Responses to Islamic TV: Between Resistance and Piety," Ehab Galal presents fieldwork research conducted on Arab-speaking audiences in Copenhagen, London and Cairo to examine their reactions to Islamic programming in TV channels and the way it affects their constructions and negotiations of Islamic identities and practices. The chapter's objective is to study the way media shapes the audiences' understanding of Islam, arguing for the existence of shared religious frames of reference and symbolic resources among Arabic-speaking audiences of Islamic

TV, though their geographical and socio-cultural locations are quite different. Furthermore, the chapter emphasizes the idea that audiences from different countries tend to use Islamic TV to pronounce and differentiate themselves in relation to religion, as their positions and reactions relate mainly to spirituality, education, authority, resistance, and piety.

The second chapter, written by Khalil Rinnawi and entitled "Cyber Religious-National Community? The Case of Arab Community in Germany" debates the degree a Berlin-based community — mainly of Palestinian and Lebanese origin — is exposed to and influenced by Arab transnational media. The main argument of this chapter is that transnational media contributes to the formation of an "imagined community" and then "imagined coherence" or "cyber nationalism and Islamic- religiousness" of a Pan-Islamic and Pan-Arab nation among the first and second generations of the Arab community in Germany who seek for a deeper sense of belonging, while forging a 'schizophrenic situation' in relation to the third generation.

The concept of belonging is still omnipresent in the third chapter "Maghrebi Audiences: Mapping the Divide between Arab Sentiment, Islamic Belonging and Political Praxis," by Ratiba Hadj-Moussa. This chapter argues that new media technology, especially satellite TV and its symbolic representations, has reframed political modes of affiliation and identity, reactivating a sense of "regionality" and calling into question the very concept of global images.

In the fourth chapter entitled "Religious Media as a Cultural Discourse: The Views of the Arab Diaspora in London," Noha Mellor argues for the contribution of religious channels to the formation and reformation of cultural and religious identities of the second-generation Arabs in London; noting the heterogeneity of Muslim Arab communities in Diaspora that makes it difficult to identify them as one community.

The fifth chapter, written by Vivian Ibrahim and entitled "Watching the History of the 'Present': Religion and National identity in the Egyptian Diaspora," shifts the book's study to the drama series genre, exploring the way it influences the Arab audiences' actions and reactions to religious and political discourse. The chapter scrutinizes the Egyptian soap opera entitled al-Gama'a (The group), sponsored by the state-run television and broadcast on Egyptian and Arab channels during the Muslim holy month of Ramadan in 2010. The drama series revolves around the Ikhwan al-Muslimeen (the Muslim brotherhood), and, as affirmed by Vivian, aimed to legitimize the leadership of the Muslim brotherhood.

A major result of this fieldwork-based study of this chapter is that the series has chiefly contributed to identity reconsideration of the two interviewed diasporic audiences: the U.S.-based group — all Copts — and the UK group, as the first group had critical tendencies toward national unity, whereas the second group showed a positive sense of unity and tolerance. The series has reshaped both groups' memories, and reflections on self, religion, nation, and historical narration.

As for the last chapter, written by Lise Paulsen Galal and entitled "Minority Religion Mediated: Contesting Representation," the focus is on the two movies: Baheb el-Cima (I love Cinema), based on a Coptic environment and screened in Egyptian and Arab cinemas in 2004, and Hassan wa Murqus (Hassan and Marcus), which was released in 2008 and shows Omar Sherif as a key Coptic figure. This chapter analyses the Arab audiences' reactions to the movies in regard to religious identities and minorities in Egypt. It portrays the role of both movies in redefining Egyptian national and religious identities, defending the rights of religious freedom, tolerance, difference, and equality, and thus calling for a culturally pluralistic yet unified Egypt.

Generally speaking, the chief objective of this book is to provide epistemic analyses of Arab audiences and to underline the ways they make use of media in their construction, negotiation, and rejection of religious identities and practices. **NM**

Opportunities for Media and Information Literacy in the Middle East and North Africa

Magda Abu-Fadil, Jordi Torrent, and Alton Grizzle, Eds. Gothenburg, SE: Nordicom, University of Gothenburg, International Clearinghouse on Children, Youth and Media. 362 pp. ISBN: 978-9187957338.

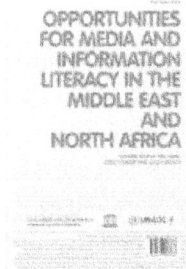

According to co-editor, Alton Grizzle, in thinking of the relevance of media and information literacy (MIL) in the Middle East and North African (MENA) region, "We must take rapid and innovative actions to fuel change" (p. 36). With *Opportunities for Media and Information Literacy in the Middle East and North Africa*, Grizzle, with editors Magda Abu-Fadil and Jordi Torrent, and contributing authors, argue that in spite of the massive impact and proliferation of digital media and information resources in the MENA region, few instructional programs have been developed about media literacy. No longer is reading and writing literacy enough, they say. To be more effective in contemporary societies, young people must be literate in media and information. They maintain that media literacy skills are teachable skills and are the responsibility of educators. Through the development of media literacy programs, individuals throughout the MENA region will be equipped to evaluate resources for bias and validity, and move forward toward stronger civic peace and an understanding of those from different religious and cultural backgrounds. Maybe most importantly, as they discuss general and state policy-specific themes related to media and information literacy (MIL), they nurture a sense of hope and optimism that these opportunities are not only available, but also necessary and designed to expand to touch lives across the MENA region.

The book, presented in both English and Arabic to widen the audience and collaboration opportunities, was published in cooperation with the International Clearinghouse on Children, Youth, & Media, UNESCO and UNAOC. The foreword, preface, and introduction provide compelling and useful data for readers because the content is written in an intelligent yet approachable manner. Although the book targets educators in the MENA region, it will likely interest educators, school administrators, and others interested in digital media, the impact of social media networks, information technology, and those involved in MIL in the USA and throughout the world. Readers learn that the purpose of the book is to inspire teachers looking for ways to bring MIL education into their classrooms, curriculum, and institutions, and that their work will lead to the greater understanding of individuals from the diverse religious and cultural backgrounds of the MENA region and the world.

The editors and contributors reach this goal through a book comprised of two main parts. Part one, largely contributed by the book's three editors, and providing a general overview of opportunities for media and information literacy in the MENA region. Part two responds to part one's general overview with country- and culture-specific perspectives. The focus is on state policy and MIL in action. Regions represented under the perspectives section include Morocco, Iraq, Egypt, Jordan, Lebanon, Oman, Algeria, and Tunisia. While it would have been difficult to bring perspectives from each and every MENA country, the countries featured provide an effective representation of the MENA region.

Following a strong introduction by Magda Abu-Fadil, part one includes a preliminary comparative analysis of MIL by Alton Grizzle. Here, readers are provided with an overview of information and media environment demographics and media characteristics in the MENA countries. Data is organized in easy-to-read tables, such as Grizzle's Table 1, which prepares readers for a fuller understanding of the book through statistics including population and numbers of libraries, radio and TV stations, and newspapers. Rationales for developing and implementing MIL programs in the MENA region are listed, and include combatting stereotypes, promoting press freedom, empowering youth to use social networks for more productive than entertainment uses, protecting local cultures, strengthening citizen journalism, quality research, and decision making, and the promotion of non-violence and peace. MIL strategies and their related implementations are also noted to provide examples and context. Jad Melki and Lubna Maaliki use the example of the Media and Digital Literacy Academy of Beirut to discuss the blossoming of Arab digital and media literacy, while Jordi Torrent writes on United Nations Alliance of Civilizations (UNAOC) workshops on MIL in Fez and Cairo.

Part two, "Media and Information Literacy in the MENA Region from State Policies to Action Research," delves into the state of MIL throughout the MENA region through articles comparing and analyzing MIL in 11 countries. This diverse and informative collection of writings opens with an overview of MIL as it relates to the Occupied Palestinian Territories to efforts to empower children and youth in Tunisia. Examples include Lebanese universities that teach MIL, the impacts of political issues on Facebook use in Philistine, and workshops offered in Morocco and Cairo that helped teachers conceptualize, and therefore, effectively teach, MIL. Far from pedantic and much more than a rehashing of data, articles offer practical recommendations, such as how and what educators should consider including in their curriculum, and list key elements that help define and describe the major discussion points, such as the key elements of information literacy and media literacy. Resources referenced include scholarly journal articles; books; UNESCO, press councils and governmental reports; research studies; masters and doctoral theses; blogs, and websites.

In spite of the scope and depth of these articles and data from across the MENA region, the editors argue that few instruction programs have been developed about media literacy. They argue that the appropriate evaluation of information sources requires skills that are teachable. For example, they suggest that educators can and should teach students how to evaluate text for bias, learn how to use social media responsibly, and through media and information literacy, develop strategies to prevent miscommunication and combat hate speech. Overall, the recommendation is to integrate media and information literacy into middle and high school curriculums. The authors maintain that while parents and church leaders also play a role, it is the educator's responsibility to teach students how to use MIL carefully and wisely so they know what to believe and learn how to distinguish between credible and incredible sources. The book emphasizes the importance of literacy knowledge for adolescents because information literacy is key to understanding and advocating for social issues, human rights, and self-expression. By bringing these local perspectives together, the editors and contributors encourage teachers to champion the development of their own media literacy programs.

In conclusion, rapidly expanding digital media and information technology in the MENA region creates a landscape that requires information literacy. By writing this yearbook, the editors and contributors seek to raise awareness, demonstrate existing shortcomings, and expand the number of stakeholders involved in MIL. Educators, school administrators, parents, and more will benefit from this informative, proactive, and perspective changing book. Through contextualizing overviews and examples of MIL from MENA countries, the book moves beyond delivering data to providing optimism and hope — an aspect suggested in the title, which focuses not on the *lack* of MIL, but rather, on the *opportunities*. **MA**

MILITARY INTERVENTION

Counter Jihad: America's Military Experience in Afghanistan, Iraq, and Syria

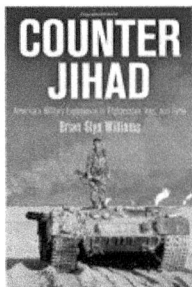

Brian Glyn Williams. Philadelphia, PA: University of Pennsylvania Press, 2017. 367 pp. ISBN: 978-0812248678.

Counter Jihad is an assessment of the military experience of the United States in the War on Terror across three Muslim majority countries: Afghanistan, Iraq, and Syria. A deeper question addressed by Brian Williams is why do terrorists hate Americans? Taking a cue from Abdul Rashid Dostum — the Uzbek warrior in Afghanistan — about foreign policy toward the Muslim world, the author is emphatic that the answer is in the pro-Israel leaning of the United States. This response explains the (at a first glance) puzzling brief discussion at the beginning of Chapter 1 of Israeli-Palestinian conflict from the Arab perspective with reference to $3 billion yearly foreign aid to Israel and the enviable lobbying power of the American Israel Political Affairs Committee (AIPAC). Starting with Afghanistan in Chapter 2, followed by Iraq, then making a full circle back to Afghanistan, the book ends with the Islamic State of Iraq and Syria (ISIS). In Chapter 3, Williams delves into a critique of the George W. Bush administration for the prelude to the 2003 Iraq War.

Following the 1979 Islamic Revolution in Iran, the author notes, the United States supported Saddam Hussein's Iraq that at the time deployed banned Weapons of Mass Destruction (WMD). Williams argues that UN Resolution 687 facilitated the dismantling of Iraqi WMDs. Also, he asserts that UNSCOM destroyed Iraqi calutrons, the mass spectrometer required for separating uranium isotopes. Furthermore, he claims that the 1998 Operation Desert Fox under the Clinton Administration "essentially" terminated Iraq's WMD program. Pointing the finger to the neo-conservative Clean Break project, the author finds it ominous that the United States played the role that even Israel distanced itself from as catastrophic. In Chapter 3, which is a valuable contribution, Williams debunks the evidence argued by the Bush administration about Iraqi WMD threat: yellowcake uranium, aluminum tubes, drones, mobile weapons laboratory, chemical-biological weapons stockpiles, and al-Qaeda linkage.

A former CIA employee tasked with tracking suicide bombers in Afghanistan, Williams is disappointed that the Blue-Sky Memo by the national security advisor Richard Clarke for massive support of the Northern Alliance against the Taliban did not see daylight. Likely to make an impression on the reader, the author sprinkles some sobering casualty figures throughout the book. The War on Terror cost the United States roughly $5 trillion and about 7,700 American lives. Also, the United States was spending $1 billion per week fighting in Iraq. In regard to Syria, by 2016 the death toll amounted to 10% of that country's population, with another 11 million people fleeing the conflict zone.

Although only 172 United States and British troops were killed in the 2003 Iraq War, about 30,000 Iraqis died in the invasion. By the time the United States forces withdrew from Iraq in 2011, the death toll for Iraqis was estimated to be 190,000. Order Number 2 by Paul Bremer, which disbanded the Iraqi military, affected the livelihood of 385,000 in the army, 285,000 in the Ministry of Defense, and 50,000 in the presidential security services. The edict also meant that 137,000 Iraqi military men could not be hired by the United States Army for post-war reconstruction. Operation Phantom Fury, the second battle for Fallujah, resulted in the limited loss of 54 American lives, but the death of 1,000-2,000 insurgents and the destruction of one-fifth of the city's 50,000 houses. Approximately 4.7 million Iraqis were displaced as the country mired in an internecine civil war. As for Iraqi Prime Minister Nouri al-Maliki, he not only rescinded the promise of security jobs to 103,000 "Sons of Iraq" Anbar Awakening militiamen, but also purged Sunnis from the army and the National Intelligence Service.

The maps of the Federally Administered Tribal Agencies (FATA) in Pakistan were useful; the map of ethnic groups in Afghanistan was insightful. Lucidly written and informative, the target audience of general population would have benefited from a list of expanded acronyms. Intended to question United States foreign policy toward the Middle East and the Muslim world, the author directly links the rise of ISIS to the 2003 Iraq War. Given the continuing challenges in Syria, Iraq, and Afghanistan, including "blowback" to the West from ISIS, Brian Williams has strong reservations about the War on Terror. **RGM**

The Soviet-Israeli War 1965-1973: The USSR's Military Intervention in the Egyptian-Israeli Conflict

Isabella Ginor, Gideon Remez. New York, NY: Oxford University Press, 2017. 506 pp. ISBN: 978-0190693480.

This is a remarkable book that should be of great interest to Sovietologists/Kremlinologists, military and diplomatic historians, and specialists on Israeli (noticeably leaving out Egyptian), American, and Russian foreign policy. A lesson that should be taken by readers of this book is that discrediting Russian military prowess should be dispelled. Anyone even with a meager knowledge of Middle Eastern politics should be able to discern that the Egyptian military could not have undertaken the cross-canal military operation it did without serious assistance from a strong military power, in this case the Soviet Union.

The intricate historical question that has been taken up many pages by analysts, commentators, and military historians of several nationalities is when did the Soviets know the exact date of the Egyptian undertaking in October 1973? To what extent were the Soviets involved in the combat operations alongside the Egyptians? And what kind of overall military support did the Soviets provide the Egyptians?

The two authors here, Ginor and Remez, are associate fellows at the Hebrew University's Truman Institute in Jerusalem. In almost excruciating detail, these authors tackle many of the statements, accorded dates, and documented conclusions found in both Western and Russian sources. Soviet military folk engaged in what they referred to by its code name, Operation *Kavkaz*, disclosed with many of the Soviet military participants named along with their rank, role, and service organization. There is a rather full description of the various military equipment supplied to the Egyptians, though with a heavy emphasis on jet aircraft and Soviet air defense systems. In this regard, there is bare mention of infantry advice, save for the provision of "advisors," or related weaponry, especially the Soviet *Malyutka* (according to the NATO designation, the Sagger, an anti-tank rocket) that on balance, perhaps caused the greatest amount of damage to Israeli armor resources.

Much of the analysis presented is sourced with Russian-language materials, and less so with English, and difficult to understand a dearth of Hebrew sources (undeniably available to the authors from all levels of the Israeli government). An indelible impression is left, if for no other reason than the lack of attention given over to an Israeli perspective at any point in time during the drama, that Israel's effort in the overall matter was ineptitude. There is also a somewhat serious matter of note regarding the involvement of the Soviets with Syria's coordinated attack on Israel, for which little is said. In addition to the overall discussion of Soviet provision of armaments, "advisors," and combat servicemen, there is little disclosure why the American intelligence community apparently failed to recognize these developments which a reader is led to believe. More intriguing is the provision of diplomatic discourse between the Soviets and the Americans (the State and Executive Departments), and the Soviets and their Egyptian counterparts or clients. An underlying theme behind the Egyptian decision to undertake a major military effort to reclaim its control over the Sinai Peninsula (but nothing more), was the failure by not only the Egyptians and Israelis to reach a diplomatic agreements on disengagement, but also the active involvement of both the Soviets and the Americans.

Interesting to note about the Soviet perspective is how much the World War II experience molded the approach of so many of the senior Soviet military officers serving in Egypt. Secondly, the extent to which the Soviet bureaucracy sought to maintain some degree of secrecy attached to whatever related activities were posed upon its military mission in Egypt is clearly demonstrated.

This is, undeniably, a contribution to an understanding of the role that major powers have played in the Arab-Israeli conflict and certainly a wealth of information is provided for use by historians for further study. **SRS**

MUSLIMS IN AMERICA

Islamophobia and Racism in America

Erik Love. New York, NY: New York University Press, 2017. 272 pp. ISBN: 978-1479804924; ISBN: 978-1479838073.

The term "Islamophobia" gained frequency in the literature after the tragic events of September 11, 2001 and the subsequent rising tidal wave of hate directed against Islam and Muslims, followed by the equally violent actions directed against Muslims in general, and certain Muslim countries, such as Iraq and Afghanistan.

Because of 9/11, Arab-American communities faced a hostile environment of "counter terrorism" activities directed against them by Western powers that view the war on terror as "us against them." Through the 1990s, FBI agents fanned out across the country in search of Arab or Middle East terrorists or sympathizers. The FBI "Watch List," "No Fly List," National Security Entry-Exist Registration System, and other measures targeted Arabs and Muslims entering the United States until 2011, when it was expanded into a biometric security measure standard for all visitors. Political and bigoted opportunists used the tragedy of 9/11 and its aftermath to aggressively advocate for law enforcement to target Muslims for surveillance under the spurious and bigoted reasoning that Muslims are more likely to commit terrorist attacks.

Mutual hostilities and distrust are nothing new to mankind. History is replete with religious as well as ethnic hostilities, some bloodier than others. Colonial forces committed countless acts of aggressions against natives and ignited ethnic and sectarian wars within and without the nations and regions they occupied. Acts of terrorism committed by Islamic groups against their fellow Christians, Jews, Hindus, and Muslims are equally repugnant and deserve the condemnation of all peace-loving people. The cowardly acts of the criminals of 9/11 and those that supported them will always be condemned by those who believe in the messages of civilized and peace-loving people regardless of religious beliefs.

It is unfortunate that the current administration in the White House — and the recently failed elections of some of the ultra-conservative nationalist

231

candidates in the US and Europe — has empowered hate and Islamophobic groups in the US and Europe. Consequently, derogatory terms are shamelessly used to negatively label the "other" fellow Americans. Islamophobia, just as religious bigotry, racism, and all other forms of "isms," along with hateful language should be eradicated, and replaced with more positive, compassionate, and civil attitude.

In his book's six chapters, Erik Love describes the various acts of incrimination and discrimination against Muslims in the US, in particular, and attributes such discrimination to the fact that Muslims come mostly from the "dark" and "yellow" (Africa and Asia) continents, and are thus, stereotyped by the white Anglo-Saxon population. Chapter 1 discusses "The Racial Dilemma"; Chapter 2, "The Racial Paradox"; Chapter 3, "Islamophobia in America;" Chapter 4, "Confronting Islamophobia"; Chapter 5, "Civil Rights Coalition;" and Chapter 6, "Towards a New Civil Rights Era." The author's objective is to point out the tragic actions and events of 9/11 which he describes as unfortunate, misguided, un-Christian, and indicates how such actions and reactions contribute to the rising Islamophobia in the United States, as well as in Europe.

Eric Love devotes the first two chapters to address the questions of racial dilemma, of ethnicity, nationality, and religiosity, and the racial and ethnic dilemma when addressing the questions of who is Muslim, Arab, Middle Eastern, or South Asian, and who among them is white and who is non-white. In Chapter 3 titled "Islamophobia in America," the author traces the fundamental tactics of early surveillance and disruption programs that the US government employed to target Middle Eastern Americans as early as in the 1950s and 1960s. He mentions, among such programs, the Counterintelligence Program, or COUNTELPRO that "actively undermine the work of all sorts of advocacy organizations" (p. 98). Follow-up spawned surveillance programs included "Operation Boulder" that began in the summer of 1972 to target Arab-American advocacy organizations, and Arab-American individuals nation-wide. The book's remaining chapters come under titles such as "Confronting Islamophobia" (Chapter 4); "Civil Rights Coalitions" (Chapter 5); and "Toward a New Civil Rights Era" (Chapter 6). Pages 209 to 265 include a Methodological Appendix, References, and Index.

Love managed to apply ethnographic methods of research to investigate the rise and impact of Islamophobia on policies and programs by focusing on the hateful rhetoric in political speeches and electoral campaigns that political opportunists used to win elections. He conducts interviews, called and/or interviewed organizations. Millions of dollars were provided by wealthy individuals and conservative political action groups and lobbyists with certain Islam-bashing agenda to self-proclaimed "Islamic experts' to trump up Islamophobic ideas, and calls for banning Shari'a law, even when such is not practiced under any present or proposed American legislation. Unfortunately, the latest American presidential election in 2016, added fuel to this fire of Muslim bashing, and divisive "us versus them" rhetoric, and acts of aggression against Muslims.

According to Love, the Islamophobic rhetoric became a prominent feature of all levels of mainstream American politics (p. 92), and an enabler to hate groups that crawled out of the halls of shame and into American town halls, state capitals, and the US Congress. As the author points out "... well-funded industry of political professionals has helped to promote Islamophobic ideas in the American political sphere" (p. 92). He describes not just the heated and bigoted rhetoric directed against Islam and Muslims, but also the secret monitoring of mosques and private homes belonging to Muslim Americans. Also monitored were American charities, a matter that had a chilling effect on philanthropic and political donations to Islamic civic and charitable organizations (p. 102).

According to the author, legislative acts such as the FISA (Foreign Intelligence Surveillance) Act, the NSA (National Security Agency) and other measures have targeted Arabs, Muslims, and others who look Arab or Muslim, and that included Hindus, Sikhs, and other individuals who looked Semitic or Middle Easterners. Such groups also suffer hateful attacks their lives, properties, and places of worship. ***MMA***

Muslim Americans: Debating the Notions of American and un-American

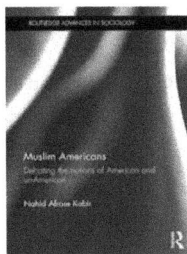

Nahid Afrose Kabir. New York, NY: Routledge, 2017. 230 pp. ISBN: 978-1138699250.

The author, a Bangladeshi Muslim, currently an adjunct senior research fellow at the School of Education at the University of South Australia, spent time in the United States as a Visiting Fellow at the Center for Middle Eastern Studies at Harvard University, but her experience also includes contacts with America that have spanned three decades. Her concern is the matter of integration and assimilation into the American cultural and political system by foreign-born Muslim immigrants. The context of her study is the effect of Islamaphobia following the 9/11 terrorist attack in the United States, by a group of Muslims, the characterization of which is colored by a cultural prism. What follows is a question of the compatibility of Islam with the American democratic model and a discussion of Muslim perceptions of what it means to be an American. The study is based on an extensive set of interviews in seven states in the United States, primarily with South and Southeastern Asian Muslim immigrants who have often been targeted as potential terrorists because of their "otherness," or non-American appearance and behavior and given the ethnic background of recent terroristic violence in the West and the United States. Strikingly absent is any substantive mention of the elephant in the room: The ethnic connection between Muslims and terrorism and the nexus to the subsequent perception of many Americans to threats to the country's national security. Integration into the American cultural society, as diverse as it is, assumes a widely accepted index that recognizes some national creed or standard. The author takes exception to the voices of some prominent conservative academicians, i.e., Samuel Huntington and Bernard Lewis, whose views towards Islam and its adherents are viewed as antithetical to western values. The evaluation by so many American observers and analysts, Kabir argues, is a contemporary return to the extremist positions of former American Senator Joseph McCarthy. This study is a useful contribution to an appreciation of the complexity of contemporary social integration in the United States. **SRS**

Muslims and the Making of America

Amir Hussain. Waco, TX: Baylor University Press, 2016. 142 pp. ISBN 978-1481306225.

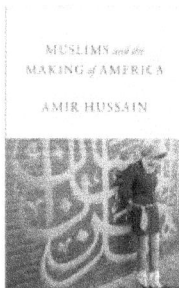

It is reasonably well recognized that the United States and pre-colonial America — but post the Native American experience — was populated by religiously distinct folk. While the amalgam was not always conducted with acceptance or even toleration, it has been what has been documented. As is the case with all multi-ethnic communities, one group tends to dominate, and in the United States, this position has been assumed by WASPS (White, Anglo-Saxon, Protestants). Perhaps but certainly not exclusively, American ethnographic studies have not always been prominently inclusive. One such case study that attempts to fill the void is the history of Muslim migration — intentional and non-voluntary — and settlement in the United States.

Hussain, a theological studies professor at Loyola Marymount University in Los Angeles, seeks to remedy this lacuna with a popularly presented collection of vignettes of Muslims who have contributed to various elements of American culture. He begins, correctly, with a brief historical coverage of pre-independent United States with black, West African Muslims forcibly brought to the continent as slave labor. There is also the diplomatic history of the United States with Muslim authorities in North Africa and the debatable fact that Morocco was the first country to diplomatically recognize the United States (possibly along with Holland and the Republic of Ragusa). What follows is a series of biographies of selected figures that have brought attention to their respective industries. Hence, we learn about the role that Ahmet M. Ertegun has played in popular music. A great deal is made of Muslims in the much-loved American, almost pathological, love with athletics. Here we learn about Ferdinand Lewis Alcinder, Jr. who converts to Islam to become Kareem Abdul-Jabbar and a star with the Los Angeles Lakers. Similarly portrayed is Chris Jackson, who also converted to Islam and whose persona became Mahmoud Abdul-Rauf. Perhaps the most controversial figure who earned prominence, as well as anger is the pugilist Cassius Clay, better known as Muhammad Ali. Also, in the ring has been Ali's fellow contender, Mike Tyson. There are others mentioned with less notoriety but nevertheless, Muslim. In the general area of contributions made to American culture, Hussain focuses on architecture and Gulzar Haidar who is best known for his work with the Masonic Shriners (whose members, although sport fezzes, the organization does not represent a Muslim identity). Fazlur Rahman Khan, another architect, introduced a number of innovative features to structural architecture. The veneer of "orientalism" has affected the marketing of cigarettes, e.g., Camel, or Donald Trump's real estate and his Taj Mahal Casino. Islam traditionally requires a place to show honor to the Prophet, the mosque. Here the reader learns about the first mosque in America to appear in Maine in 1915.

Hussain's book is a noteworthy contribution to our understanding of how Muslims have assisted, sometimes greatly, in the making of the United States. While all the information provided by the author is certainly appreciated, there is a great deal that was not covered and in need of elucidation. The author, admittedly, states that he "seeks to name a few as stand-ins for the many" (p. 19). While it is noted that many of the West African slaves that were introduced to the New World America were Muslim, little more is said of them that could have been gleaned from available slave narratives. Similarly, mention is made of the largely Muslim Arab population in Dearborn, Michigan, but nothing is mentioned of the Yemeni community in Toledo, Ohio, the story of Syrian/Lebanese travels down the Mississippi River and settlement in the lower Southland, the Muslim merchants that can be found along Atlantic Avenue in Brooklyn, or the huge Persian-speaking community in Los Angeles. *SRS*

The Oxford Handbook of American Islam

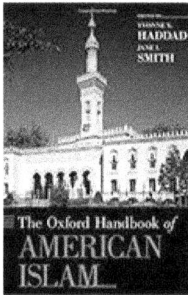

Yvonne Y. Haddad, Jane I. Smith, Eds. Oxford, UK: Oxford University Press, 2014. 560 pp. ISBN: 978-0199862634.

As Muslims in America are growing in number and becoming more organized, their political and societal impact is increasing, and general interest in their history and culture is deepening accordingly. The two editors of this volume, who have earlier devoted much of their scholarship to this issue, now offer readers a virtually comprehensive book on the subject to meet the continuing and undiminished public interest.

After an introduction by the editors, the volume is divided into three parts, logically presented to cover the history of the Muslims in America and to give an analysis of their culture and organization. The articles in the parts are written by thirty-one scholars, including the two editors. Part I is entitled "Formation of the Muslim Community in North America," Part II "Institutionalization of Islam in North America," and Part III "Integration and Assimilation of Muslims."

While there is some inevitable though innocuous duplication of information in the articles because each is independently conceived, the editors are to be complimented on having successfully brought together an encyclopedic amount of knowledge in this book, which is one of the *Oxford Handbooks* series offering authoritative and state-of-the-art surveys of current thinking and research in particular subjects.

The reader learns that from the arrival of the earliest Muslims brought to America from West Africa as slaves, to the formation of the "Nation of

Islam" under Elijah Mohammed (1897-1975) in the 1930s, and from the continuing immigration to America of Muslims from various regions of the vast Islamic world in Asia and Africa, to the conversion of Blacks and other Americans to Islam — the religion of Islam has been a continuous part of American history. Despite their different ethnic origins and languages, and despite their sometimes-conflicting interests, American Muslims eventually institutionalized themselves by building mosques, creating regional gatherings, and national organizations and publications. Each of the articles in this book deals at some length with one aspect or another of this long process which has, in the end, led to the assimilation of Muslims and their integration in American society.

The process has not been easy or harmonious, and Muslims were often thought of as a "fifth column" (p. 188) in certain circles of American society. Political events in the Muslim world reflected themselves variously on their attitudes and actions, and on their relations with the general American public. After 9/11 in particular, there was a strong feeling of unease about the presence of Muslims in America. Even American Muslims themselves debated to what extent they should assimilate or remain fully faithful to their original traditions, just as they had been debating this issue throughout their history in America. The chapters of this volume deal with many of these dilemmas and uncertainties, and give a clear picture of the state of Muslim affairs today in America.

In 2011, there were about seven million Muslims in America (p. 75) according to the estimates of the Council on American-Islamic Relations (CAIR), which is the largest Islamic advocacy organization in America; it documents cases of bias against Muslims, encourages an understanding of Islam, and helps educate American Muslims about their legal rights and responsibilities. There are many other Muslim organizations in America having other purposes, such as the Islamic Society of North America (ISNA), the Fiqh Council of North America (FCNA) that issues *fatwas* (i.e., legal rulings) on religious questions arising in the novel conditions of Muslims in America, the Islamic Circle of North America (ICNA) concerned with religious learning and character-building; and other professional organizations like the Association of Muslim Social Scientists (AMSS), the Islamic Medical Association of North America (IMANA), the Association of Muslim Scientists and Engineers (AMSE), the Muslim Students Association of US and Canada (MSA), and others.

Some articles of this book deal with specific Muslim groups in America like Sunnis, Shi'a, Sufis, Blacks and Ahmadiyya; others deal with specific topics concerning Muslims in America like shari'a, youth, women, marriage, and prisons; and still others deal with politics, Muslim-Christian relations, filmmaking, art, and architecture. Article 29 is about the effects on American Muslims of the recent war on terror, and article 30 — the last in the book — is about Islamophobia and anti-Muslim sentiment in the US. The book starts with a question: "Could a Muslim become president of the United States?" and, although Thomas Jefferson thought so, it seems that most Americans believe this question to be of great concern.

... *American Islam* is an important and timely book for Americans and all others interested in reading. It is well-planned, well-written, and well-documented; and it has a good index that makes it easy to refer to particulars in the book's encyclopedic content. Fraught with controversial issues that some of its topics entail, the book offers objective scholarship; the two editors and the contributing scholars are to be congratulated on a job well done. One slight error has to be corrected, however, and it is related to Muhammad 'Abduh on page 177, where it is wrongly said that he died in 1902 and he had been rector of al-Azhar University and a "prominent Egyptian intellectual of the late eighteenth century." In point of fact, he was the Mufti of Egypt, but was never rector of al-Azhar, nor did he live in the eighteenth century — he was born in 1849 and died in 1905. Other references to Muhammad 'Abduh in the book are correct.

This book is highly recommended to scholars and students of modern Islam, and particularly to those interested in Islam in the USA and Canada. I daresay that it is indispensable and opens new vistas for further new research.
IJB

MUSLIMS IN EUROPE

Benchmarking Muslim Well-Being in Europe

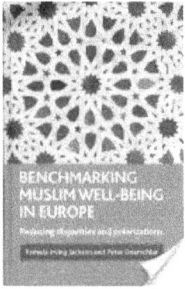

Pamela Irving Jackson, & Peter Doerschler. Bristol, UK: The Policy Press, 2012. 208 pp. ISBN: 978-1847428875.

This is a very timely book about the well-being of European Muslims, written by two American social scientists: Pamela Irving Jackson, a sociologist, and Peter Doerschler, a political scientist. Drawing on official and non-official data sets from the UK, the Netherlands, France, and Germany, the authors find that the well-being of European Muslims requires that current civic integration policy adopted by all four countries is abandoned and replaced with a full implementation of equal opportunities and civil rights. Implicitly, the book explains why xenophobic and Islamophobic parties and activists are nearly always also "EU-phobic." As the authors point out, the EU defines social integration as a *two-way accommodation* between public institutions and "minorities" — here Muslims — which contrasts with the premises of civic integration and the new "citizenship contracts" which place the responsibility for accommodation on the individual migrant. Hence, the authors advocate the view that integration policy should be moved from current national levels up to EU-level, to ensure equal opportunities and civil rights for all. These arguments are developed through the successive chapters and supported by the authors' data analysis. Together, the data sets and analysis, illustrated through tables and diagrams, make for an accessible and well-documented study.

In Chapter 1, the authors define their aim, sources and method, which reads as follows: "Our goal is to examine disparities between Muslims and others in Europe to provide a basis for reducing the polarizations that prevent full utilization of the talents of members of the religious minority. We seek to demonstrate the utility of the benchmarking (my italics) process in promoting member states' capacity for integration as defined by the European Parliament (2007:73) in its benchmarking report: 'a society's ability to integrate all its members into new arrangements of active citizenship that ensure the long-term well-being of all in a diverse society'". (p. 24)

Thus, they highlight the importance that the EU assigns to "well-being" for integration. "Benchmarking" then means to establish where countries are on the road toward this objective, and what measures are required to reach the goal.

The four selected countries are the most powerful EU member states with the largest Muslim populations, which means that their policies have a large impact both on other member states and on the well-being of European Muslims. Sources of data include both official and non-official bodies at EU level, European level, and country levels. The EU bodies are: 1) The European Union Agency for Fundamental Rights (FRA); 2) European Union Minorities and Discrimination Survey (EU-MIDIS); and 3) European Commission against Racism and Intolerance (ECRI). The non-EU European agencies include, among others: 1) The European Social Survey (ESS); 2) Open Society Institute; 3) At Home in Europe/Muslims in Europe; and 4) the Justice Initiative.

National state-sponsored data bases for the UK, the Netherlands, France and Germany are also used. Here, the authors point out that while the UK almost consistently applies "religion" as a category in data gathering, France does not wish to register data according to citizens' religious identity, which means that respondents' religion has to be surmised from their national origins or ethnicity. Given the significance of religion for Muslims' well-being (see below), the French data sets should be improved to include religion in order to meet the requirements of EU's benchmarking process.

With reference to state-of-the-art in the research field of "Muslims' integration," the authors define their contribution as a shift of focus from immigration and security toward civil rights and equal opportunities (p. 6). The method consists in comparing Muslims to non-Muslims in examining "their experiences and attitudes relating to crime and justice, and their trust in public institutions as part of our consideration of the key area of life specified by the Council of Europe (2003:7) and the European Parliament (2007:139) in terms of basic public functions, defined as including *equality, anti-discrimination*, and *self-organization*. The key areas of *culture* and *information* are also considered here, through satisfaction with democracy, evaluation of democracy as an idea, and understanding of the agencies of the government" (p. 9).

Chapter 2 investigates to what extent each state has a unique method of coordinating state identity and ethnic identity, and to what extent such methods correspond with different scopes of the nation-state in minority integration, and Muslims' ability to find a comfortable place in society. First, the authors show that any differences between the four selected countries play out within the framework of a common European strategy: "Rather than simply legislating equal access to [...] education, employment, or access to public facilities [...], European nations open state and social structures to minorities and immigrants only after they have met certain cultural gateways, or in order to ensure specific equality goals set by the state" (p. 27).

Against the background of that common framework, the findings show that while there are considerable differences between the four countries, each country has changed its policy over the last decades. In all four countries Muslims experience relative inequality, lack of political influence, and social isolation — and score higher on attachment to and practice of religion than the population average. Given that each country has changed its policy, but the results regarding Muslims' well-being are the same across the countries, the authors draw two important conclusions. Firstly, that the pervasive European discourse about set "national ways" of dealing with integration lacks empirical foundation; and secondly, that in order to improve the situation for the Muslim populations the most constructive way is to develop a uniform European policy of equal opportunities and civil rights.

Chapters 3 and 4 address the "citizenship contracts" which have been implemented in France, the Netherlands, and Germany, and are also being discussed in the UK. These contracts reflect public questioning whether non-European immigrants — especially Muslims — will be able to fit into a democratic, secular Europe, a concern which has become aggravated with the last decade's coupling of security concerns with immigration in public debates. This situation could, the authors argue, be expected to make Muslims uneasy about their place in Europe and to have reduced their trust in the police and public authorities.

Yet the findings show that, overall, Muslims report slightly higher trust in democracy, the justice system, and the police than non-Muslims, irrespective of degree of religiosity. There are two notable exceptions. French Muslims report significantly lower trust in the police than non-Muslims, which corresponds with French invasive policing of migrant communities; and British and Dutch Muslims are more worried about being subject to crime and anti-social behavior than British non-Muslims, French and German Muslims. The authors suggest this might be because British and Dutch Muslims live in more ethnically and religiously mixed neighborhoods than the more segregated French and German Muslims, hence exposing the former to a broader range of people in everyday life, some of who show hostile and anti-social attitudes.

Also interesting is that Muslims (especially British) who are born abroad show significantly higher degrees of trust in the police and justice system than those born in Europe. The authors speculate whether this is because migrants experience a "positive contrast" between the European institutions compared with the countries of origins. Another possible explanation is simply integration: Europe-born Muslims are closer to the population average regarding a degree of scepticism of public authorities and the political system.

None of the findings indicate that Muslims — neither the newly immigrated nor those who are born in the countries — are in need of special citizenship contracts or targeted actions due to distrust in the political and legal system. Rather, the results imply that the national policies target a premise, not reality. As Oscar Verkaaik's ethnographical study of new Dutch citizenship ceremonies shows, their rationale is that democracy is identified with Dutch-ness in the ethno-cultural sense, implying that people of Moroccan, Turkish or Surinamese family background have to "learn" democracy from the Dutch institutions, while the ethnic Dutch, so to speak, have it in their genes (The cachet dilemma: Ritual and agency in new Dutch nationalism, American Ethnologist, 37:1, 69–82).

Chapter 5 treats Muslims' experiences of discrimination in public institutions. Overall, Muslims report significantly higher degrees of discrimination than non-Muslims. The smallest difference between Muslims and non-Muslims is in the German data, while in the UK fewer people on average (Muslim and non-Muslim) perceive themselves as belonging to a group which is discriminated against. France stands for the highest difference between Muslims and non-Muslims — again, the authors point to French policing practices as significant factors. In France, Muslim men also report more experiences of discrimination than Muslim women, while none of the other countries show any differences between the genders in this respect. The gender difference in France might also be attributable to the police, since it is overwhelmingly (young) men who are the targets for stop-and-search campaigns, surveillance and police raids. In France, the UK and the Netherlands, to hold a citizenship makes no difference for experiences of discrimination. In Germany, however, which only recently (2001) changed its law to allow non-ethnic Germans to acquire citizenship, holding a citizenship correlates with lower degrees of experienced discrimination. Thus, it may well be that for those who recall the old German two-tier system of citizens and guest workers, acquiring citizenship is a significant raise in well-being.

According to the author's analysis, Muslims experience multiple discrimination, i.e. with reference to a range of services, authorities, the general public and the labor and housing market, and they identify religion and ethnicity as the categories with reference to which they experience most discrimination. This is important, given that Muslims also report that religion is more important to them than religion is to the population averages (Chapter 2).

On the basis of these results the authors attribute obstructive attitudes to *non-Muslims*, not to Muslims, and they detect a causal connection between policy and public attitudes: "Policies focused on keeping manifestation of religious identity out of the public arena, and the associated hostility toward those at whom such policies are targeted may serve to exclude Muslims from full membership in European states. To some extent, the impact that these policies have on non-Muslims may be the heart of the problem: such policies may send a signal that Muslims do not belong, making interactions between Muslims and non-Muslims more likely to reflect that attitude" (p. 120).

Having thus documented *relative discrimination* against European Muslims, the authors in Chapter 6 investigate Muslims' general *well-being* in respect to income, health, education, employment, awareness of political information, and access to information sources. The first group is comprised of youth 12–18 years old, the age group often considered alienated from majority society. In all four countries, this youth cohort reports the same levels of well-being, political awareness and access as the non-Muslims; in fact, they are slightly more politically engaged than the control group, both in national, EU and international politics. The only difference is that Muslim youth rate "racism" and "conflicts between cultures" highest on their lists of political issues, while non-Muslims rate the same issues as third or fourth priority.

Across all age groups, Muslims have lower household incomes, but on average, are happier than the control groups, even with regard to the economy. Yet they experience longer periods of unemployment than average, and less often work in positions of leadership and management. In Germany, France and the Netherlands, Muslims are also less likely to proceed to higher education than others. Thus, the authors' analysis is that, while Muslims are structurally disadvantaged, they are happier with public services and the economy than others, and at least as well integrated in terms of national and international political engagement and access to information. In this context, the authors caution against scholarly characterizations of Muslims as an alienated and self-segregated underclass in Europe: they are structurally disfavored but neither alienated nor self-segregated.

The concluding Chapter 7 demonstrates the significance of accurate data for benchmarking Muslims' well-being, by comparing the data with official government policy and anti-Muslim party rhetoric. Examples which the authors think counter common public prejudice include Muslims, who, while having conservative social values, have a somewhat stronger sense of social justice than others, and are more in favor of states' intervention to ensure equal opportunities than non-Muslims — not surprising, perhaps, given that Muslims are somewhat disadvantaged economically.

Summing up their results, the authors make a strong claim that current national civic integration policies rest on erroneous assumptions which should be revised on the basis of accurate data. Not only politicians but also the general public needs to be educated, since public attitudes tend to be in line with the current policy debates on civic integration and their premise, that there is a "Muslim problem."

"Widespread discussion of Muslims' 'failure' to integrate into European societies rests on the assumption that members of the religious minority were born abroad, that they are not citizens and are ethnic minorities, and that these groups do not support European values and institutions. Seen as a Diaspora, Muslims appear to have a weak claim on their European homes. Yet we have examined data from several highly credible sources and it all suggests that Muslims are at home in Europe: they trust the justice system and its officials, including police, magistrates and the courts, often to a greater degree than do non-Muslims. Where there are exceptions to this finding (as in French Muslims' distrust of the police), we have only to look at official policy (the French minority identity check and stop and search policy currently being investigated by the French and European courts for constitutionality) to understand why. Results from Gallup polls in Europe provide firm support for our findings: examinations of the Gallup survey data for France, Germany and the UK comparing responses from Muslims in the capital cities [...] to respondents in the nation as a whole indicated no statistically significant difference between Muslims and non-Muslims in their identification with the country, except for the fact that in the UK, Muslim respondents were 9% more likely to identify with the country than were respondents in the nation at large (Nyiri, 2007)" (pp. 147–48).

Civic integration policy should thus be abandoned in favor of civil rights and equal opportunities legislation, both because it does not address a real problem on the part of Muslims, and because it may even be reinforcing those attitudes among public servants and the general public which contribute to discrimination against Muslims on the grounds of their religious identity *across European countries*. This is also why it is important to research and benchmark the well-being of 'Muslims' as a religiously identified group, and not just look at the different ethnic groups that make up the European Muslim communities.

While this takes us beyond the authors' analysis, it is worth adding that their results raise questions for further research. As noted above, Muslims score higher than others on social justice and on state intervention to ensure equal opportunities; on support for the democratic political and justice system; and on general happiness. Given that Muslims also attribute more significance to religion for their lives and values than other Europeans do, it would be interesting to know more about how values identified with religion are related to these other views. **UM**

London Youth, Religion, and Politics: Engagement and Activism from Brixton to Brick Lane

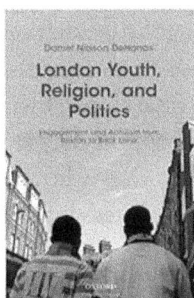

Daniel Nilsson DeHanas. Oxford, UK: Oxford University Press, 264 pp. ISBN: 978-0198743675.

This book is outstanding in that it focuses on one city, London, and compares the political and social evolution of second-generation British youth of different migrant origins: British Muslim Bangladeshis, British Christian Jamaicans and non-religious youth. It is original because no other book — to my knowledge — to date has presented such a comparative study and comprehensive findings on the integration process of youth from different immigrant ethnic backgrounds. Its comparative dimension allows the reader to examine and understand the effects of religion, citizenship, culture, migration and internal and external forces on ethnic minorities in the United Kingdom. The first major advantage of this approach is that it can be used as a model for the study of other countries and regions. The second advantage is that a number of theories are discussed with their range of concepts applied to the immigrant issues (Merton's Middle-range theory and Caldwell's theory about Muslims in Europe), and the reader is able to appreciate variation in the similarities and differences between Black British and British South Asians and the problems they face.

The book is divided into seven chapters. The first chapter shows the kinds of citizens that both groups are becoming. It reveals that both share the same relatively high level of political awareness, and the same low level of identification with British culture and citizenship. The author argues that in these two domains, religion and ethnicity do not have a significant impact. Nevertheless, both religion and politics have a major role in political participation. In fact, the data analysis shows that Bengladeshis are more active politically than their Jamaican counterparts.

The second chapter focuses on identity issues of second-generation youth, and discusses how they purposefully use self-identification to achieve their own goals. The author finds out that "deculturation" is strong among British Bengladeshis, who are more akin to move away from their Bengladeshi tainted culture toward a more universal vision of Islam. For this reason, they identify first as Muslim. By contrast, British Jamaicans display a form of fragmented cultural identity patterns in the sense that they often adopt situational and hybrid stances to identity (Chapter 3).

Chapter 4 covers the way churches and mosques contribute to the evolution of these young people as citizens. The author provides examples and case studies of varied mosques and churches in order to represent the religious diversity in the districts under study. While outlining the generation gap and the differences between youth and their parents so far as religious practices and institutions, the author argues that youth have developed their own understanding and attitudes to religious belief and self with, as they are more interested in community life than the Christian Jamaicans who are more interested in individualistic self (Chapter 5). These differences impact the ability and the degree of mobilization and participation.

In Chapter 6, the author studies the effects of religious mobilization on social and political change. Both groups of youth are involved in activism to fight against youth violence (British Christian Jamaicans) or to raise funds to struggle against poverty and hunger (British Muslim Bengladeshis).

Chapter 7 draws interesting conclusions trying to explain how political and civic participation of British Jamaicans may possibly increase in the future in order to match the strongly mobilization of British Muslim youth around religious and political matters.

Against all populist Islamophobic discourses in the West, the book reveals that ethnic minorities — Muslim communities included — participate in various degrees in British politics through their activism and participation. Today, both British Bengladeshis and British Jamaicans of the second-generation positively contribute to the common good and are becoming visible as participants in the top decision-making positions, thus emphasizing their very strong engagement and citizenship.

The analysis and comparison conclude that, despite the differences in the levels of participation and mobilization, both groups have very high rates of commitment to the British society and integration.

To sum up, I would like to state that this book is innovative and well-timed for many reasons. First, it compares Muslim and Christian British citizens of immigrant origins and sets them in context with non-religious youth.

Second, this comparative approach underscores the impact of religiosity on political change and social integration and reveals the various religious practices among Europe's second-generation youth. Third, this comparative objective study shows clearly that Muslims are not an exceptional ethnic group that is a threat to society or that requires a specific urgent treatment. Fourth, the book shows that some of the concerns and problems associated with Muslim youth in Europe are shared by other youth and migrant communities. Fifth, the book reveals that Muslim South Asians seem to be more integrated and politically active as British citizens than their Christian Black British Jamaicans. Sixth, it shows that Islam is compatible with democratic values and it can be integrated in European society and in the West in general. Seventh, it shows that it is possible to create understanding between people from different faiths and ethnicities when there is social justice and intercultural dialogue.

To conclude, this book is an interesting contribution to our understanding of the integration and political participation of British citizens of different immigrant origins, namely British Muslim, Christian, and non-religious young people in a socially and culturally changing United Kingdom. As such, it is of significant importance to readers, graduate students and researchers of migration and cultural studies, government, and sociology. *ME*

References

Caldwell, C. (2009). *Reflections on a revolution in Europe: Can Europe be the same with different people in it?* London, UK: Allen Lane.

Ennaji, M. (2016). *Muslim Moroccan migrants in Europe.* New York, NY: Palgrave.

Merton, R. K. (1967). *Social theory and social structure.* New York, NY: Free Press.

Muslims in Europe: A Review Essay

Arjana, S. R. (2015). *Muslims in the Western Imagination*. London, UK: Oxford University Press, 261 pp. ISBN: 978-0199324927. (Ebk). ISBN: 978-019932 4921.

Geelhoed, F. (2014). *Striving for Allah: Purification and Resistance among Fundamentalists Muslims in the Netherlands*. The Hague, NL: Eleven International, 282 pp. ISBN: 978-9462364936.

Peace, T. (2015). *European Social Movements and Muslim Activism: Another World but With Whom?* New York, NY: Palgrave/Macmillan, 2015. 196 pp. ISBN: 978-1137463999.

Scharbrodt, O., Sakaranaho, T., Khan, A. H., Shanneik, Y., & Ibrahim, V. (2015). *Muslims in Ireland: Past and Present*. Edinburgh, UK: Edinburgh University Press, 266 pp. ISBN: 978-0748696888.

Introduction

The rising tide of Islamophobia in the Western world, as could be judged by the outcomes of the 2016 national election results in the US, is the emergence of Islamophobic politicians and isolationists in some European countries which are indications of a widening rift between Muslims and Euro-Americans. Future studies on the subject of Muslims in general, and Muslims in Europe in particular should address — and hopefully advance solutions — to the persistent question: "why they hate us, and why we fear them?" Such studies could hopefully avoid the escalation of serious global conflicts and the rising tide of hate that can only bring harm to world peace, racial, religious and ethnic harmony.

Islam and Muslims in Europe

By examining four most recently published books on Islam and Muslims in Europe, this review essay attempts to address the long lingering question regarding the recently tenuous relations between Islam and the West, and the question: "why they hate us and why we fear them?" There are currently millions of Muslims living in the European Union, and they constitute a complex and heterogeneous population that includes believers,

radicals, non-believers, migrants, converts, ultra-religious, moderates, secular, non-practitioners, European citizens, foreigners, men and women, and
old and young. In the aftermath of the tragedy of 9/11, and the subsequent
American-Euro invasion of the two Muslim countries of Afghanistan and
Iraq, the terms Muslim and Arab have been used interchangeably to describe
or refer to such people and their countries as enemies of the Western world,
and questions were raised: "why do they hate us?"

Timothy Peace's book *European social movements and Muslim activism:
Another world but with whom?* (2015) uses the example of the alter-global-
ization movement, characterized by the slogan "another world is possible"
to explain why social movement leaders in Britain and France reacted so
differently toward the emergence of what he describes as Muslim activism.
Peace acknowledges that much previous research on Muslims has focused
on their experiences as immigrants, or the children thereof, and how they
adapt to their host society (p. 160). The author attempts to explain the political participation among present Muslim minorities while also situating
their involvement historically, thereby demonstrating the effective continuity between the migrant struggles of the first generation and those of their
children, who grew up as European citizens. The author attempts to emphasize and demonstrate that, during the current recent upheavals against Islam
throughout Europe and the US, Islam as a religion and Muslims as residents
and citizens are not necessarily the enemy of or a threat to the state. Peace
further attempts to explain the different reactions of social movements when
faced with diversity.

Using the case study method of research, Peace enhances the reader's understanding of the effects of citizenship regimes on political participation.
Between 2002 and 2006, he conducted semi-structure interviews with activists and leaders in order to asses and ascertain the context of motivations,
beliefs, and attitudes of Muslim activists and leaders.

On a similar theme, Scharbrodt et al. book *Muslims in Ireland: Past and
present* (2015) aims to "provide a complete survey of Muslims in Ireland by
combining historical, sociological, and ethnographic research approaches"
(p. 1). As with the rest of European countries, Muslim migration to Ireland
has multiplied tenfold between 1991 and 2011, as evidenced by the country's official census data. This translates to slightly more than one percent of
the entire population of the Republic of Ireland.

While most published research on Muslim migrants in Europe concen-
trated on traditional colonial countries such as France, Britain, and Germany,
Scharbrodt's book provides valuable information on the neglected topic of
Muslim migration to marginalized countries of Europe, such as Ireland. He

points out that early migrant Muslims coming to Ireland were tourists, sailors, servants, merchants, students, and academics. In contrast to the rest of Europe, most Muslim migrants to Ireland, especially during the pre-Celtic Tiger period were well educated professionals, physicians, and merchants, or business people who became part of the Irish middle and upper middle class.

Scharbrodt traces the presence of Muslims in Ireland from the nineteenth century and early twentieth century up to Irish independence in 1922, and the formation of the Muslim communal presence in Dublin in the 1950s. It continues with the massive influx of Muslim immigrants during the Celtic Tiger period, which has changed the face of both religious landscape and Islam in Ireland. Of note is the significant number of Muslims coming from Sub-Saharan Africa, primarily from Nigeria, coupled with the increase during the last decade of South-Asian Muslim communities from both Pakistan and Bangladesh. Another significant observation is the revelation about the paucity of the literature on young Arabs in the European diaspora. A hot topic of debate emerged most recently as a result of the unprovoked fatal attacks by young European Muslims on their fellow countrymen as witnessed in various European cities and capitals, and also the resultant attacks by non-Muslim Europeans on their Muslim fellow countrymen (brown skin bearded men in Pakistani, Afghani, or Saudi garb) and women (especially those wearing the *hijab* or *niqab*).

Scharbrodt's systematic and well-researched approach to the subject provides rich data and analysis on the following broad topics: 1. Muslim settlement and immigration in Ireland since WWI; 2. Communities and organizations, including their histories and the purposes for which these organizations were established; 3. State-community interaction and governance of Islam in Ireland, which explore the interaction between Muslims, the Irish state and society; and 4. Muslim women, in which he explores the experiences of Muslim women, both migrants and converts in Ireland. He concludes his book by recommending future areas of research and they include: gender issues; more research across the border between south and north; and more quantitative ethnographic research on Muslims in Ireland.

The book is a good addition to the emerging literature on the timely topic of Muslims in Europe. It is hoped that European readers, young and old, will read such literature and learn more about the contributions of Muslim immigrants to the development of their countries' economic and cultural development and stem the tide of hate and misunderstanding directed against their fellow countrymen who happen to be Muslims.

Sophia Rose Arjana adds a scholarly contribution to the modest, but gradually growing literature on the subject of Muslims in Europe, who are facing increased negative attitude toward them as the "other" in a heightened western Islamophobia. The current and hostile western anti-Islam and the campaigns of hate are fueled by some newly elected and aspiring right-wing western political figures and members of certain nationalist and conservative parties. The demonization of Muslims, Arabs, Saracens, Jews, and Africans by Christian Europeans is traced to Middle Ages Europe. Such White European discriminatory attitude continued with various levels of ebbs and flows through the ages. The tragic events of 9/11 and similar acts of violence committed by Muslim and Arab extremists are linked to past Christian-Muslim antagonism and are examined in light of historical facts described and documented by Ms. Arjana.

Arjana's book *Muslims in the Western imagination* (2015) treats the subject in six topical chapters: 1. The Muslim Monster; 2. Medieval Muslim Monsters; 3. Turkish Monsters; The Monsters of Orientalism; 5. Muslim Monsters in the Americas; and ending with Chapter 6: "The Monsters of September 11." According to the author, she follows this topical approach in order to trace the portrayal of Muslims in western culture during a period that spans roughly thirteen hundred years with many of the Muslims being portrayed by Europeans as monsters that disturb the calm of white Christianity. In Chapter 2, she provides the beginning of the genealogy that is laid out to trace how Christians created the Muslim/Saracen, African, and Jewish monster combination as shown in illustrations of European medieval texts. The killer of Christ was cast as either a Jew or a Saracen or a hybrid of the two.

In Chapter 3, Arjana discusses "Turkish Monsters" and describes the European attitudes toward the inhabitants of Ottoman territories. She provides examples from the period's European art and literature including the writings of Shakespeare such as Othello and his Muslim/Moorish identity, and describes the portrayal of the Prophet Muhammad in Elizabethan England during which time negative depictions of the prophet Muhammad were in vogue. Medieval villains encompassed Jews and they are given particular attention in Chapter 4, which describes prominent oriental monsters, including a Moor named Zofloya and a Turkish Vampire named Dracula. Dracula is described as "a product of racial hybridity, a Jew and an Ottoman Turk with a measure of Hun and Vampire thrown in" (p. 122). According to the author, Dracula's Semitic quality reveals his Jewish identity. The chapter gives special emphasis to Jewish-Muslim villains and Oriental monsters. In Chapter 5, the author investigates what European immigrants in the Americas identified as monsters, some that are similar to Plinian beasts and others that were described as devil-worshippers. These Europeans also believed that American

Indians were Moors and described their cities as New Cairo, evidence of the Maurophilia that occupied the European imagination.

Moving forward, the author engaged in analyzing the most recent clashes between Western Christianity and Islam of the East, and its continued maligning and demonizing after the 9/11 events and other acts of violence that followed and committed by both sides. These include violent portrayal and acts that were visited on Muslims in Afghanistan, Iraq, and other Muslim countries, and narratives of torture and humiliation at notorious prisons such as Abu Gharib, Bagram Airbase, and Guantanamo, among others.

Using a more positive approach, Flora Geelhoed's *Striving for Allah: Muslims in the Netherlands* (2014), presents a study of Muslims residing outside the Muslim world and in Europe in particular, and more specifically in the Netherlands. The author employs three qualitative research methods — semi-open interviews, observations, and analysis of Internet discussions. The book cites census figures from 2008 that show 95% of the estimated 825,000 Dutch Muslims, approximately 5% of the total population in the Netherlands, are from non-Western origin primarily of Moroccan and Turkish descent. Their colors and physical features make them stand out among the Dutch, predominantly white European, population — and thus, being easy targets for Islamophobic reactions. A growing number of European advocates of Islamophobia include politicians and public figures such as Ayaan Hirsi Ali, Theo van Gogh Rita Verdonk, Green Wilders, among other Dutch Muslim haters, became the loudest voices from the Dutch Liberal Party to denounce Islam after the tragic events of September 11, 2001. They espouse and advocate for the clash of civilization theory and the demonization of Islam and Muslims in their midst and worldwide.

The substance of the book is based on updated revision of the author's doctoral dissertation in the field of criminology from the University of Rotterdam, and the Netherlands. In her dissertation, she aimed to compare orthodox, radical, and extremist groups regarding attitudes, motives, reasons, and behavior, with Islamic fundamentalism. The study uses qualitative research and interviews with orthodox, fundamentalist, and radical Muslims in Europe. In the author's attempt to explore the drift or the "clash of civilization" between Dutch Muslim fundamentalists and their fellow non-Muslim countrymen, she investigates the differences in beliefs and practices and how they develop overtime, and whether they are in favor of violence, and what attracts Dutch young people to convert to Islam and especially radical Muslim fundamentalism? Geelhoed attempted to answer two main research questions: 1. how does the development of Dutch Muslims who turn to Islamic fundamentalism take place, and 2. what are the reasons for and motives of these Muslims to get involved in Islamic fundamentalism?

The theoretical framework of the study contributes to understanding the attraction of Islamic fundamentalism to individuals from Muslim families and converts. In conducting her study, the author uses criminological approach and interview technique with a number of young converts, and to answer the question "why they join [ISIS] and commit heinous atrocities against other innocent Muslims such as beheadings, and mass killings?" The author found that Dutch Muslim fundamentalists are not as "other" as is commonly assumed. The author's research demonstrates that Islamic fundamentalism among Dutch and other Western Muslims is to a large extent a Western phenomenon that has global roots. The author pays special attention to how young Muslims, and in particular, young European converts to Islam have been attracted to extremists and violent groups like ISIS.

By interviewing some of these young Muslim men and women, the author attempts to identify what drives these fighters and points to possible remedies as well as to counterproductive measures. Furthermore, the book emphasizes the need for a nuanced approach and cautioned against wrongfully labeling Muslim young people as *jihadis*. She further elaborates on Islamic fundamentalists' view in the Netherlands, by presenting findings from other research and compare such to the practice of the respondents, and distinguishes between moderate, orthodox, radical, and extremist views (Ch. 2). In Chapter three the author shows how the religious development of the respondents has taken place and thus explores issues of identity crisis and strain as well as the role of significant others, and the reasons and motives for the respondents to turn to the various fundamentalist views. Chapters 4 and 5 address the appeal of fundamentalist discourses of self-identification and resistance. Thus, collectively, the chapters deal with the question about what fundamentalist discourses have to offer to the respondents with their cognitive opening. In Chapter 6, the author reflects on fundamentalists' views, which some may find attractive, and on how the respondents internalize and express their Muslim identity, while Chapter 7 evaluates the lessons of the previous chapters and places the findings in the broader social context, and finally presents the findings in the broader social context, and the theoretical framework of the study. ***MMA***

The Oxford Handbook of European Islam

Jocelyne Cesari, Ed. Oxford, UK: Oxford University Press, 2016. 869 pp. ISBN: 978-0198779322. ISBN: 978-0199607976.

This book is essential reading for all those interested in Islam and Muslims in Europe. Written by twenty-five impressively knowledgeable contributors, including the editor, it is divided into five parts. Part I (with five chapters) deals with Islam as a postcolonial, post-second world war religion in Europe; Part II (with four chapters) deals with the arrival of Islam in Europe as a post-1974 migration of Muslims; Part III (with four chapters) is a consideration of the old, historical lands of Islam in Europe; Part IV (with three chapters) studies Islam and Muslims in the influential presence of European secularism and modernity; and Part V (with two chapters and a Conclusion) presents Islam and European politics. Each of the chapters has a distinctly large and multi-language bibliography of many pages that is, indeed, a very helpful resource to scholars needing further research.

Not that Islam was unknown in Europe in earlier times, for Europe experienced the very rise of Islam and its expansion from Arabia across North Africa into Spain in the eighth century, and it sustained the expansion of the Ottomans in the sixteenth century into Eastern Europe, resulting in the continuing presence of Muslims in the Balkans — Albania, Bosnia, and Herzegovina — and in Bulgaria and Russia. These facts are detailed in Part III of the book. However, the more engaging presence of Islam in Western Europe today is mostly the outgrowth of earlier European colonization of parts of the Muslim world, and the result of Muslim migration into Europe after World War II and after 1974, as explained in Parts II and IV of the book.

How these Muslims were received in Europe by Europeans and how they reacted to European culture and life conditions is, I think, the most important contribution of this book. Islamophobia, on the part of some Europeans, and reluctant integration, on the part of some Muslims, played into the hands of European politicians and lawmakers as well as into those of Muslim leaders in Europe. There is no doubt that Europe has changed with the presence of Muslims in it, and that Muslims have changed after they came to live in Europe. Moreover, this book is a good record of this change, and a good presentiment of things to come. *IJB*

NORTH AFRICA

Algeria

The Battle for Algeria. Sovereignty, Health Care, and Humanitarianism

Jennifer Johnson. Philadelphia, PA: University of Pennsylvania Press, 2016. 288 pp. ISBN: 978-0812247718.

The Algerian war for independence (1954 – 1962) has long provided scholarly fodder across a wide range of perspectives — military, political, social, economic, and diplomatic, to note only a few recurrent approaches. Jennifer Johnson's strategy for this volume was to comb Algerian and International Committee of the Red Cross (ICRC) archival sources and related materials, such as interviews with participants in the events described, in the belief that few such assets have yet received the attention they merit. To provide a fresh vantage point, she situates her work within the burgeoning field of decolonization studies, laying out a thesis that the conflict between France and the FLN was, above all, a contest over which side could best ensure the health, welfare, and prosperity of the Algerian people, both then and into the future. To put this another way, which party to the conflict had the more convincing claim to sovereignty over Algeria and how did it go about asserting that claim domestically and globally?

Five substantive chapters address these questions. The first focuses on the concerted French efforts, beginning in 1955, to win the "hearts and minds" of Algerians through the dispatch of Sections Administratives Spécialisées (SAS) teams attached to the French military and civilian governmental apparatus, ostensibly to offer basic care and preventive medicine information to the historically underserved Algerian populace, but whose members often also carried out the more insidious work of espionage and sabotage.

An essentially parallel chapter discusses an FLN countermeasure to the SAS — the recruitment and training its own medical teams of nationalist sympathizers, often drawn from male and female Algerian students in French universities or from allies supportive of the Algerian cause. It makes an especially important contribution to understanding how Algerians furthered, in ways not strictly political or military (but related to both) their own liberation and the sovereignty expected to flow from it.

Another chapter recounts the savvy decision by the national leadership to create the Algerian Croissant Rouge (Red Crescent) organization to solicit contributions and assistance in the dissemination of humanitarian relief inside Algeria and in neighboring countries for refugees, displaced persons, and other victims of the fighting in the face of the French-managed Algerian Red Cross' reluctance to adopt a position that would have, at the very least, created tensions with the Paris government, whose support was indispensable to its work.

Its Geneva-based parent organization, the ICRC, however, involved itself in the Algerian situation early on and, despite numerous stumbling blocks and frustrations peculiar to a colonial war and which necessitated even more delicate maneuvering than it had mastered in its work in more conventional settings over previous decades, stayed with it to the end. Johnson's chapter on this topic is the most informative, innovative, and strongest in the book. Moreover, it hints at changes then looming on the horizon for the operations of international humanitarian agencies in the post-colonial world, where conflicts like the Algerian one would become the rule rather than the exception, raising fraught questions regarding whether these were strictly internal affairs that could be shielded from outsiders' interference or were of legitimate global concern. How the principles eventually resolved these questions in Algeria influenced humanitarianism in many subsequent conflicts in Africa, Asia, and the Americas for years after the Algerian war.

The *Battle for Algeria's* final chapter recounts the persistent and skillful endeavors of the FLN to place the Algerian question on the United Nations agenda in the hope of gaining allies and pressuring France — a tactic its adversary on the battlefield fought tooth and nail. Algerian lobbying at the UN often overlapped similar (and similarly futile) efforts by Moroccan and Tunisian agents, many of which have been described at length. It would have been interesting to expand this discussion with a brief comparison among those campaigns to understand why each was successful.

An irritating, if admittedly minor, weakness throughout the book is the author's tendency to provide cursory, and sometimes slapdash, treatment of matters that fall outside her primary research concerns, but which she rightly mentions as important to the overall narrative. For example, in her background chapter on "The Long Road to War" (p.23), she mentions, among other political factions, the ulama (Algerian Association of the Ulama) without explaining who they were, why they mattered, or what role they played.

The group is peripheral to her story, but not to broader Algerian history and if mentioned, it needs to be contextualized. When she describes the nineteenth century medical work of French military officers (pp. 42-44), she too willingly accepts at face value French claims of selfless humanitarian service that are often belied by the facts.

Another example of cavalier treatment accorded to important material is the extremely weak account of the 1956 Suez Crisis (p. 174). These examples suggest the sacrifice, albeit probably not with any malicious intent, of helpful background material to foreground the author's own work. Indeed, the high quality of Professor Johnson's research and writing is not undermined by this foible, although the impression it can give might better be avoided in future work – which there is certain to be, since this first effort is a significant monograph from a promising young scholar. *KJP*

Egypt

A Coptic Narrative in Egypt: A Biography of the Boutros-Ghali Family

Youssef Boutros-Ghali. New York, NY: I.B. Tauris, 2016. 256 pp. ISBN: 978-1780769394.

Egyptian Christians — Egypt's largest non-Muslim community — have been experiencing an upsurge in attacks since 2011, which in turn had threatened the stability of post-Uprising Egypt. Consequently, it is more important than ever to highlight that Christians are an indigenous and integral part of the Egyptian nation and its heritage that must be fully incorporated into its future (see Tadros, 2013). Ghali's book does this by offering a rich archive of photographs and documents that vividly illustrate the lives of five generations of the Boutros Ghali family and how they are intertwined with the history of Egypt. The Boutros Ghali family is perhaps the most notable Coptic Christian family in Egypt, having provided a number of political figures that have been prominent not only in Egypt but also internationally. The most famous example is perhaps Dr Boutros Youssef Boutros Ghali, Secretary General of the United Nations between 1992 and 1996. The editor of this book, Youssef Raouf Boutros Ghali, was himself Egyptian Minister of Finance from 2004 until January 2011 and was elected to the Chair of the International Monetary and Financial Committee in 2008.

The Coptic Orthodox Church in Egypt represents the largest Christian community in the Middle East, but its defining feature is that it is a national Egyptian church and its history has been intertwined with the Egyptian nation. Indeed, the narrative that runs through this book highlights the point made by studies of Coptic politics, that the interests of Copts are inextricably linked to the interests of Egypt. It also shows that Copts have been pivotal to the formation of Egypt and that 'Coptic-ness' should not be understood as mutually exclusive with 'Egyptian-ness' (see Iskander, 2012a). After all, Copt — a corruption of the Greek world Aigyptos — historically simply meant Egyptian before it gained the explicit meaning of being an Egyptian Christian.

The book begins with the patriarch of the family, Boutros Pasha Ghali. He started out as a teacher, but quickly rose up through a series of government appointments to become Minister of Finance in 1893. He played a pivotal role in the development of Egypt's judicial system and was a prominent figure in negotiating many of the most pressing political issues of the time, from the Orabi revolt of 1881-82 to the question of the status of Sudan. In 1908, he became not only the first Coptic Prime Minister of Egypt, but also the first Egyptian one, so his appointment was doubly symbolic. His subsequent assassination in 1910 illustrated the tensions that would shape the trajectories of Egypt's national identity in the early twentieth century. Although his assassination was mainly a protest against cooperation with the British occupier, it also took on sectarian overtones as Egypt grappled with how to incorporate its diverse religious and cultural heritage into its national character while calling for independence and self-rule. This was made more complex because of being under the protectorate of a foreign 'Christian' power. Although Egyptian Christians complained that Muslims were favored over them, still the supposed religious affinity between Egyptian Christians and the British meant that suspicions regarding Coptic loyalties could be easily mobilized.

In fact, despite the official narratives of both church and state regarding national unity and the inseparability of Muslims and Christians as elements of the Egyptian national fabric, tensions and suspicions between individuals or communities in Egypt regularly take on a sectarian character (Iskander, 2012b). Since 2011, there is the added element of transnational terrorism, due to the penetration of Islamic State (IS) affiliates, tactics, and theology that puts Egypt's national unity under further pressure. For example, in December 2016, a bomb attack on the Boutrosiya Church, situated immediately next to the Coptic Cathedral at Abbasiya in Cairo, killed 29 and was claimed by IS. The Boutrosiya Church was built by the Boutros Ghali family in 1912 and contains the family crypt, as described in detail in the final chapter of this book.

While several of the Boutros Ghali family are well known in Egypt and internationally, other figures are less so and yet, they also played an influential role in the national life of Egypt. One such is Wassif Pasha Boutros Ghali, the second son of Boutros Pasha Ghali. He also entered politics and became one of the Egyptian delegates at the Paris Peace Conference in 1919, having been a strong advocate of Egyptian unity and independence, even in the aftermath of the assassination of his father, Boutros Pasha Ghali. He continued to be involved in politics at a sensitive time during which Egypt became officially, though not fully in reality, independent from the British and also during the drafting of Egypt's constitution of 1923. He was named Foreign Minister in 1924 and his tenure in this position spanned five Wafd governments, as well as many crucial incidents in Egypt's post-independence period and in the build-up to the promulgation of the Anglo-Egyptian Treaty of 1936.

As a result of the breakdown of the Wafd party through which so many Copts rose to political prominence in the first half of the twentieth century, in addition to the political climate introduced as a consequence of the Free Officer's Revolution, 1952 marks a temporary break between national Egyptian political life and the Boutros Ghali family. Wassif Pasha definitively resigned from the political realm and the next generation followed suit. Merrit Bey Naguib Boutros Ghali, grandson of Boutros Pasha Ghali, had been a diplomat and briefly held office as Minister of State for Municipal and Rural Affairs, but after 1952, he focused his energies on archaeological and charitable works. For him, studying Coptology was "a basis for understanding Egyptian history" (p. 127). He was also instrumental in negotiating relations between the Egyptian and Ethiopian churches. The Ethiopian Orthodox church had been under the authority of the Egyptian Orthodox church historically, leading to some disputes particularly regarding the appointment of clergy. The Ethiopian Church was eventually granted independence in 1959 and accorded its own Patriarch. Merrit was closely involved in negotiating this.

The appointment of Boutros Youssef Boutros Ghali as Foreign Minister in 1977 marked a return of the Boutros Pasha Ghali family to high political office. He took up the post reluctantly (p.153), aware of the complexities that awaited with the Egyptian-Israeli peace talks that were to unfold immediately after his appointment. It was another momentous period in Egyptian history and another member of the Boutros Ghali family would be instrumental in it. He remained in this post until 1991 and then on January 1, 1992 he officially became the sixth Secretary General of the UN, elevating the Boutros Ghali Pasha family to the international stage.

While this book is not a critical academic study of Coptic politics or history, it is a wonderful resource for scholars who are working on these topics. It would be particularly useful for those seeking to understand the interconnections between Coptic and Egyptian identity, and it also brings to life many of the processes and events that have shaped the modern history of Egypt in general. This book cleverly tells the story of modern Egypt through the eyes of this influential family. As such, it is a delightfully accessible survey of Egypt's modern history, not only from a Coptic perspective, but from the perspective of an Egyptian family with generations of experience in shaping the politics of the nation. *EM*

References

Iskander, E. (2012a). *Sectarian Conflict in Egypt: Coptic Media, Identity and Representation*. Abingdon, Oxon: Routledge.

Iskander, E. (2012b). The 'mediation' of Muslim–Christian relations in Egypt: the strategies and discourses of the official Egyptian press during Mubarak's presidency. *Islam and Christian-Muslim Relations*. Vol.23 No.1, pp. 31-44.

Tadros, M. (2013). *Copts at the Crossroads: The Challenges of Building Inclusive Democracy in Egypt*, Cairo: AUC Press.

Nassar's Blessed Movement: Egypt's Free Officers and the July Revolution

Joel Gordon. Cairo, EG: The American University in Cairo Press, 2016. 280 pp. ISBN: 978-9774167782.

This is a particularly intense history of Egypt's revolution conducted by a group of army officers in July 1952. This is an updated version of the study conducted by the author now with the perspective of a post 9/11 observation position and the availability of newly released archival materials. We know the military officers took over from the Egyptian pasha elite and the parliamentary system without understanding the unintended consequences of the political forces essential in the governing process. This is the work of a political and cultural historian of modern Egypt at the University of Arkansas, well versed in modern and contemporary Egyptian history. It is not necessarily a biographical analysis of Gamal Abdel Nasser, but delves far deeper into the intricacies of the governing processes in Egypt following the coup d'etat. Although this is a historical treatment of a momentous period in modern Egypt, it is a real contribution to comparative politics, especially to help in understanding civil-military relations. In any case, there is a full focus on the role of Nasser as he led Egypt toward becoming a leading member of the Non-Aligned Movement. While Nasser was the *eminence grise,* there is a screaming need for a political biography of the revolution's front man and first president of Egypt, Mohamed Neguib. This is an essential addition to any Middle East collection. **SRS**

The Politics of Female Circumcision in Egypt: Gender, Sexuality and the Construction of Identity

Maria Frederika Malmström. New York, NY: I.B. Tauris, 256 pp. ISBN: 978-1784531577.

Few topics strike at the heart of the Western psyche as does the subject of this monograph. It, like "honor killings" and similar practices found predominantly (though certainly not solely) in the Muslim world, is offered today by media and politicians alike as but further evidence of the extent to which the Clash of Civilizations between the developed nations and the traditional East continues unabated.

Malstrom's work is a beautifully crafted corrective to just such contentions. Her style and approach is engaging; her narratives seem to bring the reader into the discussion, offering access to the views of women which, quite clearly, few of us might encounter on our own. And were we to, our conversations would not likely take us where Malstrom seeks to go.

In short, this work enters realms very rarely touched upon by modern scholars. In part, this is due to the fact that most buy into the "Western interventionist discourse" (pp. 2, 191) when it comes to this very sensitive topic; that is, female circumcision is "mutilation," a primitive affront to women's right which must be stopped at all costs.

Refreshingly, Malstrom avoids this tack. Rather, she interrogates the issue from an entirely different perspective, names that of those who have undergone the procedure. She seeks here to better understand how and why this practice persists, and what it means not to those who wish to attack it, but rather, those who embrace and perpetuate it.

Her findings are profound and are respectfully narrated here. Influences on what is obviously a very private, personal practice are reflected, she contends, are not only local, but are found at the political and economic levels. She suggests that aspects of Egyptian identity that can be traced directly to the national level have their roots in family relations — including, control over women's reproductive organs (pp. 56-57).

Just as Westernism and modernization might be conflated if not misconstrued as one and the same thing, so too might these, in turn, be seen as forces which act concomitant with colonialist or orientalist mentalities. Thus, Malstrom seeks here to "give a nuanced picture of Egyptian women living [in] lower income areas, specifically in relation to Islam, sexuality, gender and agency against a background of growing mistrust in the West of Islam and its values" (p. 68). In other words, an attack on the practices of the body and the body politic is difficult if not impossible to distinguish. Cairo is the *Mother of the World* after all. Her body is hers alone, not open to the Western judgement or gaze.

Perhaps the most sensitive and gentle discussion in the entire volume is to be found in Chapter 3. Here, Malstrom gives voice to Egyptian women, young and old, who describe the role of circumcision in their marriages and sexual lives. They offer open discussion of their feelings and experiences in incredible detail. The chapter is written beautifully, with an understanding of both subject and reader sensibilities which I found admirable. The material is rich; rarely do I recall reading such detailed personal material (which I know is difficult to access) in such a respectful, open, yet uncensored manner.

The book's strengths do not stop here. I also found the discussion of the "hygiene narrative," (p.182) of particular interest. Purity, cleanliness, femininity, and control of the body/self are all interwoven here along with female circumcision, presenting a picture marked by remarkable complexity. Such issues have been addressed within a robust literature which far surpasses the black/white, right/wrong mindset so often utilized by feminists, human rights organizations, and the media (p.27).

It is for this reason that the volume concludes where it must. For if scholars are to understand others they must begin with the concept of agency. To assume everyone (women, minorities) is a victim of external powers is, in fact, to remove further the agency that those actors actually do hold. The women of Egypt are actors in their own lives, not passive receptacles or victims of circumstance (p.206). The sooner we in the West realize that not everyone needs saving, the better off we'll all be. **SCD**

Sinai: Egypt's Linchpin, Gaza's Lifeline, Israel's Nightmare

Mohannad Sabry. Cairo, EG: The American University in Cairo Press, 2015. 240 pp. ISBN: 978-9774167287.

This is not a typical political science or international relation book. It is a book written based on the author's extensive interviews spanning three and half years, trying to shed light on the situation of Sinai from various perspectives (see below for details), because he thinks that "in Sinai's conservative tribal community — whose history of oppression and ever-deteriorating relations with the state is coupled with a severe lack of trust in any form of media — it became clear that the most effective method for research was long, unstructured interviews and informal talks" (p. x). The book is filled with worry and pessimism typical of a good journalist. The title of the book hinted the same. The introduction reinforced the notion: "Over his thirty years in power, Mubarak succeeded in equating the Sinai Peninsula, in the minds of Egyptians and the majority of the world for that matter, to the southern beach resorts reserved mainly for foreign tourists; the cliché of the 1973 'victory' against Israel; and a lifeless desert inhabited by Bedouin outlaws and traffickers" (p. viii).

Other than the fact that "Many of the people interviewed for this book have had their names changed to protect their identities" (p. xi), the book reads like a multi-scene play with extensive notes by the playwright inserted liberally into wherever is necessary, notes based on reality and facts well researched. This is the author's first book effort, yet indeed an outstanding effort. The research and composition took the author as much as three and a half years. Under constant threat despite Mubarak's downfall, starting from 2011, the author "met, interviewed, and traveled and lived with more than 150 people from the northern, central, and southern parts of the Sinai Peninsula." He conducted face to face as well as phone and Internet "interviews in the Gaza Strip, met with Palestinian sources, including Hamas and Fatah officials, in al-Arish and Cairo, and traveled to Jerusalem and Tel Aviv to conduct interviews with government officials, media figures, and various intellectuals and experts on Israeli foreign policy and Egyptian-Israeli relations" (p. x).

The author was able to dissect the events from two perspectives, his native Egyptian one and the neighboring Israeli one. This makes the book balanced and worth reading as a high quality journalistic piece. The following is an attempt to pull from each of the ten chapters a snippet or two that has caught this reviewer's attention, but not necessarily a summary of the chapter, in order not to spoil the future readers' pique of interest.

The first chapter starts with the scene of the dramatic eruption of the Egyptian version of Arab Spring while zooming in to Sinai. Besides location by location details and person to person reactions, the author ended the chapter with Israel's reaction to the eruption and downfall of Mubarak. "Mubarak's dear friend in Jerusalem, Benjamin Ben Eliezer, Israel's former deputy prime minister and member of the Knesset, broke down in tears fearing that it might be the end for the peace with Egypt, a fear deemed legitimate by dozens of Israeli politicians and military men" (p. 30).

The second chapter covers a topic which showed up more regularly in general media covering Israel, i.e., the bombing of the gas pipeline that transports natural gas from Egypt to Israel. Due to the connection between Mubarak's ruling elite and the gas deal with Israel, when Mubarak resigned, Egyptian military establishment's attitude was ambiguous at best, eventually, they decide to "stand down and watch Israel look for alternatives to Egypt's cheap natural gas" (p. 48).

The third chapter gives the ins and outs of Sinai's role in smuggling weapons from the African continent to Hamas in Gaza. The November 2012 war between Israel and Hamas, known as Operation Pillar of Defense, was a vivid example of the rising military capabilities of Hamas. During this war, the first Iranian Fajr-5 rocket was fired at Israel, with a seventy-five-kilometer range rocket and a ninety-kilogram warhead, putting Tel Aviv for the first time ever within reach of Gazan attacks.

The fourth chapter tells the history of the development of the smuggling tunnels in Sinai, and how, as a consequence, the Gaza elements and Egyptians interact, despite the effort by both the Israelis and the US to block these tunnels.

The fifth chapter is on the law and order of the peninsula being maintained by the Shari'a laws and tribal courts. The already weak state legal system in the peninsula almost collapsed completely after Mubarak resigned.

Chapter 6 is the longest of all chapters, which described the rising and prospering of the Islamist militants in the peninsula, due to the power vacuum created by the Egyptian revolution, as well as by surrounding influences such as the Gaza Jihadists and the Muslim Brotherhood. This chapter is essential reading for scholars studying the Islamist militant movement in the region.

Chapter 7 is a detailed account of the Rafah massacre and how the Egyptian soldiers were under attack.

Chapter 8 looks at the battle between the Muslim Brotherhood leader, then president Morsi and the Army general al-Sisi through the lens of Sinai. In some sense, Morsi lost the support of the Bedouin tribes of Sinai because he never fulfilled his promise to them allowing landownership and pardoning hundreds of unjustly sentenced Bedouins.

Chapter 9 gives the reader the background of the rise of terrorism in Egypt and Sinai due to Morsi's ouster, "the military's move against the Muslim Brotherhood regime saved the country from plunging into civil strife but wasn't just a spontaneous intervention in defense of the people… it was rather a calculated plan to seize power." The rise of terrorism and consequently the cracking down needed surely helped al-Sisi to gain the presidency.

The last chapter is an account of al-Sisi's ascendency to presidency, yet the author was pessimistic by ending the book in the following statement: "Today, al-Sisi's regime is capable of ruling only as long as it maintains the iron-grip imposed by its tanks, Apache gunships, and the random fire of its AK-47s. Its only accomplishment is failing to plan to what will happen when the iron-grip loosens, and soon or later, in a country torn apart by polarization and an ailing economy, the grip will loosen" (p. 241).

This reviewer begs to differ from the author's pessimism though. Albeit the country is polarized, but the extent of the polarization is far less challenging than many of Egypt's neighbors. Sinai is the world to the author's eye, but in reality, it is only, as the author said in his book title, "Egypt's linchpin", Gaza's lifeline? Maybe but also maybe not. But Israel's nightmare? I seriously doubt that there are still that many Israelis still take this view at this stage of development of the Arab Spring in Egypt. The author might have encountered too many worried Israelis at the most worrying stage when the events unraveling while he conducted his interviews in Jerusalem and Tel Aviv. Today, after most of the dust has settled down, especially for Egypt, Israelis might be much more confident in coping with the situation on the peninsula.

Meanwhile, president al-Sisi's effort in rejuvenating the Egyptian economy, trying to solicit help from around the world, including China, is apparently genuine. If he is successful, the Arab world and beyond sure hope so, the bettering Egyptian economy will lead to a more united Egypt. This could be the solution to many of the Egyptian internal issues, including those in Sinai.

The book has a very useful chronology (pp. xvii-xxiv) that starts on June 5, 1967 when the Six Day War began, ends on June 3, 2014, when Abdel-Fatah al-Sisi was voted president of Egypt, with the period after January 25, 2011, when the revolution erupted across Egypt, in much more granulated fashion. The book has one map in grayscale covering the Sinai region. At the end of the book, besides endnotes to each chapter, there is a list of sources, which provides profiles of the key individuals interviewed by the author for the book. There are 37 profiles in total. The profiles are followed by a sizable bibliography and an index. *YC*

Tunisia

"Tunisia's Glorious Revolution" In Arabic

Azmi Bishara. Beirut, LB: Arab Center for Research and Policy Studies, 2015. 496 pp. ISBN: 978-9954028231.

The question here is why did Tunisia have a successful and smooth path toward the democratic process, whereas others like Egypt, Libya, and Yemen failed to go through the same transition?

This book provides us with firsthand account into the "Tunisian revolution" story, with extensive interviews with the activists and opposition leaders who played a role in the revolution, then try to discuss and debate the different factors who played to make this story a success one comparing to what's happened in all other "Arab spring" countries.

Bishara made his name during the "Arab Spring" as a strong advocate for the need for a Democracy in the Arab region despite the turmoil the region is going through; he was also the most productive writer about the social, economic, and political changes occurred in the Arab World during "the Arab Revolutions." He wrote at least six books about these revolutions as he prefers to call it — his most recent book Egypt's *Revolution* appeared in two volumes, provided a detailed account of the social and political changes that led to the Egyptian Revolution in 2011, then the decisions of the Egyptian army which led to the military coup in 2014 to overthrow the democratically elected President Mohamad Morsi.

His other books on "the Arab Revolutions" including his book, *Syria: The Pain Road of the Struggle for Freedom* considered as the most knowledgeable books in the subject where he relied on extensive research and tens of interviews with first hand activists who initiated the peaceful protests in Tunisia in 2010, and then, in Syria 2011.

In his book, *About the Revolution and The Need for a Revolution* (2011) tried to provide a theoretical link between the "Arab revolutions" and Democracy and why there is a need for a deeper understanding of the radical protests erupted in the Arab World after 2011.

In this book, Bishara put the emphasis on the Tunisian elites, and their role in the transition. Following the revolution in 2011 the Tunisian elites engaged in what is called "constituent negotiations" to build the face of the new political system. Given the weakness and the fragmentation of the political opposition, which is due to its subjection to 23 years of suppression, the challenges of the debate here will be tough because of the lack of negotiating entities. This current situation in Tunisia is like what occurred in Eastern Europe, a situation that experienced fragile public opinion and the absence of a political or civil entity that had the potential to build the new regime.

Of course, Tunisia benefited from having a strong middle-class, multieconomic resources, the fact that its economy is not dependent on natural resources (considered nonexistent compared to the neighboring countries such as Algeria and Libya), its strong civil society, and the society culture. Those factors would help greatly with stabilizing the democratic process.

The second factor was the role of the army or security services, which was crucial. In Tunisia, the army played the role of professional army which would not intervene in politics or to act against the will of the protesters; but in all other cases, the army and the intelligence remained loyal to the previous regime against the new incoming groups which played a critical role in turning the transition into an armed conflict or even civil war or back to the military role like the case in Egypt.

The third factor was the success of the elites to build a national coalition for the transition which acted as the boat that saved Tunisia during the troubles around Tunisia on the regional level and domestic level. Although this coalition was built on the consciences among the Islamists and secularists which made everyone happy and played a role, such consciences were absent in all other cases like Egypt, Yemen, and Syria.

The Tunisian revolution, in my opinion, represents an additional proof of Lipset's theory that associates the democratic change with the growth or development of the middle-class and civil society through economic development. Lipset has studied the democratic transition in South Korea as proof of his theory which was experienced by the students' demonstration in 1988 which led eventually to a stable democratic transition in South Korea after a series of coups and military rule that lasted between the 1950s and the 1980s. The educational and economic development statistics in Tunisia in 2011 is almost the same as South Korea in 1988.

Lipset was the first to note what he called the mutual positive relation between the economic development and democracy, according to his words "The better the nation was, the stronger the changes of supporting the Democracy are." He proved that democracies in general have stronger economic development than non-democracies.

Democracy, as he explains, will ultimately follow economic development, specifically when the income rate reaches the medium rate which will strengthen the structure of the middle class. This, in turn, will make the number of the citizens with high cultural value demands to be involved politically higher. Accordingly, a successful democratic change can be achieved, which he has managed to prove in some of the previously authoritarian states that have managed to reach the medium level of income such as Spain, Portugal in the 1970s, and later South Korea.

We can add here that the Tunisian society is in harmony religiously and ethnically, maybe there is some social diversity because of the growing gap between the ruling authoritarian elite, in addition to the majority not feeling the benefits of the revenue growth that Tunisia achieved in the last two decades under the former president Ben Ali; however, the Tunisian individual's average income is roughly the highest among the Arab countries in North Africa, which is the most significant difference between Tunisia and the other previously mentioned Arab countries that suffer an extremely high rate of poverty and illiteracy. There won't be any future democratic government that would have the capacity to solve the social and economic problems at the speed desired by the protesters who want to repeat the revolution in their countries. **RZ**

OMAN

The Bronze Age Towers at Bat, Sultanate of Oman: Research by the Bat Archaeological Project 2007-12

Christopher P. Thornton, Charlotte M. Cable, & Gregory L. Possehl, Eds. Philadelphia, PA: University of Pennsylvania Press/University of Pennsylvania Museum of Archaeology and Anthropology, 2016. 330 pp. ISBN: 978:1934-536063.

As the title states, this book is a report of the archaeological work conducted by an international team led by the University of Pennsylvania during six seasons (2007-2012) at Bat in north-central Oman. Bat, the first pre-historic site in Arabia to become a UNESCO World Heritage Site, is the best-preserved Bronze Age (3rd millennium BCE) settlement in Magan, the name given to southeastern Arabia in ancient Mesopotamian texts. The work covers the three major Bronze Age periods in Magan: Hafit (3100-2800 BCE), Umm an-Nar (2800-2000 BCE), and Wadi Suq (2000-1600 BCE). This period is characterized as witnessing "the emergence of a new socioeconomic system in which independent states became reliant, if not entirely dependent, upon other states for the maintenance of their elaborate social, cultural, and religious behavior... that eventually collapsed around 2000 BCE due to environmental, demographic, and sociopolitical factors..." (p. 1). The team's specific goal was to determine the how, when, and why of the construction of Bat's distinctive towers while adding to the understanding of the social, political, and economic conditions underlying Magan's relations with Mesopotamia, Dilmun (Eastern Arabia), and Meluhha/Harappa (the Indus Valley). The report begins with a geo-archaeological study of the site, focusing on water management and agricultural practices. The next six chapters focus on Bat's towers with detailed reports on Kasr al-Khafaji (Tower 1146), Matariya (Tower 1147), Kasr al-Sleme (Tower 1148), Tower 1156, preliminary discussion of two structures in the neighboring town of Ad-Dariz, and an overview of the five remaining towers (Kasr al-Rojoom, Husn al-Wardi, al-Qa'a, al-Khutum, and Wahrah Qala) in Bat. In presenting their findings, the authors also draw on previous, largely unpublished, archaeological work, most notably that conducted by Karen Frifelt during the 1970s and 1980s. The authors then examine the ceramics, chipped stone pieces, metal and metallurgical artifacts, and ground stone artifacts. Five appendices present information on archaeo-botanical studies, ancient water systems, Bronze Age mud bricks, radiocarbon dates, further information relative to two Wadi Suq Period tombs at Tower 1156, and a list of the field staff.

While determining the how and when of tower construction is relatively easy, the why remains elusive. All have in common an early period of mudbrick construction, usually associated with a well, during the Hafit Period, followed by the construction of a stone tower during the Umm an-Nar Period, and then a period of decline when the towers became the source of building materials for smaller Wadi Suq period grave structures. However, due in large part to their modification and re-use throughout the thousand years under consideration, their function, be it ritual, water management, or defense, is very difficult to establish. As the authors admit, they were unsuccessful in determining the exact function of the towers and "may never know precisely what the Bronze Age towers of Bat were used for" (p. 260).

What the archaeological evidence does serve to establish is Magan's interdependence with Mesopotamia and the Indus Valley and the overall decline of the region during the Bronze Age. Pottery artifacts provide evidence for both cultural and stimulus diffusion with imported wares from Mesopotamia, Iran, and the Indus Valley, followed by locally produced imitations, and then entirely local styles. Metal and metallurgical artifacts also serve to confirm Oman's importance as a source of copper for the southwest Asian region. What makes this evidence especially important is that, unlike other Bronze Age sites on the coasts of Oman and the United Arab Emirates, Bat is well inland and so demonstrates that commercial contacts existed well beyond the maritime realm. Finally, the geo-archaeological and ancient water system studies indicate steady aridification throughout the Bronze Age and a shift in water management practices from controlling excess surface water to increased dependence on irrigation.

Despite the failure to establish the function of the Bat towers, the publication of these results greatly expands our understanding of Bronze Age Oman and its world. Work continues at the site, and the preliminary data from the archaeo-botanical survey and mud brick studies provide fascinating glimpses into agricultural production and domestic life. *The Bronze Age Towers at Bat, Sultanate of Oman,* is a most welcomed addition to the literature on not just Oman but also to the broader Bronze Age period of globalization. **CHA**

OTTOMAN EMPIRE

Orphans and Destitute Children in the Late Ottoman Empire

Nazan Maksudyan. Syracruse, NY: Syracruse University Press. 264 pp. ISBN: 978-0815633181.

Orphans and Destitute Children in the Late Ottoman Empire, written by Nazan Maksudyan, sheds much needed light on the life and conditions of a "marginalized" marginal group: orphans, foster children, and destitute children. They are a "marginalized" marginal group because they are marginalized both by their society and by the discipline of history. Considering the paucity of these types of studies in the history of childhood, both in general and within the late Ottoman context in particular, this book accomplishes a significant job in bringing these children to life and making them more visible.

Nazan Maksudyan, the author of the book, is an assistant professor in the Department of Social Sciences at Istanbul Kemerburgaz University. She earned her PhD from Sabanci University and did her post-doctoral study at Zentrum Moderner Orient, Berlin. Her areas of interest include social, cultural, and economic history of children and youth in the late Ottoman Empire, as well as nationalism, urban history, women's history and gender studies. Her article "Being Saved to Serve: Armenian Orphans of 1894-96 and Interested Relief in Missionary Orphanages" appeared in *Turcica*42 in 2010, and "State 'Parenthood' and Vocational Orphanages (*Islâhhanes*): Transformation of Urbanity and Family Life" appeared in *The History of the Family*16 in 2011.

In the introduction, Maksudyan presents her critique of the mainstream approaches to the history of childhood and to children's studies, summarizes the general approaches of studies on Ottoman/Turkish children and childhood, and demonstrates her own approach to the same area. The introduction contains a literature review of children's history in the Ottoman Empire and in the Middle East, although this section could have been enriched had she included dissertations and theses as examples. Finally, the author presents her main argument, and sources that she utilized for this book. According to Maksudyan, within the discipline of history, wars, statesmen, and treaties have been prioritized by most historians, and children's history has not been "considered to have historical significance," (p. 2) and "children [have been] left out of the narrative" (p. 2). Undermining children's presence, experiences, and testimonies, therefore, causes them to be viewed as incapable of social action. For this reason, she criticizes several discourses: naturalist assumptions which ignore socially constructed relations, the perception of children as passive receptors, the perception of childhood as a period of dependency, overestimation of political significance in the discipline of history, and adultism in which children are not seen as complete and identifiable individuals.

Maksudyan also presents her critique of studies on specifically Ottoman/Turkish children and childhood. The author focuses her critique on two different themes in these studies: developmentalist approaches, which take childhood "as a period in the life-cycle" (p. 6), and discovery theory, which argues that there was no concept of childhood before modernity. By relying one of these two approaches, studies ignore another aspect of children's lives in the late Ottoman Empire — the worsening living conditions of children in modern times. Against the "adultist" approaches of dominant historiography, she, in this book, aims to "[go] beyond the rigid boundaries of importance" and "regard children as significant" (p. 4) because children's voices can be new sources for alternative history writing. Therefore, throughout the book, her main purpose is to demonstrate that children are social actors and informants, and to give voice to destitute and orphaned children in order to hear their own narrations of history.

Following the introduction, the book is divided into four chapters: The Politics of Child Abandonment, Private Negotiation of Child Fosterage, State Orphanages (Islahhanes), and the Internationalization of Orphans. The structure of the book, as Maksudyan writes, "is reminiscent of the nesting of Russian dolls" in reverse, because from the first chapter to the last, the organization flows from "the most inner/intimate sphere to the most global/international" (p. 15). In addition to giving voices to foster daughters, orphans, and destitute children through her historical approach, the chapters are also in dialog with different major fields including demographic studies, economic history, Ottoman feminist history, and diplomatic history. That makes the book useful, not only for scholars in history, but also for those who are from different disciplines. To support her main thesis and the interdisciplinary dialog, Maksudyan utilizes a broad variety of primary sources from different archives in Turkey, France, and the US, as well as yearbooks, compilations of regulations, local periodicals and memoirs, and some missionary periodicals, such as *The Missionary Herald*, *The Orient*, and *Les Missions Catholiques*.

In the first chapter, the author focuses on abandoned children and the institutionalization of foundlings. This chapter demonstrates the transformation of patterns of child abandonment in the empire-, religion- and ethnicity-based conflicts between state and non-Muslim communities, state-based and private efforts, state institutions, conditions and problems of abandoned children during the settlement process, and in the foundlings. However, the conclusions she reached that children "were victims of hospitalism" because they were "deprived of maternal attention during the first year of life" (p. 43), and that the "Ottoman Empire ignored the harmful effect of modern forms of care for the infants" (p. 44) seem somehow reductive and generalized and require more clarification.

The second part of the book is allocated to fostered children. Through fostered children Maksudyan shows how child labor was "intertwined with child raising" (p. 55), a point which presents the class aspect of this issue. Here, she gives wonderful insight into legal mechanisms vis-à-vis those children, patterns of adaptation, position and subordination of fostered children materially and legally, and problems they faced at the house they served, including sexual and physical violence. The problems they suffer caused them to resist through various means, including legal means, escape, suicide, or taking up refuge in other houses. However, her methodology of narrating their experiences through reading the legal cases, state documents and literature hampers our hearing their real voices.

The last two chapters before the conclusion focus on orphanages (ıslahhanes). In the third chapter, Maksudyan shows the state policies on orphanages, and their interaction with urban, economic, and ideological aspects of late Ottoman life. As she writes, urban reformers "stressed the exclusion of unattended children from the public sphere" (p. 85). Therefore, orphanages became important places to discipline and to impose Tanzimat values upon those children. Maksudyan also indicates how orphanages "were one of the state's new ventures to sustain and rejuvenate urban manufacturing" (p. 91) because these places turn idle and unattended children into productive workers through vocational training. The last chapter is mainly focused on the international level of the debate. She pays attention to the international diplomatic relations of the Ottoman Empire with other European powers and the US, and with the missionaries after the Armenian massacres of 1894-1896. She shows how the empire, other states, missionaries, and the Armenian patriarchate struggled to have control over the orphans after this massacre. The author gives comparative examples of the policies of the different missionary groups, the precautions of the empire (mostly preventive) to deal with the attempts of missionaries, and the position of the Armenian patriarchate during this process.

Throughout the book, Maksudyan presents a fascinating insight into the lives and conditions of fostered and destitute children and orphans. Her use of primary sources, her language, and writing style make the research more interesting and save it from the boredom of plain scientific and academic discourse. This book can be read by people who are outside of academia but interested in history. In almost every chapter, her narration was strengthened by the provision of historical background, comparing the main topic of the chapter with European counterparts, and examples from Ottoman literature. Tables, statistics, and illustrations used in the chapters facilitate the comprehension of the arguments very neatly and support them visually. Another good point related with the chapters is the wide spectrum of the debate which focuses, not only on orphans and destitute children, but also: relations between them and the state; intrainstitutional relations in the empire; relations of children, state, religious communities; missionaries with each other; and intersectional relations between different ethnicities, classes and sexes. In addition, Maksudyan also explicates how these children become significant actors in the institutionalization of welfare policies, in the economy, in internal and foreign relations, in intrareligious relations and in the transformation of legal systems and urban geography.

On the other hand, although she claims that "the original purpose of this study was to hear and see the children" (p. 164), the embeddedness of the book into the official, legal (court records), and missionary documents makes it hard to hear the children's own voices, experiences, or narrations. Related to this point, focusing mostly on institutions, state regulations, intracommunal conflicts, international relations, and intra-institutional relations, the book is far from showing children as historically active agents. Additionally, the author claims that children were assigned significant roles in the late Ottoman era and that in the same era, children-related concerns entered the agenda of the Ottoman intelligentsia and policymakers. This point seems to conflict with her criticism of the discovery of the childhood approach and developmentalist attitude in studies on Ottoman/Turkish children and childhood. In other words, she uses a discourse somewhat similar to that of the scholars whom she criticizes.

This criticism notwithstanding, overall, Nazan Maksudyan presents an amazing and well-researched book. It directs the readers to think about the current interactions between children and the state, and also about the contemporary perception of childhood. It achieves another good point by making orphans and destitute children visible in the writing of history, especially by representing these subaltern subjects through different types of sources. **AA**

War and Collapse: World War I and the Ottoman Empire

M. Hakan Yavuz, Feroz Ahmad, Ed. Salt Lake City, UT: The University of Utah Press, 2016. 1505 pp. ISBN: 978-1607814610.

A massive and encyclopedic treatment of the role of the Ottoman Empire in and its relationship to World War I. This is a collective effort resulting from a conference held at the University of Sarajevo in May 2012 and is the final component of a trilogy (following *War and Diplomacy*, 2011, edited by Peter Sluglett and M. Hakan Yavuz and *War and Nationalism*, 2013, edited by M. Hakan Yavuz and Isa Blumi). This work is segmented into seven sections with 53 reputably published scholars, each contributing an original interpretation to a wide array of subjects on levels from micro to macro.

White Christian, Western Europe, where diplomacy was created as an art, came off its high horse only in 1878 at the Congress of Berlin where the Ottoman Empire was accepted as a full negotiating partner, but only in doing so forcing it to accept autonomous Christian enclaves within which the Muslim populations were expelled.

In Part I, there is an examination of the factors that prompted Ottoman strategists to get involved in a grand European power play, sparked by Balkan nationalists. As World War II was an extension of World War I, for the Turks, World War I was an extension of the Balkan Wars. It was the decision by the Ottomans to align themselves with the Triple Alliance against the Entente Powers and the subsequent loss to the latter that spelled the dissolution of its empire and the artificial creation of a set of new states in the region in accordance with the winning forces' national interests.

Part II looks at the evolution of the Committee of Union and Progress (CUP) in how its political activities aided in establishing a secular Turkish national identity. Part III delves into state-society relations and how the Ottomans related to its many non-Muslim minority communities. Part IV represents a substantive section focusing on Armenian and Kurdish nationalist sentiments and their respective movements that ultimately brought about an ideological alliance between the Ottomans and the Russians. The ethnic and religious conflict between Christians and Muslims in the Balkans fills up Part V. While discussed substantively in other literature sources, the role of the Arabs in the eastern provinces is taken up in Part VI. Part VII contains a set of memoirs from observers on the scene in the last years of the Empire and a sort of coda on the effect World War I had on the breakdown of the historic and massive Ottoman Empire.

We learn a great deal on how, why, and what factors ultimately led to the dissolution of a major world power in the near and Middle East (assuming the geographical references established by western politicians). A comparative analysis of non-Muslim minorities and their relationship to the developing nationalist sentiment in the then emerging multi-layered complex found in the Empire. Light is brought to bear on a Turkish perspective to the Eastern Question and the Ottomans' brutal treatment of the Armenian community, which is not disputed, but put into context. The development of Kurdish nationalism interrupted, not only by Ottoman centralist policies, but also by Russian plans to expand its sphere of influence southward. A significant geographical component of the Empire was the Balkans, discussed with a host of actual and potential conflicts brewing in constant motion.

Perhaps one of the strongest contributions is the set of essays engaged in the historiographic debate on the Armenian Question, bringing to the fore the Ottoman Turkish policy of protecting the Empire's sovereignty from nationalist and irredentist elements, to include the Armenian community that sought support from the Russians in its quest for independence. The weakest component, it must be said, is the analysis of the conditions of World War I that set up what has emerged as the contemporary conflicts in today's "Middle East" within and between states artificially created by European diplomats out of the Ottoman Empire.

This is, undoubtedly, a major contribution to Ottoman studies historiography. It would have been useful to those unfamiliar with Ottoman studies to have included a collection of brief biographical statements introducing the contributors. **SRS**

POLITICS AND GOVERNMENT

America's Dream Palace: Middle East Expertise and the Rise of the National Security State

Osamah F. Khalil. Cambridge, MA: Harvard University Press, 2016. 440 pp. ISBN: 978-0674971578.

The legendary Thomas Edward Lawrence ("Lawrence of Arabia"), a British classical scholar, remarked in his *Seven Pillars of Wisdom* that he hoped to inspire a "dream-palace" of "national thoughts" for the Semitic people. In taking that cue from Lawrence, Osamah Khalil names his book *America's Dream Palace*. Alfred Mahan identified British imperial interest with West Asia and South Asia in referring to the region as the "Middle East." The Middle East became coterminous with cold war interest of the United States by the mid-twentieth century. The author claims that foreign policy doctrines of successive administrations since Harry Truman were "directly or indirectly related" to that region. Khalil argues that Middle East area studies were tied to United States vital national security interests. In particular, there was a venue shift over time from universities to think-tanks which aligned expertise and knowledge production with the United States' national security establishment. In taking a historical approach, the book is divided into eight chapters: "Missionary Knowledge," "World War II Expertise," "Overseas Universities," "Regional Studies Programs," "Modernization Framework," "Privatization of Knowledge," and "Hegemonic Limitations." Along with an introduction, there is an epilogue about the Arab Spring in lieu of a conclusion.

Missionaries and oil companies accounted for the two main sources of information about the Middle East before World War II. A secret attempt under the Woodrow Wilson Administration was the War Data Investigation Bureau with headquarters in the New York Public Library. It was renamed The Inquiry and relocated to offices of the American Geographical Society (AGS). Under the Franklin Roosevelt administration. The Inquiry was replaced by the Office of Coordination of Information, which was itself transformed into the Office of Strategic Services (OSS). In its war effort, the OSS turned to university campuses in establishing Research and Analysis (R&A)

Branch Centers for area studies and language training of military personnel. The R & A Branch was moved to the Department of State (DoS) amidst post-war security restructuring. The External Research Staff (ERS) was established within the DoS for coordinating the DoS, universities, foundations, and think-tanks. ERS took a two-way approach in sharing declassified information with universities, research libraries, and scholars.

Under Philip Hitti, the Near East Program at Princeton University became a pre-eminent Army Specialized Training Program (ASTP) Center that combined Arabic, Persian, and Turkish language training with area studies in the social sciences. Working together with the American Council of Learned Societies (ACLS) and the Social Science Research Council (SSRC), the Carnegie Corporation initially funded university-based area studies programs. The Rockefeller Foundation soon joined the efforts. The philanthropic foundations were followed by oil giants Arab-American Oil Company (ARAMCO), Gulf Oil Company, and California-Texas Oil Company. Although the American School of Oriental Research in Jerusalem was not successful, ACLS viewed overseas research centers to be mutually beneficial for both the United States and the host country. Within a framework of modernization theory amidst cold war "battle for minds," Chapter 4 is an interesting discussion of two educational institutions founded by American missionaries, what the author calls a "sheet anchor" at a time of United States military weakness in the region: American University of Beirut and American University of Cairo. The sensitivity of Israel for the Arabs played out in global-local dynamics.

There were challenges to area studies programs, however. First, such programs warranted collaboration across discipline-centered departments at universities. Second, partly compounded by the lack of institutional support, universities were losing faculty members to government agencies and the military. Faced with other challenges, the DoS made some recommendations: give military deferments for graduate students and greater support for the physical sciences in the military and Congress; expand training for current government employees; Congressional reservation about federal funding for education in creating two-tiers of brains and uniforms warranted judicial use of foundation money; and expanded international commitments demand mastery of "difficult languages," expertise of "critical areas," and analytical skills to assimilate multidisciplinary information. Another caveat was that foreign-born specialists would not pass the requisite level of security clearance.

The June 1951 *Area Studies in American University,* by Wendell Bennett of Yale University was a landmark report. A dilemma was satisfying government's expanding need for area training programs without under-mining training of research scholars. The report identified three categories of specialties: scholars with a doctoral degree, master's degree holders, and those with undergraduate or military program training. Priority was given to "integrated area programs" that prepared one for cultural comprehension. However, there was a need to shift emphasis from ancient to modern history.

David Wise and Thomas Ross argue that there are two sides to the Unit-ed States government. Drawing on that notion of "two governments," Khalil names Chapter 5 "(In) Visible Government" and takes a critical look at the national security establishment. The author traces Orientalist influence not only to immigrant British scholars Hamilton Gibb and Bernard Lew-is, but also to George Lenczowski and Halford Hoskins. Earlier in Chapter 1, Khalil observes that the Orientalist lens of AGS disavowed self-rule for "The Arab Problem." Also, the Sykes-Picot Agreement divided the Ottoman Empire into Anglo-French "direct rule" and "spheres of influence." Whereas Husayn-McMahon correspondence promised an independent Arab state, furthermore, the Balfour Declaration guaranteed "civil and religious rights" of Palestinian Arabs without assuring their "political rights." Along that line, Chapter 8 discusses neoconservative attempts to remove, what Martin Kramer calls, the "culture of irrelevance" of Middle East studies for United States national security — and Israeli interest in the region, Khalil adds. This includes the 2003 House Resolution 3077 (H.R. 3077) that countermanded the National Defense Education Act (NDEA) protection of academic free-dom from federal agencies. Even though terrorism studies date back to the 1970s, since 2003 the Department of Homeland Security has established university-based "centers of excellence." The National Science Foundation has also become a conduit for terrorism research funds.

In his 1954 report, "The National Interest and Foreign Language," William Parker of New York University made language training a national security priority. An important development was the 1958 NDEA. With ACLS iden-tifying six "critically needed foreign languages" that included Arabic, NDEA's Part-A of Title VI was earmarked for language development. Part-B of Title VI for language institutes was eliminated and moved to Title XI. However, the counterinsurgency component of Project Camelot, funded by the Ar-my's Office of Research and Development, stained relations with the social sciences in the academia. An interesting revelation was that the American Zionist Council funded the American Association for Middle East Studies (AAMES) and the Council for Middle Eastern Affairs. AAMES was shut down and replaced by the Middle East Studies Association (MESA) with funding from the Ford Foundation.

Chapter 6 is a deeper look at the modernization theory framework, which pivoted counterinsurgency with development that shaped anti-Arab sentiment within the national security establishment. In particular, Khalil addresses works by Daniel Lerner, Manfred Halpern, Walt Rostow, Lucian Pye, and Samuel Huntington. The author is especially critical of Harold Glidden for proposing "de-Arabization" in overcoming a pathology of shame and vengeance and Raphael Patai for insinuating sexual repression for hostility. Furthermore, Khalil notes a division between modernization theorists and area specialists in the academia.

Given its negative image of area studies, the United States government shifted attention from academic institutions to students. Nevertheless, under the 1991 National Security Education Program, the Pentagon funded both institutions and students for language learning. However, Title VI did not draw enough graduate students to area studies. This resulted in a further shift to think-tanks in reverting to privatization of knowledge. There were already the American Enterprise Institute, Brookings Institution, Heritage Foundation, and Hoover Institution. On the left emerged the Middle East Research and Information Project (MERIP) in 1971; on the right was established the Washington Institute for Near East Policy (WINEP) in 1985. Knowledge production has come full circle, as a private endeavor, from missionaries (and oil companies) to think-tanks.

There is an Orientalism thread and resultant anti-Arab bias decried in *America's Dream Palace* that could have been more explicitly addressed earlier in the book. The work provides a treasure-trove of background information, albeit somewhat scattered, for those in Middle East area studies. However, the forest may be lost for the vastness of the trees. The author propounds that National Security Council Intelligence Directives 2, 4, and 7 promise a future research agenda (p. 78). Three additional points warrant further exploration. First, balancing area studies training programs for national security with producing research scholars (p. 101). Second, bridging any gap between comparative politics and Middle East area specialization (p. 202). Third, promoting dialogue between area studies and security studies. Those in the emerging security studies would benefit from a better understanding of the gulf that undermines collaboration from colleagues in area studies (p. 249). By the same token, it would be incorrect to presume that university-based centers of academic excellence would succumb to "groupthink" (p. 293). Notwithstanding the aforementioned comments, *America's Dream Palace: Middle East Expertise and the Rise of the National Security State* by Osamah Khalil would be a valuable reading for the general audience, scholars, and policy-makers. ***RGM***

Arab Migrant Communities in the GCC

Zahra Babar, Ed. New York, NY: Oxford University Press, 2017. 312 pp. ISBN: 978-0190608873.

With her prior experience in the International Labor Organization and the United Nations Development Program, Zahra Babar brought together specialists to shed light on a hitherto neglected group in the literature on migration: The Arab communities in the GCC. With attention to Kuwait, Qatar, Saudi Arabia, and UAE host countries, the contributions examined Egyptian, Lebanese, Palestinian, and Yemeni migrant communities. Also, Jordanians, Moroccans, Sudanese, and Syrians were discussed. Furthermore, topics included gender, servants, sports, and teachers. In addition, the edited book presented valuable field research data.

Although supplanted by cheaper South and Southeast Asian workers since the oil price collapse of the mid-1980s, Babar observed in the introductory chapter that Arab expatriates comprised the earlier migrant communities in the GCC. The region is now the third-largest hub of international labor migration. Egypt, Morocco, and Lebanon are three ranking recipients of remittances; Saudi Arabia is the largest source of remittances. There has been a move toward "nationalization" of the workforce in the GCC, however. Not a signatory to the 1951 Geneva Refugee Convention, the *kafala* (sponsorship system) and the increasingly rising temporary worker programs deny opportunity for permanent settlement and naturalized citizenship.

In a case study of Qatar, Babar noted a declining trend for the foreign labor force. Within that context, in 2013 Arab expatriates accounted for 13% of the work force compared to 80% of non-Arabs. Egyptians comprised the largest Arab community, followed by Syrians and Sudanese in the distance. Egyptians dominated all sectors: legal and law enforcement, finance and insurance, professional and technical, media and journalism, education, and managerial and administrative services. In line with the above observation about education, Natasha Ridge, Soha Shami, and Susan Kippels found that teacher migration to Qatar and UAE was dominated by Egyptians by a significant margin. Jordanians and Lebanese followed successively in Qatar; Jordanians and Syrians comprised the next tiers in UAE, where Arab migrant teachers earned about half the salary of their UAE colleagues. Consequently, migrant teachers resorted to private tutoring to supplement their income amidst an uncertain work environment of annual contract renewal. Even though classroom management was the paramount complaint, migrant teachers were drawn by higher salary for supporting extended family and professional development opportunities.

The predominance of Egyptians was facilitated by Anwar Sadat's *infitah* (opening up) labor export policy in the early 1970s, noted by Abbie Taylor, Nada Soudy, and Susan Martin in a study of Kuwait. The influx is explained by a "chain migration" strategy. Although legally eligible for naturalization after 15 years of consecutive residency, the policy was reneged by Kuwaiti officials in practice. Also, Egyptians had to navigate the "unwritten hierarchy" in social relations: "untouchable" Kuwaitis, other GCC nationals, Westerners, Arabs, Southeast Asians, and South Asians. Furthermore, Lebanese and Egyptians were at the top and bottom, respectively, of the totem pole within the broader MENA Arab category. Historically viewed as a "destabilizing force," remarked Manal Jamal, Palestinians in UAE were expected to be apolitical and limit themselves to humanitarian activities. Generous in providing free public-school education to up to two expatriate children, there was no appeal process against UAE deportation notice. Also, in 2009, the UAE stopped issuing visas to Palestinians. Unlike those holding a Jordanian passport, it is noteworthy that Egyptian and Syrian issued travel documents record Palestinian origin. Those living under the Palestinian Authority (with a Palestinian passport) may hold a temporary Jordanian passport, but without the benefit of dual citizenship. Thus, Palestinians in the GCC opt for third country citizenship in the West.

Saudi Arabia is the most important external destination for Yemenis, noted Harry Cook and Michael Newson. A significant number of the migrants come from the Ta'iz region; most travel to Jizan in southwest Saudi Arabia bordering Yemen. Employment is primarily in the construction and agricultural sectors. Saudi government restricted migrant in-flow after the 1990-1991 Gulf War, but large-scale labor movement resumed in 1993 through irregular channels. Abdullah al-Ajmi focused on the subgroup of Hadramis "house-to-house" servants in Kuwait. The dependency relationship is elucidated with reference to not only *kafil* (legal sponsor), but also *mu'azzib* (social sponsor). The latter concept is related to intergenerational kinship and *wastah* (favoritism) by the benefactor to retired "visiting-feeding" immigrants for medical benefit and *rahah* (comfort). Second generation immigrants are disillusioned from *qalaq* (headaches) of *talabat* (demands) for consumer goods from relatives and friends amidst the bleak prospects of citizenship and economic autonomy. The 1959 Kuwaiti nationality law granted citizenship and attendant economic benefits to eligible Yemeni house servants, but they formed the most marginalized *sibyan* among Kuwaiti nationals.

Commercialization of sports in the GCC has created opportunities for athletes from the Maghreb, observed Mahfoud Amara. He proposed a five-fold typology of professional athletes: Mercenary, cosmopolitan, settler, ambitious, and returnee. Given the restriction on employment, residency, and citizenship, added Amara, settling in the GCC will be a challenge for sports migrants. Facing confessional tensions in their own country, remarked Garret Maher, Lebanese are attracted to the GCC for political stability. In moving from other GCC countries to Kuwait for higher wages and relative lifestyle freedom, the Lebanese "transnational migrants" illustrate the theory of circular migration. Francoise de Bel-Air found that a significant percentage of the women migrant workers in Kuwait were from Lebanon, Egypt, and Jordan. The Lebanese and Jordanian female expatriates are skilled or highly skilled professionals. Lebanese women reside overwhelmingly in UAE, particularly Dubai, primarily working in business and administration, followed by social sciences and health.

Although the survey of (Arab and non-Arab) students at the American University of Sharjah was interesting, it seemed artificially grafted. Also, the reference to servants as slaves reflected Western bias and lack of cultural understanding. Those two minor points notwithstanding, the book is a welcome addition to the literature on GCC labor migration. *RGM*

Civil Society and Political Reform in Lebanon and Libya: Transition and Constraint

Carmen Geha. New York, NY: Routledge, 2016. 194 pp. ISBN: 978-138184923.

Throughout the late 1990s and early 2000s, a hopeful literature grew up surrounding the impact of civil activism as a phenomenon in the Middle East. Political liberalization attended economic liberalization in states such as Egypt, Tunisia, Morocco, and Jordan. There were hopes that the expansion of economic reform in Gulf States would also lend credence to the expansion of civil society as well. Though a broad literature demonstrated the vitality of a growing civil society surviving under the cover of authoritarianism, almost no one predicted the widespread

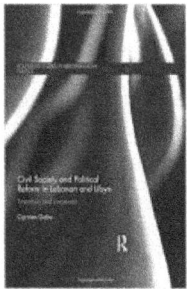

demonstrations that brought about regime change during the Arab Spring protests.

Five years later, the Arab Spring has given way to a reversal in the fortunes of pro-democracy activists throughout the region, thereby demonstrating the inability of civil society to overturn the forces of authoritarianism, Islamism, and state collapse that afflict the region. The continued resistance of the region to democratization follows directly from the inability of states to contain and respond to demands for change. It also follows from the inherent challenges to the legitimacy of states in the Middle East that arose out of the colonial period.

The failure of civil activists to effect lasting change is the topic of this book by Carmen Geha. To explore the resilience of authoritarianism amidst critical moments in which civil activists have sought to effect lasting change or reform, Geha turns to institutionalist explanations as well as the impediments presented by divided postcolonial states. As case studies, she looks at the stalled electoral reform program in Lebanon that followed the 2005 Cedar Revolution and the ill-fated efforts of Libyan activists to promote constitutional change in the wake of the 2011 overthrow of Moammar Qaddhafi in Libya.

The book begins with a discussion of institutional processes. Though the technical discussion is somewhat "jargonistic," Geha, in a nutshell, argues that civil society could not promote change in Lebanon or Libya because the existing political barriers to democratization and reform were simply too impregnable. These political patterns led to a path-dependency that simply reversed any effort at reform: "the options available to decision-makers about reform remained highly path dependent in the cases of Lebanon and Libya and, as such, limited the potential for critical moments to be turned into critical junctures. This means that any reform that favors a new type of representation or relations between citizen and state has a dismal chance of success because institutions have deeply rooted practices that have become difficult, if not impossible, to change" (p. 6).

The persistence of non-democratic and dysfunctional forms of governance in both Lebanon and Libya comes as a result of three "elements of continuity" according to Geha: weak states, communal power-sharing, and the ineffectiveness of civil society actors in achieving their ends (p. 31). Both Lebanon and Libya are countries that have struggled with postcolonial challenges to their legitimacy stemming from inherent divisions — either ethnoreligious or geographic — that undermine state institutions. What is more, power-sharing based on those divisions has created established confessional or tribal elites who benefit from the existence of the power-sharing system or from dominance of the central government, giving them little reason to support reform or change.

Geha lays out the groundwork for understanding resistance to reform in the context of Lebanon. She appropriately blames the power-sharing system for creating a rigid and unyielding commitment to institutions that simply bolstered the power of local confessional authorities, the zu'ama. She notes that "even after independence, the efforts of political leaders were geared not towards the creation of a national civic identity, but towards the fragmentation of identities in order to maintain sectarian loyalties" (p. 57). Civil war in the 1970s and 1980s did not bring this order to an end, but merely shifted the bases of power and "disrupted these networks and replaced *zu'ama* clientelism with a new and more complex mix of clientelistic networks" (p. 63). Syrian intervention following the civil war had channeled these networks to promote a pro-Syrian government. One means that the pro-Syrian elite used to dominate was the manipulation of the electoral system.

Under Syrian tutelage, civil society was managed such that only friendly political elites could cultivate the renewal of civil activism. When a popular movement arose in March 2005 in response to the assassination of Prime Minister Rafiq Hariri, it provided a brief opening for new civil groups to challenge the status quo. One of these groups was the Lebanese Association for Democratic Elections (LADE), in which the author participated as an activist. LADE worked within the system to promote non-partisan education and systemization of the electoral system over the years between 2005 and 2009. However, ultimately, the non-sectarian impulse represented by LADE was no match for the political machinations of Lebanon's sectarian elites. Rhetorical support for electoral reform among the leading political movements did not translate into real change in the Lebanese political landscape.

Moving on to Libya, Geha traces the problems of state consolidation to its early postcolonial history, when at least three very diverse regions — Fezzan, Tripolitania, and Cyrenaica — were fused into a single country. In spite of a vision for a federal structure of government, the country was subjected to a long history of centralized authoritarianism. Geha argues that Libyans were "coerced" into accepting unification, but authority would remain localized to region and tribe (p. 116). This proceeded into a deepening attempt to undermine local authority amid Arabization and Islamization under Qaddhafi. Nevertheless, the application of power under Qaddhafi's "third universal theory" created little in the way of robust political institutions. The ultimate breakdown of any form of power sharing left a void in the heart of the state once the Qaddhafi regime was overthrown: "[t]he spread of violence and complete deterioration of state institutions after 2014 reveals a path dependence on a central leadership able to oppress opposition or mitigate conflict, a leadership role that appears utterly void at present" (p. 109). The National Transitional Council therefore represented many of the regional, tribal, and religious problems that had never been resolved under the dictatorship and reproduced many of its dysfunctions.

There was, therefore, no independent civil society existing at the time of the 2011 popular movement (p. 125). Beyond the revolution, there was no existing means of pushing forward a reform agenda that would unify all Libyans under a common banner. One effort to build one was the Forum for Democratic Libya (FDL), here portrayed by Geha as a broad national organization aimed at fostering citizenship, democracy, government accountability, and the free participation of civil society (p. 145). Geha's research into the work of the organization demonstrates some of the inherent constraints on its efforts. Among other things, she found that participants revealed their distrust of national institutions in the work of the FDL as the "most repeated demand regarding the state system was for a system that could guarantee public services equitably across all regions" (p. 150). It should come as little surprise that regional dynamics played into the political division of Libya in the ensuing years.

In the final analysis, Geha argues that state weakness, coupled with the strength of identity politics in these countries, hindered the influence of civil society, ultimately limiting "citizenship and political rights… to a person's ethnic, religious, or regional origin" (p. 165). As civil society was squeezed out of the political process, it foundered in the middle of a juncture that proved to be only "partially critical" (p. 172).

Geha's book provides empirical case studies of specific civil actors that should prove particularly useful in developing our understanding of the process of transition and its relationship to civil society. She does an excellent job of summarizing the political systems and phenomena of the two societies she is studying. However, the empirical aspects of the case study are given short shrift and it would have been beneficial to reveal more of the research findings to demonstrate the truth of her claims. This might have been achieved with a more detailed account of the activities and limitations of LADE and the FDL, or with more research into the work of other parallel civil society groups involved in the transitions. It is also unfortunate that in a work with this depth of insight into institutional processes in these two states, she makes relatively scant reference to the classic works of Michael Hudson and Lisa Anderson on the institutional legacies of each country.

Given the way that civil associations tend to be dominated by the sectarian and regional groupings that impede a wider notion of nationhood in both societies, it would also be instructive to look into the work of some sectarian or sub-regional organizations in order to understand their influence on the process of transitional reform. Geha's argument is that power-sharing only serves to reinforce the cleavages that undermine a functional political space. But some civil organizations that exist to promote religious or other ends actually do serve multiple sectarian and regional populations. It would be interesting to think about the way in which such civil society groups may actually help to accelerate reform in addition to the ways that they impede it.

Institutional "path dependency" is at the heart of Geha's argument. It stands to reason that institutions tend to reinforce themselves, but such an explanation only really goes so far. What role is there here for human agency? Why is it, for example, that Lebanese and Libyan elites choose to revert to form when it is not always the best tactic? While the pattern of power in Lebanon, for example, remains bound to a small number of greater and lesser zu'ama, the cast of characters changes with the ebb and flow of power. Merely holding on to power-sharing does not always empower the existing elite. Embracing new institutional forms may well be a useful motor for one za'im to achieve relative gains. Indeed, some have embraced change for that very reason, as in the case of the radical ideology of Walid Jumblatt's Progressive Socialist Party, or the various ideologies that have driven Michel Aoun from one tactical position to another.

What is more, surely the problem in Lebanon or Libya is not simply a resistant set of institutions but the existence of extra-state violence in the hands of factional groups and revolutionaries? Geha contends that weak institutions "played into the interest of armed militias" (p. 139) but doesn't really consider their external sources of supply or their resort to brutality as a reason for the failure of the reform option. The decline of civil society in the wake of the Arab Spring owes much to the choices of militant factions in spoiling non-violent activism among the civil actors in Lebanon, Egypt, Syria, Libya, and Yemen. In every case, a peaceful pro-democracy protest movement has been eclipsed by violent reactionaries.

Geha does show concern for the agency of the civil organizations that she studies, however. Toward the end of her work, she addresses some of the tactical mistakes of civil society. It is unfortunate that these observations remain somewhat perfunctory, because her advice for civil society groups is tantalizing. She argues that civil organizations need to lay aside some of their idealism and work within the system as it is, to build partnerships with existing political players as a means of encouraging change and reform.

Though Geha argues that civil society has proven too weak to be effective in Lebanon and Libya, she remains optimistic about the potential of civil initiatives to reinforce power sharing in divided societies. For although she finds that power-sharing tends to undermine the civil sector, "an ineffective associational sector is both a symptom of weak states and power-sharing agreements but is also an enabler of these two dimensions. A strong and influential, nationally active civil society could prompt a process of reconstruction of strong state institutions and could either be an art of power-sharing agreements or maintain a strong oversight role regarding such agreements" (p. 171). If this is true, then state weakness can contribute to increasing the influence of civil society groups. As they grow in sophistication and significance, perhaps such groups could respond positively to the present malaise in Middle Eastern politics. *PSR*

Eastern Rome and the Rise of Islam: History and Prophecy

Olof Heilo. New York, NY: Routledge, Taylor & Francis Group, 2016. 149 pp. ISBN: 978-1138101388.

To properly understand the phenomenal rise and expansion of Islam in the seventh century, Dr. Olof Heilo, who teaches history at the Center for Middle Eastern Studies in Lund, shows in this book that knowing the history of Byzantium (Eastern Rome) is very helpful and even necessary. Furthermore, he offers new insights into history by showing that the religious truth perceived to come from Heaven and the historical reality humanly experienced on Earth are mutually interdependent as the human subjects associated with both make the messages of both meaningful.

Christianity in the Late Ancient world and early Islam as it rose and expanded are often viewed as two distinct and separate parts of human history, but Dr. Heilo shows that they are shared quite closely. The decline of the Eastern Roman Empire and its Byzantine civilization is shown to be a very important factor in understanding the rise of Islam and its Islamic civilization. For Muslims, the religion of Islam was, of course, initiated by God through Prophet Muhammad and was perceived as a call from God to spread His message to the world. For the Byzantines, their defeat by Muslims was perceived as a punishment by God for their lassitude in religious belief and practice. Prophecy and history are thus not defined by the apocalyptic truth of religion, but by human beings who consider them to have messages to be conveyed by their human actions and interpretations.

To come to this view and support it, Dr. Olof Heilo had recourse to an impressively vast bibliography of Latin, Greek, and Arabic sources in addition to works in German, English, and French. His short book is a veritable effort of genuine scholarship and is valuable to students and scholars of Islamic studies, especially for its new perspectives.   IJB

Egyptians in Revolt: The Political Economy of Labor and Student Mobilizations 1919-2011

Adel Abdel Ghafar. London, UK: Routledge, 2017. 236 pp. ISBN: 978-1138656109.

After thirty years as president, in February 2011, Hosni Mubarak lost the backing of the army and was forced to step down as result of mass protests against his political repression, corruption, and neoliberal economic policies in Egypt. Soon after, he faced charges of corruption and of complicity in the killing of demonstrators. While he spent a few years in jail on a corruption charge, in a recent retrial, Mubarak was acquitted of the charges for his involvement in killing protesters without any possibility of further appeal. He was subsequently released from military prison in late March of this year.

The uprising that began on January 25th, 2011and lasted for 18 days until Mubarak's downfall — one of largest Egypt had ever seen. These two weeks saw the crossing of ideological and socio-economic boundaries of a wide spectrum of protesters and social movements for a common goal, to change the way Egypt was governed. Yet as Adel Abdel Ghafar shows in his new book, *Egyptians in Revolt...*, certain features of the 2011 demonstrations have historical precedence in cross-sectional mobilizations against the Egyptian state beginning in the early twentieth century. It is this feature of mass mobilizations, namely cross-sectionality that drives Abdel Ghafar's analysis. He is particularly interested in the linkages between the labor and student movements in a historical perspective beginning with 1919 and leading up to the events of January and February 2011.

Using Alan Richards and John Waterbury's three-point model of political economy in conjunction with social movement theory, Abdel Ghafar looks at why the labor and student movements acted collectively and how political economic factors created both opportunities and threats to such cooperation (p.2). The author posits a number of arguments. First, despite the authoritarian state, both movements have been able to positively influence government policy. Abdel Ghafar also argues that the political economic context created threats and opportunities that structured why and when groups mobilized and how they framed their demands and grievances. The experience of cooperation resulted in logistical and ideological spillover between movements. The author also argues that cooperation between different groups was not always coordinated but at times occurred haphazardly. Last, Abdel Ghafar argues that both movements have consistently been co-opted by the state, which has severely inhibited the ability of activists to create long-lasting independent organizations (pp. 2-3).

For readers well versed in modern Egyptian history and contemporary politics, Abdel-Ghafar's arguments do not necessarily add a new perspective to the existing literature and can even seem redundant. For example, the co-optation of political movements is a phenomenon that has been well established within the literature on collective action in Egypt (see for example the classic *Workers on the Nile* by Joel Beinin and Zachary Lockman). Despite this drawback, Abdel Ghafar is still able to succinctly present to readers a detailed chronological overview of socio-economic changes that have propelled the cross-sectional activism of mobilizations over a broad period of time. In doing so, Abdel Ghafar supplements secondary literature with interviews with participants from all sides, such as government officials, workers, and student activists, some of who have even been active since the 1960s. The author is able to weave first-hand accounts into the narrative of social mobilizations, thereby successfully avoiding the pitfall of state-centric analysis.

Abdel Ghafar begins his book with four key developments of the nineteenth century that would continue to influence activism in the decades to come. More specifically, he looks at the dependency on the export of cotton, increasing debt, foreign economic dominance, and rapid urbanization. These factors set the stage for the growth of the labor movement and its participation in the 1919 revolt. With the expansion of the education system and the opening of universities, the student movement quickly emerged as an important player in the nationalist cause. Abdel Ghafar discusses two major demonstrations of the pre-1952 period, the mass student protests of 1935-36, and the first student-worker coordinated strike of 1946.

In chapters 3 and 4, the author addresses the Nasser and Sadat periods, respectively. Following the same layout as the previous chapter, he looks at the changing political economy of both eras. Under Nasser, this included the purging of political opposition, industrialization, and a growing public sector under state socialism. The purging of opposition necessitated state interference and control of the student and labor movements during the 1950s and 1960s. Abdel Ghafar highlights the protests of 1967 and 1968 and writes that during these years cooperation between workers and students was uncoordinated (p.76). In the Sadat era, Abdel Ghafar foregrounds the dismantling of Nasser's social bargain and the slow introduction of neo-liberal economic policy, which according to the author was actually a policy change signaled by Nasser himself (p. 85). Economic developments, including loans from the IMF, created a new elite class of business owners and a growing income gap in the country. Additionally, under Sadat, Egypt was still dealing with the aftermath of the 1967 Arab-Israeli War. The culmination of these factors led to a number of protests by workers and students throughout the 1970s. With these two chapters, Abdel Ghafar is able to present the entrenchment of certain aspects of the state-society relationship that continued to manifest in varying ways during the Mubarak years. Through this broad scope, the author is able to uncover both patterns and differences in the collective action between students and labor over the years (p. 3).

The rest of the book deals with the three decades of Mubarak's presidency. Abdel Ghafar addresses in detail the continuation of free market policies, the introduction of economic reform and structural adjustment programs (ERSAP), and the continued development of an elite class of businessmen with close connections to Mubarak's regime. This particular feature resulted in what became popularly known as "the marriage of authority to money," (pp. 151-152). In this section, the author also addresses the fascinating history of the Egyptian army's foray into civil projects such the building of factories, roads, clinics, and much more, thereby drastically altering Egypt's political economy. Mubarak's long presidency was marked by cronyism, police brutality, restriction of rights, and increasing prices. This was met with numerous protests from students and labor, especially in the 2000s. With the 6th of April movement, workers and students once again came together in 2008 to call for a general strike. Though the strike was unsuccessful, Abdel Ghafar writes that this was the beginning of the movement calling for political reform and culminating in the uprising of 2011 (p.165).

Each chapter includes an assessment of threats and opportunities created by the particular political-economic environment of the period in question. Abdel Ghafar takes into consideration a wide variety of factors such as legislative framework, educational access, social equality, regional and inter-national dynamics, master frames (such as nationalist cause of the pre-1952 period, or the slogan of "bread, freedom, social justice," of 2011), unemploy-ment, inflation, social media and much more. Abdel Ghafar addresses with clarity how each factor provided either incentives or barriers for mobiliza-tion and cross-cooperation between the labor and student movements.

With recent events in Egypt since 2011 and the severe restriction of the political environment and dangerous economic strategy, it is hard to be op-timistic about Egypt's future. The greatest contribution of this book appears in light of the developments under the current military president, where the historical legacy of state tactics as well as the inability of various social move-ments to sustain cooperation is currently evident. Cycles of repression and implementing economic policies that continue to disenfranchise the masses are repeating itself in arguably worse ways. Nonetheless, having experienced the 2011 protests himself, the author ends his book with confidence. He writes that the mobilization of 2011, "helped produce a politically empower generation of workers and students able to challenge and threaten a regime" (p.189), the potential of which the author predicts will be realized in the decades to come. **FB**

References

Abdel Ghafar, A. (2017). *Egyptians in Revolt: The Political Economy of Labor and Student Mobilizations 1919-2011*. London, UK: Routledge. 220pp. ISBN: 978-1138656109.

Beinin, J., & Lockman, Z. (1998). *Workers on the Nile: Nationalism, Commu-nism, Islam, and the Egyptian Working Class, 1882-1954*. Cairo, EG: American University in Cairo Press.

The Jarring Road to Democratic Inclusion: A Comparative Assessment of State-Society Engagements in Israel and Turkey

Aviad Rubin, Yusuf Sarfati, Eds. New York, NY: Lexington Books. 256 pp. ISBN: 978-1498525077.

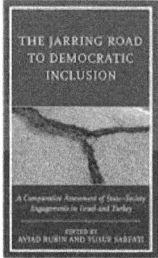

A great comparative political science collection of nine essays under the competent editorship of Aviad Rubin, a political scientist at the University of Haifa and Yusuf Safari, another political scientist, teaching at Illinois State University. Together the authors deal with Kurds, non-Sunni Muslims, Armenians, and Greeks in Turkey, while in Israel, the Jews, divided by Ashkenazim, Sephardim, and Oriental-inclined believers, are living alongside Palestinian Muslims and Christians. The question to be studied, therefore, is how do each of these separate social and religious entities get along with one another under a unified governing structure, each of which seeks to achieve some degree of power projection?

First examined is the role of religion, its spiritual dimensions, and representative institutions, placed against the theories of Jürgen Habermas, John Rawls, and Charles Taylor. Where does one find faith in pronounced secular governance? The author for this chapter, Sultan Tepe, argues for inclusion for all groups to insure inclusivity for the ultimate collective good. The next prominent theme is an examination of how public and religious school systems are employed for the process of social mobilization. While both political systems are drenched in religious fervor and embellishment, there is marked opposition shown in each and compared, anti-capitalists in Turkey, and Jewish women in Israel who seek greater autonomy from an orthodox opinion of their proper role. As is the case with any political system, there is the overriding feature of political culture. Rubin takes on this study with a finding that in Israel powerful political forces attempt to gain dominance whereas in Turkey the same elements approach power positioning in terms of hegemony. Since both political systems are parliamentary democracies, the 2015 election was chosen as a case study to examine the relative power structure of either state's party systems with the Joint List in Israel and the Peoples' Democratic Party in Turkey. A return to socio-religious concerns focuses on the important connector of marriage as an adhesive in any society. A concluding essay looks at the labor market with Turkish women as part of the *Gastarbeiter* (guest worker) phenomenon in Germany and Palestinian women in Israel, viewed with the perspective of the nature of inclusion of ethnic minorities.

One significant contribution to this book is the selective but up-to-date bibliography that is appended to each chapter which adds to the value of what may be considered an expensive addition to an interested library or researcher. The offerings of this book well serve research into social mobilization of ethnic minorities in democratic political systems. **SRS**

The Middle East: New Order or Disorder?

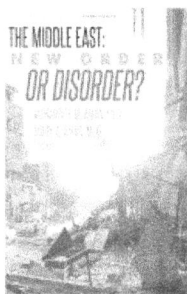

Mohammed Aman & Mary Jo Aman, Eds. Washington, DC: Westphalia Press, 2016. 476 pp. ISBN: 978-1633912847.

Six years after the first spark of the Arab uprisings, the region's future cannot be any more uncertain. With the possible exception of Tunisia, post-revolutionary Arab countries have failed in democratization, to either plunge in civil wars, or incredibly retrograde to authoritarianism. Aman and Aman's *The Middle East: New Order or Disorder?* addresses the "varied political, social issues and security issues facing the countries of the Middle East and North Africa (MENA) and the deteriorating conditions that these countries are presently facing" (p. xi). The book is a collection of twenty chapters (most of which were originally published as articles in either *Digest of Middle East Studies* (DOMES) or as proceedings from the annual conference, *Middle East Dialogue* (MED) that examines the various aspects of the region's dilemmas.

The volume exposes the different sets of challenges to stability and security in the region and the various regional ramifications of the revolutionary wave. The chapters present various aspects of the religious, historical, and political context of the Arab uprisings, as well as diverse approaches to how to conceptualize the unfolding of events, including case studies to cross-regional focus. Although the book is not subdivided into sections based on common themes, readers can easily group particular chapters together. The following review does not follow the order of the chapters in the book; neither does it cover all of them. However, it clusters number of chapters together which share either a common theme or a common perspective.

Some chapters are case-oriented. For example, a chapter by M. S. Catino suggests that the failure of the "green movement" was due to regime's capabilities that went beyond "brutal crackdown" (p. 2), reflected in "cohesive institutional backing of the state, comprehensive operational skills, mass tactical ground support and ideological strength ... which effectively mobilized large segments of Iran's population against the reformers" (p. 2). Whereas the regime's capabilities subverted the protest movement in Iran and maintained stability, Brandt Smith sheds light on how the lack of qualified leadership that satisfies the expectations of the citizens in Iraq lies at the heart of instability in the country. He argues that anarchy and chaos will continue to plague Iraq unless changes take place on the leadership level. Related to the instability issue comes the language policy in Sudan as discussed by Abderrahman Zouhir. By examining the complexity, arbitrariness and fluctuation of the Sudanese language policy in its historical, political, and educational contexts, Zouhir argues that Arabization provoked identity conflict crystallizing in the separation of South Sudan.

In contrast to this salient focus on instability and protest, Yaghi and Boateng's chapter sheds lights on the factors affecting UAE voters' preferences in the elections of federal national councils. According to their survey results, the religious, political, and personal appearance did not play a significant role in voters' decision. It was candidates' personal characteristics, campaigns, and patron-client networks that played the major role in the vote. Noureddine Miladi investigates the impact of social media with regard to political campaigning and social empowerment. Drawing on examples of social media networks in Tunisia and Egypt, he argues that online spheres mark the emergence of virtual vibrant space, particularly for the youth and the marginalized.

The political earthquake that hit some Arab countries has shaken other regional grounds too. Another group of chapters provide a regional and/or sub-regional perspective with regard to the impact of, and the reaction to, the revolutionary wave. Binhuwaidin discusses the "essential threats to the security of the GCC countries in the post-Arab Spring era." In his view, the Arab Spring has produced three main threats to the GCC countries: political liberal ideas, political Islamic movements, and sectarianism. Preserving the conservative structure of the political systems of these countries, he argues, is necessary to maintaining peace and security.

While Binhuwaidin emphasizes preserving the status quo, Sidik and Boundel investigate the political outcomes of the Arab Spring in terms of reform in the Maghreb. By focusing on Algeria, Morocco, and Tunisia, the authors show how these countries embarked on reform initiatives as a first reaction to the protest tide in the region, although the significance and sustainability of these initiatives have differed from one case to the other. Olmert, for his part, assesses the Israeli attitudes toward the Arab Spring and the implications of Israeli elections on its regional policies and evaluates the challenges and opportunities facing Israel in the new Middle East. Complementing these examples that focus on non-Arab Spring countries, Wiebelhaus-Brahn examines transitional justice politics in Arab Spring countries and concludes that retributive justice has been more common that restorative transitional justice.

The religious aspect was the hub of some other chapters. In his chapter, for instance, Wayel Azmeh argues that "corporal punishments can be reinterpreted to only represent an upper limit never to be exceeded, favoring more lenient non-corporal punishments, or even no punishment at all by the state" (p. 37). In his view, this interpretation would "contribute to eroding the ideological basis of the extremists' propaganda machine" (p. 37). Amr Osman explains the clear contradictions of Sunni Muslim scholars toward the July 3rd coup in Egypt with reference to the contradictory positions of medieval Sunni scholars toward certain events in early Islam. For her part, Michal Allon expresses gender inequality in the Israeli society with reference to the patriarchal culture and sexism of Judaism and Islam and the lack of separation between state and religion.

A fourth group of chapters focuses on the international/external aspects. Andrew Wender argues that contemporary intervention in the Middle East involves several contradictions, on top of which is the claim that intervention serves the self-interest of states, regardless of the fact that intervention transgresses the principle of non-intervention on which the modern international political order was established. In his view, the main agents of change currently in the Middle East are numerous and diverse, spanning from global to sub-state actors.

For his part, Ahmed Ibrahim argues that the uprisings were a lost opportunity for the US due to its incoherent and inconsistent policy on them. Ahmed Abushouk contextualizes the Arab Spring within the democratization wave paradigm. He discusses the causes, features, and transition process in Tunisia, Egypt, Libya, and Yemen in correlation to Huntington's theorization on the third wave. In his view, the Arab Spring is a fourth regional wave of democratization that "shares some facets with the third global wave in terms of causative factors, features, and democratic transitions" (p. 339).

The book brings various perspectives to the situation in the Middle East in a way that improves our understanding of certain topics and issues. It shows the interrelation among political, religious, and cultural aspects. Azmeh's argument, for example, is interesting in terms of its attempts to overcome the violence experienced now in the region through re-reading Qur'anic verses relating to corporal punishments. He, however, does not dig deep enough into the inherent complexity of the issue and how it involves (or should involve) the entire traditional view of Islam. Such a complexity was clearly addressed in Osman's argument where he demonstrates how opposing political stances can perfectly find reference in Islamic history, exposing thereby the sophisticated relationship between Islam and politics.

The Arab Spring, generally speaking, was an act of people's will. Therefore, understanding what affects popular attitudes and choices is important in any serious attempt to make sense of the factors contributing to order and/or disorder in the region. Here comes the importance of Yaghi and Boateng's chapter on Emirati voters. Examining voting behavior in the GCC countries is not prevalent and the chapter fills in an obvious gap in this respect. Despite the authors' remarkable results, generalizing the results to "Emirates" voters can be questioned on the basis that the overwhelming majority of the sample came from Abu Dhabi only. Regrettably, furthermore, the authors do not reflect on what these results suggest about politics in UAE.

The book also sheds light on the regional and international dynamics related to the Arab Spring. Binhuwaidin's chapter presents the GCC countries' perception of the uprisings as a threat. Such a perception explains many of the political stances taken and choices made by these countries toward the "Arab Spring" countries. While the author stresses the need for preserving the conservative structure of the GCC political systems and blames Iran for "manufacturing sectarianism" in the region, he remains silent on the impact of authoritarianism itself on provoking sectarianism and security issues. The focus of Ibrahim's chapter on the US' stance toward the Arab Spring provides an objective evaluation of this stance. However, he does not elaborate enough on the reasons for the US' fickle policy; readers would wonder if that is a result of a leadership perception or a realist approach from the Obama Administration. Tackling these questions may help readers grasp the possible change and continuity of the US policy toward the region under a new administration.

Talking about order/disorder in revolutionary contexts necessarily involves discussing transitional justice. Therefore, Brahn's chapter discusses one of the mechanisms that helps society in dealing with its past grievances and looking forward to the future. His argument would be enhanced by a discussion of the policies of transitional justice within the larger context of transition and how the modes of transition may influence the process of transitional justice.

That the volume consists of assembled articles is evident in its lack of a clear structure as well as in the (expected) disparity in the depth of discussion among its chapters. A possible organization of the volume would be dividing it into three parts, each dealing with a particular circle: domestic, regional, and international/external. An explanation of the significance of the title of the book and the relevance of its various chapters to it would have also been helpful. It is hard, for example, to locate Abdullah F. Alrebh's chapter on "The emergent kingdom in the orientalist press: Ibn Saud's authority in Western media" within the larger topic of the book. A conclusion putting together different approaches and arguments would have significantly contributed to the usefulness of the volume. Finally, readers will appreciate the typical inclusion in the volume itself of the short biographies of its contributors. Overall, the book presents an interesting collection of topics that contributes to our understanding of the complexity of change in the Middle East, as well as many aspects of the past and current situation in the region, and its future prospects. *MF*

Muslim Democracy: Politics, Religion and Society in Indonesia, Turkey and the Islamic World

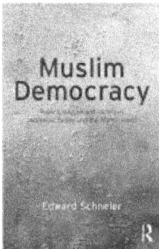

Edward Schneier. New York, NY: Routledge, 2016. 278 pp. ISBN: 978-1138928114.

This book, as the title says, is an essay on the concept of "Muslim democracy," examining the relationship between politics, religion, and society in two particular case studies, Turkey and Indonesia, but also including their regional non-Islamic neighbors and the other 47 Muslim majority countries in the world, with some tables and statistical data. It is an interesting comparative study, in which Schneier shows that the relationship between "church and state" in the Muslim world is more pluralistic than we usually think, that there is no such thing as an opposition between Islam and democracy, and that countries with similar histories and geographies have more in common than countries with similar religion. This argument is based on the evidence he found that democratization processes follow common paths in countries with different religions but dwelling in the same regions.

In a nutshell, the author shows how the political and historical factors are the real causes that shape the relationship between Islam and democracy, for example the so-called Islamic law that has more political than religious elements in its identity. What affects the democratization problems in Muslim countries, therefore, is not the variable of religion, but factors like poverty, nation-building, civil infrastructure and belonging to regions that achieved a late independence from colonial rule, and so were unable to build strong nation states or civic cultures. This is an important claim that should put an end to the old debate on the compatibility between Islam and democracy.

In the introduction, "Indonesia, Turkey and the Islamic World," the author explains the reason for his research, remembering that in the world there are 47 Muslim countries (countries where Islam is the religion of the majority of the population) but only two have been considered democracies by main-stream literature: Turkey and Indonesia. The relationship between Islam and democracy therefore has been evaluated in the past sometimes as difficult and sometimes as even incompatible and has been studied very little and mostly by a religious perspective, at least until the so-called Arab Spring. Therefore, to compare only Muslim majority countries' respect for democratization (something that is usually not done for Christian or Buddhist majority countries, for example) is not based on an Orientalist "hostile" approach, but on a comparative need for generalization, and at the same time, a need for giving to religion the importance that it rarely had in the past as key variable in studies of politics and societies (in particular, today with the resurgence of Hindus, Buddhist or Christian fundamentalism in politics of countries like India, Burma, and the US).

The first chapter, "A Brief History of the Islamic World" is an excursus on the history of the governance of the Islamic world, from the Caliphate to the "Middle Period," from the age of the Ottoman, Safavid, and Moghul empires to the shortcomings of the Tanzimat reform period in the Ottoman Empire; from the European domination with the colonial policies and the anticolonial forces, to the decolonization and the difficulties of governing systems and democratization in postcolonial Muslim majority countries, caused by the lack of strong and inclusive institutions, civil society, and multiparty systems.

The second chapter, "Religion, Development and Democratization," after a brief literature review on democracy theory (in particular Tilly and Diamond) makes an excursus of the four main comparative theories on democratization (even if the author doesn't explicitly mention them): the institutionalist theory, speaking about the importance of nation-building as independent variable to affect the democratization; the modernization theory, analyzing the importance instead of economic development; the cultural theory, considering the civic culture of civil society as crucial element; and the rational choice theory, on the importance of the elites' calculation of costs and benefits. Finally, the chapter tries to explain how religion played a role in the democratization processes, in the past as something seen as opposite to secularization and so modernization and democratization, while today with its resurgence, also as a reaction to the imposed Western secularization. Notwithstanding past generalizations, like the Huntington's idea on "Clash of Civilizations", Islamic religion is not opposite to modernization and democratization, the author claims, but we need, instead, to look at particular problems in specific regional settings to understand the relationship between Islam and democracy.

That's why in the third chapter, "The Middle East and North Africa: Strong States, Weak Democracies," the author looks at the politics of this region, making special reference to the Arab exceptionalism, asking "what, to echo Bernard Lewis's famous question, went wrong" (p. 74)? Schneier lists a series of four main elements starting, first of all, with the second wave of democratization at the beginning of the twentieth century, that in the MENA region touched only Turkey, with the revolt of the Young Turks in 1908, and Iran, with the Constitutional Revolution of 1906, but not the Arab world. The second reason for Arab exceptionalism is the artificial creation of states as ex-administrative units of empires or with lines drawn by European powers, produced strong but not inclusive institutions, supported by powerful nationalistic movements and strong militaries, which made authoritarianism an important element of stability against anarchy and revolutions and so, also, against democratization. The Third Civil society has been always very weak and this, together with the fourth element of international context based on oil interests and Israel presence, contributed to make the democratization in the MENA region more difficult. The events of the Arab Spring, and what Schneier calls the following "hot summer," showed not so much the importance of Islam in politics, but the importance of elites' authoritarian resilience, as "Islamic leaders may be complicit in these repressive acts — as were members of the Catholic clergy in Franco Spain — but they are not the powers behind the throne" (pp. 95-96).

Chapter 4, "The Road to Democracy in the Islamic World" analyzes the Muslim world, showing which problems hindered democratization in this part of the world, between Africa, with weak states, poverty, historic legacies, and ethnic conflicts; Eastern Europe and Central Asia, with the post-Soviet Union heritage; and finally the Indian subcontinent and Southeast Asia, with completely different problems, from the tribal problems and the Jihadist threat of Afghanistan to the discrimination of Muslim minorities in the Philippines, Myanmar, and Thailand. All these confirm that the issue of democratization in MENA region is not a question of Islam but a question of Arab situation, with "the more militant form of Islam, emanating particularly from Saudi Arabia and reinforced by anti-Western attitudes, moreover, is spreading in influence ... often as an anti- democratic or at least destabilizing force" (p. 136).

Chapters 5 and 6 are the two main case studies of the book, where the author makes a thorough historical analysis of the democratization processes of these two countries, showing how what he calls "pathways to democratization" for Turkey and "civil Islam" for Indonesia, are peculiar cases, that have more things in common with their regional counterparts in South West and South East Asia than with their religious counterpart in the Arab world.

Finally, in the last chapter, "Islam and Democracy," the author draws some conclusions on the relationship between faith and politics, both in the Islamic world and beyond it. He concludes that data show how Muslim majority countries in Africa, the old Soviet bloc or South Asia, have more similarities to non-Muslim majority countries of the same region than to countries that are largely Islamic in other regions. This shows that what affects the democratization problems is not the religion, but other variables like poverty, civil society and mostly, the late decolonization process, which made it more difficult to build strong institutions and civic cultures. Therefore, as the author concludes, "Islam itself is not a significant independent variable in explanation of democratization" (p. 232). **MG**

Neoliberal Governmentality and the Future of the State in the Middle East and North Africa

Emel Akçali, Ed. New York, NY: Palgrave Macmillan, 2016. 231 pp. ISBN: 978-1137546920.

Neoliberal Governmentality and the Future of the State in the Middle East and North Africa situates itself at the intersection of Foucauldian governmentality studies and the formal disciplines of International Relations and Political Science. The volume aims to explore the "societal power

relations that lead into governmental technologies, the terrains of local voices, and new forms of subjectivities, hybrid identities, transformed structures, and resistances that arise against or as a result of such governmentality techniques…[in the] MENA region" (p. 10). Taking up Foucault's definition of governmentality as "the conduct of conduct," the ten essays gathered in this collection aim to emphasize "the production of certain subjects who are expected to self-govern" through neoliberal ideologies propagated by the state (p. 6). "Neoliberal governmentalities" thus provides a lens through which the volume aims to highlight the transformations and failures of government in the MENA region leading up to and following the 2011 Arab Spring. An important part of this task is demonstrating resistance to state power, since, as editor of the volume Emel Akçali notes:

> Not all subjectivities (in the MENA region) have emerged as entrepreneurial, competitive, and/or individualistic……..A closer look at the MENA street reveals, for instance, that the understanding of political freedom and socioeconomic improvement is plural and that these concepts might be constituted in ways that differ from the liberal individualistic understanding [advanced in the West] (pp. 9-10).

Each essay in the collection takes up one or more facets of governmentality unique to the states in which they are situated in order to examine how subjects are governed, how they govern themselves, and how they deploy the resources of "freedom" to resist state forms of power.

The collection includes enlightening analysis of the society-state transformations produced by neoliberal ideologies leading up to and following the Arab Spring. Benoit Challand's chapter, the strongest in the collection, convincingly explores the limits of "transition" narratives for explaining the forms of resistance that emerged during the Arab Spring. Challand suggests that resistance took shape in ways that both exceeded the boundaries of what is understood in traditional transition narratives of social and political change and fell below the radar of those narratives since some forms of resistance took shape in unspectacular and 'mundane' ways. The anthology's theme — neoliberal governmentalities — is addressed late in the essay where the author notes that the class divisions produced by neoliberal reforms, as well as the emergence of what he calls a "transnational bourgeoisie" with intense capital investments (and conservative agendas) in the region, can help us understand the fracturing of resistance movements leading to the ultimate failure of sustained resistance.

Important to contemporary geopolitical concerns in the region, Rahman Dag's essay explores the failure of democracy (and the state more broadly) in Iraq in the aftermath of the 2003 US-led invasion and asks what role neoliberal imperatives emphasizing individual rights and freedoms (over the strong ethno-sectarian privileges central to traditional Iraqi social and political relations) played in this failure. "In such a local setting," Dag writes, "which has a completely distinctive historical experience [from those of the western powers importing neoliberal governmentalities], transforming human beings into 'homo 'economicus' does not seem so plausible, due to politically polarized identities and the continuing armed struggle among different communities" in Iraq (p. 39). For the author, the failure of the Iraqi state can, in part, be attributed to the contradiction between the strong, individualistic values associated with neoliberal reformations introduced after the 2003 US-led invasion and the local, collective identities based in tribal, ethnic, and sectarian groups. The author suggests that reforms that fail to address the deep social and ethnic divides renting the country will do little to secure the future of the Iraqi state.

Also, of interest is Ali Diskaya's chapter on Israel's nuclear "ambiguity" where the author assesses that nation's attempts to manage public discourses about its nuclear program by fostering local "nuclear subjectivities" impenetrable to "global governmentalities," such as the global anti-nuclear movement. The author argues that Israel's strategy of "secret nuclear governmentality" effectively silences internal criticism of Israel's nuclear program and prevents any outside anti-nuclear discourses from penetrating the state. The question of whether or not Israel possesses nuclear weapons remains "ambiguous" due to this form of "conducting conduct."

Most interesting, because unexpected, is Katerina Delacoura's chapter on the resurgence of the Muslim Brotherhood's political party — the Freedom and Justice Party — in Egypt and the Nahda movement in Tunisia, both in 2011-2012. Dalacoura explores the connections between Islamism and neoliberalism in the wake of the 2011 Arab Spring. She suggests that these two groups, contrary to expectations, were "readier to defend the neoliberal policies and structures that had been previously promoted by the Mubarak and Ben Ali regimes" (pp. 61-62) than may have been thought. The Islamist "embrace" of neoliberal reforms is surprising given the traditional focus of these groups on charity and helping the needy. Nevertheless, the author makes a convincing case for this shift in Islamist approaches to capitalism through an analysis of what she calls "pious neoliberalism," a notion which marks a change from the prior Islamist "idea that social justice is to something to be implemented 'from above,' by God or the state or even the Islamic group, in favor of the notion that, with God's blessing of course, the individual himself or herself will attain the position they deserve" p(p. 65-66).

The anthology ends with a reflection by Mark LeVine on the resonant call for dignity unifying all resistance movements discussed in the text. Individual dignity or *karama* had been systematically degraded, the author contends, by the very neoliberal policies adopted by MENA states to "free" the people in the region (p. 193). Instead, such policies, the author writes, are part of a broader global program evident from Latin America to the MENA region aiming to foster neoliberal subjectivities emphasizing capitalist values. The consequences of this have been seen across the world from Mexico and Central America from which refugees of poverty and political violence flow North, to Africa and the Middle East where civil war and social and political oppression have also led to a massive migration of refugees into Europe. LeVine links these problems to neoliberal reforms which strip subjects of their social identities by reconceptualizing them as "*homo economicus*, atomized individuals," whose worth is linked to the vicissitudes of 'the market" (p. 190). This way of conceptualizing the individual, LeVine further suggests, has the effect of reducing him/her to "bare life," a subject theorized by Giorgio Agamben as one who is, in LeVine's summation, "outside the bounds of social and political law and regulation, and thus prey to whatever exploitation, degradation, and even death might make him a more profitable cog or tool in the broader capitalist system" (p. 190). The Arab Spring was the popular response to these changes. The response, LeVine suggests, has been inadequate:

> ... if the world wants to end the strife across so much of Africa and Asia, stanch the flow of migrants and refugees into Europe or the United States, and drain the swamp of extremism that feeds ISIL and Al Qaeda, those who most benefit from the neoliberal globalized system must stop the flow of weapons to their clients and allies that has driven the present conflicts, support real democratic reforms uniformly and in every country of the region, and transform the economic blueprint guiding the globalization of the region from one that increases inequality, exploitation, and authoritarian rule toward one that encourages locally guided and sustainable development models (p. 195).

While aiming to bring a new lens to the study of MENA states, the collection lacks overall theoretical cohesion. The volume covers a wide breadth of empirical material in too short a space, and while the text is highly informative and relevant to contemporary events, it lacks the kind of conceptual depth and richness one might expect from such a study. The volume overall is worth a selective reading. **Me-S**

NGOs in the Muslim World: Faith and Social Services

Susumu Nejima, Ed. New York, NY: Routledge, 2015. 140 pp. ISBN: 978-1138914902. (Ebk). ISBN: 978-1315690582.

In the book *NGOs in the Muslim World: Faith and Social Services,* the editor Susumu Nejima, a professor of regional development studies at Toyo University in Tokyo, Japan, writes about an interesting subject on which little research can be found. Professor Nejima has done a lot of work on Muslim organizations and their relationships with government, private, and community-based institutions. The names of the authors of the nine chapters of the book indicate specialized expertise in the subject of the book and therefore, the writing is very engaging with rich and very informative content.

The purpose of this book as described by the editor is "to discuss the relationship of the Muslim organizations with Islamic institutions, as well as their interpretations of the contemporary issues faced by NGOs within a specifically Islamic framework." Therefore, the book comes as a useful source for researchers, students, and decision makers who deal with charitable and faith-based initiatives and activities. This book is based on a five-year group study (2006-2011) which attempts to present comprehensible ideas about Muslims' faith-based initiatives in several countries, primarily in Indonesia, Bangladesh, Turkey, Japan, Jordan, and Egypt. One of the main arguments in the book is that Muslims' NGOs is not an isolated phenomenon. Rather, it heavily relies on the value system of Islam and the profound concept of community and collective spirit; placing the interests of the group above the narrow interests of the individuals. The book discusses the meanings and applications of Islamic concepts, such as *zakat, sadaqat, tasqwa, thawab, waqf,* and *Ramadan.* However, the book brilliantly escapes the trap of labels and labeling; instead of narrowly define NGO, the book broadens the definition to include religious and non-religious organizations that operate within the Muslim framework of community-based civic activism (p. 3). Based on this, the nine chapters of the book aim to answer the following major questions: how does Islamic religious texts inspire Muslims to engage in NGO? What are the religious expectations of Muslim volunteers? And how Muslims support their NGOs? (p. 4).

In addition to a very informative *Introduction*, the book includes eight chapters. In Chapter 2 on *Charity in Islam*, Amy Singer discusses the history of philanthropy in Muslim societies with a special focus on the Ottoman era when *waqf* was a well-practiced form of philanthropy. Although NGOs did not directly emerge out of *waqf*, the popularity and long history of the latter has established a natural ground for the former to grow and continue. *Waqf* or endowments have spread everywhere in the Ottoman Empire; thus, people from different levels were familiar with the services those charitable institutions provided. The author gives many examples of *waqf* including one of the largest enterprises in Jerusalem, Mecca, Madina, and Damascus where hundreds of thousands of people benefited from diverse services the *waqf* provided. This chapter also documents some major challenges that faced *waqf*, such as financial deterioration and struggle to survive the changing governmental regulations and interactions with *waqf* activists. The official ties between governments and *waqf*, reliance of large groups of disadvantaged people on charitable services, and the recognition and lack of recognition of the status of *waqf* in the macroeconomy of Muslim states are other challenges that face this type of NGOs. In Chapter 3, Susumu Nejima writes about a case study from Pakistan where *waqf* is utilized to establish large NGOs that provide cultural, social, medical, and educational services to a growing clientele in many countries. The institutional apparatus of these NGOs indicates the level of maturity which *waqf* has achieved. The author uses interviews to collect data about this case study in addition to providing historical background of the NGOs in Pakistan. Chapter 4 is written by Sachico Hosoya who uses questionnaires and interviews to shed lights on the charitable enterprise in Tehran, Iran and discusses how providing a bathing service to senior people who have nobody to care for them. The author traces the spiritual sources of this enterprise to the religious origins of "doing well" without expecting materialistic return, except the good deeds. In Chapter 5 the author, Egbert Harmsen, uses old data from 2003 and 2004 to discuss the experience of NGOs in Jordan as re-energizing interpretation of social cooperativeness. The author explains that *Al Afaf* is a community-based, not-for-profit organization which aims to help young men and women to wed by supporting them with services which they cannot afford, such as wedding parties, first house furniture, and similar services. The weakness of this chapter though is its attempt to force the issue of women and dishonor killing without real justification or even real analysis. Takenobu Aoki writes in Chapter 6 about environmental initiatives in Indonesia with neat typology of environmentalism among Muslim Indonesians. The author explains how enterprises, such as eco-pesantren, stem its values from the Islamic values of environmental protection, environmental preservation, and environmental behavior. The teachings of Prophet Mohamed and the Holy *Qur'an* provide a rich source of environmental concepts that aim to better enhance the safe living of people in compatible way with their natural environment. In Chapter 7, Fumiko Sawae writes about gender issues in Turkey and emphasizes the interconnection between Islamic values of gender equality and environmental rights. This chapter documents the history of NGOs and provides description of their membership. In Chapter 8, Ihsan Yilmaz writes about peace-building in light of the Gulen movement. Unfortunately, however, the author puts the people in Turkey into two groups; moderates and radicals, forcing therefore political analysis in his analysis of NGOs. In the last chapter (number 9), Susumu Nejima and Idris Danismaz tell the readers about the role of Muslim NGOs in Japan and document, in doing so, the experience of global Muslim relief activities and the huge amount of donated time, effort, materials, and money in order to help the 'others' in facing natural disasters.

Finally, the book is an excellent material for those who wish to understand some of the "drivers" of NGOs in the Muslim world. The entire book is devoted to enhancing the readers' knowledge about the values, history, and contemporary developments of NGOs and faith-based initiatives in various Muslim countries. The language and methodologies utilized in the book remain valid and authentic. In a newer edition of the book, it would be further enriching if there was a chapter on the theological, *Fiqh*, aspects that drive and motivate people in the past and present to engage in non-for-profit activities. Emphasizing references from the Holy *Qur'an* and Sunna (teachings of the Prophet Mohamed) would give the discussion of NGOs significant ethical, moral, and religious dimensions that can be added to the cultural and organizational dimensions which the book has illustrated. Students, scholars, and decision makers, nevertheless, are encouraged to read this book and to use it in their specialized discussions of NGOs. *AY*

Saudi Arabian Foreign Policy: Conflict and Cooperation in Uncertain Times

Neil Partrick, Ed. New York, NY: I.B. Tauris. 336 pp. ISBN: 978-1780769141.

The book brings together original and previously published papers on aspects of Saudi Arabia (SA) foreign policy, and the overlapping relationships with states and regions in a historical context as well as their relevance to the ever-changing present. At the writing of this review, the Saudi Royal Court announced a reverse in the line of succession by naming the 31 years old Prince Mohammed bin Salman as the crown prince and next in line to the throne to succeed his ailing father, King Salman bin Abdulaziz Al-Saud. This, at the expense of his nephew, Mohammed bin Nayef, could prove to be a mixed blessing for a kingdom in transition that faces significant international challenges of its own making. The ascension of Prince Mohammed to the throne signals an attempt by the Saudi monarchy to appease the young Saudis, who view the prince as more attuned to their aspirations and potential instrument for change that the Saudi kingdom desperately needs.

The book's contributions vary in originality, as well as dates of publication. Some could be considered original contributions and other reprints or re-edits of previously published papers or articles. In the Preface to the book, the editor states as his purpose for publishing the book "to examine the motivational factors affecting Saudi Arabian foreign relations and the capacity or limitations of policy applications in key relationships" (p. ix).

The book consists of 21 chapters, and a 15-page conclusion. The first three chapters provide an overview of the domestic factors at play within Saudi Arabia, and how these impact on decision-making, external outreach, and the underlying economic and political imperatives that drive policy formulation. The remaining chapters examine relationships with key states, both in their own right and sometimes in the context of regional dynamics.

The first part of the book titled "The Internal Context" includes three chapters: Chapter 1: "The Internal Context" by Neil Partrick; Chapter 2: "Islam and Identity in Foreign Policy" by Nenno Preuschaft; and Chapter 3: "Saudi Arabia and the Politics of Oil" by Neil Quilliam.

Mindful or the Saudi foreign policy aims which include striving for legitimacy, ensuring that other regional states do not overly threaten its regional cohesion or external security, Part II of the book titled "Saudi Arabia's Foreign Relations" contains 18. Each chapter deals with a different aspect of the

Saudi foreign relations with individually named countries round the globe and the kingdom's relations with these countries. Chapters 4 to 14 deal with Saudi relations with Arab countries in alphabetical order from Egypt to Yemen. Chapters 15 to 17 deal with two East Asian countries, Indonesia and Malaysia, while chapter 18 deals with South Asia. Saudi relations with Europe, Russia, and the US are treated in chapters 19, 20, and 21, respectively.

As the chapters' authors note, the Saudis have used their petrodollars to shore up the dynasty regime, get rid of enemies or perceived threats to the system of spreading the Wahhabi's version of Islam among Muslims and converts to Islam worldwide, using the power of petrodollars. This has also resulted in supporting these autocratic regimes regardless of the will of the people, as long as these regimes fall in line with the Saudi objectives and within its orbit.

Collectively, the chapters address the various aspects and manifestations of the Saudi foreign relations in general, and with specific countries in particular. Furthermore, the contributors deal with some of the disputes and contradictions that mar the kingdom's relations with these countries, and how such contradictions serve the Saudi regime's self-interest and preservation of its absolute monarchy. The Saudi ultimate objective is what is good for the Saudi monarchy and its continued existence against all odds. As some of the book's contributing authors point out, the interests of the Saudi monarchy are different from the interests of those in its political orbit. The poorer Muslim countries look and hope to gain the approval and generosity of the largess of the Saudi financial assistance which invariably have strings attached. In Egypt's case, the Saudi largesse is conditioned upon Egypt's acquiesce to being a friendly and obedient regime, such as the present one, in return for the billions of dollars not accounted for by Egypt's leadership. The Saudi animosity toward present day Tehran, as opposed to the friendly relations with the former Shah's regime, has placed the Middle East in the unenviable position of disarray as witnessed from the current crisis between Saudi Arabia and Qatar, and the resulting weakening and disfranchisement of the GCC block for the sake of Saudi's self-interest.

As the various book's chapters emphasized, the regime's survival is uppermost in the Saudi ruling family's mind. Fear of actual or perceived external or internal influence that could result in regime change influences the Saudi red line. This is evident in the case of the Yemen war that plagued Nasser's regime in the 1960s, the first Gulf War (GW) in 1990-91 to rid Kuwait of Saddam's military invasion, and GW2 that was launched on the false pretense that Saddam was about to invade the Saudi kingdom and bring about the demise of the Saudi dynasty.

Prior to the Trump Administration's cozying up with Saudi Arabia, the Obama Administration sought to establish a balance of power between the two most powerful adversaries in the region, Saudi Arabia and Iran, as it failed to persuade Israel to negotiate a peaceful resolution to the festering Palestinian-Israeli conflict. The current Trump Administration, on the other hand, is trying to bolster Saudi Arabia as the counter to the growing Iranian influence in the region in general and in the Gulf States in particular, and to vilify the Iranian regime's nuclear agreement that was signed during the Obama Administration, and was condemned by the Saudis and Israelis. Further complicating the matter for the AGS block led by SA is the Qatar crisis, which has divided the Gulf block between those on the side of Saudi Arabia (Bahrain, UAE, Egypt) on one hand, and those trying to mediate the conflict (Kuwait, Oman and Jordan) on the other hand. The American position on the matter has varied from first blaming and condemning Qatar, to the present effort to mediate the conflict and urging the disputing parties to reach an amicable resolution.

In *Saudi Arabian Foreign Policy,* Neil Partrick and the contributing authors managed to give a thoughtful analysis of the complexities of the Saudi foreign relations with the rest of the countries. The ups and downs and the challenges that will face the young king-in-waiting Mohammed bin Salman at a time of oil glut, declining oil prices, armed conflicts around the kingdom, and internal as well as external threats can form serious challenges to the House of Al-Saud. *MMA*

Sectarianization: Mapping the New Politics of the Middle East

Nader Hashemi, Danny Postel, Eds. Oxford, UK: Oxford University Press, 2017 (1ˢᵗ ed.). 320 pp. ISBN: 978: 0190664886.

Much of the contemporary analyses on the ongoing conflicts in the Middle East, namely Syria and Iraq, takes it for granted that the violence is rooted in a 1,400-year-old conflict between Sunni and Shiʻa Muslims. This neo-oriental assumption centers religion as the main category of analysis and frames it as the primary cause and site of conflict in the region. Much like Northern Ireland and the former Yugoslavia, sectarianism is presented as a product of atavistic hatreds, which are endemic to local communities and trans-historical in nature. This approach implies that sectarianism persists despite socio-economic and political change. Hence, works like *Sectarianization: Mapping the New Politics of the Middle East* are an important and timely response to the dangerous sectarian meta-narrative that pervades much of contemporary thinking on the topic.

Edited by Nader Hashemi and Danny Postel, this volume brings together scholars from different academic disciplines to address the term sectarianism as it pertains to the Middle East. Rather than framing sectarianism as a religious problem, the authors see it as something, which is strategically and cynically deployed by different political actors, including states, to promote and advance their own parochial agendas. Hence, one of the central arguments of this book is that elites have manipulated sectarian identities as a tool to hold on to power, seemingly at any cost and to the detriment of the region.

Given the history of use and abuse of the term sectarianism, not to mention its conceptual fuzziness as an analytical category, a new term called "sectarianization" is advanced. This rightly recognizes that the mobilization around a sectarian identity is political and social. It is a contingent *process* and not, as mentioned earlier, a trans-historical phenomenon embedded in the social landscape. Following the introduction, the book is divided in two sections. Part one of the text discusses sectarianization in its historical, geopolitical, and theoretical perspectives, while part two guides the reader through various rich case studies, illustrating the processual nature of sectarianization. The rest of the review will selectively highlight the main strengths of this work.

Historical Roots of Sectarianization

In the first chapter of the book, Ussama Makdisi argues that the sectarianization of the Middle East began with the unraveling of the old Ottoman socio-political order, grounded in privilege and hierarchy on one hand and the recognition of difference on the other hand. However, the challenges and pressures posed by the various European powers led to a project of radical reform known as the Tanzimat. This series of reforms introduced new political concepts such as equality before the law regardless of religion, nationalism, and citizenship. This would dramatically alter the socio-political landscape of the Ottoman Empire, where the ideological and material relationship between the ruler and ruled was transformed. These events inadvertently lead to a dramatic, rapid rise in inter-communal violence between different religious and ethnic communities. In response to the violence, the Ottoman authorities, along with the European powers created and institutionalized sectarian political systems such as the Mutasarrifiyya of Mount Lebanon. Although a product of colonial politics interacting with local conditions and actors, sectarian systems of governance would be back-projected into the distant past and hence became a part of the "natural" political order of the Middle East.

Contemporary Sectarianization

Following the collapse of the Ottoman Empire and the formation of nation-states, the process of sectarianization in the region continued apace although with different trajectories and particularities depending on the state. For instance, Bassel Salloukh's chapter on the architecture of sectarianism in Lebanon neatly lays out the pernicious infrastructure in its material practices and legal, discursive, and ideational dimensions, which underpins and reproduces sectarianism in Lebanon. In the absence of viable political alternatives sectarianism has achieved a sort of ideological primacy in the country. Moreover, as Yezid Sayigh illustrates in his chapter any cogent analysis of sectarianization must also focus on the internal dynamics of (Arab) states and not center solely on colonial and imperial policies in the production of sectarianism. Besides affirming the agency of local actors, the analysis rightfully implicates them as well.

A major turning point in the sectarian relations in the Middle East came with the American invasion and occupation of Iraq in 2003. On a local scale this event created the conditions for the sectarianization of Iraqi society and politics. On a regional scale, the Saudi-Iranian rivalry dramatically increased with both sides playing the sectarian card, albeit in different ways. Analyzing the case of Iraq, Fanar Haddad in his chapter argues that the roots of Iraq's current sectarian moment can be found in its recent authoritarian past. Of course, this phenomenon only achieved full expression with the institutionalization of a sectarian political system implemented by the American occupation authorities. Thus, the move unleashed different sectarian entrepreneurs on the Iraqi political and electoral scene with predictably disastrous results. Interestingly, Haddad writes that with the ongoing violence in Iraq, a politicized if uncertain Sunni identity has emerged in the field as a reaction to the sectarianization of Iraqi politics, which was not present there before.

Another major turning came in 2011, with the Arab Spring, when the people demanded their rights and the end of authoritarian regimes. For a brief moment, it seemed that it would succeed, but the Gulf monarchies held the line and ferociously fought back. Leading the way was Saudi Arabia, which, as Madawi al-Rasheed in her chapter contends, invoked the specter of sectarian difference in order to divide and weaken the opposition in the country. She argues that the real threat to the Saudi regime is not the dissident Shiʻa notables of the eastern province, but a united cross-sectarian political opposition that can credibly challenge it. Ultimately, she writes, the Saudi royal family's calculations are not motivated by an innate sectarian solidarity, but the desire to hold on to power, even if it means polarizing Saudi society. In his chapter on Syria, Paulo Gabriel Hilu Pinto argues that the process of sectarianization proceeded from different vectors, but it was the Syrian regime's framing of the initial uprising for freedom and dignity as a Sunni Salafi uprising and positioning itself as the defender of religious minorities that greatly contributed to the current civil war. This discursive move, backed by the selective distribution of physical violence according to the sect, gave an opportunity to Islamist and jihadi actors to claim that they are the defenders of Sunni lives and interests. Moreover, their actions have been buttressed by the financial largesse of the Gulf monarchies, which have also been promoting sectarianism in the region. Sectarian violence has become a self-fulfilling prophecy and as the civil war grinds on, sectarianization serves as a tool of mobilization and indoctrination.

Like in the former Yugoslavia, the deployment of sectarian language, rhetoric, and practices by different actors (supported by outside powers) has had the effect of masking deep social, economic, and political cleavages in a given society. It was and remains a route to power and wealth as the case of Bosnia illustrates. What this empirically rich and theoretically sophisticated volume shows is that there are multiple processes that drive sectarianization in the Middle East, and not religious fanaticism. It decisively rejects simplistic and orientalist depictions of Middle Eastern societies and history. I would highly recommend this book for both undergraduate and graduate courses in contemporary Middle Eastern politics. **MK**

Shifting Sands: The Unraveling of the Old Order in the Middle East

Raja Shehadeh, Penny Johnson, Eds. Northampton, MA: Olive Branch Press, 2016. 262 pp. ISBN: 978-156656056.

This compilation of previously published essays is a boon for educators looking for accessible and important articles contained in one concise volume. Penny Johnson's essay, "The Significance of a Screwdriver," introduces the volume. She begins with the tragic story of Ra'ed al Hom, a hero to Gaza residents for his years of successfully defusing unexploded ordinance with little protective gear or equipment, who had just been killed in Gaza trying to defuse a 500 kg bomb with a screwdriver. To understand today's realities, she argues, we need to go back to World War I, when the Ottoman Empire was collapsing and British and French diplomats divided up its eastern territories into their spheres of influence. In the first essay, Avi Shlaim states convincingly that in pursuing their own imperial interests in World War I and its aftermath, the French and British, in effect, created the basis for today's regional struggles. After retelling the story of conflicting British and French promises and interests in World War I, James Barr wonders what would have happened if the Arab provinces of the Ottoman Empire had been allowed to form their own governments. It might, he supposes, have led to a better transition. But great power politics held sway over local aspirations with consequences that we see today in the seemingly unending conflicts in Israel Palestine, Syria, and Iraq. Salim Tamari reminds us that the war in the eastern Mediterranean was far from a minor episode; a sixth of the population perished, new nations were artificially created, and local identities are resurfacing in today's identity conflicts, ethnic ambivalence, and national dualisms. By studying three World War I diaries, he observes that the significance of Gallipoli — is believed by the Australians — that it led to Australian nationhood; and to the Turks that it was its first great victory. In reality, most of the Ottoman fighters and war dead came from non-Turkish regions of the empire, and most of the troops in Mustafa Kemal's (later Ataturk) two battalions were Syrian Arabs. The Ottoman idea of a common citizenship and multi-ethnic homeland came to an end in World War I, replaced by exclusivism and chauvinistic nationalism.

Khaled Fahmy wonders what the Tahrir demonstrators really wanted. Were they calling for constitutional and civil rights, or protesting the existence of the modern Egyptian state itself? Muhammad Ali had created a tyrannical state with no social contract and no rule of law. Egyptians however resisted the tyrannical state by every means possible. How to deal with British and later American interference, with the Egyptian military, expanded to struggle against Israel, but now a domestic economic and political monopoly, with petrodollars, with lack of a golden age held up as a symbolic goal, and finally with political Islam? For Fahmy, historical movements and events may point the way.

Tamim al-Barghouti points out that states in the region have failed to protect and defend their citizens from civil war and invasion. New forms of political existence and new networks and ideas that can form and dissolve are replacing the more rigid failed states. Justin Marozzi offers a pessimistic view from Iraq and also Libya but hopes that the current cycle of violence may turn into a more peaceful era. Ramita Navai argues that Iranians are constrained by the government and disillusioned and discontented by their social options. Nevertheless, Iran may yet come in from the cold and join in international partnerships. Alev Scott's essay on Turkey was written before the attempted coup of July 15, 2016 changed everything, but it offers useful background and context to the current authoritarian trends.

Mai al-Nakib, a Kuwaiti writer, mourns an earlier, more cosmopolitan era in Kuwait, when citizenship was offered to all nationalities and educational standards were high. She has a book published by the Kuwaiti government in 1969 in which there are photos of a service at the Catholic Church, of women waterskiing, and women university students in class, none of whom wore the hijab. She includes a photo of Andy Warhol exhibiting his work in Kuwait in 1976. Through her novels, she is able to recreate a pre-1991, more cosmopolitan Kuwaiti society in which 380,000 Palestinians lived. Selma Dabbagh, a British-Palestinian novelist, created a fictional Gaza, and in so doing, put Gazans on the literary map. She sees a growing cosmopolitanism and global identity free of ethnic, religious, and racial tensions. Through the novels of Arab Women writers Marilyn Booth locates an alternative history of communities in which young people and women dream of social equality and fulfilling lives. She is heartened by the many new writers on the Arab literary scene, but worries that too many young people suffer from malnutrition, poor education, war, disease, sexual violence, domestic abuse, and in general the inequalities of the global system.

Dawn Chatty expects that a coalition of Beduin tribes and Kurds will bring the destruction in Syria to an end and the various ethnoreligious societies will remain whether or not the borders established after World War I remain in place. Robin Yassin-Kassab argues that the Syria she visited in 2011 and

2012 does not resemble the country presented in the Western media. There is a cultural revolution in which artists, TV shows, radio stations, internet poets, independent newspapers, and hip hop and heavy metal musicians are creating popular art that has replaced the government-sponsored top-down art of the past. Malu Halasa identifies a cultural revolution in the region and abroad, in which Syrian artists are producing music, videos, cartoons, and posters that advocate for rights and democracy.

In a brief conclusion, Raja Shehadeh observes that today despair is the dominant sentiment and optimism is in short supply. The essays, however, demonstrate that there is a creative energy pulsating throughout the region that offers exciting alternatives to the depredations of the past and present. ***NEG***

Spheres of Intervention: Foreign Policy and the Collapse of Lebanon, 1967-1976

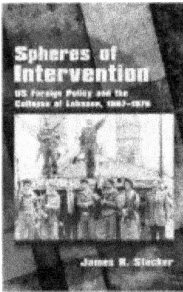

James R. Stocker. Ithaca, NY: Cornell University Press, 2016. 296 pp. ISBN: 978-1501700774.

James R. Stocker's *Spheres of Intervention: U.S. Foreign Policy and the Collapse of Lebanon, 1967-1976*, is a welcome addition to the literature concerning Lebanese politics during a turbulent time in the Middle East. Within this carefully research and balanced text the reader is presented not only with a detailed examination of Lebanon's domestic politics but also how various non-Lebanese actors (Israel, the Palestinians, Syria, and the United States) that influenced Lebanon's internal affairs.

Lebanon has always been a fragile state, possessing a complex political system based upon balancing various confessional and ethnic groups. Identity politics is diverse, for it involves not only an individual being the member of a particular confessional and ethnic group but also entails the sense of being Lebanese. Left to its own devices, Lebanon, no doubt, would have made its own way during the period Stocker considers. Unfortunately, as this work clearly points out Lebanon is rarely left alone.

Although Stocker's primary focus is on the relationship between the United States and Lebanon between 1967 and 1976, from the beginning it is clear that the Washington-Beirut connection is not simply bilateral. Rather it is the one tested by events largely outside of the control of either the United States or Lebanon. The easy connections of the past are no longer relevant.

Historically the United States and Lebanon had a pleasant relationship. The good works of American missionaries in the nineteenth and twentieth centuries in Beirut created fond feelings for Americans among the Lebanese people. Yet, Stocker is quick to point out that his work is no nostalgia trip. Rather the focus is Lebanese politics from 1967 to 1976. This time period involved two wars between Israel and its Arab neighbors as well as Lebanon's own decay into Civil War.

Washington's policy toward Lebanon must be seen within the context of three issues: first, the Cold War between the United States and the former Soviet Union and their respective competition for influence in the Middle East; second, the need to secure Western access to the oil resources of the Middle East; and third, the Arab-Israeli conflict. As Stocker tells his story it is the first and third factors (the Cold War and greater Arab-Israeli Conflict) that occupy the majority of Washington's efforts in Lebanon. The second issue, access to oil reserves, has little relevance to the Washington-Beirut connection. Although the United States will welcome the flow of petrodollars from wealthy Persian Gulf States into Lebanon, this issue is largely outside Stocker's concern. It is the Cold War and the Arab-Israeli Conflict that dominate the analysis.

This point is clearly brought to mind when Stocker examines the impact of both, the Six Day War in June 1967 and the October War of 1973, upon Lebanon. These conflicts showed the overall weakness of the Lebanese military, exposed Beirut's political structure to stresses between opposing elites in the country and laid bare the critical importance of the Palestinian refugees and the various groups associated with the Palestinians (Fatah and Popular Front for the Liberation of Palestine, for example). Of course, above all this floated the United States, first during the waning days of the Johnson Administration, and then under the Nixon and Ford Administrations, with Henry Kissinger first as National Security Advisor and then Secretary of State guiding Washington's policy in the region.

That policy revolved around the major combatants of the region (Egypt, Syria, and Israel) and when possible reducing the influence of the Soviet Union. Kissinger's "Shuttle Diplomacy" and resulting Disengagement Agreements between ignored Beirut. Lebanon was viewed as a side show within this context. The United States of course wanted a peaceful and stable Lebanon. Washington did provide limited military and political assistance when needed and tried to bring a measure of peace to the country when the

Lebanese Civil War broke out. An example of these efforts at peace making involved the mission of Special Envoy L. Dean Brown in 1976, which Stocker devoted a significant part of Chapter 7 to examining.

Washington also served as a useful go between for Lebanon and Israel as well as Israel and Syria throughout the period under examination. This communication channel did much to prevent direct conflict between Damascus and Tel Aviv, especially when the former moved forces into Lebanon in 1976. Never, though, did the United States address the key factor of the Palestinians, in terms of their impact upon Lebanese politics or the larger Middle East peace process.

As Stocker notes in his insightful *Epilogue*, the end of his analysis does not mean an end to Lebanon's woes, nor Washington's involvement in this country. The United States will return to Lebanon again during the Reagan Administration and have as little to show for its efforts as it did between 1967 and 1976. This reviewer hopes that Professor Stocker will bring his insightful analysis to the post-1976 period of Lebanese politics in the future. **WLR**

Statecraft in the Middle East: Foreign Policy, Domestic Politics and Security

Imad Mansour. New York, NY: I. B. Tauris, 2016. 282 pp. ISBN: 978:1784535803.

Political scientists, especially international relations and foreign policy specialists, are well aware of the theoretical approach of linkage politics, which for some reason is not mentioned in this work. Introduced by James N. Rosenau[1] and followed soon thereafter by Joseph Franke,[2] the efforts of state decision makers toward the external environment are dependent to some degree on their respective domestic political structure and set of condition.

Government policies dealing with the external environment and domestic demands must, the author (an Assistant Professor in the Department of International Affairs at the University of Qatar) argues, operate within an ideological and social context. His theoretical foundation is a social narrative that is essentially political culture (another comparative political theoretical formula not mentioned though applicable), the place of the state in history and its place in the world. Statecraft, as opposed to diplomacy, is understood to be a combination of local, regional, and even state-building processes. There is brought forth then a complex relationship between statehood, state-craft, and narratives. But it is the basic societal narrative that serves as a building block for statecraft.

In pursuit of the effort, Mansour selected six states in the Middle East, Muslim, Arab, Persian, and Jewish, hence a wide range with a temporal period of the latter part of the twentieth through the early twenty-first[1] century. Each of the countries selected for an empirical examination against the theoretical construct — Egypt, Israel, Syria, Turkey, Saudi Arabia, Iran — are treated to a perspicacious, but not necessarily balanced, review.

Credit must be given to the author to parlay a rich understanding of the political dynamics of such an array of Middle Eastern polities and providing a relatively extensive bibliography to further guide the reader. Despite the few deficiencies noted, this work should be considered a valued contribution to international relations theory and the comparative politics literature. **SRS**

References

[1] James N. Rosenau ed. *Linkage Politics.* New York, NY: Free Press, 1969.

[2] Joseph Frankel. *Contemporary International Theory and the Behavior of States.* New York, NY: Oxford University Press, 1973.

SAUDI ARABIA

King Faisal of Saudi Arabia: Personality, Faith and Times

Alexei Vassiliev. London, UK: Saqi Books, 2015. 528 pp. ISBN: 978: 0863561290.

The book *King Faisal of Saudi Arabia Personality, Faith and Times* is a magnificent work by Alexei Vassiliev. Vassiliev, who has authored the award-winning book, *The History of Saudi Arabia* has outdone himself in this book, which is a biography of King Faisal bin Abd al-Aziz of Saudi Arabia, and aptly covers all aspects of Faisal's life. Vassiliev delivers and fulfils the objectives he sets for himself in the preface. Probing the issues in-depth, Vassiliev provides the most sophisticated explanation, providing factual details and objective analyses. He fills in the details that help put things in perspective so that readers can understand Faisal's take on issues. Not many authors would admit to the inherent bias in their work while Vassiliev warns the readers beforehand of any prejudices. However, one does not come across any as whatever position he takes is supported by substantial evidence. He shows great expertise on politics, history, economy, defense, and sociology of the Saudi Kingdom.

The book has twenty-nine chapters, a preface and an epilogue. Only a work of this magnitude and caliber could do justice to King Faisal. Vassiliev keeps the reader hooked to the last. He takes the readers on a journey through Faisal's life as if living his life, sharing his experiences, learning his lessons and understanding the rationale behind his decisions. What a joyous ride! With his powerful descriptions, he transforms the reader into the world of Faisal, strolling through the streets of Najd into the mud houses and the lives of the Najdi's. He introduces readers to the life of Faisal from the early years, his upbringing and how two great figures left lasting imprint on the personality of Faisal — his father, King Abd al-Aziz ibn Abd al-Rahman and his maternal grandfather Sheikh Abdallah ibn Abd al-Latif, a revered religious scholar. Faisal's religious convictions were instilled in him by his grandfather.

No story of Faisal can be complete without King Abd al-Aziz and Vassiliev discusses Abd al-Aziz to a great degree. Aziz was a political strategist first, and then a warrior. Aziz played any political gambit that helped. He would play two great powers simultaneously but would never risk coming on hostile terms with them. He would make peace with adversaries when the circumstances demanded and when the conditions became favorable, struck them hard.

Faisal was tutored by the best military commanders, aided by the most seasoned diplomats and exposed to the foreign world from an earliest. Possessing a curious mind, a keen Faisal absorbed information and learned quickly. Faisal was an "all-rounder" and successful in everything. He secured victory in his first military expedition in Asir. His first appointment as Viceroy of Hijaz instilled in him governance skills which would later be replicated later in the country. He ruled Hijaz, the most sacred place for the Muslims, with much devotion. As a foreign minister, he displayed deep knowledge of history and law beyond his age.

Vassiliev goes to great length in explaining the controversy behind Faisal's taking over from his brother, Saud. Abd al-Aziz acknowledged the potential in Faisal, stating that he wished he had more sons like Faisal. Abd al-Aziz knew that, between Saud and Faisal, Faisal was the smarter one. Abd al-Aziz could foresee a feud developing over succession after his death. He, therefore, took a pledge of loyalty from Faisal and asked Saud to take counsel from Faisal. Soon after the two would develop a rift over how they would govern their people that gained strength. Faisal, however, stayed true to the word given to his father, but did not compromise on his principles even if it meant giving up his position. Saud could not keep up on many fronts. The family intervened and asked Saud to step down. On assuming power, Faisal rectified Saud's policies and took new initiatives.

Faisal embarked upon a wide range of reform programs, paving the way for development and modernization. Undertaking reforms was not the easiest job in a conservative society like Saudi Arabia. There was resistance and opposition to everything, whether big or small, for example, putting women's photographs on their passports. He laid down the infrastructure for change and welcomed new ideas and expert opinion and selected the most competent people for his team. He was careful in making a move toward modernization at just the right pace. Understanding the significance of information and propaganda warfare, he introduced radio and TV into the mix. Faisal was concerned for the welfare of the people. As soon as oil money became available, Faisal put them to good use through provision of municipal, health, education services etc. He took upon himself the restoration of holy places. He steered the Kingdom through domestic turmoil, economic crunch, and international threats. Had it not been for King Faisal, the story of the

Kingdom would have been very different. If Abd al-Aziz founded the Kingdom, it was King Faisal who was behind the political and economic success of the Kingdom.

Faisal's life was not without challenges and he would work assiduously to overcome all these challenges — the war in Yemen, Arab nationalism, and taking over ARAMCO, etc. He resolved these issues in the best way possible. Regarding the Palestinian issue, he reached out to Muslim countries and laid the framework for Muslim cooperation. King Faisal was a unique combination of modern and traditional culture. For Faisal, two things were of utmost interests — Islam and national interests of Saudi Arabia. His opposition to Communism was driven by his religious beliefs. But did this belief stop him from cooperating with the West? Not quite. Time and again, he was proven wrong on his earlier assessment of the US. However, common interests continued to bind the two countries in a "special relationship." He initiated lobbying in the US to show a favorable view of his country.

Faisal possessed traits of great leaders. He was disciplined and diligent. As a King, he would work for longer hours, never taking a day off despite his failing health. He was an experienced politician and well-versed in the art of governance, financial management, and international politics. He was polite and modest. Many leaders would testify to his wisdom and competence including his enemies. Vassiliev does a good job in getting the readers know this great King. The book is a must-read for anyone who is interested in Saudi Arabia or the regional politics. *MS*

Modern Woman in the Kingdom of Saudi Arabia: Rights, Challenges and Achievements

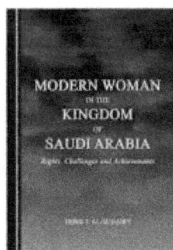

Hend T. Al-Sudairy. Newcastle, U.K.: Cambridge Scholars Publishing. 150 pp. ISBN: 978-1443872812.

Modern Woman in the Kingdom of Saudi Arabia: Rights, Challenges and Achievements was written by Hend T. Al-Sudairy and published by Cambridge Scholars Publishing in 2017. The book documents the Saudi woman's aspects of life, achievements, and challenges, notably shaped by Saudi conservative traditions and social structures that have restricted her opportunities and played a major role in making her unfamiliar to the world.

Divided into six chapters, this book portrays the Saudi woman's life journey from the nineteenth century up to the present time, scrutinizing the way she has been located within her family, society, and nation in general, and thus highlighting the major empowering governmental policies and the social changes which contributed to her progress and development.

According to the book, the twenty-first century Saudi woman is much more than the mystery stereotypically represented to the masses as either an ignorant oppressed woman or an extravagant and luxurious creature. She revolts against social destructive traditions that inhibit her success, yet honorably embraces others. The Saudi woman is an active pioneering subject in her society leading national and international roles.

The book's first chapter focuses on the Saudi woman's history, describing aspects of her social and economic life and contributions to her community that differed according to geographical space as well as social strata. It is an attempt to unveil the Saudi woman's life facets described by the writer as "aspects […] of pride, while others were gloomy and hectic" (p. 22), especially amid the change and development of the country advocated by the Saudi government in the last hundred years to allow much more socio-economic space for female citizens who, according to the writer, have " always had [their] status given within [their] home and among [their] family"(p. 2), yet not equally "granted a role outside it"(p. 2).

In the second chapter, the writer tackles the issue of the Saudi woman's early education and compares it to the modern era, and affirms that education problem has been worldwide and not a dilemma that has existed only in the area that would become known in the early nineteenth century as Saudi Arabia, asserting that "the early women's education problem is not confined to Saudi Arabia only, as education is one of the most important paths towards the empowerment of women everywhere. It is also an area where discrimination against women exists everywhere" (p. 27). This chapter describes the progress of Saudi woman's education and its modalities throughout history, as well as the role education has played in developing the Saudi women's critical thinking and thus attitudes toward themselves, traditions, rights, and demands.

The flow of the Saudi woman's personal, social, and economic development would be widely examined in the third chapter that depicts the way Saudi women have abandoned their traditional role for a more successful and assertive one, though heavily challenged by a variety of obstacles.

In the fourth and fifth chapters, the writer provides a general view on Saudi women's early and contemporary writings, drawing major lines of conversion in writing conditions and then interests and tones, as early female writers used to "exemplify an anxiety in many different periods of their writing journey, and an awareness of their status, rights, struggle, and the social pressures upon them" (p. 55), and hence documented Saudi women's personal development as well as political, economic, and social awareness, whereas contemporary writings are stronger and more liberal in their modes of expression, "seeking social reform, criticizing the social laws regarding women or simply attempting to climb the fame ladder through stepping on forbidden territories" (p. 69). According to the writer, contemporary novels are an optimistic female response toward a powerful writing tradition that reflects Saudi women's consciousness of their own existence. A selection of contemporary female Saudi novels is studied in the fifth chapter to familiarize the reader with their themes and artistic values, such as *Malamah (Features)* by Zainab Hufni, *Jahliah (Pr- Islamic Era)* by Layla Aljahni, and *Alwarfah (The Lush Tree)* by Omaimah Al-Khamis.

The book's sixth chapter is devoted to examining the Saudi woman's achievements in the fields of education, politics, sports, and mass media, as well as the impediments she is still challenging, some of which are "not limited to Saudi women but are shared by other women worldwide" (p. 123). The chapter stresses the fact that Saudi women have had major leading roles as social and political decision makers, and that they have always been active subjects in their society, yet in the modern era, their active political role "has entered a hibernation period for social and custom-related reasons" (p.113). *NM*

Of Sand or Soil: Genealogy & Tribal Belonging in Saudi Arabia

Nadav Samin. Princeton and Oxford: Princeton University Press, 2015. 304 pp. ISBN: 978-0691164441.

Both popular media and academic writing have recently focused attention on the retribalization of the Middle East, attributing the reversion to the traditional socio-political structure of Arab society to the collapse of central state authority throughout the region. All such analysis would be advised to consult Nadiv Samin's *Of Sand or Soil*. In this revision of his

2013 dissertation "The Dark Matter of Tribal Belonging: Genealogical Representation and Practice in Saudi Arabia," Samin, a lecturer in anthropology at Dartmouth College, argues that since the 1960s, a culture of genealogy, strongly encouraged by the Saudi government's genealogical rule of governance, has led to an assertion of tribal identity throughout Saudi society.

Samin develops his thesis through an examination of the life of Hamad al-Jasir (1909-2000), a Wahhabi legal official with Arab nationalist tendencies turned educator, journalist, philologist, geographer, and historian whose professional life balanced criticism of the Wahhabi establishment and occasional exile with Saudi patronage and financial support, who became, in the author's telling, the leading Saudi genealogist of the twentieth century. Chapter 1 outlines al-Jasir's life within the context of twentieth century Saudi history. In Chapter 2, Samin examines the function of genealogy in central Saudi Arabia from the early Wahhabi period (late 18th century) through the twentieth century. Chapters 3-5 return to Hamad al-Jasir and the development of a methodology leading to the culture of genealogy from the 1970s on, including the struggle between oral tradition and written documentation in validating genealogies, a case study of the Bahila tribe, in which al-Jasir utilized marriage patterns in order to determine tribal status and reputation, and a case study of the town of Ula and the influence of newly settled Bedouin populations pressing a largely non-tribal settled population to claim tribal identity, but introducing the whole issue of race into the tribal equation. Chapter 6 traces the role of the Saudi government in supplanting the security and political functions of the tribes with a genealogical rule of governance that emphasized tribal association in establishing personal and national identity. Samin concludes by discussing the relationship between the culture of genealogy and Wahhabism, the Saudi state, and the economic system heavily dependent on foreign labor.

The archetype of Arabian society is a unit comprised of all males descended from the same grandfather. Its function is to define those to whom one is obligated in any conflict (in such matters as a blood feud), who one should marry (the ideal being your father's brother's offspring), and from whom one inherited. It might also define one's occupation and status. It provides one with the *nisbah Āl, Banu, Awlad* (among other terms), Fulan (the name of the grandfather), or Fulani attached to the end of the name, thereby establishing one identification. By design, the unit is dynamic since as an individual ages, he (it is paternalistic) potentially has three different *nisbas* as he moves from his grandfather's, father's, and his own unit. Finally, it associates one with a larger unit (known in English as "tribe") of all males descended from a more distant common ancestor. The tribe provides a higher order of protection and political authority, expands marriage opportunities, and access to property, as each tribe claimed a more or less clearly defined territory (*dirah or dār*). It also added another *nisbah* to one's name. The system provided for the inclusion of foreigners and other non-tribals who were not biologically related, but living within the territory, who could be brought in as a *mawlā* (client). Since it's an archetype, it is very fluid. For example, there might not be a sufficient number of individuals of one or the other gender to form a viable paternal unit. Groups simply adjusted accordingly. The larger tribal unit might be less fluid, but they, too, adjusted to circumstances, as individual or collective paternal groups joined or split off.

Samin's focus is on the fluid nature of this social structure with specific attention to the external factors that influence it and the genealogical factors that validate it. In particular, during the last 60-some years in Saudi Arabia, Samin argues that the tribal unit has become much more important as the basis of individual identity across a wider spectrum of the Saudi population than was the case historically. Samin identifies a variety of pressures, among them the religious elite's opposition to tribal identity in favor of Muslim identity and general disdain for lax Bedouin religious observance; a centralized state authority that provided the security and material goods previously provided by the tribe, added a higher level of political authority, and physically set out to destroy the Bedouin through forced settlement; and economic development which served to create employment and status opportunities and pressured archetypical marriage patterns, that all served to weaken tribal institutions.

However, Samin observes that paradoxically, many of these same factors served to reinforce the tribal system. Emphasis on Islam still left the practical issue of national identity, and Wahhabi opposition to local religious practices encouraged groups to look to alternative sources of identity. Town-dwelling populations who tended to be less concerned with tribal culture came into contact with and were influenced by newly settled Bedouin for whom tribal identity remained salient. Economic patterns, too, while having the potential to lessen tribal identity, raised new identity issues as the country was flooded with foreign laborers and Saudis sought a system to establish their own nationality. Furthermore, marriage arrangements continued to take into consideration status, and while cross-tribal marriages became more acceptable, the relative status of the tribes became a factor in the decision. The Saudi royal family may have wished to lessen tribal authority, but tribal identity provided an important source of its own legitimacy. Even foreign policy, most notably the 1950s Buraymi dispute among Saudi Arabia, Abu Dhabi, and Oman, revolved around tribal identification and loyalties. Eventually the Al-Sa'ud adopted policies, such as the national identity paper that required a *nisbah,* although it was not legally required to be a tribal identity that institutionalized the tribal heritage as central to Saudi national identity.

Tribal identity required verification, and that came through genealogy. This created a great challenge, especially as the focus was on the extended tribe rather than the four/five generation base unit for, while nearly everyone knew his/her grandfather and most tribes have elaborate genealogies that link the usually long-distant eponymous ancestor with the two great tribal founders — i.e. Qahtan and Adnan — all of the generations in between are generally quite vague. Historically, it was of minor importance, and given the fluid nature of tribal structure there were advantages to imprecise linkages. However, validating one's tribal affiliation became central to what Samin calls the culture of genealogy as scholars, most notably Hamad al-Jasir, had to develop a methodology to recreate long-lost family trees. A particular challenge in the process was the balancing of oral traditions, upon which genealogy had been based historically, and a greater emphasis on written documentation. The government also became part of the process, employing tribal *mu'arrif* (experts) to monitor and validate identities. What had once been a fluid social institution became much more rigid.

This is an outstanding addition to the literature of modern Saudi Arabia that also serves to put the whole contemporary analysis of retribalization into a much broader context. Samin successfully demonstrates that despite religious, political, and economic forces that diminished tribal institutions, cross-pressures countered those trends, and in the process a culture of genealogy combined with a bureaucratic genealogical rule of governance to lead Saudis to assert tribal descent…and so establish their ancient roots in the Arabian Peninsula (pp. 2-3). **CHA**

The Other Saudis: Shi'ism, Dissent and Sectarianism

Toby Matthiesen. Cambridge, UK: Cambridge University Press, 2014. 306 pp. ISBN: 978-1107043046.

Toby Matthiesen, Research Fellow in Islamic and Middle Eastern Studies at Pembroke College, University of Cambridge, is to be commended for his timely and wide-ranging examination of the Shia minority in Saudi Arabia. For this text provides readers with an opportunity to gain greater awareness, not only of the Sunni-Shi'a divide within the Kingdom of Saudi Arabia, but also a better understanding of the nature of Shi'ism throughout the Middle East.

Matthiesen examines the nature of Shi'ism in Saudi Arabia by focusing upon two communities, those of Qatif and al-Ahsa in the Eastern Province. Both are ancient communities with histories stretching back thousands of years. Prior to the coming of Islam, many of the people of this area were Christian, with a strong connection to the ancient Christian communities residing in Bahrain at that time. After the arrival of Islam, the new faith was adopted but as the locals held a strong understanding of self in terms of religious identity, it would be Shi'ism not Sunni Islam that won their loyalty.

Yet, for Matthiesen, the tendency for Westerners to identify Shi'ism as a sect (as in sectarianism in the Christian use of the term) and as an expression of communalism (as is applied to the Hindu-Muslim conflict in former British India) are both incorrect understandings. Within the context of the Middle East, Matthiesen considers sectarianism to be the preview of the elite and privileged attempting to maintain their power (think the various elites in Lebanon). The Shi'a, though, are not members of Saudi Arabia's elite. Taken as a whole, they are an oppressed religious minority. As for communalism, one might very loosely describe the position of the Shi'a in Saudi Arabia and their relationship to the larger Sunni majority within this context, but it is important not to stretch the comparison too far. Numerous alternative identities exist within Saudi Arabia that intersect and cross through the "Sunni-Shi'a divide." These include (but are not limited to) gender, class, profession, and educational level.

The Shi'a of Qatif and al-Ahsa have been subject to discrimination since the area was conquered by Ibn Saud in the early twentieth century. Considered *rafida* (rejectionists) by Ibn Saud's most extreme followers the *Ikhwan*, a *fatwa* was issued requiring the people of Qatif and al-Ahsa to convert to the "true Islam." This was refused and after Ibn Saud defeated the *Ikhwan*, pressure for conversion relaxed.

Nevertheless, the Shi'a in the Eastern Provinces found themselves economically and politically disadvantaged. Economically, the Shia became subject to special taxes called the jihad tax. This tax was especially difficult as revenue from the pearl trade declined but the benefit of oil production has yet to begin.

Politically, Ibn Saud known to cement tribal alliances through marriage never took a wife from any of the Shi'a tribes. This cut off the Shi'a community from the close political access other groups enjoyed. Political discrimination also expressed itself through the oppression of Shi'a religious courts. As law and religion are virtually inseparable in Saudi Arabia, Wahhabi *ulama* resisted the appointment of Shiʿa judges and the existence of Shiʿa courts.

Of course, the coming of oil wealth to Saudi Arabia was not only transformational for the kingdom as a whole, but also for the Shiʿa. With major oil reserves located in the Eastern Provinces it was inevitable that local Shiʿa would find work in the oil field. It was also inevitable that those Shiʿa workers would be exposed to individuals and ideas from other countries and adopted other class and ideological identities.

Matthiesen's analysis of the growth of leftist and Arab nationalist identities in the 1950s and 1960s is quite interesting. As Arab workers from other countries (Egypt, Syria, Iraq, and Lebanon) came to the oil fields for employment, they brought not only their technical skills for a range of ideological flavors. Examples included the Arab Socialist Baath Party in Saudi, the Marxist-Leninist Popular Democratic Party in the Arabian Peninsula (PD-PAP), and the Socialist Action Party in the Arabian Peninsula. The latter was formed by Saudi students in the United States in 1972.

Although able to ferment unrest among ARAMCO workers and engage in limited violence, none of these groups presented a real threat to the regime. Many members, drawn from notable Shiʿa families, found themselves in jail for their political activities. By the time they were released, the oil wealth was flowing into Saudi society and the new generation of Saudis (those born in the late 1950s and early 1960s) were not willing to risk the force of the state upon them. The new generation would find its identity in religion.

Matthiesen notes the overwhelming importance of the January 1979 Iranian Revolution of Saudi Shiʿa. The manifestation of a radical Shiʿa state across the Persian Gulf from the Eastern Provinces held a powerful emotional and ideological pull for Saudi's Shiʿa. The new Iranian regime came at a time when the Kingdom's Shiʿa were determined to bring their Ashura processions during the month of Muharram out of the shadows and into the mainstream. These public displays of Shia beliefs were quickly oppressed, and violence ensued. The tensions of 1979 were only increased by the seizure of the Grand Mosque in Mecca by Sunni extremists. Following these events, Shiʿa left the country rather than risk arrest and imprisonment.

The 1980s would be a decade of tension. Iran would serve as a place of exile and training for disgruntled Shiʿa from Saudi Arabia. Tensions between Iran and Saudi Arabia spilled over into the annual pilgrimage to Mecca and Medina, when Iranian pilgrims routinely clashed with Saudi security forces. The Kingdom was clearly open about its backing of Baghdad during the Iran-Iraq War, Saudi Arabia and Iran also challenged each other in Lebanon. The Lebanese conflict would inspire the creation of *Hizbullah al-Hijaz*, a group that would carry out violent attacks against Saudi interest, but to little real success.

The period after the 1990s has brought a greater level of dialogue between Saudi Arabia and its Shi'a citizens. Reforms within Saudi Arabia allowed the return of some exiled Shi'a activists and greater tolerance on the part of the state for Shi'a-based civil society institutions. Football clubs, private schools, youth centers, and various low-level religious structures operated with greater openness. Shi'a mourning rituals also become more public, at least in Shi'a-only communities.

Most significant were the post-2003 petitions from prominent Shi'a representatives to Crown Prince Abdullah. The Prince received the petitions and promised to consider the requests but security concerns after the 9/11 attacks have slowed this process, leading to increased Shi'a protests between 2003 and 2012 and further repression by the state.

Matthiesen's text ends prior to King Salman al-Saud coming to power in January 2015. It is unlikely King Salman will make any significant changes to the position of the Shi'a in Saudi Arabia well into the future. This is especially true given Riyadh's concerns over Iran's growing nuclear program and the current unrest in Syria. Nevertheless, Matthiesen's text is a timely and important work that should be included in every university library. The reviewer strongly recommends the text for your consideration. **WLR**

***

Saudi Arabian Foreign Policy: Conflict and Cooperation in Uncertain Times

Neil Partrick, Ed. New York, NY: I.B. Tauris. 336 pp. ISBN: 978-780769141.

The book brings together original and previously published papers on aspects of Saudi Arabia (SA) foreign policy, and the overlapping relationships with states and regions in a historical context as well as their relevance to the ever-changing present. At the writing of this review, the Saudi Royal Court announced a reverse in the line of succession by naming the 31 years old Prince Mohammed bin Salman as the crown prince and next in line to the throne to succeed his ailing father, King Salman

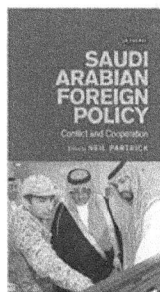

bin Abdulaziz Al-Saud. This, at the expense of his nephew, Mohammed bin Nayef, could prove to be a mixed blessing for a kingdom in transition that faces significant international challenges of its own making. The ascension of Prince Mohammed to the throne signals an attempt by the Saudi monarchy to appease the young Saudis, who view the prince as more attuned to their aspirations and potential instrument for change that the Saudi kingdom desperately needs.

The book's contributions vary in originality, as well as dates of publication. Some could be considered original contributions and other reprints or re-edits of previously published papers or articles. In the Preface to the book, the editor states as his purpose for publishing the book "to examine the motivational factors affecting Saudi Arabian foreign relations and the capacity or limitations of policy applications in key relationships" (p. ix).

The book consists of 21 chapters, and a 15-page conclusion. The first three chapters provide an overview of the domestic factors at play within Saudi Arabia, and how these impact on decision-making, external outreach, and the underlying economic and political imperatives that drive policy formulation. The remaining chapters examine relationships with key states, both in their own right and sometimes in the context of regional dynamics.

The first part of the book titled "The Internal Context" includes three chapters: Chapter 1: "The Internal Context" by Neil Partrick; Chapter 2: "Islam and Identity in Foreign Policy" by Nenno Preuschaft; and Chapter 3: "Saudi Arabia and the Politics of Oil" by Neil Quilliam.

Mindful or the Saudi foreign policy aims which include striving for legitimacy, ensuring that other regional states do not overly threaten its regional cohesion or external security, Part II of the book titled "Saudi Arabia's Foreign Relations" contains 18. Each chapter deals with a different aspect of the Saudi foreign relations with individually named countries round the globe and the kingdom's relations with these countries. Chapters 4 to 14 deal with Saudi relations with Arab countries in alphabetical order from Egypt to Yemen. Chapters 15 to 17 deal with two East Asian countries Indonesia, and Malaysia, while chapter 18 deals with South Asia. Saudi relations with Europe, Russia and the US are treated in chapters 19, 20, and 21 respectively.

As the chapters' authors note, the Saudis have used their petrodollars to shore up the dynasty regime, get rid of enemies or perceived threats to the system of spreading the Wahhabi's version of Islam among Muslims and converts to Islam worldwide, using the power of petrodollars. This has also resulted in supporting these autocratic regimes regardless of the will of the people, as long as these regimes fall in line with the Saudi objectives and within its orbit.

Collectively, the chapters address the various aspects and manifestations of the Saudi foreign relations in general, and with specific countries in particular. Furthermore, the contributors deal with some of the disputes and contradictions that mar the kingdom's relations with these countries, and how such contradictions serve the Saudi regime's self-interest and preservation of its absolute monarchy. The Saudi ultimate objective is what is good for the Saudi monarchy and its continued existence against all odds. As some of the book's contributing authors point out, the interests of the Saudi monarchy are different from the interests of those in its political orbit. The poorer Muslim countries look and hope to gain the approval and generosity of the largess of the Saudi financial assistance which invariably have strings attached. In Egypt's case, the Saudi largesse is conditioned upon Egypt's acquiesce to being a friendly and obedient regime, such as the present one, in return for the billions of dollars not accounted for by Egypt's leadership. The Saudi animosity towards present day Tehran, as opposed to the friendly relations with the former Shah's regime, have placed the Middle East in the unenviable position of disarray as witnessed from the current crisis between Saudi Arabia and Qatar, and the resulting weakening and disfranchisement of the GCC block for the sake of Saudi's self-interest.

As the various book's chapters emphasized, the regime's survival is uppermost in the Saudi ruling family's mind. Fear of actual or perceived external or internal influence that could result in regime change influence the Saudi red line. This is evident in the case of the Yemen war that plagued Nasser's regime in the 1960s, the first Gulf War (GW) in 1990-91 to rid Kuwait of Saddam's military invasion, and GW2 that was launched on the false pretense that Saddam was about to invade the Saudi kingdom and bring about the demise of the Saudi dynasty.

Prior to the Trump's Administration's cozying up with Saudi Arabia, the Obama Administration sought to establish a balance of power between the two most powerful adversaries in the region, Saudi Arabia and Iran, as it failed to persuade Israel to negotiate a peaceful resolution to the festering Palestinian-Israeli conflict. The current Trump Administration, on the other hand, is trying to bolster Saudi Arabia as the counter to the growing Iranian influence in the region in general and in the Gulf States in particular, and to vilify the Iranian regime's nuclear agreement that was signed during the Obama administration, and was condemned by the Saudis and Israelis. Complicating the matter further for the AGS block led by SA is the Qatar crisis, which has divided the Gulf block between those on the side of Saudi Arabia (Bahrain, UAE, Egypt) on one hand, and those trying to mediate the conflict (Kuwait, Oman and Jordan). The American position on the matter has varied from first blaming and condemning Qatar, to the present effort to mediate the conflict and urging the disputing parties to reach an amicable resolution.

In *Saudi Arabian Foreign Policy,* Neil Partrick and the contributing authors managed to give a thoughtful analysis of the complexities of the Saudi foreign relations with the rest of the countries. The ups and downs and the challenges that will face the young king-in-waiting Mohammed bin Salman at a time of oil glut, declining oil prices, armed conflicts around the kingdom, and internal as well as external threats can form serious challenges to the House of Al-Saud. *MMA*

Saudi Clerics and Shi'a Islam

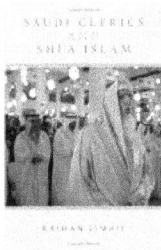

Raihan Ismail. New York, NY: Oxford University Press, 2016. 328 pp. ISBN: 978-010233310.

The theological disputes over "true Islam" between Salafi Sunnis and Shi'a Muslims, once an obscure issue of interest only to specialists and academics, has entered the mainstream consciousness of Western media and general audiences, thanks in large part to the ongoing conflicts in Iraq and Syria. The 2003 US and British-led coalition invasion and subsequent occupation of Iraq, following the toppling of the Iraqi Ba'ath Party government of Saddam Hussein, marked the beginning of Western fascination and often, misunderstanding, of this increasingly bitter set of disputes between competing groups among the global Muslim population. At the forefront of this conflict are Saudi Salafi religious scholars (*'ulama*), who represent arguably the most vocal and influential segment of anti-Shi'a Sunnis today, and their Twelver Shi'a clerical opponents, some of them independent and others aligned with the Iranian Shi'a Islamist state. Neither group, however, represent a unified front and are divided into a number of sub-groups or intellectual/ideological currents. Disputes between Salafi Sunni and Shi'a clerics and scholars are also often shaped by current events and contemporary politics as well as medieval theological disputation and the clash of historical narratives. In the book under review, Raihan Ismail provides a major contribution to the scholarship on both Salafi, and specifically Saudi Salafi,

Islam and historical and contemporary ideological differences and conflicts between Salafi and Shi'a Muslim theologians and *'ulama*. She does this, however, with a careful eye to how modern politics impact how these seemingly obscure theological disputes.

Ismail utilizes an extensive array of primary sources including audio and video recordings of sermons and lectures, written publicans, and juridical opinions (*fatawa*) and rulings (*ahkam*) from Saudi Salafi *'ulama* related to their positions on Shi'ism and modern conflicts in places such as Yemen, Iraq, and Bahrain. She examines materials not only from mainstream *'ulama* aligned or even employed by the Saudi state but also materials produced by a diverse group of Saudi Salafi religious scholars including more moderate voices, such as that of *Shaykh* Salman al-Awda, and more extreme anti- Shi'a voices, such as that of *Shaykh* Nasir al-'Umar. This second group include *'ulama* from the non-establishment clerical elite, a collective that is loosely referred to generally as the Sahwa or "Awakening" movement, though it is not a single organization but rather an intellectual/ideological current of *'ulama* not employed by the state and who are willing to sometimes criticize the monarchy when it fails to, in their eyes, maintain proper Islamic positions on a range of issues.

Beginning with a brief historical overview of the Saudi Salafi *'ulama* and their relationship with the Al-Sa'ud family, Ismail details how the *'ulama*, particularly the state-aligned clergy, became institutionalized within the modern Saudi state. Understanding this relationship is critical to understanding the ways in which state *'ulama* both use and are used by the monarchy and how dissident and non-establishment *Sahwa 'ulama* see themselves as being separate from the state-sanctioned clergy. Many of the *Sahwa* clergy were influenced not only by the Najdi Salafism of Muhammad ibn Abd al-Wahhab and his clerical descendants but also by aspects of the political thought of the Muslim Brotherhood organizations in Egypt and Syria through ideologues such as Muhammad Qutb, the brother of Sayyid Qutb, many of whom fled their home countries to escape government persecution and were allowed to settle and work in Saudi Arabia in the 1970s. Some Saudi *'ulama* therefore draw not only from a particular form of Salafism, but also from political aspects of the Muslim Brotherhood.

In the book's second chapter, Ismail provides a historical overview of the division and differences between what would become Sunni and Shi'a Islam. The origins of the theological/doctrinal disputes between Sunnism and Shi'ism, such as the debates over the Prophet Muhammad's decision (or not) to name a specific successor as leader of the Muslim community and the status of his companions (*Sahaba*), are discussed in detail. Criticisms of Shi'ism from Sunni *'ulama*, though today often blamed solely on "Wahhabis"/Salafi, have been made historically, as Ismail shows, by many mainstream Sunni scholars, many of them predating the emergence of Salafism, broadly speaking, as a recognizable intellectual current within revivalist Sunnism in the eighteenth and nineteenth centuries. These include Malik ibn Anas, one of the founders of the four surviving schools of Sunni jurisprudence, the famous *hadith* compiler and commentator al-Bukhari, and the medieval Syrian Hanbali jurist Taqi al-Din ibn Taymiyya, though the latter is now often accused of being a sort of "Wahhabi"/Salafi godfather figure. Ismail also discusses the more accommodating views of more modern Sunni *'ulama* such as Mahmoud Shaltut, the grand rector of Al-Azhar mosque and seminary in Cairo between 1958 and 1963 and the Egyptian Muslim Brotherhood-affiliated Yusuf al-Qaradawi based in Qatar. Shaltut accepted the Ja'fari school of jurisprudence as a legitimate legal school of thought and al-Qaradawi has generally taken a more inclusive view of Shi'a Muslims, though his views have hardened since the execution of Saddam Hussein in Iraq and even more so since the sectarianization of Syria's ongoing civil war.

Moving beyond the theological and creedal disputations of Saudi Salafi *'ulama* with Shi'ism, which she covers in great detail in chapter three, Ismail also recognizes the role of politics and social competition as drivers of anti-Shi'a sectarianism. Saudi Shi'a, who make up a significant and even majority of the populations in the oil-rich Eastern Province of al-Ahsa, spark demographic fears of an internal "enemy" among many Saudi Salafis, both *'ulama* and non-clerics. The history of anti-Shi'a discrimination in the Saudi state from its founding in 1925-26 is long and continues to this day, despite a relative loosening under the late King Abdullah (2005-2015). Though Abdullah was relatively more tolerant toward the kingdom's Shi'a citizens, there remained certain limits imposed on Saudi Shi'a social and political activism, employment discrimination, and public denigration of Shi'ism by state *'ulama*. Ongoing conflicts in Iraq and Syria, both beset with mounting levels of violent sectarianism, also had an adverse effect on Saudi Shi'a. In addition, even relatively more moderate Saudi Salafi *'ulama*, such as al-Awda, still do not accept the legitimacy of Shi'a theology and creed, thus limiting the nature of any acceptance of Sh 'ism by a Saudi Salafi religious scholar.

Saudi Shi'a are also negatively affected by the state's geopolitical rivalry with Shi'a Islamist Iran. They are seen by many Sunnis as a potential "fifth column" of Iran in the domestic space. Iranian involvement in conflicts in Lebanon, Bahrain, Syria, Iraq, and Yemen are seen by Saudi *'ulama* and many Saudi Sunnis and Sunnis in the Arab Gulf states as being a part of a broader attempt to spread Shi'ism in Sunni majority countries. Thus, the Saudi state has harnessed the official Salafi religious establishment as yet another tool to use against Iran. Through financial support for religious institutions, building projects, *da'wa* (missionary propagation) campaigns, and political actors across the globe, the Saudi state is engaged in a sustained anti-Iran campaign designed to counter Iranian state interests and attempts to broaden its popularity among the world's Muslims. The Saudi state form of Salafism has thus been able to spread through official and semi-official Saudi religious institutions to Sunni communities from North America to Indonesia. Modern political disputes often shape the nature of Saudi Salafi *'ulama* criticisms of Shi'ism and Shi'a actors, but Ismail argues that it is primarily Salafi objections to Shi'a theology, creed, and ritual practices, such as mourning rituals during Muharram and Arba'in, that form the basis of the former's anti-Shi'ism. The intensity, timing, and specific parameters of anti- Shi'a sectarian discourse, however, is influenced significantly by geopolitics.

Ismail's book fills a gap in the literature on Saudi Salafism and Salafi- Shi'a theological disputes and also makes a significant contribution to the understanding of the utilization and contours of sectarianism in modern conflicts in the Middle East. It is thoroughly sourced and includes many fascinating details while remaining clarity and highly readable prose. **CA**

THE SUDAN

Networks of Knowledge Production in Sudan: Identities, Mobilities, and Technologies

Sondra Hale, Gada Kadodae, Eds. Boulder, CO: Rowman and Littlefield (Lexington Books). 2016. 318 pp. ISBN: 978-498532129.

At first glance, compendiums of essays presented at academic conferences rarely make for compelling reading. Often papers that are interesting, cogent, and well-presented at an international forum may fall a bit flat months later when bound into book form. Further still, topics which worked well together when they were presented may fail to weave together well within the edited volume. When the topics are narrow in focus, still other questions arise: will lessons learned in the specific cases set forward hold relevance for other locations, peoples, and experiences?

The volume considered here, edited by scholars Hale and Kadoda, defies every concern noted above. At first blush, the material presented — products of symposia directed toward specialists in Sudanese studies — is clearly defined to a single place and region. And yet, though the topics found here are perfectly suited to the African and Muslim cases, the volume offers numerous lessons with broad application to a multitude of regional and disciplinary interests which extend well beyond this specific case. The writing is lucid; the research both solid and compelling. In this regard then, this is one of the most successfully edited volumes I have ever encountered, and one which should be of interest to a variety of readers in addition to scholars of the Sudan.

The themes of the volume well-situate not only young Sudanese but indeed, young people of all religions and ethnicities around the developing world who are now experiencing the pressures brought on by global social and economic change. New communication technologies, primarily social media transmitted via the mobile phone, inform virtually every aspect of today's evolving youth culture. The chapters presented here recognize this fact, but with a twist; mobility has always been inherent in societies such as those of the tribal peoples of the Sudan. And while "modernity" assumes a certain level of settlement and geographic stability fixed lifestyles, in truth, are becoming less common.

Thus, the mobility of humanity in combination with the flexibility of borderless technologies allows for (if not, encourages) socio-psychological mobility as well. Put differently, identities are becoming less fixed than ever, more fluid and, in turn, more ambivalent and ambiguous (p. 33). This reflects, as well as facilitates, a society on the move, in which the porosity of borders, both real and imagined, has increasingly become a forgone conclusion.

The chapters here well reflect the degree to which the "in-flux" nature of identity formulation and "borderlessness" is both cause and effect within this dynamic set of processes. New value systems, new ideas, new images — new everything, it seems — are produced and disseminated faster than ever, defying time and space with little potential or any level or degree of sorting, slowing, discerning, or mollifying. It is noted, for example, that messages are coming at Sudanese youth from religious leaders to pop stars alike with the same degree of frequency and intensity, with little to no filter in terms of which is which, who is who, and what is more genuinely "Sudanese" (or for that matter, what is genuinely more "genuine"). At a time when "fake news" is making headlines daily (on Facebook and websites which are, one hopes, *not* fake), the production of uncertainty is the one certainty which appears to be universal. While the chapters in the first half of the volume deal primarily with such questions, the second changes nuance somewhat, addressing a different albeit related issue: the question of authenticity. Here the chapters' contents deal with a fascinating array of examples of the ways in which the virtual world tends by definition to be a world of disruption, if not outright "deceit." As Katarzyna Grabska writes, "The social media are a source of knowledge production directly used by potential and actual [Eritrean] migrants [to the Sudan]. Social media allows for creating alternative identities, or multiple identities, lived simultaneously, flickering back and forth between what is desired (on Facebook) and what is experienced (wearing *abbayas*, marginalization, poverty, everyday abuse, suffering)" (p. 149). Of course, social media are notorious for such deceptions and dishonesty. But is that not the point? In the past, for example, potential European immigrants may have *believed* that the streets of the New World were paved with gold, but they did not experience a constant daily barrage of fabricated images to support their wishful thinking.

While the case of the Sudan is emphasized throughout, the questions found in this volume are clearly universal in scope. Concluding with chapters on present and future conflicts over identity and resource-sharing in an era of blurred and confused stakes and stakeholders, the volume serves to raise numerous issues worthy of further discussion and debate in the years ahead.

Clearly this volume has potential classroom use in the area of Development Studies, Communications Studies, and other fields. As for this reader, I intend to incorporate many of the lessons found here into my own personal research and writing. It is well written, well documented, and for those of us seeking a better understanding of the role of social media and communications technologies upon developing communities, offers much about where we are now as well as hints of where we are heading. *SCD*

SYRIA

Palestinians in Syria: Nakba Memories of Shattered Communities

Anaheed Al-Hardan. New York: Columbia University Press, 2016. 272 pp. ISBN: 978-0231176361.

Anaheed al-Harden has produced a powerful testimony of a community that — although she could not have known when she began her research — has been swept away by a destructive civil war, a second Nakba for Palestinians in Syria. A Palestinian refugee community has existed in parts of Syria, and especially in Damascus, since the exodus of 1948; on the whole, it has been a relatively tranquil and contented part of the diaspora. Al-Hardan's book celebrates the lives of these people in terms of generational memories of al-Nakba, the founding event of Palestinian history. It is important and interesting on several levels. First, it documents a somewhat unfamiliar aspect of Palestinian communities in exile; second, it contrasts 'Nakba memories' with more contemporary activism; and, third, it builds on a wide range of theoretical understandings as a way of enriching our understanding of Palestinian loss and identity. It also highlights the stories and reflections of individuals, which provides a fascinating insight into a community now almost completely obliterated.

Before the war, Yarmouk, the largest and most important of the Syrian camps was, by all accounts, a special place, a comfortable environment where Palestinians were able to build homes and families, a place they could call home. For many of those forced to flee by the violence, it felt like a second Nakba, the destruction of all that had become familiar. It is an odd and intriguing thought that some of the Palestinians who left their homeland in 1948, and successive generations might come to regard the destruction of Yarmouk as a similar catastrophic event. At the same time, as al-Hardan remarks: "Palestinian communities belonging to both Palestine and Syria, the source of the demand of a return to them, challenges us to think beyond the British and French colonial era-carved nation-states that have so violently failed in the Arab East."

The book relies on narrative, in the shape of "Nakba memories" and later practices of commemoration and mobilization. It is a methodological approach that permits the voices of the refugees themselves to emerge, with their complex and often disruptive stories. The Nakba, as al-Hardan reminds us, started as "a pan-Arab nationalist catastrophe;" only later was it reclaimed and re-imagined as a Palestinian liberation project. Memory does not start with the 1948 Nakba, but rather before, in the shape of memories of homes and lands now lost. The catastrophic events of 1948, when thousands of Palestinians were forced to flee and were transformed into a stateless nation, are difficult to discuss for many of those who survived; however, in this respect, al-Harden relies on her own insider status; she too is a member of a Palestinian family that endured the horrors of flight.

A positive attribute of this book is its insistence throughout on the terrible injustice that befell Palestinians and the ensuing brutality of the Israeli settler-colonial regime. However, as the author notes, the idea of 1948 as a "Zionist-inflicted catastrophe" was not universally accepted in its immediate aftermath; some accused the Palestinians of bringing it upon themselves through various forms of "collusion." These feelings occasionally emerge in conversations with several generations of refugees when younger family members express incredulity that their elders voluntarily left their homeland in 1948; in the words of one of al-Hardan's interviewees: "The question that I would always ask myself was why did they leave… They should have remained like those who are still there now." As the "generation of 48" — referred to here as "the guardians" — points out, their leaving was believed to be only temporary; they expected to return within weeks.

Starting with "the Nakba in Arab thought," the book goes on to explore fully and originally the Palestinian refugee community in Syria, memories — in the past and the present — of what the Nakba means and the right of Palestinians to return, the stories or narratives of Palestine, in terms of loss and grieving, and finally "post-memories" of Palestine, as deployed by the second and third generations, those with no direct connection to the land.

There is a rich and diverse existing literature about Palestinian refugee communities, whether in exile in the countries bordering Palestine or still residing "on the land," in the state of Israel itself and in territories occupied by Israel in 1967 and now envisaged as a future Palestinian state. The notion of a state is clearly and increasingly unfeasible, and what is highly interesting about this current volume is its reference to the work of the Right of Return Movement in Syria; as al-Hardan observes: "In commemorating 1948 and mobilizing for the eventual return, activists also created pervasive popular memory discourses in their communities;" these have become a source of strength among scattered and demoralized Palestinian refugees who continue to insist on their "right of return" yet are aware of the fading reality of this right in a world of realism in which Israel and the US hold all the power and are able to dictate the terms of any eventual settlement between Israelis and Palestinians. The act of memory, therefore, serves as a movement of empowerment (I myself have interviewed Palestinians from Syria, now residing in Lebanese camps, who mentioned with pride and hope their innovative work on mobilizing young people about their "Palestinian-ness"). Far from the Israeli expectation that "the old people will die, and the young will forget," Palestinian youth are more determined than ever to keep alive the link with 1948 and their land. The terrible tragedy here is that al-Hardan's book, far from simply being a useful addition to the existing ethnographic literature on Palestinian refugee communities, instead has become a testimony to a community now lost forever to the forces of violence which have, deliberately or not, created a new Nakba. *MH*

Syria: A Way of Suffering to Freedom, a Foray into Current History

Azmi Bishara. Doha, QA: Arab Center for Research and Policy Studies, 2015. 688 pp. ISBN: 978-9953027654.

The Syrian Revolution has now entered its sixth year. Since March 15, 2011 the Syrian people have paid an enormous price in their struggle for freedom from the authoritarian rule of Syrian President Bashar al-Assad. To date, international human rights organizations estimate that more than 450,000 Syrians have been killed due to the conflict. Additionally, the United Nations reports that more than five million Syrians have fled the fighting and are registered or are waiting to register as refugees in Turkey, Lebanon, Iraq, Jordan, and Egypt. Some six and a half million Syrians have abandoned their homes, but remain inside the country as internally displaced persons.

The level of destruction to infrastructure and public and private property across the country is appalling. Entire towns have been leveled thanks to sustained regime bombardment and continuous fighting between different rebel groups.

As the battle against the regime continues, rebel forces will be hard-pressed to gain more territory. The conflict has reached a stalemate. Perhaps Syria is doomed to suffer in the violence of the conflict for many years to come.

In light of the current state of the revolution, now dominated by news of clashes with rebels and regime airstrikes, it's easy to overlook its peaceful beginnings. However, in hindsight, it is clear that for months, Syria's revolutionaries were loathed to engage in any sort of violent activities. It took until August 2011 (and the death of at least 6000 Syrians) before any numbers of armed individuals began accompanying protesters to demonstrations. And even then, the purpose was solely to defend protests — no opposition forces engaged in offensive operations against regime soldiers or positions. It was not until January 2012 that one could say that the revolution truly began to transform into an armed conflict.

The book covers only three years of the revolution but provides an excellent insight to the revolution through hundreds of first-hand interviews with activists and local leaders.

This book also represents a compelling argument on how the Syrian revolution turned into violent, what brought about this transformation from peaceful, non-violent revolution to open, armed struggle? First and foremost, the blame lies with the Syrian regime according to the author, which conducted a calculated and determined campaign of violent repression against demonstrators with the explicit aim of undermining the peaceful nature of the opposition's activities. Assad security forces arrested, tortured, and murdered key youth leaders in the early months of the revolution with the clear goal of removing proponents of nonviolence from opposition ranks. Additionally, the Syrian army regularly targeted women and children to solicit a violent reaction from Syria's husbands, brothers, fathers, and sons. The incomprehensible brutality of the regime in this respect, ultimately drove many Syrians to take up arms to defend themselves.

The blame also lies on the international community. For months, the Arab League and the United Nations stood idly by while Bashar al-Assad killed his own people. Meanwhile, al-Assad himself had found allies in Iran and Russia. Strong assurances of support from these two nations, in conjunction with vacillation on the part of the rest of the international community, convinced al-Assad that he could act with impunity. During this time, revolutionaries lost all hope that the international community would defend the people from Syrian government forces. As a result, some revolutionaries gradually resorted to violence to act to defend themselves and their fellow Syrians after concluding that no other government would come to their aid.

The book is comprised of thirteen chapters, the first five chronologically documenting and examining the revolution over the span of two years, following the arrest of the school children in Dara'a, a small city in southern Syria; these events have transformed the country forever. A week later, thousands of protesters gathered at the al-Omari Mosque and marched at security forces, demanding the release of the children, greater political freedom, and an end to government corruption. When riot police failed to stop the protesters, they advanced with batons and water cannons; additionally, members of the security services opened fire on the unarmed crowd with live ammunition, killing at least four citizens. On March 26, protests spread to the coastal city of Lattakia then all over Syria.

On March 30, President Bashar al-Asad spoke in a televised address to the nation from the Syrian parliament. The speech was widely expected to be conciliatory in tone; many believed the president had no choice but to proffer a timeline for significant changes in government policy, including an end to a four-decade-old emergency law banning public gatherings. Instead, al-Asad chose to double down, insisting in his speech that reform would occur, but at a deliberate pace.

Syrians reacted poorly to their legitimate grievances being treated with such levity. Not only had al-Asad refused to commit to a timetable for instituting governmental reform, but to add insult to injury, had neither apologized nor taken responsibility for the spilling of Syrian blood. That week, after Friday prayers, Syrians took to the street by the thousands in towns and cities across the country. The barrier of fear had been broken —– the Arab Spring had arrived in Syria. But the Syrian government had faced popular revolt before.

Six years into the Syrian revolution, it is easy to forget the chants of *Silmiyeh* (Peaceful) that echoed across the streets of Syria for months in 2011 before succumbing to the sound of explosions and gunfire. It was not until January 2012 that the revolution truly began to transform into an armed conflict. It is also expected to forget the massive peaceful demonstrations in which protestors held nothing but signs and olive branches. In hindsight, perhaps it is even logical to claim that an armed conflict was inevitable in Syria.

Some activists argue that the current perception of the conflict in 2015 was pursued by the strategy of the Syrian government from the outset.

With huge civilian devastation and loss of a quarter of a million individuals, so far, and open-ended suffering of half of the population between refugees and internally displaced persons, the blame goes everywhere, and lies, on the international community for not intervening at least to protect civilians. Bloodshed is the norm of the day across Syria; and the Western media has reached a stage of coverage fatigue regarding Syrian violence. Syria's return to normal life seems impossible in the foreseeable future. **RZ**

Syria in World War I: Politics, Economy, and Society

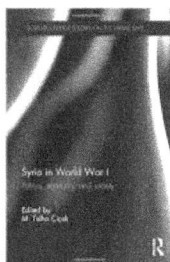

M. Talha Çiçek, Ed. New York, NY: Routledge/Taylor & Francis Group, 2016. 264 pp. ISBN: 978-1138944541.

This is a very important book which covers a significant chapter in Syria's history. *Syria's history? Whither Syria?* This is a book on Ottoman Syria, so it naturally includes important contributions about Lebanon and Palestine, which are not part of today's Syria. This is not a minute issue, as was made clear just recently, by none other than the terror group ISIS, vowing to do away with the Sykes-Picot Agreement and the dismemberment of historic Greater Syria. This is a theme that has never been neglected by successive Syrian regimes, from its independence in 1946 through the reign of the House of Assad (1970-), and as such, merited a special chapter explaining the differences between WW1 Syria, and the Syria as known to the average reader.

I also expected a chapter/essay on what could be the connections between WW1 Syria and the current implosion of the Syrian state. Some may think that any such reference is by definition somewhat speculative, but here again, it is a question of expectations of the average reader. With the unprecedented mayhem taking place in Syria as of 2011, the question of what can be the Ottoman legacy over, for example, sectarian issues in Syria, is a fascinating food for thought and research. All this is presented by way of suggestions for an updated edition.

The book deals with sensitive issues, such as the fate of the Armenians, but may be lacking clarity as to what exactly is the Armenian issue. There is much detailed discussion by Hilmar Kaiser on "Shukru Bey and the Armenian deportations in the fall of 1915" (pp.169-233). This is the longest chapter of the book, but the word "Genocide" does not appear there. An omission of major significance, one which arouses questions. The "Genocide" word does appear in the article by Roberto Mazza, "We shall treat you like the

Armenians"; Djemal Pasha, Zionism and the evacuation of Jaffa, April 1917 (pp.99-106).

Altogether, though this is a very important contribution to the study of Syria in a crucial period. Articles by Salim Tamari on the Syrian-Palestinian intelligentsia (pp.37-61), and Elizabeth Williams on the economy, with an emphasis on famine (pp.150-167) were particularly interesting and illuminating, though the latter did not deal with Lebanon and the terrible conditions there, and that was missing in the overall description of the horrific conditions in Syria. I definitely recommend this book and will personally use it in my reading lists about Syria. *JO*

TERRORISM

Essentials of Counterterrorism

James J. F. Forest, Ed. Santa Barbara, CA: Praeger/ABC-CLIO/Praeger, 2015. 456 pp. ISBN: 978-1440832833. (Pbk). 2015. ISBN: 978-1440834707.

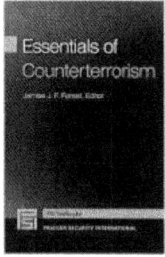

This is a textbook designed to educate future counterterrorism professionals enrolled in university courses and training programs. There are 18 chapters by 18 different authors representing a broad diversity of backgrounds, including retired and active duty military, intelligence and law enforcement officers, and research scholars at universities and think-tanks (p. ix), with half of these from the United States. Most of the chapters were originally published in the more comprehensive three-volume (60 thematic essays) *Countering Terrorism and Insurgency in the 21ˢᵗ Century* (Praeger Security International, 2007), and have been updated for this 2015 single volume textbook.

The preface gives each chapter a half-page long one paragraph summary. Then the editor wrote an introduction to the study of counterterrorism. In it, he discussed various definitions of the term "terrorism" and "counterterrorism", critical lessons from history of terrorist activities and counterterrorism efforts from countries around the world, with a focus on the post-9/11 US. Since the editor is not only a researcher, but also a seasoned practitioner in the US antiterrorism scene, the book is distinctively US-centered with information from other countries playing a supporting role. By asking a very essential question "what resources are committed to our nation's … counterterrorism efforts, and how are these resources distributed?" the author introduced to the reader the roles of over two dozen relevant offices across the White House, seven departments, and the Office of the Director for National Intelligence.

There are seven categories of efforts — military, intelligence, diplomatic, informational, economic, financial, and law enforcement that need to work together to achieve the goal of counterterrorism. The author succinctly explained each aspect and linked these together to demonstrate the interconnectivity among them. The author correctly considered that the most important element of counterterrorism is intelligence, as he stated that "none is more crucial to the success or failure of counterterrorism than intelligence.... Effective action in military, diplomatic, law enforcement, financial interdiction, and all other areas of counterterrorism requires deep levels of knowledge, insight, and understanding — the intended products of any national intelligence service" (p. 23). Last but not least, the author drew attention to the lone wolf type terrorists and called for friends and family members to be part of the society's antiterrorism force.

The author concluded his introduction with two optimistic points. The first is historical data that shows that some terrorists disengage themselves from terrorist activities and groups; therefore, a nation's counterterrorism strategies should incorporate research-based initiatives to encourage this type of disengagement (p. 25). The second optimistic point is that terrorism ends someday and in one way or another and terrorism is not, and has never been, a winning strategy.

The rest of the book is divided into three parts, they are policy and strategy (7 chapters), tactical and operational dimensions (3 chapters), and case studies (8 chapters).

Jennifer Holmes' chapter on "Developing and Implementing Counterterrorism Policy in a Liberal Democracy" starts the first of three parts of the textbook. In it, she argues for the case of patiently creating an effective intelligence community, increasing security, and maintaining principles of good governance are essential to democracies confronting terrorism.

Christopher Jasparro's "Geographic Perspectives on the Sociocultural, Economic, and Demographic Aspects of Counterterrorism" argues that applying the geographic approach can help situate terrorist social network and their origins in actual space while adding granularity to the understanding and sociodemographic conditions that add resonance to extremist messages and locate terrorist source areas, which in turn can help focus counterterrorism strategies and policies where they are most needed.

Daniel Byman argues in his chapter "Combating State Sponsors of Terrorism" that it is easier to stop state support for terrorism before it starts than to halt backing after it begins because existing supporters would rather not to back down than losing face.

Paul Smith's "Terrorism Finance: Global Responses to the Terrorism Money Trail" describes the extremely versatile and creative ways for terrorists to transfer money, their capability of adapting to changing regulations. Simply starving terrorists their money by itself is not sufficient to fight against them.

Joseph St. Marie, Shahdad Naghshpour and Samuel Stanton Jr.'s "The Shadow Economy: The Forgotten Infrastructure of Terrorist Financing" states that shadow economy can provide an infrastructure for terrorist organizations to operate in, whereby financing becomes easier and detecting it becomes more difficult.

J. P. Larsson's "Organized Criminal Networks and Terrorism" treats the two as similar concepts and suggests combatting them with the same group of resources, with minimal distinction.

Jennifer Sims' "The Contemporary Challenges of Counterterrorism Intelligence" notes that the human intelligence, all-source data fusion, and collaboration with law enforcement worldwide are three essential elements of counterterrorism, and they all need further improvements.

Michael Kraft's "The U.S. Government's Counterterrorism Research and Development Programs" gives insights into the interagency coordinating body, the older Technical Support Working Group and the newer Department of Homeland Security. He also suggested that budget makers need to be patient with these R&D efforts.

Robert Pauly Jr. and Robert Redding's "Denying Terrorists Sanctuary through Civil-Military Operations" tells how US military Special Forces working in Afghanistan, Iraq, Mongolia, Yemen, and the Philippines achieved strategic objectives in counterterrorism.

The eight case studies of part three of the textbook are: David Scott Palmer's Countering Terrorism in Latin America: The Case of Shining Path in Peru; Sixty Years of Counterinsurgency in Colombia: From 'La Violencia' to the 'Sword of Honor' Plan by Roman Ortiz and Janneth Vargas; "Italy and the Red Brigades: The Success of Repentance Policy in Counterterrorism" by Erica Chenoweth; "Countering West Germany's Red Army Faction: What Can We Learn?" by Joanne Wright; "The Role of Democratization in Reducing the Appeal of Extremist Groups in the Middle East and North Africa after the Uprisings" by Francesco Cavatorta; "India's Response to Terrorism in Kashmir" by Behram Sahukar; "Capturing Khalid Sheikh Mohammad" by Robert Wesley and "The Madrid Attacks on March 11: An Analysis of the Jihadist Threat in Spain and Main Counterterrorist Measures" by Rogelio Alonso.

These case studies provide not only overall details of each region/country's counterterrorism case(s), but also evaluations of each government's measures and pitfalls. On one hand, each student, based on his or her regional focus, can use these case studies as a launching pad to dig deeper into their specific target of work, on the other hand, general policy and strategy makers will also benefit from combing through all eight cases with a comparative perspective.

Each chapter is followed by its own endnotes. The book has a bibliography of 20 pages, and detailed biography for all authors. The book has a standard index at the end.

No matter what the opinion one has regarding the state of Israel, no one will challenge the fact that this country is among the top sufferers from terrorism. It is a pity to find Israel's experience in counterterrorism is almost not mentioned at all by any of the authors in any of the chapters (see, e.g., p. 450, index). This reviewer can only guess the editor might hesitate to define some of the Palestinian attackers as terrorists. Terrorists are terrorists, no matter what political cause they are fighting for. Such a comprehensive textbook on counterterrorism having no text drawing from Israel's expertise and experience might put some provoking minds in an awkward situation discussing materials in it in a classroom setting. And the counterterrorism community around the world certainly cannot ignore all the technology and expertise developed by the state of Israel in this field.

Nevertheless, this is a voluminous textbook (with relatively small print types), authored by the top-notch experts in the field, and covers almost exhaustively all possible aspects of the international counterterrorism endeavor (except the one mentioned in the previous paragraph), with a focus on the US aspect. All students and practitioners should have it handy in their reference collection. **YC**

ISIS: A History

A HISTORY

ISIS

FAWAZ A. GERGES

Fawaz A. Gerges. Princeton, NJ: Princeton University Press, 2016. 384 pp. ISBN: 978-0691170008.

A formidable force of carnage, the Islamic State exercises a rare combination of order and brutally unparalleled among those on history's list of non-state actors. The Al-Qaeda offshoot remains, by any reasonable measure of humanity, an unconscionably ruthless organization intent on ushering in its apocalyptic vision of world's end through the most dreadful examples of butchery. Yet, the group's high-profile bloodlust belies the ideological complexities and cultural intricacies that define it.

Acclaimed scholar, Fawaz A. Gerges sets himself apart from the bevy of stale and unimaginative work on ISIS flooding the market these days by digging deeper into the religious particulars and fleshing out the nuances of an organization that many define merely by its violent pageantry. His latest work *ISIS: A History* goes beyond the hysteria that surrounds their ferocious response to a post-modern world by challenging the generic explanations that reduce the Islamic State to a caricature of its vicious behavior.

Gerges offers a systematic analysis of the group's motivation, philosophy, and perceived purpose, laying out with precision and readability how social order, political dysfunction, and Islamic doctrine came together to help shape the organization's identity. Gerges' diligent work reveals that ISIS was bred from within a complicated web of hyper-Sunni identity, political intrigue, and human suffering — a revelation that allows the reader to appreciate complexities of the Islamic State and the region it operates in without rationalizing its appalling behavior.

Perhaps the greatest contribution Gerges makes to the field involves his ability to use ISIS to show that jihadist organizations cannot be treated as one "undifferentiated constituency" (p. 245). He does this, in part, by retracing the evolution of the organization in a way that distinguishes it from its predecessor in Al-Qaeda. Although adhering to a similar worldview as global jihadist movement, "[ISIS's] social origins are rooted in a specific Iraqi context, and, to a lesser degree, the Syrian War that has raged since 2011" (p. 6). As a result, the Islamic State harbors the familiar anti-Shi'a, anti-Iranian proclivities of "Al-Qaeda Central" but prioritizes its objectives much differently — targeting the near enemy in the Islamic lands first versus the far enemy of the western world, for instance.

Gerges points out that ISIS is best known as an extension of Al-Qaeda. But the group formed a wholly separate identity early on and fought against the perception of operating as a step-child to its parent organization. Moreover, it owed its rapid ascendance to the chaos that engulfed the region after 2011, more so than capitalizing on the residual influence of Al-Qaeda Central. ISIS's tyranny expanded with the fracturing of the post-Saddam Hussein establishment and the subsequent widening of the Shi'a-Sunni divide, the institutional collapse within Syria and the chaotic aftermath of the Arab Spring, Gerges argues. The clash of identities melded with existing anger over years of political repression and social marginalization, which altogether attracted "thousands of embittered Iraqi and Syrian Sunnis to fight under ISIS's banner even though many do not subscribe to its extremist Islamist ideology" (p. 13).

In Chapter 1, Gerges immediately sets himself apart from other scholars and self-declared experts on ISIS by highlighting those features that truly define the group. "ISIS possesses a totalitarian, millenarian worldview that eschews political pluralism, competition and diversity of thought," he writes

(p. 27). They blend puritanical Salafist-jihadism and identity politics with social institutions and territorial control, which allows their version of "true Islam" to be exclusively practiced in physical space and within what adherents see as a fractured religion. ISIS aimed to function like a state early on, he surmises, whereas Al-Qaeda did not.

In Chapters 2 and 3, Gerges retraces the lineage of the organization through the life of its founder Abu Musab al-Zarqawi. He goes into great detail to catalog Zarqawi's brutal rise to power in Iraq in a narrative that offers more than the standard retelling of Iraq's demise under American occupation. Most notably, the chapters recount how the schism that began between Al-Qaeda Central and Zarqawi ballooned into an organizational rupture after his death, leading to the eventual rise of an independent ISIS. The organization learned from the mistakes of a predecessor that choose to emphasize the far enemy and avoid state creation, Gerges argues, and capitalized on the Sunni discontent and institutional collapse that engulfed both Iraq and Syria.

Chapters 4 and 5 offer a window into the often-overlooked conversion from Al-Qaeda in Iraq and the emergence of ISIS under Baghdadi. This rocky transition saw Zarqawi's old group failing, Gerges writes, desperately clinging to the power it had before his death. But the quiet, yet equally ruthless Baghdadi found opportunities to resurrect the organization by exploiting the social and political turmoil caused by the Arab Spring, a Syrian civil war, and institutional collapse within Iraq.

Here again, Gerges stands out by challenging specific assumptions regarding Baghdadi's surge in followership from among former Baathist officers. He retraces Hussein's own Islamic emphasis campaign in the early 1990s, arguing that the event actually encouraged a religious awakening among fellow Sunni officials long before ISIS. In this light, the Baathist attraction to the militant organization (coupled with its hyper-Sunni identity) would appear to be more natural — as opposed to the narrative that assumes ISIS was either co-opted by secular officials or infiltrated by opportunistic converts. The simple but profound observation better explains ISIS' ability to successfully exercise military prowess, secular governing abilities, and religious conviction simultaneously.

Chapters 6 and 7 speak directly to how the civil war in Syria and the Arab Spring fed the ranks of the Islamic State. Gerges helps readers by exploring those nuances that clarify the otherwise complicated story of religious affiliation, jihadist rivalries and geopolitical maneuvering that dominated the period. This section is remarkable for its detail and especially beneficial for those having to negotiate their way through this increasingly complex phase in the history of the Islamic State.

Gerges wraps up his treatise with Chapter Eight and a conclusion that expertly ties everything together. The Islamic State, Gerges concludes, "is both a symptom of the breakdown of state institutions in the heart of the Arab World and a clash of identities between Sunni and Shi'a Muslims" (p. 260). The two-pronged "social and sectarian violence" allowed ISIS to fill a governing void as the defender of Sunni identity in a region of expanding Salafi-jihadism. ISIS' success has as much to do with its strategy as it does with the unpredictable events that aided in its rise, his work concludes. In that light, it is not hard to see why some in ISIS believe the group to be divinely appointed.

Gerges goes to great lengths to explain the complexities surrounding the evolution of ISIS and the nuances of its philosophy. Although dry at points, his work challenges media and academic commentary, which too often treat "jihadist as one undifferentiated constituency" (p. 245). If all else was stripped away, that conclusion alone should make this book required reading for scholars, government officials, and lay people alike. **DG**

Jihad and Death: The Global Appeal of Islamic State

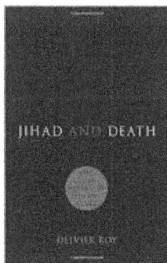

Olivier Roy. Oxford, UK: Oxford University Press. 136 pp. ISBN: 978-0190843632.

In his latest book, the noted French scholar of religion and Islam, Olivier Roy, turns his attention to the phenomenon of jihadism and the appeal of militant Islamist organizations such as Islamic State. Expanding upon his earlier work in studies of secularism and fundamentalism, Islam, and modern and globalized religion, he argues, as he has in the past, that the specifically "Islamic" elements of the appeal of *jihadi* groups are much less than often assumed and that many disaffected, marginalized youth attracted to them bear much in common with the target audiences attracted to other subaltern and fringe movements. Roy previously published pioneering fieldwork-based studies of Afghan *mujahideen* rebel groups in 1970s and 1980s Afghanistan as well as influential, if also contested, theoretical interventions positing the "failure of political Islam" and its devolution into "neo-fundamentalism" rather than a sophisticated political movement. A vocal opponent of fellow French scholar of Islamism Gilles Kepel, with whom he has an often public and vitriolic rivalry, Roy calls into question the heavy cultural explanations favored by other scholars and analysts, including Kepel, who in turn, has dismissed Roy's work out of hand. The book, which is written in the form of a lengthy essay or short monograph, provides an interesting counter to the culture and Islam-heavy analysis of jihadism and *jihadi* movements.

The book's central argument is that events such as the Paris attacks in November 2015 planned and carried out by an Islamic State cell mark not a radicalization of Islam but rather the "Islamization" of radicalism and nihilism, that is, the attempt to justify nihilism and an obsession with death by attaching it to a "higher" power or purpose. Basing his argument on the biographies of homegrown European *jihadis*, Roy argues that the majority of them are not deeply religious nor particularly well, or even minimally, educated with regard to the intricacies of Islam as a complex, multifaceted, and lived religious tradition. Instead, the majority of homegrown militants come from previous lives of crime and debauchery and attempt to continue on a similar path within jihadism, which represents a fringe current within Islam more broadly and political Islam more specifically.

One of the shifts with newer generations of domestic *jihadis*, Roy argues, is the growing attraction of death as an end goal in itself rather than the use of violence and terror to achieve political ends while, ideally, living to fight on. In the 1970s and 1980s, militants tended to plan attacks in a way that included an escape after the deed was done instead of seeking "martyrdom" as the majority of contemporary *jihadis* do. Today's *jihadis* are also overwhelming young, making up what is essentially a youth movement that draws upon aspects of mainstream rebellious youth culture and which attempts to forge an identity independent of older generations. These young radicals attempt to start from scratch, to erase past real or perceived humiliations and defeats through violent assertiveness that includes not only acts of political violence and terrorism but also religious and ideological iconoclasm. The latter is where the iconoclasm of Salafism is particularly attractive.

Revolution, which was seen by past political activists as the means to an end, is seen by today's *jihadis*, Roy argues, as being an end in itself, a desire for "pure revolt" against the status quo. Driven by utopian and unrealistic fantasies, which he terms the "jihadi imaginary" (p. 41), today's *jihadis* see violence not as a strategic tool but rather as the underlying point. Violence, death, and self-sacrifice are the goals rather than the belief that these are only a means to achieve a political end such as the overthrow of an existing government or fundamental changes in the state. This current stage is only the latest in the evolution both of jihadism and terrorism; it is temporary rather than permanent and is linked intimately to the current situation in the Middle East where Islamic State emerged as a powerhouse. Roy downplays significantly the role of indoctrination and socialization by charismatic figures and in small groups, focusing primarily on individual and "self" radicalization, which is contested by studies on the importance of social networks in the radicalization process.

Roy's latest book presents a useful counterpoint to other studies, such as the work of his rival Gilles Kepel and much of the terrorism studies literature, which focuses much more on cultural ("Islamic") explanations for the phenomenon of jihadism. The book is well written, and an engaging read, though it is light on end notes and presents primarily a theoretical argument rather than an empirics-heavy study. It will be of interest to readers, both general and more specialized, following political Islam, jihadism, the modern Middle East, and religion and modernity. *AZ*

Jihadism Transformed: Al-Qaeda and Islamic State's Global Battle of Ideas

Jihadism Transformed

Simon Staffell, Akil N. Awan, Eds. New York City, NY: Oxford University Press, 2016. 273 pp. ISBN: 978-0190650292.

Al-Qaeda and Islamic State's Global Battle of Ideas

Simon Staffell & Akil Awan (eds.)

President Donald Trump announced the redeployment of 4,000 troops to Afghanistan in August 2017, signaling that the War on Terror would continue indefinitely. Likewise, the flurry of published research since September 11th addressing Islamic extremism shows no signs of slowing. A problem persists, however, as far-reaching analysis and intense historical studies remain the primary avenue for explaining modern Islamic extremism. The information saturation is difficult to absorb. That is why *Jihadism Transformed: Al-Qaeda and Islamic State's Global Battle of Ideas* is such a refreshing change.

Editors Simon Staffell and Akil Awan bring together a list of contributors who dissect the elements of extremism by looking at how two organizations, tied together by history and ideology, tackle the meaning and implementation of jihad — a thesis that quickly narrows in scope to the advantages of a current Caliphate versus abstractions about a future one. Despite its particularity, the topic exposes readers to broader discussions on the rationale

for violence, apocalyptic interpretation, and recruitment, among other issues. *Jihadism Transformed…* avoids the overwhelmingly comprehensive
and instead takes aim at core ideas as testified to by those involved, which
illuminates greater truths about the growth of terrorism.

Getting right to it, the editors open the book by highlighting the effects of
the Arab Spring on jihadist ideology. The launching off point is not entirely
original as scholars agree that the political upheaval represented a significant
turning point in the history of global jihad. But they pinpoint a central idea
that goes on to define the entire book: the Islamic State focused on a simple
narrative of "utopia in the here and now," whereas Al-Qaeda took inspiration
from unresolved "grievances" (p. 15). The Islamic State's creation of a "concrete" empire was more appealing than the "abstract eschatological vision"
of their parent organization. Turning the "abstract millenarian notion of the
Caliphate" into a "present, tangible reality" proved to be an "unprecedented
material success" in the global battle of ideas (p. 17). This concept is fundamental to the web of jihadist thought.

Contributor Nelly Lahoud immediately revisits this central thesis in
Chapter 2 and adds an interesting sub-argument, contending that the Islamic
State's violence is not "whimsical, random or crazed," as Al-Qaeda suggested and as many Western leaders believe. ISIS' actions are instead deliberate
"abominable savagery" intended to terrorize. Al-Qaeda positions itself as the
"regretful terrorist" in the Islamic World, whereas ISIS sees extreme violence
as the purest form of jihad, he argues. The physical Caliphate then lends further credibility to the violence as a tangible representation of divine favor.

In Chapter 3, Donald Holbrooke focuses on Al-Qaeda's poor messaging in
the face of a physical Caliphate, pointing out that Ayman Al-Zawahiri failed
to adequately address the citizen-led Arab Spring that humiliated Al-Qaeda
and undermined its reputation as the organization to lead revolution. Simon
Stafell follows in Chapter 4 with a similar analysis on messaging, explaining
that the Islamic State's otherwise attractive narrative has not quite resonated
within Egyptian Salafi-jihadist circles since they take inspiration from different grievances.

An opposite result occurred in Tunisia as Jonathan Githens-Mazer explains in Chapter 5. The Islamic State's political violence found traction there
due to the incomplete nature of the 2011 revolution, which called into question secular strategies and gave the Islamic State fertile ground to spread the
seeds of Islam's incompatibility with "democratic political practice" (p. 84).
Chapters 6 and 7 dive further into the battle of regional messaging in Yemen
and the Maghreb, respectively, both arguing that "belonging" to an existing
Caliphate plays a major role in attracting IS recruits.

In Chapter 8, Virginia Comolli unravels Boko Haram's shift from an Al-Qaeda affiliate to Islamic State loyalist by demonstrating how operational benefits yielded from a physical Caliphate provided enormous incentive. Chapter 9 continues the regional theme as Martha Turnbull observes how ISIS and the Syrian jihad pulled attention away from the Afghanistan jihad, pushing a Taliban desperate for resources and new messaging closer to Al-Qaeda.

Christopher Anzalone contends in Chapter 10 that the sectarianism brought on by the Arab Spring gave rise to not only the hyper-Sunni identity of the Islamic State but a resurgence in organized Shiʻa intent on defending against minority repression. Akil Awan closes the anthology with a salient point about jihadist messaging: the individual's context and personal circumstances remain central to whether a narrative resonates. He points out how IS was able to project an image as the defender of Islam thanks in part to a physical Caliphate.

The contributors show that the Islamic State succeeded by traditional means of preying on feelings of victimization but separated itself from Al-Qaeda by erecting a physical Caliphate. Borders and governance alongside the right message attracted not only those seeking belonging but those who believed the Caliphate fulfilled Islamic eschatology. Going forward, Islamic radicals will not likely fight for abstract ideas in perpetuity. This winning combination suggests the world could see future extremist organizations seek to build physical empires as a means of attracting recruits. For that realization alone, *Jihadism Transformed…* is a must-read for anyone seeking greater understanding of Islamic extremism and the future of international terrorism. **DG**

Salafi-Jihadism: The History of an Idea

Shiraz Maher. New York, NY: Oxford University Press, 2016. 256 pp. ISBN: 9780190651121

David Kilcullen (2015) noted the difference in strategy between Al-Qaeda and the Islamic State. Fawaz Gerges (2016) followed with a history of the latter. At long last, Shiraz Maher sheds light on the theological underpinning (or lack thereof) of Al-Qaeda and the Islamic State. Arguing against perceived irrationality, the author is emphatic that Salafi behavior

is grounded in a particular interpretation of the *Qur'an*. In tracing the intellectual history of the Salafi movement, Maher points to its three subgroups: quietist, activist, and jihadist. With attention to the locutionary, illocutionary, and perlocutionary influences of words, the author is particularly interested in perlocutory aspects of Salafi-jihadism in influencing followers. The book is organized into five sections like peeling an onion: *jihad, takfir, al-wa-la' wa al-bara', tawhid,* and *hakimiyya*. Salafi-jihadis associate the first three concepts with protection of Islam and the last two with its promotion.

Jihad (struggle) was the second obligation after faith for Taqi ad-Din Ahmad ibn Taymiyya. Abu Zakaryya al-Dimashqi al-Dumyati ("Ibn Nuhass") declared it a "pillar" and "pinnacle" of Islam. Muhammad ibn Abd al-Wahhab blessed Ibn Saud family's battles against rival tribes. Sayyid Qutb invoked Prophet Muhammad in endorsing the concept. Abdallah Azzam made it legally equivalent to fighting in defending "Muslim lands." Ayman al-Zawahiri gave jihad precedence over feeding the hungry. Like Ibn Taymiyya, Abu Musab al-Zarqawi placed jihad second only to faith.

The sixth pillar of jihad is added in incorporating two principles of Islamic jurisprudence: *dalatat* accepting inference from the scripture and *mafhum al-mukhalafa* allowing understanding of the opposite. The latter concept is disavowed by most scholars, but Salafi-jihadis do away with restrictions in the interest of flexibility, including indiscriminate violence against civilians. Another relevant concept is *qisas*, which permits equal retaliation based on the principle of reciprocity. However, Salafi-jihadis expanded the scope from private individuals to international relations and ignored the restricted application to known aggressor. Furthermore, *tatarrus* (human shields) has been discarded in favor of the lesser of two evils or *fiqh al-muwazanat* (jurisprudence of balances) in asymmetrical conflict.

Given a nuanced acceptance by Ibn Taymiyya in his Mardin decree against the Mongol legal system that replaced *shari'a* (Islamic legal system), *takfir* (excommunication) is a process of declaring another Muslim to be outside the fold of Islam. It relates to the question of who is a Muslim or, conversely, who is a *kafir* (disbeliever), observes Maher. While *Kufr* linguistically means to cover or veil, legally it connotes absence of faith. Abd al-Wahhab declared it a great sin that negates faith itself. Originally attributed to Hassan bin Muhammad bin al-Hanafiyya, grandson of Ali ibn Abi Talib, Imam Abu Hanifa developed the doctrine of *irja'* (postponement) instead of excommunicating another Muslim. Salafi-quietist scholar Rabi ibn Hadi Umayr al-Madkhali is also identified with the postponement camp. However, Salafi-jihadis adamantly disagree with the postponement thesis in demanding that faith be demonstrated with action.

Khaled Abou el-Fadl, a scholar of Islamic jurisprudence, noted that Islamic theology allows confrontation in dealing with three categories of people: apostates, bandits, and rebels. Salafi-jihadis broaden the scope in permitting *takfir* against the following: tyrant or apostate Muslim rulers, criminal transgressors or oppressors, and heretics or rejecters. Maher observes a division within the Salafi-jihadi movement between theorists and fighters, with the latter ignoring restrictions on declaring *takfir* for jihad. Al-Qaeda has declared jihad against Muslim despots; the Islamic State has targeted the Shi'a in sectarian violence.

Maher traces *al-wala' wa al-bara'* (loyalty and disavowal) to the Emirate of Diriyah (1744-1818), the first Saudi state, under Muhammad ibn Saud. In return for sanctifying the reign of the House of Saud, the family of Abd al-Wahhab was given autonomy over moral, social, and education matters. Sulayman ibn Muhammad ibn Abd al-Wahhab, the grandson of Abd al-Wahhab, declared the Ottomans polytheists in dissuading Hijazi tribes from collaborating with the Turks. With Arabs fighting Soviet forces in Afghanistan in the 1980s, Abu Muhammad al-Maqdisi transformed the concept from omission (denial of support) to commission (affirmation of support) that required an act of *bara'* (disavowal). In rejecting *isti'ana bi al-kuffar* (help from non-Muslims) in fighting the Soviets in Afghanistan, Azzam left open a narrow window. That was based on the concepts of *maslaha al-mursala* (public interest) and *akhaff al-dararayn* (choosing the lesser of two evils).

However, the Qur'anic injunction of *'amr bi al-ma'ruf wa an-nahy 'an al-munkar* (enjoining right and forbidding wrong) gives pause to this utilitarian approach to shari'a, remarks the author. The context was the emergence of the *sahwa* (awakening) in Saudi Arabia in the 1980s that combined Salafi conservatism with political activism. The first test case was the 1990 Operation Desert Shield and the 1991 Operation Desert Storm against Iraq with the *sahwa* submitting to the House of Saud two petitions: *khitab al-'ulama'* (letter of the scholars) and *mudhak-kirat al-nasiha* (memorandum of advice). With the Taliban regime demonstrating loyalty toward Al Qaeda (and disavowal of the United States) leading to the 2001 Operation Enduring Freedom, a few Saudi Salafi clerics aligned themselves with the Al-Qaeda position of uncompromising loyalty of Muslims toward Muslims. Al-Zawahiri made jihad an obligation against Muslims who accept help from non-Muslims. After 9/11 Osama bin Laden even remonstrated Saudi intellectuals for proposing coexistence with the West.

Abd al-Wahhab ensconced *tawhid* (monotheism) as the conceptual apex in Islam and identified its three components: *tawhid al-rububiyya* (oneness of Lordship), *tawhid al-uluhiyya* (oneness of divinity), and *tawhid al-asma' wa al-sifat* (oneness of attributes). It is the oneness of divinity, what Ibn Taymiyya also called *tawhid al-'ibada* (oneness of worship), that couples faith with practice in everyday life. In the 1990s Salafi-quietists like Rabi ibn Hadi Umayr al-Madkhali and Muhammad Aman al-Jami opposed questioning the faith of the ruler and leaving that judgment to God. After 9/11 Bin Laden conjoined monotheism and faith with dissociation from Muslim tyrants for *'aqida* (doctrinal purity). The rigidity of political absolutism was demonstrated for Maher with Al Qaeda opposing the Saudi sponsored 2007 Hamas-Fatah Makkah Agreement for a Palestinian unity government because it was endorsed by the United States.

Relevant for understanding *inghimas* (plunging into the enemy) tactics, Maher illustrates Salafi-jihadi doctrinal rigidity with reference to three concepts: *al-qada' wa al-qadr* (divine will and predestination), *tawakkul* (entrusting oneself totally to God for everything), and *khawf* (fearing God alone). The author notes that entrusting oneself totally to God for everything encapsulates three components: *iman* (faith), *halaat* (resigning oneself to God), and *amal* (righteous deeds). Azzam propounded that entrusting oneself totally to God is to be by jihad in practicing loyalty and disavowal. Thus, fearing God alone was linked with the righteous deed of jihad that included practicing loyalty and disavowal in resigning oneself to God as a demonstration of faith.

The concept of *hakimiyya* (God's sovereignty) relates to establishing political authority in an Islamic state. Generally attributed to Abul A'la Maududi, Maher traces the idea to Imam Abu al-Hasan al-Mawardi who reserved legislative, judicial, and executive rights for God. Whereas Qutb was influenced by Maududi, the author makes a point that Maududi himself owed to Muhammad Iqbal. The fear of Western secularism that agonized all of them was developed into a *jahiliyya* (pre-Islamic polytheism) doctrine by Qutb. After the 1991 Gulf War the ideas of oneness of God and God's sovereignty were intertwined by Saudi Salafis into a new concept of *tawhid al-hakimiyya*. Salafi-quietists are status quo oriented and advocate absolute obedience to the *wali al-amr* (legitimate ruler) in objecting to God's sovereignty as a separate category of oneness of God. Salafi-activists are reformists and propose that *shura* (consultation) be limited to *nasiha* (advice). Salafi-jihadis place all executive authority in the *khalifa* (successor). In particular, Salafi-jihadis couple *shari'a* and *tawhid* in an uncompromising view of *hakimiyya*. The politics of *tawhid al-hakimiyya*, remarked Abu Hamza, is its potential use for ascertaining the sincerity of a Muslim ruler.

Shiraz Maher argues that major doctrinal shifts have been precipitated by wars. It is not the Islamic State, the author adds a caveat, but Al-Qaeda that has significantly contributed to the Salafi-jihadi doctrine. The glossary is helpful; the bibliography will be useful. While keeping Arabic words the book is lucidly written with the general audience in mind. *Salafi-Jihadism: The History of an Idea* is a monumental contribution to the literature on political Islam in general and Salafi movement in particular. Scholars and practitioners in security studies, including those in counterterrorism, will find the book an invaluable and worthwhile reading. **RGM**

State of Terror: How Terrorism Created Modern Israel

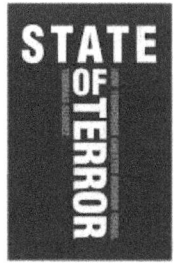

Thomas Suarez. Northampton, MA: Olive Branch Press (Interlink Pub Group), 2016. 418 pp. ISBN: 978-1-56656-068-9.

The politically violent orientation of two Jewish organizations operating in mandated Palestine is the focus of *State of Terror*. Suarez, a writer and musician, based in London strains credulity by taking the obviously odious activities of the Irgun and Lehi, aka Stern Gang, and equating them to the overall effort of the Jewish Agency in Palestine to seek and work for an independent Jewish state. Each attack by these two focused groups is highlighted with graphic exaggeration in an attempt to sour the entire Zionist enterprise. There is a contribution to be credited, namely the documentation of some number of incidents during the mandate period, supported by a wealth of British archival material, however without consultation with the relevant Irgun and Lehi archival outlets. Palestinian Arab-initiated violence is characterized as opposition to Zionist plans or retaliation for Jewish violence against Arab targets. To be sure, there was Jewish pressure on the British mandatory regime to respect the general intent of the Balfour Declaration, certainly after 1922 when the territory west of the Jordan River was excised to create an Arab Transjordan. There certainly was also a violent component to the organized Jewish presence, some of it devoted to self-defense against Palestinian Arab violence directed toward the Yishuv (the Jewish community), initiated for a number of perceived inflicted injustices.

The author's arguments are taken beyond Israel's creation to the current Israeli defense policies and criticized accordingly. This is a clear and intense attempt to delegitimize Zionist ideology and in doing so, change the traditional historiographic interpretation on the creation of Israel. The author would have the reader consider that there has been a pattern of settler colonialism qua imperialism in place. Some will view this work as a polemic while others can reach a reasonable conclusion of revisionist historical interpretation. **SRS**

Terror in France: The Rise of Jihad in the West

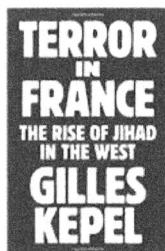

Gilles Kepel, Antoine Jardin. Princeton, NJ: Princeton University Press. 240 pp. ISBN: 978-0691174846.

In this updated study and expansion upon previously published work, Gilles Kepel traces the contemporary history and evolution of Sunni radical Islamism and militancy in France from 2005 up to the launching of attacks by Islamic State in Paris and other locations in the country in 2015. The backdrop of the book is not only the rise and increasing radicalization and organization of European *jihadi* cells on the continent, but also the growing popularity of far-right wing political parties such as Marine Le Pen's National Front in France and Geert Wilders' Party for Freedom (Partij voor de Vrijheid; PVV) in the Netherlands, which have drawn on public alarm and anger over terrorist attacks at home to push their anti-immigration and extreme nationalist and ethno-racial ideologies.

Kepel is uniquely placed to write such a study as one of the foremost academic experts on radical Sunni Islamism and the author of several important and influential earlier studies in the 1980s and 1990s on the history and trajectories of Sunni jihadism in Egypt and the wider Muslim world. In this book, he draws upon his several decades of fieldwork and observation of the outlying neighborhoods of France's major cities, the *banlieus*, which tend to be home to immigrants and other groups from lower socio-economic classes and who are less connected to mainstream French society. It is in these neighborhoods that feelings of alienation, anger, and a desire for the utopian ideal promised by jihadi ideologues has partially taken root, producing groups of youth susceptible to the media messaging and propaganda of radical organizations such as Islamic State and Al-Qaeda. Kepel also makes use of selected primary source materials produced by these organizations, most of them in Arabic, but some of which are translated into other languages including French, English, German, and Spanish.

What France and other countries are experiencing now, Kepel argues, is the "third wave" of jihadi militancy that builds upon the first set of waves of Afghanistan, Bosnia, Egypt, and Algeria in the 1980s and 1990s and the "second wave" represented by Al-Qaeda Central's attacks inside the United States on September 11, 2001. In Europe, this "third wave jihadism" began in 2005 and was marked by jihadi recruiters targeting second-generation immigrants from Muslim majority countries living in Europe, whose personal and communal identities remain, to a large degree, separate from the rest of national society. He also argues that 2005 was a pivotal year in the emergence of a new form of jihadism in France because it also saw the breakout of the most widespread riots in the banlieus, riots which were also based on an "enclave-based ethnic-racial logic of violence" (p. xi) that came to form the basis of third wave jihadism's exhortations to militancy. The riots themselves marked a major shift in French society and politics as the children of first-generation immigrants from North and West Africa emerged for the first time as significant political actors.

France's Muslim communities are divided along generational, social, political, and economic lines with many different groups competing for influence over an estimated eight percent of the country's population of nearly 65 million people. A greater percentage of first-generation immigrants and second-generation French Muslims are younger and poorer than the national average. The numbers of the country's Muslims have also increased due to the conversion of "native" French to Islam, particularly from the working and lower middle class. Since the early 2000s, France's once dominant Muslim organizations, many of which were offshoots of the Muslim Brotherhood movement, have lost more and more ground to grassroots Salafi preachers and groups who have built large followings in the banlieus. On the political side of developments, French Muslims also began to play a more prominent role in national politics, establishing their own civic organizations and lobbying groups that supported an array of different candidates for public office.

French jihadism specifically built upon the opportunities for indoctrination and recruitment presented to imprisoned militants such as the French-Algerian Djamel Beghal, who was jailed on charges that he was planning an Al-Qaeda attack on French soil before being released to house arrest in 2009 after the government was unable to deport him to Algeria. Some of these militant voices went on to indoctrinate younger generations of militants such as the Kouachi brothers, Saïd and Chérif, who carried out the January 7, 2015 attack on the offices of *Charlie Hebdo* in Paris. These shifts in French Islam and the evolution of French jihadism are discussed in the book's first three chapters.

The outbreak of mass demonstrations followed by civil war in Syria presented jihadis with arguably the most significant recruitment opportunity in modern history. Graphic footage and reports of government atrocities, which were later backed by Russian and Iranian military interventions, served as an emotional catalyst for many Muslim youth around the world including in France, with estimates ranging from 1,500 to 2,500 of individuals believed to have traveled to Syria or Iraq to join organizations including Islamic State and Jabhat al-Nusra. Although only an estimate, these numbers are the highest in Europe. The poorer integration of France's Muslims into mainstream society has probably played a role in the attractiveness of militancy among segments of the population. Recruitment into Islamic State and other jihadi organizations was also aided by individuals who had joined during earlier periods and later served as recruiters in their own right, such as the notorious Islamic State member and recruiter Rachid Kassim, who was featured in the organization's media operations and his own social media accounts before he was killed in early 2017 in a US air strike near Mosul, Iraq.

The book is rich in detail and includes a useful chronology of events as an appendix. Citations, however, are scant and it does not include either substantial footnotes/end notes or a bibliography, which makes it difficult to verify or follow up on sources of information cited in the main text. The absence of substantial in-text citations or footnotes and a bibliography are particularly surprising in an academic study published by a university press. Despite these important omissions, the book provides one of the most extensive histories and set of analysis on the history and evolution of French jihadism and will be of interest to the general public as well as scholars and analysts. **AZ**

TURKEY

Images of Istanbul

Veronika Bernard. Vienna, AT: Lit Verlag GmbH, 2015.
133 pp. ISBN: 978-3643906878.

From the outset, Veronika Bernard's recently published collection of photographs is clear about its purpose: "*Images of Istanbul* is a photographic album devoted to the permanently changing urban face of Istanbul and trying to catch the manifold character of the city" (p. 7). Taken over the course of a decade, from 2005 to 2014, Bernard's photos are presented in color, black and white, as well as some that have had filtration effects applied to them. In terms of organization, the book is divided into nine chapters, six of which are actual photographic themes that begin with "The Changing Face of Taksim Square" and ends with "Istanbul Styles & Arts".

The number of photos included in this volume could plausibly range anywhere from 55 to 110, a span that unquestionably requires some explanation. There are 55 individually numbered and titled plates in this album, which corresponds with the author's statements at the start of the book, notwithstanding the description on the back cover that leads the reader to expect 63 photos. However, each numbered plate is actually a two-page spread with each page of the spread featuring a different version of the same photograph. Thus, a pattern is repeated for all 55 plates: On the left facing page is a small (8.5 x 11.5cm or 9.5 x 12.5cm), full frame black and white rendering of a photo and on the right facing page there is an enlarged, manipulated variation of that photo which has been cropped to the dimensions of the page (20 x 20cm). Therefore, it is hardly an abuse of arithmetic to state that when each of the 55 plates offers two interpretations of a photo, the sum of 110 images is entirely within the bounds of reason.

When turning to the photographs themselves, it is perhaps significant to note that *Images of Istanbul* is a product of Veronika Bernard's other projects — as listed in her text — and that the name of one of these undertakings seems like a fitting description of the overall aesthetic represented in *Images…*: Snapshots. Accordingly, many of the same merits and drawbacks that can be attached to the whole conception of snapshots as its own sort of photographic grouping are visible here. For instance, it might be said that while the spontaneity of a snapshot approach to Istanbul can provide a degree of novelty to the visual records of this much-photographed city, there are also certain deficiencies like underexposures and blown highlights and limited tonal range that make some of the provided samples lean toward simply being too emblematic of a pedestrian snapshot. Likewise, while the lack of an overarching pictorial premise to tie all the photos together can be refreshing, it can also make the set seem disjointed and more suggestive of how Istanbul might look through the pages of a family holiday scrapbook.

As for the subject matter in *Images…*, Istanbul is obviously the center of attention; yet, as already mentioned, it is a vision of the city as an almost random collage of photographs. So, indicative of this arbitrariness, there are views of taxis, pigeons, a squirrel, an insect, storefront window displays, empty outdoor café tables, graffiti, and tulips. Of course, this is not to imply that uniformity is necessarily good or even desirable; nevertheless, some cohesive elements — whether stylistic, thematic, or technical — could easily add some semblance of interrelatedness to this visual narrative of Istanbul. But again, like with the snapshot aesthetic, it is very likely that this mixture matches exactly with the artist's mission as she describes it in her own words: "The… photos of this photographic album try to catch the very special Istanbul atmosphere and take the reader on a journey to the author's favorite places" (p. 9).

Ultimately, though, there is the underlying and much broader issue that Veronika Bernard's photographic reading of Istanbul brings to mind. Given the snapshot techniques and the haphazard arrangement of Bernard's book, it does make one curious to know how hardcopy sets like this are going to compete with — and be differentiated from — all of the other similarly shot journeys to favorite places that are already assembled in a scattershot manner online. The fundamental reality is that with the ubiquity of camera phones bolstering the widespread usage of sites like Instagram, Facebook, Flickr, and Pinterest, experiencing someone else's snap shooting an uncoordinated path through foreign cities is as easy as a keyword search. Hence, from the vantage point of today's digital era of photography, it must be asked: Is there anything outside of price and a printed format that distinguishes an artist's snapshots from those of an amateur, or is such a distinction already obsolete?
JCAR

Queering Sexualities in Turkey: Gay Men, Male Prostitutes and the City

Cenk Özbay. London, UK: I. B. Tauris. 194 pp. ISBN: 978-1784533175.

Based on over a decade of fieldwork and interviews with male sex workers and their clients in Istanbul, Cenk Öz-bey's extensively researched study provides a much-need-ed insight into the issues of masculinity, (homo)eroticism, sexuality, gender and class in the world of transactional gay sex in neoliberal Turkey. His work will prove invaluable reading for those re-searchers across various disciplines interested in queer studies, sexuality and gender studies, masculinity, and sex work. The primary focus of Özbey's re-search, the "rent boy," is typically a lower-class, straight-identified man from the Istanbul's outer suburbs who travels to the city center in order to engage in sex work with upper-class gay men. Many of these men insist that they are heterosexual (or "normal"), that they are "top-only" (only playing the role of penetrator, never penetrated), and that they do not experience any sexu-al pleasure or desire in their encounters with gay men. As Özbey recounts, one of the most common questions he experienced the most often was as follows: "Why do they not just quit sex work and stop being rent boys if, as they say, they do not like having sex with men or gay culture" (p.153)? He recounts that many believe that rent boys are "really" gay men.

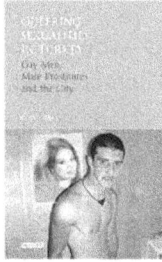

Özbey's research, however, intentionally eschews the problematic ques-tion of a "real" sexual orientation and rather looks at other benefits for rent boys, such as material benefits. Furthermore, he explores some of the con-tradictory discourses, practices, and anxieties around desire and pleasure experienced by rent boys. For example, rent boys, in his description, devel-op intricate practices in order to navigate these sexualized spaces. In some of his interviews, some rent boys speak about experiencing pleasure when having sex with younger, attractive men. One of the biggest anxieties which Özbey describes is the anxiety of getting penetrated — for this reason, they must avoid getting too drunk at the bar, they must closely monitor the kinds of contact and interaction they have with other rent boys, etc. (The fear of attraction between two rent boys, for instance, is one which he discusses ex-tensively, as is the fear for a rent boy that another rent boy may touch his ass while dancing at the bar.) There are many risks for rent boys, which threat-en to destabilize their extensively cultivated masculinity. One of the biggest fears is the fear of "becoming gay," that by spending too much time with gay men, getting too close to them, they risk becoming one. In fact, there are examples of rent boys who eventually came out as gay. At the same time, there are also rent boys who eventually quit and went back to their heterosexual, "normal" lives.

Rather than essentializing rent boys as "really gay," (as many of his gay informants do), Özbey shows how rent boys destabilize the apparently self-evident categories of "heterosexual" and "homosexual." He cites Halberstam's concept of queer spatiality and temporality to argue that "rent boys in Istanbul subvert the imagined balance between erotic practices, sexual identities and regulations… while they embody an inconsistent, in-between and oscillating position, through which they produce sexual subjectivities" (p.108). He argues that "rent boys are queer subjects because they simultaneously expose how homosexuals *become* homosexual and heterosexuals *become* heterosexual … in addition to their distanced and unscrupulous attitude towards these two sexually regulating categories, discourses and erotic regimes" (p.109). Rent boys trouble the categories of "heterosexual" and "homosexual" through their transgressions — which, in turn, makes them a particular kind of queer subject. While Özbey's book helps problematize these categories, it also exposes the ways in which "gay" as a category references class as much as sexuality. Lower class boys from the suburbs are not allowed to be "gay" even if they experience sexual desire for male bodies, precisely because "gay" is a class position from which they are excluded.

Central to the book is the concept of "exaggerated masculinity." Rent boys, Özbey argues, perform exaggerated masculinity as a way of keeping their heterosexual identity intact despite having sex with men. They do this for multiple reasons, but one of the primary reasons is that middle-class gay men fetishize the "authentic" masculinity of lower-class rent boys. The sexualization of lower-class masculinity puts rent boys into a delicate situation: on the one hand, they must maintain this performance of masculinity, and not "become gay"; on the other hand, it is precisely through engaging in sex with men that the very masculinity they must sell becomes threatened. In fact, as Özbey demonstrates, both middle-class gay men and lower-class rent boys are performing certain scripted gender roles. At the beginning of Chapter 5, Özbey shares a quote from Judith Butler: "The thought of sexual difference within homosexuality has yet to be theorized in its complexity" (p.125). This book accomplishes exactly that.

"Exaggerated masculinity" is tied to another key component of Özbey's argument: the idea that this kind of performance is also tied to the production of a neoliberal, cultivated, marketable self. It is at this step in the argument, however, that I find a problem in an otherwise well-written and researched book. Although he does draw in the historical trajectory of Turkish neoliberalism, these connections remain somewhat unconvincing. The book could have stood to delve a little more into theories of neoliberalism, and what neoliberalism looks like in a Turkish context, in order to connect it with the production of neoliberal selves on the part of rent boys. Furthermore, is it not the case that sex work has always involved a kind of self-fashioning and self-marketization? Is this aspect of male sex work in Istanbul really a manifestation of neoliberalism or is it simply a product of capitalism? In order to address these questions, however, Özbey would have had to expand the scope of his research to include oral history or other historical research, and there is only so much one can do in one book.

Another weakness which makes the book somewhat difficult to follow at times are the inconsistencies between discourse and practice which are often described but sometimes left hanging, in need of more conceptual connections. At times, the book describes certain socio-cultural archetypes and practices in great detail (how rent boys dance in clubs, what kinds of cologne they wear, what their relationships are with other rent boys, to name a few examples) while, a few pages later, interviews and examples show us the exceptions to these rules (rent boys experiencing pleasure in their sexual encounters with gay men, rent boys having sex or forming romantic relationships with other rent boys, for example.) If the book seems to contradict itself, however, that is because Özbey is dealing with a very contradictory subject. There is a larger methodological question, here, then, of how to present the reader with socio-cultural or discursive archetypes which have certain truth-value, while also exploring the contradictions and inconsistencies of these discourses. Overall, the book does a good job dealing with these questions, but there are moments when the reader may get confused. But perhaps this is also a testament to the book's strengths, as many careful readers will come away from the book with even more questions for further research and exploration.

Finally, at the risk of over-criticizing an otherwise well-written and researched book, there is one more critique which bears mentioning. Özbey situates rent boys as troubling the discourses of homosexuality and heterosexuality in Turkey. However, there is a wide range of literature on the history of sexuality in the Balkans and Middle East which demonstrates that historically, masculinity in the region was defined in terms of penetration, and not the gender or body of the penetrated — that is, the "queer" was only the one being penetrated, that the "man" maintained his "normal" masculinity so long as he was the one penetrating, regardless of whether it was a man or woman he penetrated. From this perspective, doesn't the rent boy's sexuality represent more of a continuation with a historical norm than a transgression? If sexuality in Turkey really is otherwise conceptualized along the lines of a (western) heterosexual/homosexual binary — a background against which the rent boy intervenes — doesn't that transformation require accounting for? From my own ethnographic research in both Turkey and Greece, I can say that the western heterosexual/homosexual binary is not as fully hegemonic as in the west.

Despite the aforementioned limitations, *Queering Sexualities in Turkey* will prove vital reading for anyone interested in issues of gender, sexuality, and sex work in Turkey, the Middle East and Balkans, as well as students of gender and sexuality more generally. His demonstration of the ways in which "gay" serves as a signifier of class along with sexuality will provide a compelling case for the field of queer studies, and his last chapter, documenting how the marketplace of male sex work in Turkey shifted drastically during the last years of his research, will provide interesting material for anybody interested in the rapidly shifting terrain of contemporary Turkish politics. His exploration of the middle-class fetishization of lower-class masculinity will prove interesting for anyone interested in the intersections of class and sexuality. This is a book which will provide a wealth of insight for researchers with a wide variety of interests. ***SP***

VIOLENCE

Whether to Kill: The Cognitive Maps of
Violent and Nonviolent Individuals

Stephanie Dornschneider. Philadelphia, PA: University of Pennsylvania Press, 2016. 328 pp. ISBN: 978-0812247701.

Why do people take up arms? How do individuals with violent and nonviolent behaviors arrive at their decisions to act? In bringing back the cognitive mapping approach (CMA) by Robert Axelrod, Stephanie Dornschneider takes a political psychology perspective in addressing these questions through an examination of beliefs (factors) and systems of beliefs (mechanisms) for decisions of political activism. The book is divided into six chapters: CMA, research design, group history, cognitive map construction process, computational analysis, and counterfactual alternatives. With ethnographic interviews of 27 individuals, the research design is a double-paired comparison: half are Muslims from Egypt, a "poor authoritarian state;" the other half are non-Muslims [Christians] from Germany, a "wealthy democratic state." Both violent and nonviolent activities are examined. The groups associated with violent activities category are Al-Jama'at al-Islamiyya and Al-Jihad in Egypt and Rote Armee Fraktion (RAF) and Bewegung 2. Juni (B2J) in Germany. Those associated with nonviolent activities are the Muslim Brotherhood in Egypt and Socialist German Student Union (SDS) and Kommune 1 (K1) in Germany.

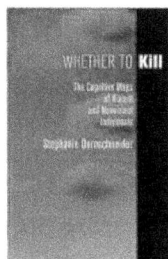

The study has two major findings. First, both violent and nonviolent behaviors by individuals are responses to the beliefs about an aggressive state. Second, the absence of beliefs about threatening state behavior would dissuade both violent and nonviolent behaviors by individuals. In addition, the hypotheses questioned four prevailing theories. First, violent behaviors by individuals are not explained by religious beliefs (cultural-psychological theory). In particular, political violence is not explained by Islam. Second, violent behaviors are not explained by beliefs about economic deprivation (environmental-psychological theory). Third, violent behaviors are not explained by beliefs about violent groups (group theory). Specifically, violent individuals are not alienated from society or influenced by social networks. Finally, violent behaviors are not explained by mental illness (psychopathological theory).

In applying CMA to the study of political violence by individuals the work breaks a new ground, Dornschneider claims. Cognitive mapping involves a two-step process. First, identify the components from interview notes. Second, abstract direct speech into a coding scheme. The three components of cognitive mapping are beliefs, belief connections, and decisions. Belief systems help to identify the motivating factors for political behaviors. The propositional contents distinguish among three types of beliefs: true, intersubjective, and subjective. With true beliefs as the most important for cognitive mapping, political violence is a response to the external world (rather than being associated with culture or mental illness). The subjective probability of belief connections points to coherence and logical consistency within given belief contexts. Decisions connect beliefs to actions or political behavior. Of course, planning is not to be equated with performance. However, actions are related to goals, which are coterminous with desired outcomes. A coding scheme facilitates comparison of beliefs among different individuals.

Dornschneider drew on theme analysis by James Spradley for the coding scheme. Attention to semantics (questions and issues) and syntax (words and grammatical constructions) allowed identification of assertions by the interviewees. Beliefs were abstracted into successive tiers of generalization for comparison. At the fifth-tier of belief "super-superclasses" there was no distinction in the reasoning process between either violent and nonviolent individuals or Muslims and non-Muslims. The latter observation led the author to hold that Islam itself did not explain political violence.

Computational analysis of cognitive maps in Matrix Laboratory (MATLAB) revealed ten mechanisms (reasoning processes): five for taking up arms and five for engaging in nonviolent activism. In the second phase, Dornschneider transformed the cognitive maps into directed acyclical graphs (DAGs). Devoid of self-loops DAGs allowed a new way of studying counterfactuals, the author argued, by intervening on internal factors instead of the external world. Findings from counterfactual alternatives supported earlier findings that both violent and nonviolent activisms occur as a response to threatening state behaviors of aggression and repression.

The author defined political violence with reference to four characteristics: use of physical force, civilian perpetrators (with a focus on individuals rather than groups), state targets (including government officials), and political goals. However, it would have added clarity with goals included for features of political violence instead of listing brute force and means as two separate items (p. 18). Tables and diagrams were helpful. The appendices will delight those with computer programming skills. Scholars in Islamic studies will rejoice from the empirical evidence that decouples Islam from political violence. That very point should provide food for thought to scholars and practitioners in security studies. The book is a significant contribution to the literature in political psychology. **RGM**

YEMEN

Hadhramaut and Its Diaspora: Yemeni Politics, Identity and Migration

Noel Brehony, Ed. New York, NY: I. B. Taurus, 2017. 320 pp. ISBN: 978-1784538682.

Noel Brehony, a retired British diplomat and author on Yemeni affairs, has joined with eleven other specialists to present an examination of the Hadramaut, Yemen's eastern province, and its many emigres dispersed throughout the Indian Ocean basin. The collection of articles seeks nothing more than to "illuminate many aspects of Hadhramaut, Yemen and the diaspora" while showing that research "is still comparatively underdeveloped" (p. 14), and has in common with much of the literature on the Hadhramaut foci on the Hadhrami diaspora and the traditional social stratification that divides Hadhrami society among the *sada* (s. sayyid, i.e. religious elites claiming descent from the Prophet Muhammad), *mashayikh* and *qaba'il* (tribal elites and tribemen), and the *masakin* (common people). However, two common themes, the close relationship between the Hadhrami homeland and the diaspora and an effort to establish a theoretical basis for the examination of Hadhramaut and its diaspora, distinguish the volume.

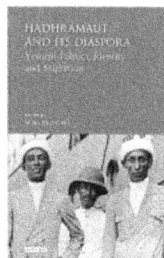

The book is divided into three sections, covering Hadhramis in Yemen, Hadhramis in the Diaspora, and Research Issues. The introduction by Editor Brehony and Abdalla Burja, Director of the Institute for Cultural Heritage at the Muslim University of Morogoro (Tanzania) and a leading scholar on Hadhramaut, provides general historical background. Brehony and retired Yemeni politician Saadaldeen Talib then turn to the limited role, with a few noted individual exceptions, that Hadhramis have played in Yemeni politics, economics, and culture since 1960. Yemen specialist Thanos Petouris analyses Hadhrami identity, arguing that Hadhrami "exceptionalism" grew from tribal and territorial attachments to a sense of nationalism under the influence of anti-colonial and nationalist movements in Yemen and the diaspora. Helen Lackner, an expert on rural development in Yemen, concludes this section with an analysis of the land redistribution enacted under the South Yemeni government and subsequently undone after unification in 1990, which served to exacerbate the traditional social divisions mentioned above. The six articles on the Hadhrami diaspora begin with Professor Nico Kapstien's, Leiden University and a specialist on Indonesia, examination of the Indonesian Hadhrami Sayyid Uthman bin Abdallah al-Alawi (1822-1914) and his *Atlas Arabi*, a collection of three maps (world, Arabian Peninsula, Hadhramaut) and a stylized representation of a Hadhrami village, that drew the attention and admiration of both Hadhramis and Dutch scholars and colonial officials. Kazuhiro Arai, Keio University in Japan, continues the focus on Indonesia with a study of the expanded contacts between Hadhramaut and Indonesia since the unification of Yemen in 1990. Professor William Clarence-Smith, University of London and a widely-published specialist on the Hadhrami diaspora, analyzes Hadhrami activities in the economic, political, and religious life of Spanish and American colonial Philippines. James Spencer, a consultant on the prevention of and recovery from conflict, discusses Hadhramis as foreign mercenaries throughout the Indian Ocean. Iain Walker, a Senior Researcher at the Max Plank Institute in Halle, Germany, examines the issue of identity as expressed in citizenship among Hadhrami residents of Kenya. Philippe Petriat, Sorbonne, examines non-Sayyid Hadhrami merchants in Jeddah and their development of commercial networks that went beyond intra-Diaspora linkages.

The final section comprises two articles. Professor Leif Manger, Bergen (Norway), discusses research problems derived from his own work on Hadhramaut and the Hadhrami diaspora, identifying the conceptual challenges associated with the terms diaspora, globalization, and agency. Burja concludes the book with a call for more research on the history of Hadhramaut, itself; more in-depth analysis of the causes of migration, the choices of destination, and integration into those destinations; the impact of emigration on Hadhramaut; and Hadhrami relations with the rest of Yemen.

As observed in both the introduction and conclusion of the book, the scant literature on Hadhramaut has largely focused on the Hadhrami diaspora, a fact due in large part to the region's isolation and only exacerbated by Yemen's current chaotic political situation. While some effort is made to address that deficiency with the three articles focusing on internal conditions in Hadhramaut, the overwhelming majority of the articles in this collection focus on the wide-spread Hadhrami expatriate community. However, a distinguishing factor of these writings in the conscious efforts to link the diaspora with the homeland. For example, in describing the *Atlas Arabi*, Kapstein observes that, "Through its maps, travel to and within Hadhramaut was facilitated" (p. 96). Spencer observes that throughout the long history of Hadhrami mercenaries abroad, it was not uncommon for those identified as Hadhrami to have originated from elsewhere in South Arabia and to have used their newfound status to "break back into Hadhramaut" (p. 159). More recently, Walker documents the transnational identity of Hadhrami-Kenyans who hold dual nationality and sometimes even claim a kind of tri-nationality with papers from the old Hadhrami Sultanates. Even in the chaos of modern Yemen, strong ties continue to exist between Hadhramaut and Indonesia as documented by Arai.

The second main theme is the effort to establish a theoretical basis for an examination of Hadhramaut and its diaspora. These are not case studies written by narrowly focused specialists on the Hadhramaut. Instead, the various authors bring wide-ranging theoretical and territorial perspectives to their work and present their studies within that broader context. For example, Walker's discussion of Hadhrami-Kenyans draws on the much broader question of identity while Petriat's article on Hadhrami merchants in Jeddah draws on broader theoretical discussions of diaspora and network analysis, a discussion reinforced by Manger, most specifically in his analysis of the concepts of diaspora and agency.

Given the paucity of publications on the Hadhramaut, almost any new work is a welcome addition to the literature. However, *Hadhramaut and Its Diaspora* stands out by expanding our knowledge of the recent history of Hadhramaut, if only briefly, and focusing on the linkages between the Hadhrami homeland and the diaspora within a much more rigorous theoretical framework. **CHA**

The 'Magic Carpet' Exodus of Yemenite Jewry

Esther Meir-Glitzenstein. Eastbourne, UK: Sussex Academic Press, 2014. 265 pp. ISBN: 978-1845196165.

In 1949, they came from all over Yemen, from 1,000 villages, travelling often on foot on more than 77 roads to reach camp. "It was a desert place without any sign of vegetation. Refugees living in matted huts, like sardines, living a base, primitive life. The camp has 4,000 people and babies are born every day" (p. 61), recalled Ethel Slonim, a nurse who had arrived in Aden — now Yemen — in 1948. Many died enroute and in the camp. Yet,

even more than half a century later, the traumatic immigration is thought of as a miracle. Why has the myth of the Yemenite migration not been fully understood for what it was, a massive tragedy in which a community was uprooted, the scars of the operation having never been healed? Esther Meir-Glitzenstein, an associate professor at Ben-Gurion University of the Negev seeks to set the record straight, and provide readers some nuance on this formative historical event in the founding of Israel.

Meir-Glitzenstein sets out to ask several important questions about the migration of Yemenite Jews in 1949. Who initiated it, what caused the Jews to suddenly leave en masse, why was there a humanitarian tragedy and was some of the tragedy underpinned by racism or bigotry among the officials charged with running the operation? She notes that the Yemenite immigration was part of the larger immigration of hundreds of thousands of Jews from both Europe and the Middle East who poured into Israel after the War of Independence. From December 1948 to March 1949, some 5,000 Yemenites arrived. Then an additional 45,000 were airlifted by 1950. Israeli representatives and the Joint Distribution Committee (JDC) played a key role in the operation.

The operation took on a Janus face in Israel's history. For years after the event, many Yemenite Jews claimed that their children had disappeared or been kidnapped. In 1994, Uzi Meshulam and some of his Yemenite followers became so enraged at what they saw as an official state cover-up, they barricaded themselves with weapons in a house in Yehud. In 2001, a commission of inquiry was still investigating what became of the children. Yet for the primarily European-born Israeli establishment, this was anathema to the national narrative of redemption. "This type of exodus story is also found in Golda Meir's autobiography... she describes how the life of suffering and despair led by the Jews of Yemen motivated them to leave, and she emphasizes that they fled spontaneously, clinging to their Hebrew biblical texts" (p. 5). Children in Israel learned in textbooks that claimed that "Yemen is a poor land, dry and barren. When the miracle occurred, and when Israel overcame her enemies and the State of Israel was established in perpetuity, the sound of shofar (ram's horn) announcing the coming of the Messiah was heard even by the Jews in far-away Yemen" (p. 6).

One of the reasons for the lack of an inquiry into what happened was that so few books on the subject were published. Yosef Zadok, an emissary of the Jewish Agency, who was born in Yemen, wrote a book about the events in 1956. But as the author notes, most research has only been done in the last two decades.

Yemenite Jews had lived in Yemen since the time of the Second Temple. Even Maimonides had intervened to save them. This was an ancient community, scattered in more than 1,000 villages — mostly in the highlands of the country. As the author notes, by the first half of the twentieth century there were some 50,000 Jews living among 3.5 million Muslims. In some areas they suffered great discrimination, being confined sometimes to collect human waste or animal carcasses. By 1914, some 5,000 Yemenites had already made their way to Palestine, where they played an integral role in the development of the Zionist economy; founding several communities.

During the Second World War, due to a famine and other issues, around 10,000 Jews fled from North Yemen to British-administered Aden (South Yemen). The British interdicted these Jewish refugees who wanted to make it to the Holy Land. "The British wanted to expel these refugees to [North] Yemen, as they had done with the Muslim labor migrants, but they feared that the Jewish Agency would oppose such an expulsion" (p. 46). Later, the number of refugees would continue to swell. Then in December of 1947, a pogrom broke out in Aden in which Muslims, supposedly protesting the UN partition of Palestine, slaughtered 80 Jews.

The author argues the Jewish Agency and others did not do enough for these refugees. In one instance in Qa'tabah, the graves of hundreds of Jews were discovered. "Why was insufficient help not sent to save these refugees...first and foremost because the Jewish Agency did not show any interest in their fate" (p. 57), she argues. Other authors, such as Tudor Parfit,t have linked this dismissive attitude to a "colonial" mindset among the European Jews of Palestine.

The text takes the reader through the tragic story of the deterioration of the situation in Yemen; the Muslim hostility, British indifference and the lack of organization by some Israeli officials. The author concludes that the inability of the state authorities and others to admit that something had gone wrong led to years of denial and lack of compassion or compensation for the hardships. Later in 1984, a repeat of the disaster took place when more than 4,000 Ethiopian Jews died on the way to Israel. One is compelled to ask whether this tragedy might have been averted had the lessons of the Yemenite immigration been learned, while the tragedy of European migrant ships to Israel, like the Egoz and Sturma that sank, are commemorated, the suffering of the Yemenites is not part of the Israeli consciousness. It is an important lesson raised by this book: the need for an Israeli society that can be both introspective and acknowledge all its diverse communities. **SJF**

A Spectre Is Haunting Arabia: How the Germans Brought Their Communism to Yemen

Miriam M. Müller. Germany: Transcript-Verlag Political Science, 2016. 440 pp. ISBN: 978-3837632255.

Ein Gespenst geht um in Europa—das Gespenst des Kommunismus [A spectre is haunting Europe—the spectre of communism] (Marx & Engels, 1970: 415).

Obviously, the title of Miriam Müller's book, which is her PhD thesis, is inspired by the *Communist Manifesto* of Karl Marx and Friedrich Engels. Though in this book the spectre is (or was) haunting South Yemen, instead of Europe. Linking Yemen with communism sounds unusual. In today's media coverage, the country is usually connected to terrorist groups, to the Houthi movement, and finally to the proxy wars of Iran and Saudi Arabia in the region. But part of the history of Yemen is connected to communism, and this is strongly linked to Müller's book. A few decades ago, in the south of the county — following its liberation from colonial Britain — its tendency to Arab nationalism and the impact from the consequences of the Cold War led it to become a social communist state, the "People's Democratic Republic of Yemen." The book deals with four major topics, which intersected in South Yemen:

(a) it analyzes different dimensions of the South Yemeni society;

(b) it brings to light untold dimensions of the foreign policy of East Germany in the Cold War era;

(c) it deliberates the creation and establishment of South Yemen as an independent state and a process of nation- and state-building;

(d) it discusses the role of East Germany in building a socialist state in South Yemen; and

(e) it analyzes the relationship between the Soviet Union and East Germany.

Müller's book is rich in the use of literature from fields such as nationalism, identity, nation-building, foreign, and international and regional policy. However, the reader rarely feels alone, and without orientation. The varied theories are applied competently.

The book presents arguments in three main parts, which are structured throughout 17 chapters. The first part presents the analytic framework in three chapters. The methodology, theoretical approaches, and hypothesis of the research are presented here. One of Müller's key theoretical frameworks are Jochen Hippler's three preconditions of successful nation- and state building (Hippler, 2005). Müller summarizes them as follows: "firstly the communication and acceptance of an integrative ideology, secondly the integration of society, and lastly, the establishment of a functional state apparatus in the sense of state-building" (p. 70).

The second part deals with internal and external determinants of the foreign policy of East Germany and its activities in South Yemen, in 12 chapters. It makes up more than half of the book (275 of 440 pages). It provides a detailed overview on the foreign policy of East Germany, which was influenced by two external factors: the activities and policies of the Soviet Union, and the competitive relationship with West Germany. On the one hand, East Germany had to accept the political guidance of "Big brother" Moscow to survive politically. An interesting example are the "Moscow cadres" of the Communist party of East Germany. They were exiled communists who fled to Moscow from the Nazi regime during the 1930s. When they returned after WWII, they competed with those Germans who fought against the Nazi regime but had not been in exile. The Soviet Union favored the Moscow cadres. It took some years of conflict till the Moscow cadres won and a new Marxist Leninist party (SED) was established, backed by Moscow (p. 87-88). On the other hand, East Germany had a problem achieving its foreign policy goals, when West Germany did not respect its political legitimacy in the international era. An example is the *Hallstein* Doctrine, which was introduced by West Germany in 1955. It became a "stumbling block" for East German foreign policy until the 1970s (p. 92). West Germany, according to this doctrine, would not establish diplomatic relations with any state that diplomatically recognized East Germany. Finally, the *Grundlagenvertrag*, a treaty between both countries, based on the existence of two German states in Germany (1972), made the doctrine obsolete. In these times, South Yemen gave East Germany room to maneuver and to illustrate that it was going to take a step forward in its foreign policy. Müller uses the analysis of Fred Halliday of a "reciprocal relationship" (p. 158), to clarify that in the Cold War era, not only relationships in the international, but also in regional levels were important for the Eastern Block. This was especially true in the Middle East. For many reasons, including economic ones, the Soviet Union did not deal directly with all its partners in the Third World. Among the Arab countries, South Yemen seemed to be a good opportunity for the foreign policy for East Germany — it was small enough to allow trying to build a socialist nation and state. Also, "Arab nationalism" against British colonialism at that time was on the rise in Arabia. It "absorbed Soviet and Maoist" thoughts (p. 215). Müller presents and analyzes East Germany's engagement in South Yemen in four phases. They are as follows:

Phase I, sampling and creation, from 1963 to 1970. In this period, East Germany was still struggling for international recognition. South Yemen was in a radical political path to become a Marxist state. However, the South Yemen state was young and rather weak; but it did show a clear willingness to accept East Germany as a partner.

Phase II, establishment and expansion, from 1969 to 1978. In this phase, East Germany attempted to integrate the tribal society of South Yemen into Marxist-Leninism. The major fields of engagement were "military and ideology" (p. 293). This engagement was promoted from two dynamics. On the one hand, West Germany had withdrawn from South Yemen; on the other hand, some advisors and experts of the UN and some Western countries were involved in affairs of the new state of South Yemen.

Phase III, continuity and consolidation, from 1978 to 1986. In this phase, East Germany provided its guidance and strengthened its position in South Yemen through its party-centered political system, economic aid, the media and security apparatus. Despite the Soviet Union's and East Germany's increased engagement in this period, the results were not promising. For instance, they had hoped to discover more oil fields. However, it was not fulfilled. Moreover, the South Yemeni intelligence agency was still inefficient.

Phase IV, neglect, from 1986 to 1990. This was a phase of cold relations between East Germany and South Yemen and included the end of socialist state-building in South Yemen. The conflicts between North and South Yemen resulted in the "January crisis" in 1986. Even though political chaos in South Yemen were brief, East Germany lost its trust in the South Yemeni state. It was no longer accepted as an unquestioned socialist state and nation. In this phase, East Germany engaged in South Yemen political affairs reluctantly. However, the decline of Soviet Union and East Germany was near.

The third part of the book presents findings of Müller's research. On the one hand, East Germany's foreign policy was fragmented; on the other hand, tribalism of South Sudan was a major obstacle. The majority of the population of South Yemen has come from tribes. That made a change of ideas and identity difficult. Müller argues that nation-building is a policy that is pursued from the inside and outside. Referring to Hippler's analysis — that nation building from outside is harder — Müller concludes that East Germany had difficulties initiating some developments, regarding ideology in South Yemen. Hence South Yemen failed to become a Marxist state in the end.

The book has many strong points. The topic of the book is multi-objective. It includes numerous theories and relevant literature. Nonetheless, the author has successfully managed to present these complex discussions in a clear way. Her critical approach to dominant academic debates is admirable as well. For instance, Müller challenges the idea that just interests of the foreign policy of East Germany were determinative in the nation-building of South Yemen. She argues that firstly, South Yemen, like other Arab countries was not "helpless" with "no agency at all" during the Cold War (p. 391). Secondly, the regime in Aden was not as weak and insufficient as Moscow and East Germany assumed. Another strong point of the study is its rich sources and materials. Besides reviewing the relevant literature, it is based on 1) archival texts, like material of the East German Foreign Intelligence ("Hauptverwaltung Aufklärung", HVA); 2) monographs and published interviews of key political figures of East Germany; and, 3) personal interviews with former diplomats and members of staffs of relevant organizations of East Germany.

The book has very minor weaknesses. The table of content could be presented in a clearer structure and numbering. I highly recommend the book because of its original topic, its rich critical appraisal of literature, and its exploratory approach to historic facts. Those who have an interest in issues around South Yemen, foreign policy generally and foreign policy of Communist countries in the Cold war era specifically, and nation-building should read the book. *FKC*

References

Hippler, J. (2005). *Nation-building: a key concept for peaceful conflict transformation?* London, UK: Pluto Press.

Marx, K., & Engels, F. (1970). Manifest der Kommunistischen Partei [Manifesto of the Communist Party] *Karl Marx/ Friedrich Engels Ausgewählte Werke in 6 Bänden* (Vol. 1, pp. 415-464). Frankfurt, DE: Marxistische Blätter GmbH.

Tribes and Politics in Yemen: A History of the Houthi Conflict

Marieke Brandt. New York, NY: Oxford University Press, 2017. 466 pp. ISBN: 978-0190673598.

The ongoing civil war and humanitarian catastrophe in Yemen has brought to the world's attention the previously obscure Zaydi tribal and Islamist movement Ansar Allah (God's Partisans) founded and led by the al-Houthi family, currently headed by Abd al-Malik al-Houthi since the killing of his brother, Husayn, in a strike by the Yemeni military in the summer of 2004. The complex array of social groups, competing loyalties, political intrigues, and regional and international geostrategic maneuverings are today seen predominantly through the lens of the narrative frame of Iranian-Saudi competition for power and influence across the Middle East with the Yemeni conflict being simplified and described as merely a "proxy war" between the two countries. This frame distorts far more than it explains, and it is this problem that Marieke Brandt, an anthropologist at the Institute for Social Anthropology at the Austrian Academy of Sciences, contests in her most recent book. Rather than examining the Houthi phenomenon and the rounds of conflict between it and the Yemeni government, the first under the Ali Abdullah Saleh and currently under the Saudi-backed government of Abd Rabbuh Mansur Hadi, her research is instead focused on laying out the local, grassroots, and "bottom-up" dynamics at play from within the Houthi movement's home region of Sa'da in northern Yemen.

Drawing on years of field work among Yemeni tribes and other societal actors as well as Arabic sources and digital anthropology, her book is the most detailed study of the history, dynamics, and evolution of the Houthis published to date. She argues that the roots of the current conflict involving the Houthis predate the early years of the twenty-first century, which is where most accounts of the movement begin, and instead can be traced to the major sociopolitical and religious events that transformed Yemen beginning in the 1960s and 1970s. Major societal shocks had significant impact on Yemen's tribal system as did the emergence of new religious and ideological currents in the regions of Yemen including in Sa'da where Salafism first emerged during the 1980s. Brought to the country's Zaydi heartland in the north by Yemenis, some of them born into Zaydi families from non-*sayyid* lineages, which limited their upward mobility in Zaydi areas, such as Muqbil al-Wadi'i, Salafism proved to be attractive for many in parts of northern Yemen because it seemed to be more egalitarian in that it prioritized personal religious knowledge and study over heredity in social advancement. Contemporary Yemeni Salafis have also drawn upon the writings and scholastic legacy of Muhammad al-Shawkani, an influential Yemeni Sunni jurist and religious scholar of the eighteenth and nineteenth centuries who, though born into a Zaydi family, adopted a more "Salafi"-like form of Sunnism.

The Houthis also did, and do not enjoy a monopoly on Zaydi loyalties in the country, with many Zaydis having historically actively opposed or distanced themselves from the Houthis. These included the powerful al-Ahmar clan from among the Hashid tribal confederation as well as the late Yemeni president, Ali Abdullah Saleh, himself. Yemen's conflict is not one pitting all Zaydis against all Sunnis and, despite reported Iranian state support for the Houthis and the shift of segments of Ansar Allah toward ritual aspects more frequently seen among Twelver Shi'ites than Zaydis, the Houthis are not an exact replica of other Iranian allies and proxies in the Middle East. Instead, the Houthi leadership draws upon support from Iran and also, reportedly, Lebanon's Hizbullah and attempts to mimic the media stylings of the latter in pursuit of its own domestic interests and goals.

The book's first chapter introduces the geographical and geological landscape of Yemen and discusses how these have historically impacted the development of Yemeni culture and the tribal system of kinship ties and politics. The chapter also discusses the general contours of the country's tribes with a focus on the Sa'da region and how tribal politics and conflict resolution work. Brandt argues that the Sa'da conflicts between 2004 and 2010 were the results of several simultaneous dynamics including power struggles between local tribes, a populist social revolution of the parts of the region's population who were politically and economically marginalized, and the result of sectarian conflict following Zaydi revivalism.

The second chapter examines how Yemen's civil war between 1962 and 1970, which is often referred to as the "September 26th Revolution," between royalist supporters of the Imamate and republican supporters of the Yemen Arab Republic profoundly impacted the social landscape of the country. Many of the families, individuals, and tribal groups who continue to play an influential role in the Yemeni conflict today emerged as key players during this period and Brandt traces the continuities of who was and continues to be a local powerbroker. These local and regional notables continue to wield significant power because of the failure of the revolutionary republicans to build a durable or authoritative national state. The government's clientelist alliances and social ties and uneven economic patronage alienated segments of Sa'da's population. Victorious tribal leaders emerged from the civil war with expanded power and resources and used these against their tribal rivals, which in turn led to continued instability.

Yemen has long fallen under the influence of its powerful neighbor to the north, the Kingdom of Saudi Arabia. The Saudis and Egypt under the champion of Pan-Arabism, Gamal Abd al-Nasir, fought a proxy war in Yemen in what the late Middle East studies scholar Malcolm Kerr dubbed the "Arab Cold War." Yemeni students such as Muqbil al-Wadi'i studied Salafism in Saudi universities and brought it back to Sa'da and other parts of Yemen. The book's third chapter explains how Saudi Arabia has pursued its own interests in Yemen through the provision of patronage and increasing attempts to establish its writ over the mountainous borderlands between the two countries. The fourth chapter traces the history of sectarian conflict between Zaydis and Salafis in Sa'da and what role this has played in the region's conflicts and the emergence and evolution of the Houthi movement. The book's fifth and six chapters cover the history of the Sa'da conflict beginning in 2004 and ending in 2010, including periods of negotiations and ceasefires or periods of détente between the Yemeni government and the Houthis. Brandt concludes with brief analysis of developments up to the September 2014 Houthi takeover of the Yemeni capital, San'a.

Brandt's study of the Houthi movement and the Sa'da wars is meticulous and even exhaustive in its detail and is geared toward specialist readers and researchers. Indeed, lay non-specialist readers will likely find the book dense and difficult to follow without significant prior knowledge of Yemen and its recent history. This does not lessen the book's quality or the author's contribution to the literatures on Yemen and its history, Zaydi Shi'ism, the social and political dynamics of the Yemen's tribes, and the clash of competing sectarianisms in Sa'da. The book includes extensive end notes as well as a stand-alone bibliography, the latter of which has regrettably been increasingly absent from more and more recent academic publications. Readers will find many sources and studies of interest for further reading in these two sections. **CA**

REVIEWERS

SA = Sadiq Alabbas, ABD; University of Nebraska at Omaha; Omaha, NE

AA = Atacan Atakan, MA; University of Arizona; Tucson, AZ

CHA = Calvin H. Allen, Jr. PhD; Shenandoah University; Winchester, VA

MLA = Michal L. Allon, Phd; Tel Aviv University; Tel Aviv, Israel

MMA = Mohammed M. Aman, Phd; University of Wisconsin; Milwaukee, WI

MA = Murfet Alnemr, EdD; Western Michigan University; Kalamazoo, MI

e-Se-A = el-Sayed el-Aswad; United Arab Emirates University; Al-Ain, UAE

CA = Christopher Anzalone, ABD; McGill University; Montréal, Canada

FB = Fadia Bahgat, PhD; McGill University; Montreal, CA

IJB = Issa J. Boullata, PhD; McGill University; Montreal, Canada

MSC = Martin Scott Catino, PhD; Security Consultant; Richmond, VA

YC = Yiyi Chen, PhD; Shanghai Jiao Tong University; Shanghai, P. R. China

FKC = Fatemeh Kamali Chirani, MA; Augsburg University; Minneapolis, MN

JJC = John J. Curry, PhD; University of Nevada; Nevada, LV

GDD = G. Doug Davis, PhD; Troy University; Troy, AL

SCD = Steven C. Dinero; Philadelphia University; Philadelphia, PA

DD = Damian Doyle, MA; Australian National University; Canberra, Australia

AD = Adis Duderija, PhD; Griffith University; Queensland, Australia

ME = Moha Ennaji, PhD; University of Fes; Fes, Morocco

ROF = Robert O. Freedman, PhD; Johns Hopkins University; Baltimore, MD

NG = Nancy Gallagher, PhD; University of California; Santa Barbara, CA

MG = Maurizio Geri, MA; Old Dominion University; Norfolk, VA

DG = David Grantham, PhD; National Center for Policy Analysis; Dallas, TX

EH = Elhum Haghighat, PhD; City University of New York; New York, NY

MH = Maria Holt, PhD; University of Westminster; Westminster, UK

FK = Feras Klenk, ABD; University of Arizona; Tucson, AZ

JDL = Justin D. Leach, PhD; Troy University; Washington, DC

NM = Najah Mahmi, PhD; Sidi Mohamed Ben Abdellah University, Morocco; Sophia Antipolis University, France

RGM = Rolin G. Mainuddin: North Carolina Central University; Durham, NC

UM = Ulrika Mårtensson, PhD; Norwegian University of Science and Technology; Trondheim, NO

DCM = David C. Mason, PhD; Zayed University; Abu Dhabi, UAE

EM = Elizabeth Monier, PhD; University of Cambridge; Cambridge, United Kingdom

JO = Josef Olmert, PhD; University of South Carolina; Columbia, SC

AO = Amr Osman, PhD; Qatar University; Doha, Qatar

CO-P = Claire Oueslati-Porter, PhD; University of Miami; Coral Gables, FL

KJP = Kenneth J. Perkins, PhD; University of South Carolina; Columbia, SC

SP = Saffo Papantonopoulou, PhD; University of Arizona; Tucson, AZ

MR = Mizanur Rahman, MD; Bangabandhu Sheikh Mujibur Rahman Science and Technology University; Dhaka, Banglades

JCAR = James C. A. Redman, PhD; Zayed University; Dubai, UAE

PSR = Paul S. Rowe, PhD; Trinity Western University; Langley, BC, CA

MFAS = Marwa Fikry Abdel Samei, PhD; Cairo University; Cairo, Egypt

Me-S = Maryam el-Shall, PhD; Embry-Riddle Aeronautical University; IL

SRS = Sanford R. Silverburg, PhD; Catawba College; Salisbury, NC

MS = Maria Syed, MA; The Australian National University; Canberra, Australia

AMW = Andrew M. Wender, JD, PhD, University of Victoria; Victoria, BC, Canada

AY = Abdulfattah Yaghi, PhD; United Arab Emirates University; Al-Ein, UAE

BY = Bassam Yousif, PhD; Indiana University; Bloomington, IN

RZ = Radwan Ziadeh, MA; Arab Center Washington D.C; Washington, DC

AZ = Abderrahman Zouhir, PhD; Wayne State University; Detroit, MI

ABOUT THE EDITORS

Mohammed M. Aman, PhD, author, consultant, Professor of Information Studies at the University of Wisconsin-Milwaukee (UWM), and Editor-in-Chief the peer-reviewed journal, *Digest of Middle East Studies (DOMES),* published by Wiley-Blackwell. He has held a number of academic leadership positions including Dean of the School of Information Studies at UWM (1979-2002), Interim Dean of the School of Education and Vice Chancellor for Partnership in Education (2000-2002). His prior positions include Dean of the School of Information Sciences at Long Island University (1976-79); Director and Professor, St. John's University, New York, Division of Information Sciences (1972-76); Information Officer, Arab League Mission to the United Nations. He was also UNESCO, UNIDO and AID consultant to several Arab, African, and Latin American countries. Professor Aman is the author of many books, journal articles, and book chapters, and the recipient of numerous national and international honors and awards.

Mary Jo Aman, MLIS is Associate Editor of the peer-reviewed journal, *Digest of Middle East Studies (DOMES).* She has held several positions in New York — among them Director of Library Promotion at Viking Press; Consultant, Nassau County, N.Y. Library System, Assistant Coordinator, Brooklyn Public Library; Member of the Board of International Board of Books for Young People (IBBY) and Editor of IBBY's *Newsletter.* Mrs. Aman was Director, University of Wisconsin-Milwaukee Education/Curriculum Library, Coordinator of Outreach, School of Continuing Education and Outreach, Director, Technology Department, Division of Student Services. She also taught courses at St. John's University in New York, and Cardinal Stritch University, Glendale, Wisconsin. Mrs Aman is the recipient of several awards including citations of merit from the Milwaukee Board of Supervisors and the Wisconsin State Senate, and most recently the University of Wisconsin-Milwaukee's Spaights Award for Outstanding Contributions to UWM.

www.ingramcontent.com/pod-product-compliance
Lightning Source LLC
Chambersburg PA
CBHW072133090426
42739CB00013B/3175